MW01048989

The Rowell-Sirois Commission
and the Remaking
of Canadian Federalism

C.D. Howe Series in Canadian Political History
Series editors: Robert Bothwell and John English

This series offers fresh perspectives on Canadian political history and public policy from over the past century. Its purpose is to encourage scholars to write and publish on all aspects of the nation's political history, including the origins, administration, and significance of economic policies; the social foundations of politics and political parties; transnational influences on Canadian public life; and the biographies of key public figures. In doing so, the series fills large gaps in our knowledge about recent Canadian history and makes accessible to a broader audience the background necessary to understand contemporary public-political issues. Other volumes in the series are:

Grit: The Life and Politics of Paul Martin Sr., by Greg Donaghy
The Call of the World: A Political Memoir, by Bill Graham
Prime Ministerial Power in Canada: Its Origins under Macdonald, Laurier, and Borden, by Patrice Dutil
The Good Fight: Marcel Cadieux and Canadian Diplomacy, by Brendan Kelly
Challenge the Strong Wind: Canada and East Timor, 1975–99, by David Webster
The Nuclear North: Histories of Canada in the Atomic Age, edited by Susan Colbourn and Timothy Andrews Sayle
The Unexpected Louis St-Laurent: Politics and Policies for a Modern Canada, edited by Patrice Dutil
Canadian Foreign Policy: Reflections on a Field in Transition, edited by Brian Bow and Andrea Lane

The series originated with a grant from the C.D. Howe Memorial Foundation and is further supported by the Bill Graham Centre for Contemporary International History.

C.D. Howe Series in
Canadian Political History

The Rowell-Sirois Commission and the Remaking of Canadian Federalism

ROBERT WARDHAUGH
AND
BARRY FERGUSON

UBCPress
1971–2021

© UBC Press 2021

All rights reserved. No part of this publication may be reproduced, stored in a retrieval system, or transmitted, in any form or by any means, without prior written permission of the publisher, or, in Canada, in the case of photocopying or other reprographic copying, a licence from Access Copyright, www.accesscopyright.ca.

30 29 28 27 26 25 24 23 22 21   5 4 3 2 1

Printed in Canada on FSC-certified ancient-forest-free paper (100% post-consumer recycled) that is processed chlorine- and acid-free.

Library and Archives Canada Cataloguing in Publication

Title: The Rowell-Sirois Commission and the remaking of Canadian federalism / Robert Wardhaugh and Barry Ferguson.
Names: Wardhaugh, Robert Alexander, 1967- author. | Ferguson, Barry, 1952- author.

Series: C.D. Howe series in Canadian political history.
Description: Series statement: C.D. Howe series in Canadian political history | Includes bibliographical references and index.
Identifiers: Canadiana (print) 20210178906 | Canadiana (ebook) 20210178965 | ISBN 9780774865012 (hardcover) | ISBN 9780774865036 (PDF) | ISBN 9780774865043 (EPUB)

Subjects: LCSH: Canada. Royal Commission on Dominion-Provincial Relations. | LCSH: Federal government—Canada—History—20th century. | LCSH: Intergovernmental fiscal relations—Canada—History—20th century.

Classification: LCC JL27 .W37 2021 | DDC 321.02/30971—dc23

Canadä

UBC Press gratefully acknowledges the financial support for our publishing program of the Government of Canada (through the Canada Book Fund), the Canada Council for the Arts, and the British Columbia Arts Council.

This book has been published with the help of a grant from the Canadian Federation for the Humanities and Social Sciences, through the Awards to Scholarly Publications Program, using funds provided by the Social Sciences and Humanities Research Council of Canada.

Printed and bound in Canada by Friesens
Set in Univers Condensed and Minion by Artegraphica Design Co.
Copy editor: Joanne Richardson
Proofreader: Judy Dunlop
Indexer: Noeline Bridge
Cover designer: Will Brown

UBC Press
The University of British Columbia
2029 West Mall
Vancouver, BC V6T 1Z2
www.ubcpress.ca

for John Kendle

Contents

Note on Sources

Our book is grounded in primary sources, including records and correspondence of individuals and government departments. Archival records from many places across Canada were consulted, and a few were of crucial importance. The latter include the papers of Robert A. MacKay and the correspondence, diaries, and memoranda of Mackenzie King held in Library and Archives Canada, and the voluminous papers of John W. Dafoe held in the University of Manitoba Archives. Less voluminous but significant were the Premiers' Papers in the British Columbia Archives and the Archives of Manitoba and key records in the Bank of Canada Archives.

Also central to the book was the rich array of contemporary published work that constituted the debates of the 1930s and 1940s about government and politics. Most important were the many studies the commission prompted, including the research studies and the report itself, the provincial government briefs prepared for it, and many other contemporary government inquiries from that prolific age of public inquiries.

We have relied on a broad array of secondary sources including the work of political scientists, legal and economic historians, and political historians. The Canadian historical studies we have been most oriented in were written over a particularly lengthy period of time. These range from work in the "old" or traditional political history to the "new" more explicitly multi-disciplinary political history. Each historiographical approach has been valuable in framing our arguments and interpretations.

Foreword

ROBERT BOTHWELL and JOHN ENGLISH

The Rowell-Sirois Commission is one of the landmarks in Canada's political and constitutional history. Landmarks are often best studied from a distance, bathed in the rising or setting sun. When the Royal Commission on Dominion-Provincial Relations was appointed in 1937, many Canadians thought the sun was setting. Canada's economic problems seemed to be insurmountable, and ordinary politics had failed to find a solution. On a more fundamental level, many suspected that the Canadian federal constitution had made matters worse, linking not only disparate geographies but possibly incompatible economies.

Finding a solution transcended ordinary politics. Mackenzie King's Liberal government in Ottawa had significant problems of its own. Civil war in Spain presaged a larger European conflict. In 1937, Canada began slowly and prudently, according to King's taste, to rearm. There problems arose with nationalists in Quebec, bumptious Ontario-firsters, economic evangelism in Alberta, a dustbowl in Saskatchewan, and aggrieved provincial leaders in the Maritimes and British Columbia.

To look into these many problems and suggest solutions, Mackenzie King appointed a classic Canadian inquiry, later named Rowell-Sirois after its two functional heads, Newton Rowell and Joseph Sirois. The name was justified: these two individuals headed an extraordinary collection of personalities – lawyers, economists, political scientists, historians, and sociologists, who trundled across the country meeting an equally extraordinary gaggle of politicians.

Robert Wardhaugh and Barry Ferguson's book might have been a dry recitation of the facts and the dates of the commission. Constitutional history, after all, is not usually considered a scintillating study. Important, to be sure, even fundamental, but lively? But so it is. Canada's condition in 1937 was dire – breadlines, abandoned farms, demagogues to the East, West, and centre. The authors never lose sight of the very real despair and discontent that was the backdrop to the commission.

The commission is also a take of personal encounters and interactions. The commission and its staff and Canada's political class are very real in this volume. Constitutional politics are fought out over banquet tables and bars. The premier of Alberta evicts the province's lieutenant-governor; not to be outdone, the premier of Ontario does the same. The premier of Quebec, meanwhile, tipples his favourite beverage, Geneva gin. The premier of Ontario entertains the commissioners with the 1930s version of karaoke, with songs that even now we hesitate to repeat. In the background to the commission's travels, there is the tinkle of ice cubes – a cross-section of 1930s society, as lived by Canada's political class, or many of them.

The Rowell-Sirois Commission and the Remaking of Canadian Federalism is a serious book, certainly. It has a serious theme. It deals with the levers of power in the Canadian federation. But it also gives life and colour to those who wielded those levers. The consequences of the actions of drunken buffoons like the premiers of Ontario and Quebec were grave. Too often, however, historians fail to deal with the extraordinary and the irrational. That is not the case here. Wardhaugh and Ferguson have expanded our knowledge of how Canada has worked, what Canadians thought of it, and what they did about it. It is political history at its best.

* * *

The C.D. Howe Series on Canadian Political History is supported by a grant from the C.D. Howe Memorial Foundation. The grant was given to promote greater research and publications on Canada's political history. The Bill Graham Centre for Contemporary International History also supports this series, which has already published important biographies and analytical studies that have attracted academic and popular interest.

Acknowledgments

We have received a great deal of help over the years in which this project has occupied our attention. Several institutions, and their archivists, across the country have been of great help. The original impetus for our work was provided by Mike Moosberger, then at the University of Manitoba Archives, with a tip about newly acquired "family papers" in the John Dafoe collection. When we read them, we saw a new side to Dafoe and to federalism in the 1930s and 1940s. We have received great assistance from knowledgeable and efficient archival staff at the BC Archives, the Provincial Archives of Alberta, the Provincial Archives of Saskatchewan, the Archives of Manitoba, the Archives of Ontario, Library and Archives Canada, the Bank of Canada Archives, the York University Archives, the Queen's University Archives, and the University of Manitoba Archives. The task of retrieving images has been aided by Catherine Fancy at the Acadia University Archives, Lisa Gauthier at the Queen's University Archives, Karsh collection curator Jill Delaney and archivist Jean Matheson at Library and Archives Canada, Nicole Courier at the University of Manitoba Archives, and Carmen Tiampo at UBC Press.

In conducting the research, we have benefitted from the assistance of a number of our students. Western University students Stephen Grandpre and Graeme Phillips, and University of Manitoba students Ian McKay, Savannah Van Dongen, Maria Gheorghe, and Lora Ibragimova each dug up valuable material. Further research was contributed by Daniel Sims in Edmonton, Thirstan Falconer in Ottawa, Ian Peach in Fredericton, Scott MacNeil and Jody Perrun in Winnipeg, and Klavdia Tatar in Ottawa.

A grant from the Social Sciences and Humanities Research Council and research funds from the Duff Roblin Chair at the University of Manitoba provided the funding that facilitated our own work and defrayed costs of graduate research assistants. Invaluable administrative support from our departments was always cheerfully provided, but we owe particular thanks to Sandra Ferguson, Cathy Dunlop, Sheri Miles, and Mary Harder.

Colleagues at our respective institutions have consistently proved valuable soundboards and support, including Rory Henry, Derek Hum, Adele Perry, and Len Kuffert at Manitoba, and Keith Fleming, Alan MacEachern, and Peter Neary at Western. Royce Koop, as chair of the Political Studies Department, greatly assisted Barry Ferguson by his help in scheduling teaching duties in political studies and by offering thoughtful commentary about federal government and politics. Foundationally, we have had the benefit over some years from our association with Gerald Friesen and John Kendle – Wardhaugh's mentors and Ferguson's colleagues. Their ideas and knowledge about regional politics, about federalism, and about government broadened our perspectives in many important ways. None of these people are implicated in our views!

We have had the opportunity to present several papers over the years on themes related to this book, and some paragraphs in this book were first published in our chapter, "Thinking Confederation: St-Laurent and the Rowell-Sirois Commission," in the volume edited by Patrice Dutil, *The Unexpected Louis St-Laurent: Politics and Policies for a Modern Canada*.

Our work with UBC Press has been a pleasure. The acquisition and review processes have been as smooth as could be. The editorial team – senior acquisitions editor Randy Schmidt, production editor Meagan Dyer, assistant editor Carmen Tiampo, and our copy editor Joanne Richardson – has been helpful, efficient and, in this challenging period, resourceful. The three manuscript readers were thorough and positive and offered invaluable comments that have helped strengthen the book. We gratefully acknowledge the financial support of the Aid to Scholarly Publications Program.

Our debts to our close families are of course as important to us as any others. They have had to hear us out and put up with our preoccupations with the work, but these debts we shall keep within our own circles.

The Rowell-Sirois Commission
and the Remaking
of Canadian Federalism

Introduction

*Canadians spend as much or more time as do other peoples
in major debates about ends and means, about the rich and
the poor, about freedom and equality, and about change
and the status quo. But they do so in the strange vocabulary
of the political elites, in terms of changing the structures and
responsibilities of their systems of government – in short
in terms of different concepts of federalism.*

– Edwin R. Black, 1975[1]

Why write a book on a Canadian royal commission established in the
1930s? Royal commissions are infamous for providing the appearance of
governmental action while providing little substance. This view perme-
ates both the popular and the academic responses to public inquiries. And
not without reason. Canadian political history is filled with public inquiries
that produced few substantial policy results. Some commissions, however, are called at critical junctures in a nation's or a province's history to
deal with essential matters of state. And a few are worthy of study because
their work has meaningful impact not only in the short term but for many
years to come.[2]

In the 1930s the Canadian state confronted the most serious economic
crisis the country has ever experienced. The market economy during
the Great Depression was in tatters and Canada's federal political system

was feeble in response. Policies put forward by federal and provincial governments to deal with the situation seemed to worsen rather than to alleviate the problem. The Royal Commission on Dominion-Provincial Relations, dubbed the Rowell-Sirois Commission after its two chairmen, was called in 1937 to deal with the political and economic crisis. Its three years of work reveals several aspects of mid-twentieth century Canadian government that are worth pondering today, a time when politics in many liberal democracies once again wallow in problems of legitimacy, scepticism about government, and fears about democracy.

The story of the Rowell-Sirois Commission emphasizes the extent of the political and economic crisis caused by the Depression, and the conditions of "modern" government that accompanied it. The commission's work demonstrates how a disparate group of talented if orthodox members of the legal and academic elites conducted a massive inquiry and then arrived at remarkable recommendations, unexpected in their originality. Their recommendations avoided the paralysis of constitutional change, reinterpreted the economic and political problems and goals of the country, and described a striking vision for the reset of federal government in Canada.

Moreover, the commission's extensive consultations and research left a trove of public evidence, private correspondence, and writings that provide rare and detailed insights into the inner workings of government. In its two and a half years of activity, the Rowell-Sirois Commission experienced its share of serious problems. These included the stubborn resistance of the most powerful provinces, serious clashes between federal and provincial "first ministers," the manipulative agenda of the federal government, and the inquiry's serious internal disagreements and conflicts. Any one of these obstacles could have destroyed Rowell-Sirois. But none did.

The Commission's Report is usually described by those who write about the era as one of the most important state papers in Canada's political history. The depths of its innovations and the issues it raised about federalism, however, have not always been fully appreciated.[3] To reconsider one of the few deep examinations of federal government in Canada reminds us that these issues reverberate still, perhaps now as much as ever. Drawing on both the "old" and the "new" political history, the life of the commission takes on new and broader meanings.[4]

When most Canadians think of the Great Depression, two images come to mind: the sepia-toned photographs of the drought-stricken Prairie dustbowl and the stark images of unemployed men seeking jobs and lining up for relief. Over the past half-century, popular histories such as James Gray's *The Winter Years* and Barry Broadfoot's *Ten Lost Years* have etched the impact of the Depression onto the collective imagination.[5] But most Canadians may not realize that these two conditions – the economic collapse of the Prairie West and rampant unemployment – seriously threatened the viability of the Canadian political and economic order. Most Canadians today know little of the politicians at the federal and provincial levels who struggled to come up with solutions to these dire threats.

By the mid-1930s, problems worthy of the word "crisis" afflicted the Canadian federal system. Since Confederation in 1867, conflict between the dominion and the provincial governments characterized Canadian politics. By the decade of the Depression, however, governments were unable to meet their obligations to the citizenry. Observers expressed doubts about the capacity of the federation to provide effective government. The country's most powerful civil servant, Oscar Skelton, warned Liberal prime minister William Lyon Mackenzie King in 1936 that "the disintegration of Canada is proceeding fast." Reflecting upon the period years later, economist Henry Angus recalled "a profoundly discontented country, every region of which was obsessed with a sense of injustice ... and self-pity." Angus and Skelton were not suggesting that Canada's governmental structures were in imminent danger of collapse. They were seriously disturbed by the ineffectuality of the country's political and governmental institutions. As Canada's under-secretary of external affairs, Skelton knew how the absence of consensus vitiated Canadian foreign and defence policies. As political economists, Angus and Skelton were well aware that the failure to coordinate federal and provincial policies had hamstrung all governmental responses to the Depression.[6]

Beyond sketching out the looming threats, Angus and Skelton could have gone further and pointed to the many ways in which public life in Canada had become imperilled. The problems of the economy were obvious and their impact on the well-being of Canadians was deeply troubling. The failure of the country to find a clear foreign policy was another disturbing matter. Less obvious were the ways in which the institutions of government, politics, and society had deteriorated. The failure of the dominion government to take concerted action against the collapse in world trade demonstrated the limited capacity of the international system for cooperation and indeed a strong tendency for predation. The national two-party system had fractured during the crisis of the Great War, and, despite a return to majority government in 1926, the new multi-party system revealed the extent to which the old politics and traditional parties no longer represented Canadians. The new reformist parties emerging in the 1930s (the Co-operative Commonwealth Federation and Social Credit) attracted enthusiastic adherence but limited broad support, while revolutionary parties such as the Communist Party demonstrated that Canada was not immune to radicalism. By the mid-1930s, provincial political leaders rode the waves of a new populism and became far more compelling figures than their federal counterparts. Premiers such as "Bible Bill" Aberhart, Maurice Duplessis, Mitch Hepburn, Angus L. Macdonald, and Duff Pattullo seemed much more dynamic in responding to public issues than the erratic R.B. Bennett, the crafty Mackenzie King, or the earnest J.S. Woodsworth.

The international trend towards economic protectionism among Western countries in the late 1920s and 1930s gutted international trade. This shift intensified and prolonged the economic crisis for a trading nation like Canada. To make matters worse, collapsing markets and drought devastated the crucial Prairie wheat economy. As trade and commerce collapsed, industrial unemployment emerged as a formidable socio-economic problem that plagued urban centres. Local governments from school boards to town councils were on the front lines in dealing with the economic disaster. They buckled under the weight of mounting costs and plummeting tax revenues, and they turned to provincial governments for aid. The provinces staggered under the weight of relief costs, while the federal government in Ottawa tried to avoid or minimize financial responsibility for what, according to the British North America Act, 1867, was constitutionally a provincial concern. The economic malaise was complicated by the fact that the Canadian federal state was unbalanced. The provinces were not all the same, and the Depression brought regional disparities into sharp focus. The Prairie provinces in particular teetered on the edge of bankruptcy (literally in default on debt), while the Maritimes went from despondence to despair regarding their conditions and prospects. Despite measures undertaken by both Conservative and Liberal governments in Ottawa to deal with these problems, along with efforts by their provincial counterparts, governments were mired in the conventions of economic orthodoxy and the rules of a federal system of government immune to major changes starting with effective coordination between Ottawa and the provinces. By the mid-thirties, the federal system was broken. By 1937 something had to be done.

Canada's federal system had changed fundamentally over the seventy years since its founding in 1867. It began as a highly centralized order with the extraordinary tools of legislative review, disallowance, and residual power vested in the dominion government. Ottawa enjoyed wide taxation powers and fed off rich fields of "indirect" excises and tariffs. This "quasi-federal" state of dominion priority was challenged relentlessly almost from its inception. Provincial governments exerted their legislative powers and challenged the original fiscal dispensation in critical ways as early as the 1870s and 1880s. Their fiscal concerns often sounded like mere financial pleading for more money from Ottawa, but their strategies grew more sophisticated as they challenged for revenues from business licences and, most important, natural resource outputs. These challenges were supported in the main by judicial decisions from the Judicial Committee of the Privy Council, Canada's final court of appeal until 1951.

By the 1920s, Canada had become a typical, or "classical," federal state characterized by two coordinate levels of sovereign government, neither superior nor inferior to the other. It was an arrangement that prompted fierce and unresolved constitutional and political disagreements during the 1930s. While Ottawa possessed the fiscal resources to deal with unemployment, poverty, and public health, the constitutional responsibilities to address those matters remained in the provincial realm. Despite occasional fiscal adjustments, the provinces lacked the necessary resources to deal with what were now seen as "modern problems." In addition, Canada was both pleased with and dismayed by the full implications of constitutional autonomy that led to the Statute of Westminster in 1931. The country possessed the capacity but not the will to make substantive changes to its federal system let alone to its foreign policy, where the effects of national disunity were evident on the world stage. The result was a federation that seemed incapable of decisive policy action.

After Confederation, the "purposes of the Dominion" evolved into a broad program of economic development described later as the "national policy." This policy was not a coordinated program but, rather, a cumulative settler-colonial project of the federal government devised in the 1870s and 1880s. It comprised massive westward territorial expansion and the simultaneous dispossession of Indigenous peoples, the construction of a transcontinental railway system, and the adoption of protective tariffs. Territorial expansion led to the settlement of the Prairie West as a major grain-export region and the creation of three constitutionally subordinate provinces, hamstrung fiscally and administratively by their lack of control over natural resources yet aware of their economic importance. The protective tariff nurtured a large manufacturing economy centred on the core areas of Ontario and Quebec. By the 1920s, the realization of this national policy program resulted in a continent-wide state and economy, but it also created deep regional and provincial disparities, social inequalities, and political conflicts. Throughout the period of expansion leading up to the Depression, both the Prairies and the Maritimes, with limited results, railed against national economic policies.

The international economic cataclysm of the Great Depression in the 1930s intensified the consequences of the transformed federal system and transcontinental national economy. The Depression has become such a cliché in popular culture that it is easy to elide its relentless impact over the course of the decade. But that impact was so grinding that it led Canadian politicians at both the federal and provincial levels to agree that a national inquiry into the federal system might provide an escape from the economic and constitutional labyrinth. The result was a paradox. The federal government had been motivated for seventy years by a clear national purpose of economic expansion and was supported by relatively stable taxation and revenues. The provincial governments, meanwhile, had increasingly taken up responsibility for these unprecedented "modern conditions," including education, transportation, health, and welfare. During the 1930s, however, the provinces found it increasingly difficult not just to balance budgets but even to meet their governmental obligations. The nineteenth-century institutions of government and the old ways of governing no longer worked. The crisis epitomized the "break with the past" emphasized by many twentieth-century commentators to describe the unprecedented technological, organizational, and economic transformation of the "modern age."[7]

The Royal Commission on Dominion-Provincial Relations was established in August of 1937 and reported to the federal government in May of 1940. It was created to confront the evident failings of federalism in Canada. To an extent it was established to deal with the prospect of Confederation's failure. Much had changed in the seventy years since 1867 and, as policy-makers repeatedly pointed out, the "Fathers of Confederation" could not have foreseen the rapid transformation of the nation. Most emphatically, the Great Depression made it glaringly apparent that the provincial governments (except Ontario) could not shoulder the increasing costs of their constitutional responsibilities, including relief for the unemployed, the building of new roads and infrastructure, and new expenditures on social programs. Canadian federalism had to be reconsidered and, if possible, remade.

While Canada has produced more than three hundred commissions of inquiry, the Rowell-Sirois Commission holds a distinctive place. As noted at the outset, it has been described in many works as the most important royal commission in Canadian history. In the words of political scientist Neil Bradford, it was "the greatest state paper of the twentieth century," and "the most comprehensive investigation of a working federal system that has ever been made." Its "radical prescription" was "set forth against a background of history and analysis the likes of which Canadians had never seen." It represented a unique attempt to "weigh up at one stroke the economic, political, and financial progress of an organized system of government from its inception and to chart its future course." Perhaps Lord Durham's famous report, published a century before, might be comparable, but it was a British blueprint for a colony lacking full governmental powers. Rowell-Sirois was one of those rare governmental projects, identified by Max Weber, that "realign the thought and behaviour of social and political interests" and therefore "reset" national policy.[8] Yet despite the importance of Rowell-Sirois having been recognized by historians and political scientists alike, its main findings have not been fully understood.

The Royal Commission on Dominion-Provincial Relations articulated a new role for the state in Canada and a new relationship between Ottawa and the provinces. The process was orchestrated by some of the most impressive policy-making minds in the country. This intelligentsia, described at the time as a "Brain Trust" and by historians since as "the Ottawa Men" and "the Government Generation," advocated a major shake-up of the Canadian federal system. The agenda was referred to by contemporaries as a "plan of re-federation."[9] But federalism, by its very nature, is built upon power and competition among different levels of government. Even though dominion and provincial officials agreed that the system was broken, finding a way to repair and even rebuild it would prove difficult to say the least. The Rowell-Sirois Commission was supposed to find the way.

Almost immediately after the report was delivered to the Canadian government in May 1940, its recommendations, and ultimately its direct impact, began to slip away. The report was released during the darkest days of the Second World War, when Ottawa was undertaking an extraordinary expansion of the state's role. With its impressive research output and storehouse of proposals, and above all its specific recommendations for changes to Canadian federalism, the Rowell-Sirois Commission became one more victim of the war. Released during a particularly bitter and acrimonious period in the history of dominion-provincial relations, the path set out by the report was quickly obscured. Yet federalism moved in a direction that most analysts assumed was guided by Rowell-Sirois. They were correct about its significance but wrong about its direct impact. This book shows how the commission recast ideas about the foundations of the federal system and the nature of government in ways that would be at the core of public life for the next forty years.

Commissions of inquiry in the Canadian federal system are temporary institutions that fill a specific task for the government of the day. They are of two general types. Most are investigative commissions. These are inquiries into specific governmental or administrative problems, fact-finding studies of administrative failures or wrong-doing. A few, like the Rowell-Sirois Commission, are advisory commissions serving as broad examinations of general policy problems. The political scientist Alan Cairns noted that any inquiry is a "bureaucracy" but "ephemeral." Commissions are administrative extensions of government with no extraordinary legal or legislative power beyond that of senior agencies and officials, but they allow full access to government records and offer the ability to call on witnesses as in civil not criminal cases. They have considerable flexibility in operations, including the right to shape their program of inquiry within their terms of reference. They often include public hearings, research, and a public report, and, as a result, face considerable public scrutiny. Commissions are usually appointed under an Inquiries Act, whether federal or provincial, but they may be appointed under a variety of departmental guidelines. They disclose their findings to the government but the reports are tabled in the legislature and become part of the public agenda as well as the policy record.[10]

The Rowell-Sirois Commission was called at a time when governments heavily relied upon inquiries, particularly in newer British dominions like Canada and Australia, which were facing seemingly intractable problems and weak administrative and research capacities. The 1920s and 1930s was a period in which the interventionist, social service state was growing rapidly despite an ideology of laissez-faire. The federal government created commissions with remarkable frequency in the 1920s (forty-five in total) and 1930s (fifty-five in total). Most were formed to address administrative and legal bungling, but some advised on major political and economic questions.[11] The use of commissions declined in the decades after the Second World War. To an extent, this was inevitable. Their usage in the United Kingdom declined after 1900, and it was assumed that, as Canada built up competent public sectors and underwent civil service reform, the need for them would also decline.[12] But the importance of big public inquiries has remained notable in Canada and the provinces, even as their frequency has diminished.[13]

Many of the inquiries in the interwar period were called to deal with regional problems from two particular sections of the country. In the Maritimes, regional protest arose from what was perceived as the deleterious effect of national economic policy. In the West, vociferous demands were raised for compensation from half a century of quasi-colonial subordination and unfair national policy. These sectional protests resulted in royal commissions on Maritime claims, the marketing of grain, and Prairie natural resources. There were also more general "dominion" problems in the 1930s, most notably the stability of the banking and credit system, and the calamity of the unemployment crisis. Inquiries were vital policy tools of the times, although none were as extensive as Rowell-Sirois.[14]

The Royal Commission on Dominion-Provincial Relations undertook an extraordinary and indeed unprecedented task. It was the most extensive of its time and became the prototype for the later, multi-year broad policy inquiries. These inquiries have continued to punctuate national political life since the 1940s, on themes ranging from cultural policies and French-English relations to the fundamentals of economic and social policy, and most recently Indigenous issues.[15] A careful examination of Rowell-Sirois reveals much about the workings of mid-twentieth-century government and also about how large-scale public policies were developed during the era.

This book explains the origins, the activities, and the outcomes of the Rowell-Sirois Commission. The first three chapters examine the national political framework and key federal policy problems that led to the decision to form the commission. The following five chapters explore the commission's organization and deliberations, particularly in relation to the views of the nine provinces, as the inquiry worked towards writing a report. The final three chapters provide an analysis of the report and the significance of its recommendations. The book concludes by reviewing the ways in which the commission's recommendations were considered by the federal and provincial governments in the 1940s and argues that it was at first shelved and then gained influence for decades after.

1

A Federation Turned Upside Down

The most difficult and complicated domestic question for every government and every political party in Canada is how to establish a satisfactory relationship between the federal and the provincial authorities.

– J.W. Pickersgill, 1962[1]

For the Canadian state, the politics of federalism are the politics of survival.

– Edwin R. Black, 1975[2]

The Rowell-Sirois Commission was created to resolve the dominion-provincial conflicts that plagued Canada during the 1920s and 1930s. But it was also formed to deal with the inability of government to deal with the crisis of the Great Depression. The origins of dominion-provincial conflict went back to the creation of the Canadian federal state in 1867.

The so-called Fathers of Confederation produced a constitutional outline, the British North America (BNA) Act, which divided legislative responsibility between the federal and provincial governments. The intentions of the founders and the meaning of the BNA Act inspired heated debate that has continued over many decades. Adherents of centralization and decentralization alike found credence for their positions, but in 1867 greater authority was available to the dominion.[3] The mechanisms that granted crucial powers and all residual authority (as well as the rights of review and disallowance) to the dominion government emerged from a centralist conception of federalism that was widespread in mid-nineteenth-century Great Britain and Canada. This conception was grounded in a specific set of governmental and constitutional practices that have not always been recognized by scholars as time-bound. In recent decades, a number of important academic studies have shown rather persuasively that the centralist position was not overwhelmingly accepted even at the time of Confederation and that it has given ground to a pluralist "classic" federalism in subsequent decades of both practice and interpretation.[4]

The original division of powers reflected a centralizing hierarchical order spanning provincial legislatures, the dominion parliament, and the imperial government of the United Kingdom.[5] Under section 91 of the BNA Act, the dominion parliament was responsible for twenty-eight areas. These were mainly crucial economic functions such as trade, commerce, and transportation but included military and naval defence. Fiscal powers included all areas of taxation, and regulation of banking and currency, among others. Federal powers included all matters "not ... assigned exclusively to the Legislatures of the Provinces." The "exclusive powers" of the provincial legislatures under section 92 were more limited and were confined to fifteen areas. These were mainly in social policy realms such as education, health, and welfare, vital fields for the preservation of the long-standing institutions and identities of each of the contracting colonies. The list of powers also included direct taxation, public lands and resources, municipalities, and various forms for the regulation of businesses, including "property and civil rights." The two sections were framed by the "Peace, Order, and good Government" clause directly tied to "all Matters not coming within the Classes of Subjects by this Act assigned exclusively to the Legislatures of the Provinces."[6]

There were some areas of joint or overlapping authority, specifically regarding education (denominational schools), agriculture, justice, and, most crucially, taxation. Provincial authority over direct taxation, however, was almost moot in 1867 whereas federal authority over indirect taxation gave Ottawa access to the lucrative fields of customs and excise duties. The dominion through section 91, clause 2, was entitled to "the raising of

Money by any Mode or System of Taxation," which seemed to envelope the provincial powers of direct taxation. In practice, the federal government did not tap major direct taxes such as income taxes until the First World War.

To deal with the entrenched revenue imbalance, Ottawa instituted a system of unconditional grants to the provinces. These grants were based on a per capita amount that provided limited revenues to the provinces even by the standards of the mid-nineteenth century. There was no proviso for revision of these terms or for the specific grants in the 1867 agreement. They were determined entirely by political negotiations, particularly for new provinces that entered the federation in the years that followed. In 1867 the dominion government relieved the existing provinces of their public debts, which was of greatest benefit to Ontario and Quebec, who had built up a large debt as the United Province of Canada after 1841. Debt relief was offered to the later entrants as well. But neither the unconditional per capita grant nor the debt relief were enacted with provisions for regular review. This rigidity meant that federal-provincial finance was a political matter subject to negotiation and side deals, a facet of national politics that would lead to controversy and conflict.[7]

The centralizing bias of the Canadian federation was reinforced through the federal powers of reservation and disallowance over provincial legislation as well as the original impetus regarding the appointment of lieutenant-governors. The twist in this bias was that legislative and judicial review extended from Ottawa to London, which remained for decades the imperial parliament and the top court of appeal, the Judicial Committee of the Privy Council (JCPC).

The Canadian legislative minds that were responsible for the BNA Act were more fixated upon the doctrine of centralizing sovereignty than in recognizing that governmental authority could be divided between legislatures such as the federal and provincial governments. In the 1860s, the emphasis on centralized sovereignty in Ottawa seemed to trump the federal idea. That emphasis, however, would change over time.[8] It would be most influenced by a crucial institutional aspect of the centralization of sovereignty vested in the United Kingdom Parliament – specifically, British judicial review of Canadian legislation. Decisions from the JCPC in London changed the balance between Ottawa and the provinces, moving it away from centralization towards greater provincial rights and therefore decentralization.[9]

Changing economic and social conditions, and vast changes in the duties of governments, led to clashes between the provinces and the dominion. These clashes were not just territorial and legislative quarrels between antagonists but rather contests between two levels of government over economic development strategies, social policy agendas, and their fiduciary duties to their citizens. Despite the attempts of Prime Minister John A. Macdonald and others to create a centralized federation, the efforts of provincial-rights advocates such as Premier Oliver Mowat of Ontario and Premier Honoré Mercier of Quebec turned the momentum in the opposite direction. They were aided and abetted by smaller provinces, above all Manitoba, with its many battles over railways and subsidies and, later, educational and language rights. Mowat, through persistent legal challenges, "probably came out on top" in the "intergovernmental skirmishes" that dominated the 1880s. Mowat's Ontario did this by winning most of the key constitutional cases ultimately decided by the JCPC against the dominion in the crucial areas of control over natural resources, taxation, and the regulation of business. Tiny Manitoba harried the dominion over railway policy through failed challenges to the Canadian Pacific Railway's (CPR) monopoly in the 1880s. In the 1890s, it successfully gutted the 1870 Manitoba Act and federal rights of disallowance in regard to "minority rights" of language and religion in the legislature, courts, and schools.[10]

In 1892, in a case regarding the insolvent Maritime Bank and the Province of New Brunswick, the JCPC summarized its view of federalism. Lord Watson explained that the "object" of the BNA Act "was neither to weld the provinces into one, nor to subordinate provincial governments to a central authority, but to create a federal government in which they should all be represented, entrusted with the exclusive administration of affairs in which they had a common interest, each province retaining its independence and autonomy."[11] A new constitutional die was cast. Federalism was gaining the upper hand over parliamentary sovereignty.

The First World War significantly recast the role of the state in Canada and ushered in what were called at the time "modern conditions." Canada was transformed by the cumulative impact of prewar national expansion, western settlement, and industrialization and urbanization. The growth of a "national" economy was largely based upon western Canadian agriculture and central Canadian manufacturing, and highly focused on international trade in wheat, newsprint, and lumber. As a result, it became increasingly difficult to achieve a balanced economy and a national policy "on the old model" that was mutually acceptable to Canada's diverse regions and provinces.[12]

The Great War led to a more centralist and interventionist state under the impetus of wartime needs, but none of the underlying sources of federal-provincial discontent were resolved. Few of the Union government's agencies, boards, or commissions aiming at tighter federal economic direction, such as the first Canadian Wheat Board or the Commission of Commerce, survived beyond the government's defeat in 1921. A major institutional survivor was the government-owned Canadian National Railway (CNR), created in 1919 to bail out the two bankrupt transcontinental railways. The other major legacy was the federal government's move into the field of direct taxation of business and personal incomes, a wartime measure to strengthen federal government finance that proved so lucrative it was not thereafter relinquished.[13]

A dominion-provincial conference was held at war's end in 1918 in an attempt to appease regional concerns. Only the second such gathering ever called, the conference addressed the long-brewing discontent of the Prairie provinces over federal control of natural resources and soldier settlement issues, but not the issues of tariffs and income taxes. Prime Minister Borden's attention was elsewhere, and he was soon off to London in preparation for the postwar peace settlements. He left Finance Minister Thomas White in his stead, but White did not even chair the sessions. The conference ended after desultory discussions that focused mainly on the natural resource issue.[14]

The Liberal leadership convention of 1919, which selected William Lyon Mackenzie King, produced a progressive party platform that included "an adequate system of insurance against unemployment, sickness, dependence in old age, and other disability, which would include old age pensions, widows' pensions, and maternity benefits."[15] But the federal party system in Canada was splitting along regional and socio-economic lines. The new minority parties (the Progressive Party along with a group of

Labour members of Parliament) were sure to remind the minority Liberal government elected in 1921 of the party's promises. The Progressive Party emerged to protest the traditional party system and its treatment of the agrarian economy. With a base of support mainly from the Prairie West, the populist Progressives squandered their influence due to internal divisions. They proved more interested in economic liberalization, non-partisanship, and regional concerns than social legislation. Labour support was critical during the Liberal minority Parliament of 1925–26, and the resulting Old Age Pensions Act, 1927, represented the first permanent involvement of the federal government in income security. Under its terms, Ottawa reimbursed provincial governments for half of the costs of means-tested pensions for those aged seventy and over. Within nine years all provinces opted in, although the poorer ones in eastern Canada waited until after 1930 when the federal share of the costs was raised to 75 percent. The pensions program, however, was the exception to a general rule of inaction.[16]

These new circumstances shifted the balance of economic and political power away from the federal government and towards the provinces. Constitutionally, the provinces (except for the Prairie provinces) controlled many of the new economic industries, such as hydroelectricity, forestry, and mining, but all the provinces were responsible for most of the social consequence of economic growth and population expansion. The 1920s, however, were anything but "roaring" in parts of Canada, and the inter-war period began with a stubborn recession. The fiscal capacity of municipal governments was severely strained during the decade, particularly when confronted with these new responsibilities. Municipal governments, meanwhile, were the subordinates of the provinces. Large-scale urban unemployment became a serious issue. Poverty was not new to Canada, but, according to nineteenth-century convention, it was regarded as a local problem. Aid, through charity, was administered privately or publicly through municipal institutions. By the 1920s, such thinking was in the process of being abandoned and the shift was well under way from "residual" to "institutional" responsibility for social welfare. This change in comprehension meant that government, specifically the provinces, had to devise policies and programs to address social problems.[17] In the early 1920s, it was assumed that unemployment was a temporary postwar phenomenon. It was such a serious matter, however, that the provinces had to provide "relief" and sustain their social welfare regimes. Even the federal government became involved, providing emergency grants for unemployment over a three-year period.

The forces of modernity transformed life and government in Canada in the interwar period, but most of these changes fell under provincial jurisdiction. New natural resources were developed, such as hydroelectric power and mining, but they were under provincial control and so the provinces had to deal with emerging private corporate interests. New social services and institutions – ranging from welfare to education to municipal government – had to be created, and they were costly. In 1930, after a decade of negotiation and three royal commissions, control over natural resources was transferred from Ottawa to the Prairie provinces.[18] While federal expenditures in the realm of social welfare declined during the 1920s, provincial expenditures nearly doubled. The nine provinces in 1921 spent an amount equal to just under 20 percent of the federal budget. By the end of the decade, this proportion had doubled. The growth of provincial spending – like the spike in federal expenditure during the war – shook up conventional ideas and practices.[19]

One of the best examples of new government activity in the 1920s was the push for road and highway construction, a result of the vast expansion of motor vehicle transportation. Provincial revenues came mainly from vehicle licences, gasoline taxes, and the profits from liquor monopolies, although Ontario, Quebec, and British Columbia also did well from natural resource revenues and British Columbia found that provincial income tax revenues were as strong as those from natural resources. Provincial governments were now under increasing pressure to raise more revenue for expenditures in transportation, city-building, and education. The pressure showed no signs of lessening: "All provinces had revenue increases between 1921 and 1929, but because the economic development of the 1920s was regionally uneven there was a considerable disparity among these increases nationwide." Ontario and Quebec, the two most powerful provinces in the federation due to their rich natural resources and strong manufacturing economies, enjoyed increases of 150 percent and 120 percent in provincial revenues, respectively. The average increase for the other seven provinces was a more modest 65 percent.[20] The dominion meanwhile strained to pay down war debt and the heavy railway debt, but it enjoyed a reliable new revenue stream from direct taxation sources amounting to approximately 15 percent of total revenues by the end of the 1920s.[21] The increasing burdens on provincial coffers to cover the costs of mounting government programs combined with regional disparities to further strain dominion-provincial relations.

Unsurprisingly, Quebec and Ontario led the way when it came to pressing for provincial autonomy. These two provinces, while uneasy allies based on a long and contentious history of religious and cultural animosity, found common cause in challenging the influence of the federal government. Ontario and Quebec had come together to champion the provincial position throughout the 1880s under the premierships of Oliver Mowat and Honoré Mercier. While this common front collapsed over issues of French-English/Catholic-Protestant antagonism (such as when Ontario restricted the educational rights of its French-speaking minority in 1912), the alliance was "resurrected" in the 1920s under Premiers Howard Ferguson and Louis-Alexandre Taschereau, particularly when it came to economic issues such as advancing hydroelectric development. At the centenary celebrations of the University of Toronto in October 1927, Ferguson and Taschereau shared a platform. The Quebec premier reminded the audience that "every Canadian must understand that sixty years ago we formed not a homogeneous country but a confederation of different provinces for certain purposes, with the distinct understanding that each of these provinces should retain certain things." The two premiers espoused what became known as the "compact theory" of Confederation. According to this theory, Confederation in 1867 was a compact, or treaty, among sovereign and equal provinces. All powers not specifically given to the federal government in the BNA Act remained in the preserve of the provinces: "Neither Ferguson nor Taschereau felt he was demanding new provincial rights at Ottawa's expense. In their minds they were simply restoring the correct interpretation of the dominion-provincial relationship, perverted during the Great War, and defending themselves against further federal encroachments."[22]

The alliance between Ontario and Quebec presaged the Dominion-Provincial Conference held in November 1927. Formal consultation between federal and provincial leaders was extremely rare but harkened to

1887, when Premier Mercier of Quebec suggested to Prime Minister Macdonald that a meeting of the first ministers was necessary to review the first twenty years of federalism in Canada. The centralist Macdonald balked at the proposal and refused to attend, but the meeting went ahead regardless. The attending premiers, led by Mowat and Mercier but aided and abetted by Nova Scotia's W.H. Fielding, urged Ottawa to amend the British North America Act to increase the subsidies paid to the provinces by tying them to current population levels rather than those of 1860. The provinces urged the federal government to recognize that, as the nation expanded and economic and social conditions in Canada changed, the federal system had to adapt accordingly. The provinces lost the political debate but led by Ontario, they made considerable gains in the courts.

Despite the resistance of the federal government, intergovernmental conferences eventually emerged as a mechanism of federalism. The first formal dominion-provincial conferences between the premiers and the prime minister occurred in 1906 and 1918.[23] The provinces continued to push for increased subsidies to bolster their revenues, a share of the customs and excise revenues, and recognition of the costs they bore due to federal policies. Prime Ministers Laurier and Borden approved of the conferences but gave only minor concessions. Even though the provinces shouldered so many of the mounting costs of government resulting from national policies and national expansion, federalism in Canada functioned largely without their being consulted. According to historian Christopher Armstrong:

> The federal government really did not seek consultation but a forum in which to announce policies already decided upon. Provincial co-operation was deemed desirable but by no means essential. Thus, the first half-century of Confederation ended without the provincial leaders having attained any formal right to pronounce upon vital constitutional issues. Even the BNA Act could be amended without any reference to the provinces.[24]

The new "forum" meant that Ottawa was being drawn into consultations.

In the late 1920s, dominion-provincial conferences took on a more entrenched role. Federal politicians, starting with Liberal prime minister

Mackenzie King, realized not only that these gatherings served their own purposes but also that Ottawa needed provincial support to deal with the changed governmental and constitutional landscape. Federal governments may have hoped that merely holding such meetings could provide "a substitute for action or a means of legitimizing actions already planned to which the provinces would not consent," but the provincial premiers were also learning important lessons. An interprovincial session was held in 1926 without federal representation. United Farmers of Manitoba (UFM) premier John Bracken strongly supported this tactic, arguing in favour of an organized provincial approach to Ottawa. He hoped that "if the Provinces could come to an agreement with reference to some problems and then discuss those upon which they were agreed with the Federal authorities, a great deal more would be accomplished."[25]

The Dominion-Provincial Conference of 1927 gained attention for several reasons. It occurred in the wake of the significant changes in Canada's constitutional status announced at the Imperial Conference of 1926. It reflected the remarkable expansion of intergovernmental issues, including social insurance, that were permeating the boundaries of federal and provincial responsibilities. Finally, it provided a forum for premiers from the Maritimes and Prairies to advance the voices of protest that had overturned governments and the party systems in their regions. The examination of crucial areas of long-standing federal-provincial disagreement was under way. The provinces seemed reasonably sympathetic to each other's concerns.[26]

The agenda of the 1927 meeting emphasized the many issues requiring federal-provincial accord.[27] Prime Minister King had appointed a commission of inquiry the year before – the Royal Commission on Maritime Claims – to deal with the Maritime Rights movement. The commission came up with a list of increased provincial subsidies for the region. The increases were temporary and the meeting in 1927 was intended to produce a more permanent arrangement. Agitation and protest continued from the Prairie provinces, particularly in their sustained critiques of the tariff and railway rates, as well as the crucial natural resources question.[28]

Anticipating adjustments for the Maritimes, the prospect of the transfer of natural resources to the Prairies, and the resolution of British Columbia's long-standing complaints about control of CPR lands in the province, the premiers used the 1927 conference to emphasize that they were facing new pressures and new forms of spending. How would these expenditures be financed? When the King government suggested "conditional" grants by which Ottawa would share costs for programs starting with old age pensions, every premier was opposed on the basis that programs clearly within provincial jurisdiction "should have no strings attached."[29]

The conference also discussed constitutional matters – specifically, an amending formula. After the declaration of constitutional equality between the dominions and the United Kingdom expressed in the Balfour Report at the 1926 Imperial Conference, it was embarrassing for "autonomous" Canada to have to request that the British Parliament change its constitutional arrangements or even implement many of its international obligations. The broad constitutional issues, ranging from amendment to Senate reform, proved divisive, based as they were on increasingly divergent interpretations of the Confederation agreement between and among the premiers of the day.[30] Canada remained embarrassed for many decades.

By the end of the 1920s, and despite the absence of any agreement on principles, "Canada's federal system became more truly federal as the provinces acquired an authority and prestige co-ordinate with rather than subordinate to the national government."[31] Ottawa continued to occupy and benefit from the area of direct taxation (a realm left to the provinces by custom but not law) through the income tax. Precipitated further by economic issues, ranging from transportation and trade policy to fiscal questions, dominion-provincial relations were well on their way to becoming the most difficult issue in Canadian politics. Mackenzie King congratulated himself after the 1927 conference, noting that it had been "the greatest possible success" due to a fine spirit of debate.[32] Nothing had been settled, but the main issues were placed on the table.

Leading constitutional authorities in Canada decried the absence of substantive resolutions to problems and the impediments to constitutional change and effective government. Some were particularly disturbed by the limitations on federal initiatives in domestic policy and Ottawa's conduct of foreign policy, both contained in the continuing deadlock over constitutional amendment. W.P.M. Kennedy proclaimed in 1934 that there was a "crisis" created by the simultaneous arrival of constitutional autonomy and coordinate federalism.[33]

Other experts, including Vincent MacDonald and Frank Scott, were somewhat more measured, but they agreed that the federation was hamstrung by undesirable constitutional limitations. J.A. Corry argued a few years later that the trend was clear. Due to the "unified and inter-dependent economy" and the "rapid extension of government intervention, the politico-economic system strained toward political centralization." Advocates of state intervention among the intelligentsia, such as Frank Scott and his confreres in the social democratic League for Social Reconstruction, argued for stronger federal action and intervention.[34]

Some observers viewed the problems from a different perspective. Queen's University political scientist Norman Rogers wrote in the mid-1930s that the Constitution was caught by the "dead hand" of 1867 and could not adapt to the new era of joint provincial and federal responsibilities. Economists such as the University of Manitoba's William J. Waines and Robert McQueen and the University of Toronto's Vincent Bladen and D.C. MacGregor entered the debate. Bladen and MacGregor examined the effects of unequal fiscal arrangements, such as the tariff, while McQueen railed against the absence of redress for regional inequities. Waines went even further and argued for basic institutional changes. The Constitution had "canalized" government finance so that "onerous financial obligations" had been placed on the provinces while the dominion had used the old constitutional framework to "encroach upon the limited sources" of provincial revenues. A new institutional balance was needed and he pointed to the Australian case as a model.[35]

New ideas about government, federalism, and the fiscal system were under review by a new generation of social scientists. These experts reflected a pluralistic concept of the state, an important innovation among liberal and social democratic thinkers in the interwar period that challenged the older centralist, sovereignty-centred doctrines.[36] This shift in thinking and practice about the modern state pushed a reconsideration of the relations between governments within a federation. And it was increasingly these experts and their ideas that were being drawn upon to advise governments at both the provincial and federal levels in Canada.

The Great Depression delivered another and much more severe blow to the governmental status quo. Canada reeled from a global economic crisis that most seriously affected the United States (one of Canada's two main trade and investment partners) and spent a decade dealing with the effects of the disaster.[37] The Depression left the provincial governments staggering from social, economic, and political problems. It severely disrupted fiscal capacities. The Mackenzie King Liberals were knocked from power in the general election of July 1930 and replaced by Richard Bedford Bennett and the Conservatives. Bennett hoped that the sharp economic decline would be brief. The government he led spent the next five years trying to deal with the repercussions on Canada of a severe, mutating world crisis.

For Canada, the Depression was a national economic disaster with even worse regional effects. The country was hit by the collapse in international trade, which hurt grain growers as well as pulp and paper and lumber exporters, and the automobile and allied industries. The international trade crisis in turn precipitated declining domestic demand for other resources and manufactured goods, all then marked by declines in the transportation sector. The problem of unemployment grew month by month, reaching the devastating level of more than one-quarter of the workforce by mid-1933. Thereafter, unemployment levels declined but very slowly, remaining at the extraordinary level of one-sixth of the labour force in 1938. The unemployment catastrophe also led to worsening conditions for most of the industrial and agricultural labour force since wage levels fell and conditions of work deteriorated. The collapse of export industries created widespread distress and indeed impoverishment among commodity producers, particularly Prairie grain farmers. The collapse led to the heavy burden of unemployment in urban and industrial centres. Banks tightened credit. Private- and public-sector investment in every area from housing to business to public finance became a quagmire. The impact of high and persistent levels of unemployment, the extraordinary credit squeeze on municipal and provincial governments (as well as business and individual debtors), and the relentless demands for emergency relief measures by municipal authorities strained provincial governments and their municipal clients to the point of fiscal collapse.[38]

The effects of this lengthy economic crisis varied by region. The Prairies were devastated for most of the decade, while British Columbia, Ontario, and Quebec experienced a wave of serious economic decline followed by recovery and, in some sectors (automobile and machinery manufacturing, mining and forestry), buoyant growth by the late-1930s. The Maritimes faced the intensification of a longer-term struggle, already apparent by the mid-1920s, to maintain industrial activity while also dealing with the upheavals and decline in fishing, agriculture, and forestry. In the 1930s these adverse conditions worsened.[39]

The federal response was based upon orthodox fiscal thinking that included curbing spending, supporting the financial system, maintaining a strong dollar, and waiting for recovery. The strategy made conditions worse for some sectors and regions while easing conditions in others. International cooperation was difficult to achieve in areas such as trade, exchange rates, and capital investment. Trade protectionism was revived and intensified, the gold standard remained the ideal in theory if not in practice since Canada abandoned it in 1929, and efforts floundered to revive Canada's crucial international trade and investment ties.

Despite signs of recovery in some manufacturing sectors and expansion in mining and forestry (chiefly benefitting Ontario, Quebec, and British Columbia), the crisis intensified over the five years that the Conservatives were in office. The Bennett government reacted to the economic problems by trying to maintain a semblance of fiscal stability both for itself and the nine provinces, several of which faced perilous conditions.

The federal response was twofold. First, there were irregular interventions to prop up provincial finances, particularly those of the Prairie provinces, as the effects of collapsed world markets and mass unemployment increased. Second, there were a few important institutional changes and initiatives undertaken by the dominion itself. These included the protectionist direction of Canadian trade policy in 1932 at the Imperial Economic Conference, the formation of a national (but not yet nationalized) Bank of Canada in 1935, and a myriad of policy initiatives, including commissions of inquiry addressing the Depression in such areas as banking and retail trade. Some but not all of these efforts involved consultations between the dominion and the provinces. The consultations included not only meetings between treasury officials but also, on four occasions between

1931 and 1934, formal dominion-provincial conferences to deal with the issues of unemployment, relief, and provincial finances. These were private and informal meetings among small groups of officials, and they led to no communiqués or précis.[40] There was consultation, but Prime Minister Bennett tended to dominate the meetings and there was no consensus. Coordination between Ottawa and the provinces was befuddled by the sheer variation of provincial economic experiences, the fixation on orthodox fiscal and monetary policies at both levels, and the inability of governments to address the crucial issues of unemployment and social assistance costs.[41]

Prime Minister Bennett promised at the outset of his term in office that "the Conservative party is going to find work for all who are willing to work, or perish in the attempt."[42] And perish it would, but not before it was dragged kicking and screaming into the complexities of social policy legislation in such areas as unemployment relief and insurance.

The Unemployment Relief Act provided $20 million for grants of 25 percent of the cost of municipal work projects and for one-third of the cost of direct relief paid by municipalities. Faulty administration and disorganization led to only $4 million being disbursed by the end of the 1930 fiscal year. In July 1931 the Unemployment and Farm Relief Act was passed, but responsibility for relief remained with the municipalities and provinces. The drought-stricken Prairie region was particularly hard hit, and by the end of the year an independent relief commission was distributing aid in Saskatchewan. The four western provinces called on Ottawa to assume at least 75 percent of the cost of transient relief. The Bennett government responded by agreeing to pay half the cost of approved municipal relief projects and to lend the western provincial governments what they needed to make up the difference. Tensions increased as the federal government criticized the provincial administration of relief. Time and again, Bennett pointed directly to what he perceived as the mismanagement of provincial fiscal resources.[43]

Manitoba premier John Bracken led the charge in pressing the federal government for more relief money. On the Prairies, drought, dust storms, grasshoppers, weeds, and rust joined with the terrible economic crisis in the wheat economy to cripple the regional economy. Environmental conditions were exacerbated by a wheat glut in other exporting countries and the utter collapse of grain prices. Since 1929, the Bracken government had grappled with an unemployment problem that seemed directly tied to immigration and other national policies. The Manitoba premier asserted that the costs of unemployment must be shared or assumed by Ottawa.[44]

Immigration was one contributing factor, but it was part of a larger issue associated with the movement of people within Canada. How could the provinces implement services, and the provincial population be taxed to support these services, if people could move from province to province as conditions varied? Otherwise, how could Ottawa ensure a fair distribution of services across the diverse provinces of the dominion? Mobility was already a concern for provincial governments in the 1920s. The crisis of the Depression only exacerbated provincial differences. New Brunswick, for example, was for some decades affected by the out-migration of people. This problem diminished during the Depression, and the province suffered less, relatively speaking, than did growing and wealthier provinces like Ontario and BC. Incomes did not drop sharply in New Brunswick in the 1930s because they had not risen dramatically during the 1920s, and the economy was not as specialized as those of Saskatchewan or Ontario.[45] The provincial situations and responses would not be the same.

There was also the constitutional problem. The move towards dominion autonomy within the British Empire, marked by the Balfour Report of 1926 and the Statute of Westminster of 1931, increased the pressure on Canada to formulate an amending formula for constitutional change. An autonomous country, it was widely argued, should be able to amend its own Constitution without British approval and therefore address its problems of governmental responsibility. Yet the 1927 Dominion-Provincial Conference had merely agreed that a clear amending "procedure" was desirable: it was not actually achieved. The draft statute in 1931 appeared to permit the modification of any British enactments that applied to Canada (such as the BNA Act) without any reference to the provinces. This enactment would have allowed the division of jurisdiction between the two levels of government to be altered unilaterally by Ottawa. The 1931 Dominion-Provincial Conference committed both levels of government to ensure that constitutional amendments were assessed before they were made.[46]

In April 1932 the premiers met in Ottawa with federal leaders. Economic problems and the relief situation dominated the gathering. An agreement was ratified that shifted policy from "relief work" to "direct relief." The establishment of relief camps was intended to ensure that men did not sit idle while they collected relief payments. But 1932 witnessed the worst ravages of the Depression and a rise in the severity of unemployment. The number of people on direct relief increased from approximately 600,000 in May to 1.2 million in December. Criticism increased regarding the administration of relief programs.

Bennett gave Bracken a stern and condescending lecture on fiscal responsibility as a condition for assisting the provinces. "No convincing evidence has been adduced to show that every possible effort is being made by the Legislature and Government of your province to adjust your affairs and work into a position of self-reliance," he asserted. It seemed, Bennett went on, "that your course has been pursued without due regard to the ever-increasing difficulties involved, not only for the Province but for this Government." The prime minister ended by warning Bracken that if Manitoba did not economize even further, the province would face supervision by a "financial controller" (in other words, a bankruptcy trustee), and one "satisfactory to the Government of Canada."[47] Adding insult to injury, Bennett sent the head of the Canadian Council of Child Welfare, Charlotte Whitton, to investigate the situation out west. After a four-month tour of the Prairies and BC, she reached the conclusion that almost 40 percent of those receiving relief did not need it, at least in the sense that they might survive without it. With the direct relief program discredited, Bennett moved to impose further "economy" upon the provinces.[48]

On the policy side, the Conservative government pursued more constructive measures. These followed upon Bennett's notorious promise to "blast" Canada's way back into the markets of the world. This project was undertaken most notably through the Imperial Economic Conference, held in Ottawa in the summer of 1932. It was there that the dominions and Great Britain, upholding the new era of dominion autonomy following the 1931 Statute of Westminster, gathered to face the world economic crisis. Admitting the failure of the gold standard and measures to enhance imperial trade, the conference devolved into an intensification of the very protectionism that had led to the world slump in the first place. Bennett dominated proceedings and pressed for a series of tariff increases that irritated the other participants, particularly Great Britain. Various tariff agreements offered a measure of support for some Canadian manufacturing export industries, but they did not address the problems of Canadian agricultural and natural resource industries. It all left a sour taste for Canada's potential international trade and investment partners. It was also further evidence that the federal government was stuck in the rut of traditional policies and indeed worse since tariffs had increased to unprecedented levels.[49] Natural resource exporters, especially grain exporters, were left to fend for themselves in the collapsed world markets.

The other major economic policy change adopted by the Bennett government did not come into effect until March 1935. The federal government had hitherto relied upon a consortium of the chartered banks in consultation with the Department of Finance and the Senate Banking Committee to formulate monetary policy and oversee the national credit and currency system. Plagued by ineffective policies, responding to popular although not business pressure, and buttressed by a 1933 commission of inquiry chaired by a British law lord, Hugh Macmillan, Ottawa moved to create a national bank that would oversee the credit and banking system. The Bank of Canada was from its outset a crucial governmental institution.[50]

Despite these policy changes, unemployment relief costs remained an unyielding problem. The Dominion-Provincial Conference in January 1933 again focused on the issue of relief. The four western provinces presented a united demand that the federal government accept the cost of financing relief. By this time, both the banks and the federal finance department denied the extension of credit for further loans sought by the western provinces. Ottawa's position was that the provinces had to get their financial houses in order and set up a cooperative scheme with the Canadian bond houses to establish a program of long-term financing. The conference did succeed in resolving that the federal government should continue to assist the provinces with matching grants covering one-third the cost of direct relief. In addition, it was decided that the dominion would cooperate with any province that set up a commission to administer relief (as in the case of Saskatchewan). All provinces agreed that certain particularly hard-hit provinces should receive better terms from the federal government.[51]

Unemployment relief was an abiding political issue and Bennett's energies were focused on resolving it. As early as April 1931 the prime minister had promised a national system of unemployment insurance. This promise was easier to make than to fulfil. The issue of jurisdiction was the major obstacle, not to mention the costs to an already strained treasury. In a memorandum prior to the 1933 conference, R.K. Finlayson, Bennett's private secretary, recommended that a royal commission should be appointed to make a thorough statistical and actuarial survey before the federal government made proposals on unemployment insurance. Clifford Clark, newly appointed as deputy minister of finance, agreed with Finlayson. They both urged the separation of unemployment relief from any insurance scheme. In the end, the 1933 conference broke up on the shoals of jurisdiction. Bennett urged that the provinces agree to transfer jurisdiction and contribute to an insurance scheme. The provinces refused.[52]

The 1933 conference revealed another serious problem for both levels of government: the lack of factual and statistical information about the economy. The arrival of Clifford Clark in Ottawa as deputy minister of finance signalled a new attention to this matter, but it would take time. Alongside O.D. Skelton, who had recruited him, Clark became one of the leaders of a new elite of experts in government. These men were only a few dozen in number but they were determined to gain public influence and confident they could reshape federal policy. Unlike their predecessors, they had been trained in the new social sciences, often economics, and their education was burnished by graduate studies outside Canada at elite institutions in the Anglo-American world. Educated at Queen's and Harvard, where he began but did not complete a PhD in economics, Clark had for a decade taught economics at Queen's University, one of the centres of the new political economy in Canada. His arrival in Ottawa signalled a generational shift in government circles.[53] Almost immediately, Clark looked to establish a much-improved system of national economic statistics. This vital foundation of modern macro-economic policy-making took more than a decade to complete.[54]

As the Depression reached its worst point in 1933, Prime Minister Bennett again put the fiscal squeeze on the provinces. He refused to recognize the provincial situation as "a continuing emergency beyond their control." Bennett informed the western premiers that, in order to obtain further federal aid, they would have to agree to balance their budgets or at least prevent their deficits from increasing. When Watson Sellar, comptroller of the Treasury, visited the western provinces in April, he reported that their financial prospects were "balanced on hope." Manitoba seemed in the worst situation and managed to secure loans from Ottawa for relief and other purposes amounting to $2.5 million.[55] The other western provinces received loans as well as federal relief.[56]

In July the federal government signed fiscal agreements with the provinces. Both levels of government would contribute one-third towards the costs of direct relief while the municipalities would provide the remaining one-third. Most were in dire circumstances already and would have to borrow or beg the money. The continuing regional drought and depressed world wheat markets meant that Saskatchewan was brought to the brink of default. By the end of 1933, the western provinces were requesting another dominion-provincial conference. Led by Manitoba, they pushed for "a complete federal takeover of relief for homeless transients and a constitutional amendment to establish unemployment insurance."[57]

Another dominion-provincial meeting was held in January 1934 with relief at the top of the agenda. The federal minister of labour informed the premiers that by spring Ottawa would cut off all federal contributions to the cost of direct relief. A national program of public works would be implemented "to take up some of the slack." Bennett used the opportunity to once again "launch into a diatribe against the provincial leaders for their extravagance and sloppiness." He also indicated that he was, in his words, "sick of being abused for the amount of assistance we have given the Provinces to discharge their duties. They should do the maximum possible to discharge their own obligations, and only then should we be asked to say what we should do." United Farmers of Alberta premier John Brownlee argued that the West was not guilty of financial mismanagement and had "cut further" than the eastern provinces. He asked what more the western provinces could do. They were under the same obligation to provide services to their citizenry as the other provinces and had not been "extravagant."

Brownlee indicated that it was "humiliating" to be "treated as a poor sister." John Bracken questioned whether any western province was financially capable of sharing in a public works program, and he requested that the decision on direct relief be postponed. The Ontario representative indicated that his province would "not be critical of the assistance given the West and [would] not be critical if it [were] continued." If the western provinces needed more loans, Bennett responded, they should "get the money from the market." Premier Brownlee was frustrated: "In conclusion I must say frankly – we cannot go on and pay relief and maintain our services from present revenues. We cannot increase taxes. We have tapped every available source. Therefore we must either get assistance from some source or we must default."[58] Saskatchewan and Manitoba were in the same bind as Alberta.

The Quebec Liberal premier, Louis-Alexandre Taschereau, proposed a commission of inquiry to study the entire relief question. Brownlee was in full agreement: "I would be most happy to see a complete analysis of all Public Accounts of all the Provinces," the Alberta premier responded. "We in the West are quite prepared to take our chances in the result of any such enquiry to show the whole financial relationships of Dominion and Provinces." The Liberal premier of Nova Scotia, Angus Macdonald, agreed. He was armed with information from the province's recently published inquiry into fiscal federalism. The *Provincial Economic Inquiry* that Macdonald drew upon was a serious analysis of the long-standing economic and fiscal problems faced by the province, many if not most of which were attributed to the federal system.[59]

While not strictly opposed, the prime minister did not place much hope in the idea and claimed that the provinces themselves would be the sticking point:

> We have given the assistance covered by the agreements and I wish to make it clear that the Provinces have always been jealous of their jurisdiction and never would give us power to set up a commission. It has been apparent ever since 1931 that the Provinces would not surrender any control or jurisdiction, and a Federal Commission could only operate as agreed to by Provinces. Our assistance, therefore, has been only by grants in aid.

Bennett proposed that, in order to maintain the financial integrity of the country, the Prairie provinces surrender to the dominion control over old age pensions, telephones, and electrical utilities. Once again, the prime minister lectured the provinces on the need for fiscal restraint, and now he proposed to strip them of some of their constitutional authority. More practically, federal officials discussed provincial debt conversion and the idea of a "loan council" based on a model used in Australia.[60]

The condition of dominion-provincial relations frayed in the summer of 1934 when the federal government came into conflict with British Columbia, led by Liberal premier Dufferin Pattullo. The BC Liberals were elected in 1933 on their promise to attack unemployment. But Pattullo's interventionist plans (dubbed the "little new deal") ran into federal obstacles when Ottawa demanded that the province reduce its deficit in order to receive federal loans for relief costs and debt obligations. Pattullo wanted Ottawa to make large, interest-free loans available to the provinces for public works that would be paid off while the works were under way. He also pushed for a royal commission. The Liberal premier warned that if federal loans were not forthcoming, the province would default on its interest payments. The deadlock between Pattullo and Finance Minister Edgar Rhodes continued for several months until an improvement in the province's economy reduced the deficit. In the meantime, BC drew on its long-standing argument that the province deserved "better terms" from Ottawa in the form of a special grant. This proposal, the latest of a dozen over the decades, was labelled BC's "Claim for Equality of Treatment in the Confederation of the Provinces." Surprisingly, Bennett more or less agreed and promised an additional $750,000 to BC, justifying this extraordinary grant in part because the Prairie provinces had made further demands for subsidies (from claims emerging from the 1930 agreement to transfer control of natural resources). The award to BC was a prime example of a fiscal system based on tactics of the moment rather than on broad strategies, on politics rather than on policies.[61]

That same summer the federal government revised the terms of relief payments. The federal contribution was altered from a share of the actual payments to a round-sum grant-in-aid for relief. At the end of July 1934, the premiers came to Ottawa for another meeting. Beginning on 15 August each province would be given an "unconditional" grant to be used for relief.

The amount would be determined by Ottawa. Each premier met with the prime minister separately and was informed of the province's award. In almost every case the provincial grant was reduced from previous levels.

Bennett also intended to proceed with a constitutional amendment to have the provinces surrender jurisdiction over unemployment insurance. The premiers refused to attend a conference to discuss the issue.[62] Grant Dexter of the *Winnipeg Free Press* wrote that he had "never known a Dominion-Provincial Conference which went so deep in stirring up resentment."[63] Relations between Ottawa and the provinces were hitting a new low point. The provinces demanded that the federal government increase its aid while the federal government sought to protect its own treasury while arguing that the costs were not its responsibility. Not surprisingly, meetings were "rancorous." Bennett's aggressive style and position only made the situation worse. According to historians Thompson and Seager, "little real discussion took place, for Bennett called the premiers together to announce his policies, not to invite provincial guidance in shaping them."[64]

The magnitude of relief costs now exceeded the fiscal capacities, and not just the fiscal preferences, of the provinces and municipalities, and this crisis was exacerbated by the regional incidence of social needs. As a result, those with the worst problems had the least resources with which to respond. The federal government was forced to come to the rescue with relief efforts based on grants-in-aid and additional loans for the western provinces. The federal contributions amounted to almost half of total relief expenditures and over 70 percent of expenditures in the western provinces. Across Canada, the municipal governments, responsible for about one-third of the total population, had to shoulder three-quarters of the total direct relief costs for all of Canada. They too faced the prospect of defaulting on their large debts, which would have redounded against the provinces.[65]

Out of the political blue there appeared an astounding federal proposal. This project was R.B. Bennett's "New Deal," a major social insurance and regulatory program announced by the prime minister in January 1935. The plan had been devised in late 1934 by Bennett's confidante and brother-in-law, W.D. Herridge, who was Canadian ambassador to the United States and an enthusiastic student of President Franklin Delano Roosevelt's New

Deal. Herridge's outlines and Bennett's plan had involved no substantive consultations with senior officials or cabinet ministers.[66] The New Deal was announced in a series of four half-hour radio broadcasts. In the first of his broadcasts, Bennett famously declared that "the old order is gone. It will not return."[67] He admitted that capitalism was in crisis. "I am for reform," he announced. "And, in my mind, reform means government intervention. It means the end of laissez-faire ... I nail the flag of progress to the masthead. I summon the power of the State to its support."[68] In his speeches, the prime minister proposed unemployment insurance, a new contributory old age pension system, health insurance, and farm credit and agricultural marketing regulation. Although these issues had been discussed in dominion-provincial conferences for some years, they had never been embraced by R.B. Bennett. Now his New Deal – an obvious attempt to adopt the rhetoric and replicate the impact of the Roosevelt administration's response to the Depression – brought only further trouble.

The Conservative caucus was divided between would-be reformers such as H.H. Stevens, a Vancouver accountant and economic populist who left the caucus in late 1934, and defenders of orthodoxy like C.H. Cahan, a Montreal corporate lawyer. Not only was Bennett turning his back on the norms of the market economy, he was abjuring fiscal and constitutional order and orthodoxy in Canada, not to mention his own party's fundamental positions. The package was exceptionally bold but its constitutional validity was questionable from the outset. The package was later referred by the successor Liberal government to the courts for adjudication. The legislation fared poorly in the Supreme Court of Canada. Greater protection for farm debtors was declared valid, but key interventions in regard to agricultural marketing, labour conditions, and unemployment insurance were declared invalid. The Canadian decisions were upheld by the Judicial Committee of the Privy Council.[69]

The court decisions were in keeping with a half-century of practice that had adjudicated in favour of the more decentralized conception of federalism with watertight compartments. The capacity for intervention by each level of government was tightly bound: the provinces by fiscal weakness, the dominion by jurisdictional limits. The constitutional binding of each level was so tight that intervention had become "not so much an exalted concept of provincial powers as 'a no man's land'" in the Constitution. In regard to the practical effect on government action, historian P.E. Bryden has argued that, "by the 1930s, the balance had tilted so far in favour of the provinces that there was little the federal government could do on its own – even had Prime Ministers R.B. Bennett or Mackenzie King been willing to try – to alleviate the effects of the Depression."[70] Bennett recklessly tried and failed. Mackenzie King was seldom reckless.

2

Towards a Royal Commission
1935–37

It is what we prevent, rather than what we do that counts most in Government.

– Mackenzie King, 26 August 1936[1]

When the Liberals were returned to office in October 1935, they faced the same grinding economic and political problems as their Conservative predecessors. But there were signs of economic recovery in international commodity prices and a revival in domestic manufacturing. There were also encouraging trade talks with the United States. The two countries agreed to scale back on tariffs, indicating an important reorientation in cross-border trade and transportation. Further talks led to a second round of tariff reductions in 1938. These were important changes, but the recovery of trade and increased American investment in Canada did not alleviate the fundamental economic debilitation or the fiscal crisis in certain provinces.

The King government was as fixated as its predecessor with controlling public spending and limiting unemployment aid to the provinces. There was no hint of expansionist or what would later become known as Keynesian policies.[2] The economic crisis created a severe gap between provincial revenues and expenditures that eviscerated the finances of most provinces and forced the dominion to provide bailouts. The aim of the new Liberal government was to recalibrate, under federal control, the entire system of public borrowing. This approach led Ottawa to contemplate both a

The original commissioners, 1937. *Library and Archives Canada 010403*

joint federal-provincial loan council system and a form of unemployment insurance.

The pursuit of these measures took up a great deal of federal and provincial energy throughout 1936 and 1937.˙ And both created difficulties for Ottawa. The proposal for a loan council was marred by contentious negotiations with the provinces and a tepid legislative launch in 1936. The unemployment crisis, among many other matters, led to the appointment of the National Employment Commission, but its activities and recommendations irritated the King government. The pursuit of each of these initiatives helps explain the move to call a royal commission into the entire condition of dominion-provincial relations.[3]

Almost immediately after the 1935 general election, Finance Minister Charles Dunning and his staff examined various proposals for joint federal-provincial coordination through a new agency to adjudicate and administer public borrowing. Deputy Minister Clifford Clark was most involved, but he was aided by Graham Towers, governor of the newly created Bank of Canada, and abetted by his own small cadre of officials. Clark supported the intriguing potential of what was termed a loan council proposal, the reference being to a recent Australian innovation. Clark had previously suggested federal supervision of provincial finances and viewed the new proposal in light of that aim. He provided Dunning with background papers on the idea.

The proposal for a loan council was inspired by the Australian system created in the late 1920s in response to its own intergovernmental "state-commonwealth" fiscal crisis. Australia was a more clearly demarcated federation than Canada, and national action in Australia required federal-state cooperation. Australian governments were moved to action by the serious threat of secession that emerged from prolonged fiscal crises in the 1920s. The plan was adopted by each legislature, supported by a constitutional amendment, and then implemented as the basis for national fiscal planning. It resulted in joint federal-state management of all governmental borrowing. The resulting loan council was an extraordinary body due to its administrative autonomy and powers over both the states and the commonwealth governments, and its reliance on administrative expertise rather than legislative politics or financial markets.[4]

For a time, the loan council proposal became the panacea favoured by Charles Dunning and the Department of Finance. A decade removed from his career as a Saskatchewan farmer, cooperative leader, and provincial premier, Dunning had become the voice of Montreal business rectitude, tolerated but not admired by Mackenzie King as an effective minister.[5] Dunning channelled the scheme through the assessments of the increasingly influential mandarins of finance, Graham Towers and Clifford Clark.[6] The Towers-Clark plan called for the consolidation of federal and provincial debt through separate agreements between the dominion and each province rather than through a pooled program as in Australia. Although consultation was the mantra, the mandarins' plan aimed at a high level of intervention in provincial fiscal autonomy. For a time in 1935 and 1936 it gained a measure of provincial interest, even though the most sympathetic provinces and the prime minister were lukewarm at best.

The intergovernmental review of the loan council idea began at the Dominion-Provincial Conference convened in December 1935. Annual meetings had been held since 1931 but this was only the fourth formal conference of first ministers ever held.[7] Unlike its predecessors, the meeting had a broad agenda, including constitutional amendments, unemployment insurance, and relief costs. Prime Minister King attempted to use the opportunity to demonstrate that much of the blame for the poor relationship between Ottawa and the provinces was due to the policies of the previous government as well as to the combative personality of R.B. Bennett. The issues of public finance dominated the proceedings. By 1935 the traditional balance between revenues and expenditures at all levels of government was disrupted. The federal government carried a debt of $3 billion, an increase of $1 billion since 1930, and much of it was the result of bailouts to the fiscally vulnerable provinces.

Officials in finance and the Bank of Canada convinced themselves that there was sufficient consensus about the loan council for a "continuing committee" of provincial and federal bureaucrats to work out details. Between January and March 1936, the outlines of a scheme were put together. An executive committee of finance ministers would constitute a "national finance council," and specific loan council agreements would be set up between Ottawa and each province. Some provinces would be able to opt out. The system would ensure council (federal) controls over future borrowing in return for federal guarantees of provincial debts. It was a severe bargain. The provinces would pledge to the dominion certain revenues as security for Ottawa's guarantee of provincial borrowing. The dominion would seek a constitutional amendment to allow provinces to enact retail sales and amusement taxes because they were deemed indirect taxes.[8] Dunning received cautious support for the loan council from the desperate provinces, such as Manitoba and Saskatchewan, but he heard reservations from provinces favoured with strong revenue streams, notably Ontario and British Columbia. There was general agreement that the proposal constituted neither a systematic nor a totally desirable means to resolve the crisis. But the provincial treasurers agreed to continue discussions.[9]

Manitoba was intrigued by the proposals and well prepared for discussions. The provincial treasurer, Ewan McPherson, admitted that the key issue was "how far a province should divest itself of financial control in advance of a default, and how far the Dominion should go in assuming control." Dunning responded that he did not want the federal government to have to assume control of provincial finances: "Democracy being what it is that would probably cause the rise of a Party to fight such a state of affairs." Instead, in the case of default, he preferred to assign "certain specific revenues such as subsidies, and perhaps other taxes." Subsidies, however, were not enough to solve the problem, so he suggested that "the Dominion collect all incomes taxes and pro rate the proceeds after expenses to the Provinces, and then these also could be made readily available to the Dominion."[10]

Dunning stated that Ottawa might be prepared to transfer certain tax fields to the provinces and to back provincial bond issues by a federal guarantee, which would make it easier for provinces to borrow money and possibly reduce interest charges. The finance minister did not go into details, but he linked this offer to a refunding operation that would involve federal supervision of provincial finances. The proposed councils would also seek agreement for joint security from each province on a fifty-fifty basis.

Manitoba's finances were perilous, but McPherson asked whether the scheme was a stopgap measure rather than a complete plan for balancing budgets and sound finances. "Does this present a solution of our problem?" McPherson asked. "Is the Loan Council a factor unless the Provinces are first put in a position to balance their Budgets? How does a Loan Council help if we are going to go bankrupt a year or two years from now in any event?" Manitoba indicated that it would support the idea but did not think it presented a long-term solution: "We must tackle the whole problem, otherwise collapse is inevitable and default will come just the same, and in spite of us." McPherson emphasized the severity of the fiscal crisis faced by Manitoba. He said he had "fought default – and have taxed to avoid it – and am now seriously wondering if it has been worth it."[11]

Nova Scotia's premier Angus Macdonald reminded those gathered that two inquiries – the federal government's *Royal Commission on Maritime Claims* of 1927 and Nova Scotia's 1934 *Report of the Royal Commission, Provincial Economic Inquiry* – had already plumbed the depths of Maritime economic grievances. He pointed out that the region's problems were the result of both the cumulative effects of national economic policy and the current federal fiscal system.[12] He warned that provincial defaults would be understandable in the absence of a systematic solution to the fiscal crisis.

Ontario countered the federal proposal by arguing that the fundamental issue was not debt but the cost of borrowing. Ontario favoured a
system of compulsory debt conversions. A reduction in interest from 5 to
3 percent would save Ontario approximately $10 million a year and enable
a balanced budget. If refunding were not possible Ottawa should move out
of the field of direct taxation. Ontario's debt totalled approximately $700
million and was consuming 25 percent of provincial revenues. Apart from
Ontario, most provinces expressed difficulty in bearing the burden of debt
charges. They urged the dominion to come up with increased aid. But the
federal government "sang a similar tale of woe." The federal debt was $3
billion and the deficit was $116 million in the past year alone.[13]

In March, Clifford Clark informed Charles Cockcroft, Alberta's first
Social Credit treasurer, that "representatives of all the provinces agreed
that the Dominion should take immediate steps to secure the necessary
constitutional authority to make such an arrangement effective." Clark
assured Alberta officials that the dominion did not intend to control provincial finances but simply to ensure fairness and the financial system's
security in cases of provincial profligacy. Cockcroft went along and Premier
William Aberhart seemed to support the loan council. Clark and Towers
envisioned an agency that would control provincial borrowing more than
it would oversee the provision of credit facilities.[14] Provincial reactions
hardened, however, starting with Alberta. Facing political problems of
his own, Aberhart turned from the moderates within his government like
Cockcroft to Social Credit devotees like Solon Low, who soon replaced
Cockcroft as treasurer. The premier rejected the scheme and Alberta moved
resolutely towards its own solution to its debt problem. On 1 April 1936,
Alberta unilaterally revised and in effect defaulted on portions of its provincial debt.

By mid-April, the Bank of Canada was also souring on the loan council. It had undertaken several assessments of the federal-provincial fiscal
situation starting in late 1935, most written by its chief economist, Alex
Skelton. As early as March 1936, Skelton and Graham Towers had begun
to rethink the entire policy proposal in strongly written memos. The fiscal
benefits were not all that clear and the political consequences could well
be disastrous. "No Province stated definitely that it would participate

in the plan," Graham Towers admitted, "although no Province objected to the creation of the necessary machinery."[15] Three premiers, William Aberhart of Alberta, Duff Pattullo of British Columbia, and Mitch Hepburn of Ontario, found arguments to avoid a commitment. By May, even as the loan council legislation was approved by the House of Commons, the King government was backing away. The loan council was allowed to die in the Senate.[16] The scheme continued to be bandied about among some of the provinces as they grappled with their fiscal crises in 1937 and 1938.[17] But it was never more than a counter-example and it was not raised again as a solution to Canada's problems.

The other major federal proposal for economic reform involved tackling the problem of high unemployment and the costs of relief that fell to the provinces. At the 1935 Dominion-Provincial Conference, Prime Minister King identified unemployment as the "most urgent national problem." He wove unemployment into a complex fabric of dominion-provincial fiscal issues, each "formidable" but together "all the more baffling and difficult of solution." King indicated that the federal government would like to see a comprehensive solution that sounded like support for a form of national unemployment insurance.[18] Depression-era unemployment not only ravaged the well-being of the Canadian working population (unemployment was above 20 and even 25 percent of the labour force during the worst period of 1932–33), it also gutted provincial and municipal finances, thereby threatening the solvency of the Prairie provinces in particular. Federal finances were regularly distorted due to Ottawa's reluctantly given but necessary emergency aid packages to the provinces.

In May 1936, the King government appointed the National Employment Commission, charged with inquiring into the means to alleviate unemployment and to recommend systematic relief measures. The proposal for the commission was championed by the reform-minded minister of labour, Norman Rogers, previously a political scientist at Queen's University and before that a Privy Council Office advisor to Mackenzie King. The commission was headed by the British businessman Arthur B. Purvis, then residing in Montreal as president of Canadian Industries Limited.[19]

The National Employment Commission was no routine inquiry and it raised a great deal of controversy. It worked at a steady pace from mid-1936 to mid-1937. Purvis was a savvy businessman and other members, notably the Queen's University economist William Mackintosh and Trades and Labour Congress president Tom Moore, were strongly committed to resolving the problems of unemployment relief and insurance. The commission assembled important information about the nature and extent of the unemployment problem in each province, including the issue of "unemployable" as well as "employable" workers. The inquiry tried to shape informed public support for a measure that governments had more or less favoured for some time. It released an interim report in July 1937 that discerned the beginnings of a recovery in the labour market but did not gloss over the serious problems that remained. The interim report was followed by six "information service bulletins" issued from July to December 1937. These bulletins showed that effective federal involvement had to be permanent and required labour market research, administrative planning, and new programs devised in concert with the provinces. The bulletins addressed the complexities of the Canadian labour market. Alleviating the unemployment situation required full-scale revisions of dominion aid to the provinces, a reappraisal and implementation of training and apprenticeship programs, appreciation of the distinctive requirements of female workers, and aid for housing, including low-income rental housing. The commission warned that expenditures in public works projects should be limited in order to avoid displacing private investment during the recovery that was now under way. It touched on the issue of a national system of unemployment insurance (which was left for the final report of January 1938) and emphasized the necessity of federal-provincial agreement in all matters.[20]

The National Employment Commission did more than offer a policy fix. It called for an expansion of the federal government's involvement in labour market planning. It also made it clear that national programs, above all unemployment insurance, involved agreements with the provinces. The deliberations, bulletins, and report, however, put the prime minister on guard about support for a federal government program since that would mean constitutional change. King's concerns intensified in December 1937. He was tipped off by one of the commissioners, Mary Sutherland, a former editorialist at the *Grain Growers' Guide* and a King loyalist. She handed over a draft of the final report, which supported federal responsibility for the funding and administration of unemployment insurance. The prime minister was irate. He vented about the Minister of Labour, Norman Rogers and he put pressure on the commission, specifically Purvis and Mackintosh, to tone down the recommendations. Even in its muted final form released in January 1938, with its terse recommendation for a national unemployment insurance plan, the commission's proposals opened up cabinet conflict between Norman Rogers and C.D. Howe, on one hand, and Charles Dunning and Ernest Lapointe, on the other. King raged against what he perceived as impractical reformers like Rogers and dangerous academic advisors like Mackintosh. The prime minister was determined to steel himself against what he now perceived as a cabal of Queen's University political economists among his closest advisors, Rogers and O.D. Skelton, Clark and Mackintosh.[21] Yet the report, even blunted as it was, argued that resolving the unemployment problem involved more than just waiting out the business cycle with emergency measures. Serious action involved the full weight of long-range planning, coordination, an insurance plan, and public investment in selected areas such as housing and training. As with the loan council project, the approach was not supported by the majority in cabinet or by the prime minister. Fiscal orthodoxy and political caution prevailed.

The underlying problems remained. The financial plight of the Prairie provinces revealed a fiscal system that continued to deteriorate despite a partial recovery in many sectors of the economy. The Bank of Canada was alarmed by the chaotic fiscal situation. An alternative strategy to the cycle of interim refinancing, one that might prepare the ground for a systematic and permanent resolution, was to reconsider the whole structure of fiscal federalism. The bank's support for such a fundamental reconsideration emerged from its work in 1936. It began with a memorandum from Alex (Sandy) Skelton, the head of the research department at the bank. Skelton's perch at the Bank of Canada meant that he was deeply involved in dominion-provincial fiscal relations and monetary policy, and sat in on dominion-provincial meetings as well as federal committees.

Sandy Skelton's thinking changed course during the year of 1936. In January he had argued that the provinces no longer had the capacity to deal with the financial crisis and that "greater centralization of control" was essential:

The important consideration must be the efficient and economical government of the country as a whole. It is perhaps time to return to what should be, from the financial point of view at least, the guiding principle of federal finances. National, provincial, and municipal governments are all fulfilling the same function for (and at the expense of) the same people. Presumably they should attempt to divide the functions of government in the most efficient manner possible, regardless of their respective legal, political, and historical vested interests.[22]

At that point, like his boss Graham Towers, Skelton was engaged in planning for a Canadian loan council. By March, Skelton was pushing for a reconsideration of the whole approach to federal-provincial debt. Rather than the loan council proposal, he advocated a much more robust "National Finance Council" that would vest greater power in an expert body of the council, a "secretariate" that would be somewhat insulated from federal and provincial politicians. This council would reduce provincial fiscal manoeuvrability and strengthen the dominion's capacity to make long-term fiscal decisions. The new mechanism would limit and control provincial demands for fiscal support. Moreover, it would offset the distinct possibility of a more decentralized federation and the still-muted threats about the viability of secession coming from British Columbia and Alberta. Ontario presumably did not need to be named as a potential rival to Ottawa since its economic strengths and political clout were blatantly obvious. Skelton summarized his case: if the dominion paid the financial "piper," it was "entitled to at least call some of the notes."[23] The Bank of Canada should cut the Gordian knot of fiscal federalism.

Reflections on provincial fiscal disabilities had already led to somewhat different conclusions at the provincial level. In 1934, Nova Scotia appointed an inquiry into its economic problems. The Provincial Economic inquiry was led by a University of Leeds professor of economics and commerce, John H. Jones, supported by two other commissioners: former federal deputy minister of fisheries Alexander Johnstone and University of Toronto economist Harold Innis. The report was a systematic and well-researched treatment of the province's present burdens as well as historical grievances with the federal system. It presented a tough critique of national policy regarding tariffs, transportation, and federal finance. While not assigning deliberate malevolence, the report emphasized that national policy, not market forces, had primarily shaped the economic problems Nova Scotia had faced since Confederation. It argued also that Nova Scotia had been harmed by policies to "integrate" the regional economies into a "single economic unit." The Nova Scotia inquiry received praise from the opposite side of the country. British Columbia economist and senior civil servant W.A. Carrothers agreed with the commission that the provinces were in "an impossible financial situation." Moreover, he pointed to the signal lesson that it was not constitutional interpretation but economic policy that was at the root of the crisis in federalism. Carrothers called for a national economic inquiry along the lines of the Nova Scotia study.[24]

In the summer of 1936, the Bank of Canada hired economist A.E. Grauer from the University of Toronto to produce a comprehensive summary of the distribution of taxation powers in Canada. By the time Grauer went to work, Alberta had defaulted on loans and the other western provinces indicated that they were about to default as well. The BC-born and educated Grauer, who did advanced work in economics at Oxford and Berkeley, provided a systematic review of federal, provincial, and municipal taxation. The study cited the leading British proponents of the new economics, including J.M. Keynes and Evan Durbin, who argued that economic policy should be based upon demand management rather than supply factors. Grauer's report concluded that Canada had created an ineffectual and inefficient patchwork of revenues that neither met the fiscal needs of the various levels of government nor provided the economic incentives to strengthen economic activity.

Grauer had argued that a "business upswing" was under way but warned that it was not strong enough to counteract the effects of the serious deficits experienced by municipalities and some provinces. He recommended that the provinces should yield exclusive use of direct taxes, principally the income tax, to the dominion but asserted that they should expect that revenue be redistributed across the country: "It was his view," Robert Bryce summarized years later, "that the main direct taxes on income and wealth should be vested in the central government as a means of offsetting regional inequalities and meeting regional fiscal requirements." This conclusion was music to the ears of federal officials. Grauer's other conclusions about the need for tariff reform, greater reliance on direct taxation, and larger unconditional transfers to the provinces were less melodious. In addition to his rigorous overview and defence of contemporary "equity" and "efficiency" in taxation, Grauer tossed in the suggestion for a royal commission to deal with the "possible inequalities" faced by the western provinces.[25]

The continuing crisis convinced the top civil servants in Ottawa that measures had to be found to allow the federal government to "secure major improvements in the division of responsibilities for expenditures and of revenue sources." Graham Towers and Alex Skelton discussed the idea of a commission of inquiry with Clifford Clark. Towers then took the idea officially to the finance minister on 20 October 1936. He wrote to Charles Dunning that he was fully behind the idea of a royal commission and that, if it was done, "a policy of temporizing with the public debt situation of the western provinces could be justified." Towers included a copy of a memorandum from Sandy Skelton arguing in favour of a full-scale national inquiry. The finance minister was open to the commission proposal and he broached the topic with the prime minister on 14 November. Two weeks later, Skelton produced a further memorandum entitled "The Case for a Royal Commission Inquiry on Provincial Finances."[26] "No one can pretend," Skelton asserted, "that the present distribution of governmental functions and tax powers is giving Canada the most efficient and economical government possible ... Ostrich-like tactics will no longer do; 1937 should become as memorable a date in Canadian history as 1867."[27]

On 7 December 1936, on the eve of what had become an annual gathering of federal and provincial finance ministers, Clifford Clark wrote a report that elaborated on Sandy Skelton's memorandum. Entitled "Royal Commission on Economic Basis of Confederation," the brief argued that a commission was the best means to provide a comprehensive overview of fiscal federalism. It should examine "the economic and financial basis of Confederation with special reference to the allocation of governmental burdens on the one hand and revenue sources on the other hand to Dominion, provincial and municipal governments." Clark emphasized a historical perspective because it was essential to understand the "allocation of responsibilities and powers in the light of the developments over the last seventy years." This description was similar to Skelton's memo and to the terms eventually adopted.[28] Clark suggested Newton Rowell as chair and possible members such as prominent lawyers Louis St-Laurent and J.L. Ralston, and economists like Henry Angus of the University of British Columbia (UBC), Jacob Viner of the University of Chicago, and his old Queen's University colleague, William Mackintosh. Clark emphasized the need for a particularly able secretariat and research staff due to the breadth of what was being proposed.

Clark went even further and pointed to some of the "inevitable" issues that such an inquiry would examine. Social expenditures, including relief, were growing at a rate never contemplated at the time of Confederation. The taxation powers given to the provinces by the BNA Act were inadequate to meet present and future demands. The dominion would have to assume some of the provincial financial burdens and the provinces would have to be compensated for fields of taxation taken on by Ottawa. Clark's memo also listed the inevitable challenges to such a commission, the main one being provincial obstructionism: "It is certainly true that the difficulties at present surrounding a Constitutional amendment and arising out of narrow 'provincial rights' attitudes on the part of one, two or three provinces, form a serious obstacle to any major constructive change. Nevertheless, sooner or later these difficulties must be faced and, as the present situation is intolerable, the sooner the better." There was a danger that political dissension and friction would be intensified. Such a royal commission would "stir up sleeping dogs in the form of every long-cherished or temporary grievance possessed by every province, and every minority within a province, since Confederation."[29]

Clark foresaw that the most formidable opposition would come from Ontario and Quebec. They would correctly assume that, in his words, "any redistribution of governmental burdens in this country must inevitably be at the expense of these two central provinces, in which population and wealth are abnormally concentrated, and these provinces may, therefore, take the view that it is preferable to let the Western Provinces go bankrupt and allow the Maritime Provinces to decay gradually." This opposition had to be "tackled" by demonstrating the consequences of allowing the have-not provinces to go under. Provincial default would "impoverish" the central provinces by leaving them with a larger share of the national debt and damage to their credit in the long run. It would also lead to further dominion loans to these regions which would produce a "continuation of federal doles, largely paid for by Ontario and Quebec." It was, "in fact, just because Ontario and Quebec ha[d] the most to lose from mishandling or failure to handle the matter that they should be particularly interested in a thorough examination of the problem."[30]

The inability of the federal system to deal with the expansion of new governmental functions, expenditures, and revenues, Clark concluded, had "seriously disturbed the financial balance" of the nation. The Depression had aggravated the situation to the point that drastic action was necessary. In particular, the "hazardous" situation facing the Prairie region had recently led to the "extremes" of Social Credit in Alberta: "In the West particularly we have a steady deterioration of public morale, the immediate and ultimate consequences of which are difficult to contemplate." For the pragmatic Clark, the federal machine was breaking down and needed rebuilding. At the very least, it was not running smoothly and required major repairs. The "Topsy-like structure of Canadian public finance" had to be replaced, and the job of designing a comprehensive scheme should fall to "a competent and impartial Commission."[31]

The failed attempt to proceed with a constitutional amendment and the ensuing asphyxiation of the loan council also played a significant role in demonstrating how essential it was that substantial changes occur in the federal system. Clark and Dunning recognized this need. They emphasized the importance of the National Finance Committee so that dominion and provincial officials could meet twice a year to discuss such issues as tax collection, administration, and duplication, as well as the raising of public funds through borrowing.[32] These issues would become central to a proposed royal commission. Indeed, when Premier Aberhart later opposed the creation of the royal commission, his objections to its terms of reference revolved mainly around the belief that the dominion was merely seeking a more devious way to revive the loan council.[33]

In December 1936, the National Finance Committee (consisting of federal finance and provincial treasury officials and ministers) again convened. The agenda for the meeting called for discussions about a fundamental restructuring of the dominion-provincial tax system, but Dunning decided not to raise the issue of a royal commission. Instead, the federal strategy was to encourage the provinces to reach that conclusion themselves. The federal "tactics worked well" and federal officials heralded it as "one of the most successful Dominion-provincial meetings of the decade."[34] In truth, some of the provinces had already reached the same conclusion and were again discussing the need for a royal commission on dominion-provincial relations. The commission idea was not exclusive to federal officials.

Dunning stated that the purpose of the meeting was not to serve as a full-scale conference or to prepare for specific policy initiatives; instead, it was "a means of pooling our knowledge and experience with respect to financial problems." Some of the discussion focused around the role of the Bank of Canada, still unfamiliar to the provinces. Its role, Dunning explained, included dealing with provincial finances, particularly in assisting with marketing the securities of provincial governments, as it did for the dominion. "I think," Dunning noted, "we have this afternoon clarified the basis on which any province can approach the Central Bank. And it is very evident that you cannot use the Central Bank merely to get money from it; you have to use it as a general financial adviser."[35]

The delegation from Manitoba gave a forceful presentation. Premier John Bracken and the new treasurer, Stuart Garson, dominated the proceedings and advanced the strongest and most sophisticated positions among the provinces. Bracken came to the meeting with two clear objectives. After outlining his province's financial difficulties, which he had reviewed many times, he proposed that the federal and provincial governments cooperate to secure adjustment of interest rates on provincial and municipal bonds. This long-standing provincial request was aimed at both the Department of Finance and the Bank of Canada.

Bracken recommended a full review of "the economic basis of Confederation" in order "to see whether, in the interests of the people of the Dominion of Canada, the provinces should not be relieved of some of the many responsibilities that were given to them at Confederation." In 1867, he pontificated, the provinces received one-quarter of their revenue from the customs and excise; at present they were receiving one-eighth. The cost of services, meanwhile, had increased in Manitoba nine times over: "I am not building up a case for it now, except to state that I think there is a case for an inquiry on that point." He directly asked the other premiers: "Are we prepared to endorse the idea of a Royal Inquiry into the economic basis of confederation with a view to changing that basis in the light of conditions as they are to-day, and as they have developed during the last seventy years?" If a commission to study the situation across the nation was not possible, Bracken suggested an examination of the situation in the four western provinces along the lines of the Duncan Commission of 1927, which had investigated the condition of the Maritime provinces. "There were difficulties there, and I think they were great," Bracken observed, "but I think our difficulties in western Canada to-day are greater than the difficulties of the Maritime Provinces at that time."[36]

Bracken received strong support from the Liberal premier of Saskatchewan, W.J. Patterson, who stated that his province was in much the same position as Manitoba, "but ours is somewhat more aggravated because of having had a very much more serious drought situation which has persisted in the province for seven years." Patterson supported the idea of a royal commission since Canada had developed "along lines which probably the Fathers of Confederation in their wisdom could not possibly have foreseen." Like Bracken, he argued that the growth of social services now placed a burden on the provinces "which no one looking into the future sixty years ago would ever have dreamed possible." At the same time, extreme limitations were placed upon provincial powers of taxation that made it impossible to carry the burden of services. Saskatchewan desperately needed adjustment and relief with its debt interest. Patterson hardly had to allude to the possibility of a Saskatchewan default, which was obvious to federal officials.[37]

The delegations from Quebec, Ontario, and British Columbia focused on the issue of income taxes and urged the federal government to return the field to the provinces. Ottawa had first imposed income taxes in 1917 as a war measure but had more or less suggested it might be reviewed. While the federal government was within its constitutional rights, direct taxation had traditionally remained in the realm of provincial control. Ottawa had already invaded provincial areas of taxation, the Union Nationale premier of Quebec complained. Ottawa may have a legal right to income taxes, Maurice Duplessis noted, but "they certainly have not a moral right to it." A decade earlier, Quebec alone among the provinces had mounted a serious challenge, *Caron v. the King*, over the constitutionality of the federal move. Quebec lost at both the Supreme Court of Canada and the Judicial Committee of the Privy Council.[38] Duplessis agreed that the dominion should take over the costs for unemployment relief but he was quite concerned over the accumulating costs of borrowing: "I do believe that if one of our provinces went into bankruptcy – which they probably will – those provinces will have a direct bearing on the solvency of this Dominion, because the weakest link must be considered." Dunning, however, remained steadfast: "I may say at once and quite frankly, that I am sure that no Dominion government ... would for a moment consider getting out of the income tax field."[39]

Dunning was quick to scotch the idea of a regional commission along the lines proposed by Bracken: "Our experience as a Dominion with localized commissions, dealing with what after all is the basis of the confederation of the whole has not been a particularly happy one ... Every localized inquiry has merely created or intensified problems elsewhere in relation to the whole body." Dunning alluded to the effects of the Duncan Commission on entrenching Maritime grievances. Surprisingly, the premier of Alberta supported the idea of a national commission. "I think it is most important," Aberhart argued. "It could do no harm, and we could at least get expert information from an unbiased quarter ... On the part of Alberta I express the wish that we could agree upon asking for such a commission." Aberhart returned to Edmonton and proclaimed to the press gallery journalists that Alberta and indeed most provinces favoured a royal commission "probe" into the fiscal problems of the country.[40] British Columbia, New Brunswick, and Prince Edward Island offered their support as long as the inquiry was broad enough. Premier Macdonald of Nova Scotia jauntily remarked that "there is no province in the Dominion that is more willing to agree to commissions than Nova Scotia." Ontario had only a junior minister present and offered no opinion, indicating that such a commission was not an agenda item and therefore did not merit official comment. Quebec, meanwhile, was opposed. "All governments, Conservative and Liberal," Duplessis noted,

> favour commissions to make investigations when it would be better to take action. The present problems are well known ... Now, why should there be a commission? ... The questions that a commission would take up have been discussed time and time again since confederation, and we have had numerous commissions ... There have been commissions on

this and that. But all the time the provinces are going from bad to worse and the people are suffering ... I say, speaking for the province of Quebec, give us the income tax and we will free you of unemployment relief in Quebec.[41]

Duplessis, however, was an outlier.

Dunning wished to avoid a specific commitment to a commission so he did not mention it in the official statement to the press; instead, he urged the Manitoba delegation to discuss the matter further with the other provinces. The seeds had been planted. As Robert Bryce later noted, "in the end there was no consensus for or against the inquiry proposal but there had been enough debate to pave the way for the Dominion to act."[42] Federal officials now claimed that the loan council and its administrative overseer, the National Finance Council, were "half-measures." The real objective should be constitutional reform prior to fiscal reform. According to Doug Owram's study of the bureaucratic minds of the age, "the financial experts within the government bureaucracy thus worked to keep the issue alive at a time when most politicians were working hard to avoid such a contentious issue."[43]

The federal officials may have viewed the December meetings as a partial success, but Premier Bracken was frustrated with national inaction and realized his province was approaching the end of its financial rope. He warned Ottawa that Manitoba would soon have little choice but to approach its creditors and ask for an adjustment regardless of the impact on the principal value of its bonds. The province would not oppose a loan council or any other federal oversight as long as it resulted in a balanced provincial budget. In other words, Manitoba was approaching default.[44]

The dominion-provincial meetings had taken place amidst the distractions of the abdication crisis of King Edward VIII. Dunning made arrangements during one session for the premiers to listen to the British monarch's momentous radio address. Prime Minister King's mind was focused on the potential dangers in the abdication crisis, but he did attend a dinner with the premiers on the evening of 9 December. Three days later King met with Tommy Davis, attorney general of Saskatchewan and a close political ally, who confirmed that the province was effectively bankrupt and unable to meet its payments. According to King: "[Davis] thought it was better to let them, as a Province, square the debts with their own creditors, and not bring the Dominion into the picture. It was the only way we would work out of the financial depression. This is what Bennett's Government should have done, while still in office, with all the Western Provinces."

Days and weeks of flip-flops ensued. On 15 December the federal cabinet discussed the dire financial situation in the western provinces, in particular whether Saskatchewan and Manitoba should be allowed to default. Dunning favoured further loans but, according to King, "he did not seem to know that Saskatchewan Ministers were in Toronto now seeking to arrange a voluntary reduction of interest on securities, and the issue of new certificates and bonds of its own to meet the payment later on. This would be a step toward a reduction of interest all around." The cabinet was opposed to more loans, seeing them "as simply sending good money after bad money, continuing the error made by Bennett." While Dunning feared the impact on Canadian credit of two provincial defaults, King argued that "Canada's credit would be strengthened by it being seen through the world that we were ceasing to try to bolster up impossible conditions."[45] The cabinet moved towards countenancing provincial defaults.

King spoke with Towers the following day. The Bank of Canada "strongly opposed" allowing the two Prairie provinces to default on loans. Towers "thought that a loan of seven hundred thousand dollars in one case, and a million in the other would tide over the situation." He used the opportunity to propose yet again a royal commission: "He thought there should be enquiry by Commission into the financial position of these provinces, and in their relation to provincial and federal services." When Towers met with Dunning, he reiterated that "a Royal Commission and temporary assistance in the meantime was the best method of dealing with the western problem (and the general problem)." The dominion should try to secure "the maximum possible protection" for a temporary guarantee of interest by "laying its hands" on any moneys payable by Ottawa to the provinces, such as subsidies.[46]

The cabinet met on 18 December and the consensus was that Saskatchewan and Manitoba "should try to work out their own salvation." The banks and insurance companies could help the situation and look to Ottawa "for financial grants or loans. They [were] likely to lean on the Federal Treasury." The cabinet wrestled with the situation over the next few days. It was suggested that the dominion could secure certain provincial bonds at a lower rate of interest for a fixed period of time. The issue was further complicated by the rising costs of unemployment relief. Mackenzie King was becoming more disgruntled with the Purvis Commission, particularly as he felt the pressure from the Prairie provinces. "The Commission," he complained, "is really turning out to be a spending body instead of one to effect economy." Again, discussion on the Saskatchewan-Manitoba crisis proved fruitless: "Most of the members present were in favour of taking chances on what the banks might be prepared to do to save them from default." It was decided to introduce legislation "to free the provinces and municipalities from paying bonded indebtedness in gold but permitting payment in existing currency."[47]

The Manitoba-Saskatchewan situation was discussed again on 6 January 1937. The cabinet was by then opposed to the idea of the dominion undertaking to guarantee provincial securities if they were reissued at a lower rate of interest, although the move would have gained the favour of the Prairie premiers. King admitted that "the problem is a very large one as there is little saying of what might follow from default of two or more Western Provinces in payment of their interest ... sooner or later default has to be faced." King concluded, with some complacency, that: "the only question that remains in my mind is whether having large refunding operations to meet in Canada this year, we should incur the additional financial sacrifice for the Dominion which would be incurred by letting the Provinces go into default this year." Like many in cabinet, he hesitated on the brink of that momentous step.[48]

Two days later, when Premier Mitchell Hepburn in Ontario announced a surplus and proposed a reduction in provincial taxation rates, King decided that it was "ludicrous that the Federal Government should be regarded in financial problem with respect to unemployment at a time when we were willing to go a million dollars into debt to help Ontario, and are unable to consider reduction in the enormous dealings we already have, especially in addition to the vast sums being paid out to unemployment relief." The cabinet was now "fairly evenly divided" on the issue of provincial bankruptcy. J.L. Ilsley, Norman Rogers, J.C. Elliot, and Arthur Cardin were prepared to let Saskatchewan and Manitoba default. But King argued: "it would be much too great a risk to take at this time when we have vast refunding operations on war debt account, and when the world is in the disturbed condition it is, and when unrest in Canada might assume alarming proportions at any time." The prime minister had the support of Charles Dunning, T.A. Crerar, and Ernest Lapointe. C.D. Howe was absent but King was sure he had Howe's support. It was finally decided that they "should allow Dunning to seek to make an arrangement with Manitoba and Saskatchewan which would enable them to issue securities at a lower rate, to be guaranteed by the Dominion, taking, however, the subsidies and some of the revenues of the Province as security for any amount which might have to be paid out on the Dominion's guarantee."[49]

According to Mackenzie King, "[The default issue was] the most difficult decision which I have had to make this year. It was clearly up to me at the end, and I took the step which I believe was wisest, everything considered."[50] The issue of a royal commission came up during the discussion. Lapointe now opposed the idea but King and Dunning supported it. The decision was made to leave the issue for the time being. The prime minister noted that "it is a step which I suggested six years ago, and which should then have been taken." Clearly, however, the cabinet was pressed to support the commission idea. By mid-January T.A. Crerar was leaking to the *Winnipeg Free Press* editor, John W. Dafoe, that a royal commission was the likeliest outcome of the current crisis.[51]

Dunning, Clark, and Towers met with Premiers Bracken and Patterson on 18 and 19 January 1937. The federal officials were opposed to any unilateral reduction of interest rates on provincial securities. Any temporary benefit would be offset by "long-term distrust in provincial obligations that such a repudiation would generate in the foreign and domestic bond markets." The Department of Finance had just arranged to sell $85 million worth of bonds in the New York stock market. This position could not be jeopardized by allowing Manitoba and Saskatchewan to unilaterally lower the interest payable on their outstanding issues. Dunning's objective was to come to an agreement with Manitoba and Saskatchewan that would enable them to issue dominion-guaranteed securities at lower interest rates. The federal government would take the subsidies and some of the revenues of the provinces as security for any amount that might have to be paid out on the dominion's guarantee.

That was fine as far as Bracken and Patterson were concerned, but it failed to address the absence of alternatives. The two provinces were sliding into bankruptcy. Further efforts to increase taxation would lead to public upheaval. There could be no federal loaning of the provincial share of relief, the provinces were out of money and options, and time was running out. Still, the federal officials refused to guarantee the interest on new refunded securities, to assume any more of the costs for relief, or to increase provincial subsidies: "The upshot of the meeting was an understanding between the parties that if Manitoba (and Saskatchewan) refrained from defaulting on their indebtedness, the Dominion would appoint the proposed royal commission, and during the time the inquiry was being conducted, would provide the two provinces with funds to meet their obligations."[52] On 20 January, King addressed the Liberal caucus and expressed serious concern about the effects of provincial distress. He spoke of "the disintegration that was taking place in Canada on the part of the Provinces, Alberta becoming isolated, and Manitoba and Saskatchewan emphasizing sectional interests through financial embarrassment, Quebec talking of separation, New Brunswick of itself as a Province of the United Kingdom, etc."[53]

Dunning was prepared to take the commission idea to his fellow ministers. It would be proposed as a solution to the Manitoba-Saskatchewan problem. The cabinet was well primed on the fiscal crisis in the Prairie provinces but the prime minister was undecided. Dunning and Towers met with King on 21 January. They put forward a proposal that the Bank of Canada should "report upon the financial relations between Manitoba and Canada." But this was not yet a concrete proposal, and Towers immediately indicated that such an action might embarrass the bank. He returned "to the old idea of grants being made to the Provinces with a Commission to investigate financial relations."[54]

Mackenzie King's engrained caution flared up. He agreed that the Bank of Canada should not jeopardize its position by getting involved in dominion-provincial relations. But the prime minister indicated that there was "no chance of a Commission." Towers reiterated that the bank would like to report on the financial position of Manitoba and examine steps to remedy its parlous condition, while keeping its role confidential. King met with Clark, and the finance department was instructed to work with the bank on the Manitoba situation. The deputy minister seemed relieved, but King suspected that his officials were pressing for another broader strategy:

All I can say is there must have been some effort between the two to try and get me to go further on the matter of subsidies to the Provinces, and when they found they were up against a wall, found a way to take this step which is the necessary preliminary to Manitoba disclosing its financial conditions to its creditors. The more I think of it, the more I believe the quicker the old situation is known and understood, the sooner we will be rid of it.[55]

The major opponent was King's Quebec lieutenant, Ernest Lapointe, who opposed a federal commission to solve what he perceived as provincial problems.[56]

Yet the cabinet continued to discuss the possibility of default on 22 and 23 January, focusing on the consequences of such action. Constitutional niceties were yielding to the threat of fiscal doom. "I again strongly urged that we do not allow default there," King recorded, "also that we have enquiry into the financial relations at least of the Western Provinces, if not the entire Dominion. The discussion was helpful in getting matters moved along a stage further toward final settlement."[57] Dunning, Towers, and Clark had succeeded in convincing the prime minister to approve a bank review of the Prairie provincial governments. The key was to allow King to come to their conclusion while believing that he had led the way. The prime minister received more advice in this direction when he met with a representative of the Royal Bank on 27 January who advised "not letting the West default." Once the Bank of Canada was put to work, the financial situation would stabilize for a time.[58]

Meanwhile, Dunning and his officials reassured the premiers of Manitoba and Saskatchewan that something was in the works: "Dunning and Clark gave Bracken assurance that by the time his train reached Winnipeg, they would be able to advise him if the Bank of Canada was to proceed with the financial investigation." Even though Towers had proposed that the bank investigate Manitoba's fiscal situation, he was still not fully comfortable with the actual decision to act. Towers "was reluctant to have the bank employed as a mere device to serve a political purpose." Nonetheless,

Alex Skelton went to Winnipeg to begin the examination of provincial finances and was joined a few days later by Towers. They reviewed provincial materials and conferred with Bracken, Garson, and senior provincial officials. In the midst of these discussions, Towers made it clear that the loan council idea was "out." Even before completing their work the bank's officials admitted that the problems of the Prairie provinces, starting with Manitoba, were rooted in a systematic failure of the federal system.[59] The subsequent reports, however, were much less contextual than judgmental about the three Prairie governments.

The Bank of Canada's "Report on Manitoba" was completed with dispatch and sent to Bracken on 11 February. It chastised the Manitoba government for reducing tax loads in the late 1920s, for not building up a surplus during these more prosperous years, and for making unduly large capital outlays from 1929 to 1932. Overall, however, the report concluded that Manitoba had "made strong and commendable efforts to keep its budget balanced" despite the pressures it faced. The province's revenues had increased less than almost any other province in the country despite commendable efforts, including a small income tax to raise revenues, and it had undertaken every effort to control expenditures. Public services were now in grave jeopardy. Manitoba's dire situation was largely beyond its control. Low agricultural prices and drought had devastated the economy: "The province is either not in a position to carry on, or is able to do so with assurance for no more than a short period, unless some unexpected favourable factor should appear ... It seems to be the case that revenues are not adequate, or are not sufficiently elastic, to enable the province to bear the burdens which modern practices of government and the force of the depression have placed upon it."[60]

In letters of conveyance sent to the finance minister and premier, Towers remarked: "Manitoba does not stand alone in its difficulties as other sections of the country may differ in degree but are not in other respects much dissimilar." He concluded: "we do not see any solution other than that which might be provided by a comprehensive enquiry into the financial powers and responsibilities of all our governing bodies, and we are therefore led to the unqualified recommendation that a Royal Commission should be appointed for this purpose." Pending the appointment of such a commission, the report advised that Ottawa "would be justified in extending temporary financial aid." Fully aware that King and Lapointe would review his conclusions, Towers drew upon Bracken's own veiled threats:

> I believe that Mr. Bracken feels that he must present a definite programme of some kind to his Legislature when it meets on February 18th, and that if a decision in regard to the appointment of a Royal Commission has not been reached by that time, he will probably announce his Government's intention of cutting interest rates. Once such a position is taken, it is difficult or impossible to retreat from it and this emphasizes the urgent necessity for a decision by the Dominion Government prior to the 18th instant.[61]

Armed with this report, the federal cabinet acted. On 16 February 1937, King recorded: "inside of half an hour, [we] decided that we would have a Royal Commission investigate financial relations of the Provinces and assist Manitoba and Saskatchewan pending report." King now justified the decision on the following grounds: "our refunding and other matters have sent down the price of bonds considerably; to have two Western Provinces default today might lead to extremes of legislation and to a worse condition than any up to the present." Characteristically self-serving, King noted in his diary: "I have all along wanted a commission on financial allocations and responsibilities of the provinces and the Dominion."[62] Even one of King's most unyielding critics, historian Donald Creighton, acknowledged that King "made a move which, though characteristic of his cautious approach to difficult issues, was at once more original and more courageous than anything he had done since taking office nearly two years before."[63]

The prime minister announced the cabinet decision to the House of Commons, referring somewhat vaguely to a federal inquiry into taxation. The primary justification was the plight of the Prairie governments. The financial crisis was "acute" in Manitoba and Saskatchewan. "The depression, intensified by drought," King noted, "has drastically reduced the income of the people of these two provinces and consequently the revenue-raising capacity of their governments, while at the same time it has given rise to steadily mounting relief costs and fixed charges. These two provinces have thus far met their obligations but we have been advised that it is impossible for them to continue to meet their present burdens with the sources of income available to them." The prime minister implied that temporary grants would be provided pending the inquiry, and a recommendation would be made to the House when the supplementary estimates were brought down. While the Prairie West was in deep trouble, "other sections of the country are not free from problems of a similar character, although they may not be so acute."[64]

The Bank of Canada issued reports on the fiscal problems of Saskatchewan and Alberta in March and April 1937. The Saskatchewan report confirmed that conditions and prospects in Saskatchewan were even worse than those in Manitoba. While Saskatchewan had also been somewhat extravagant in its public spending and borrowing during the later 1920s, the scale of the economic "disaster" the province had experienced since 1930 could have been neither anticipated nor dealt with at the provincial level. The conclusion was sombre. There was "no possibility" that the provincial government could deal with the severity of its relief problems or its cumulative debt. The Saskatchewan case reinforced the conclusion reached in Manitoba. It was necessary to conduct a "complete enquiry into the financial powers and responsibilities of all our governing bodies."[65]

The Bank of Canada's report on Alberta, issued one month after the Saskatchewan study, cast the province in a very critical light. According to the bank, Alberta was responsible for its own fiscal vulnerabilities due to profligacy during the period from 1905 to 1922 and ineffectual fiscal management between 1925 and 1930. Despite the onset of depression, for several more years Alberta had not taken significant measures to address its debt and revenue problems. The bank's argument was that, although the failures of governments past contributed to the responsibilities of government present, Alberta possessed the fiscal capacity to address its problems, yet had not done so. Its economy was more buoyant than those of the other two provinces, and the Alberta government did not face the same level of fiscal vulnerability. Alberta could maintain its level of governmental services with no "temporary financial aid" from Ottawa and without further adjustments to taxation or expenditure. The report made no mention of the need for a broad national inquiry into fiscal relations, though perhaps by mid-April the point was moot.[66]

In order to deal with the immediate fiscal crisis, temporary grants of $750,000 to Manitoba and $1.5 million to Saskatchewan were initiated in early April, while Alberta's request was denied. Alberta would not soon forget the slight, which further soured relations between Ottawa and the province. Reacting to the initial decision about the appointment of the royal commission in Parliament, R.B. Bennett, speaking "as a citizen of Alberta," immediately pointed to what appeared as overt favouritism towards Saskatchewan and Manitoba. He charged that Dunning, the former premier of Saskatchewan, had allowed the Social Credit-run Alberta to default but was now providing Saskatchewan and Manitoba with assistance that would save them from having to follow the same course.[67] "In retrospect," Robert Bryce observed, "it is hard to judge whether Bennett's charge of discrimination against Alberta was justified ... Alberta was unlucky in the timing of its critical need for financing in March 1936 and the result certainly looked like discrimination." A later analysis, conducted in the 1950s by the economist Eric Hanson, argued that the managers of Alberta's public finances had been unduly criticized for failing to anticipate the worst economic crisis in a century.[68]

The Conservatives opposed the creation of the royal commission in principle, not just for being discriminatory against Alberta. Bennett wanted a constitutional conference rather than a "long academic discussion on reconfederation." He argued that Canadians needed "something more effective than an anodyne royal commission."[69] Bennett ignored the fact that the Alberta premier favoured the proposal for a commission and publicly welcomed its announcement.[70]

Privately King shared some of the concerns raised by the Opposition. The prime minister envisioned "an inquiry of limited scope and duration. He preferred a fact-finding mission that would compile technical information on public finances and not recommend a plan of action." Royal commissions could be harmless advisory bodies, but they could also force the government's hand when it came to policy. King wanted a commission that would serve as a "preliminary step in what would be a prolonged process." The real difficulties, he pointed out, would emerge "after the commission had reported and the various governments would have to be persuaded to agree on the necessary constitutional amendments." King's caution, however, ran up against "the ambitious design of the bureaucrats who saw the commission as the necessary catalyst for sweeping reforms to Canadian federalism and, to some degree, the market economy."[71]

By early 1937 economic distress, regional tensions, and political conflict had been roiling through Canada for seven years in the form of the Great Depression. Increasingly discordant notes were coming from the provincial capitals, and national policies were perceived across the country as largely incoherent. Indeed, the provincial governments had become more effective critics of the federal government than the federal opposition parties. There was a popular sentiment that governments were incapable of dealing effectively with these serious matters. The emergence, yet again, of new political parties – the Co-operative Commonwealth Federation, Social Credit, the Union Nationale, and the Reconstruction Party – served as examples of a breakdown of basic trust in political and economic institutions. This loss of trust was of serious concern and reflected more ominous signs of a possible break between civil and political society. Since its foundation in 1867, Canada had a fragile sense of political unity; seventy years after Confederation, the nation was in an era of political doubt. This fragility was cancelling out much of the nation-building politics and economic policy cultivated over the previous decades.

From his position at the apex of the federal public service, O.D. Skelton, the under-secretary of state for external affairs, was deeply worried by these national and regional conflicts. Much of Skelton's distress was rooted in what he described to the prime minister as the "chaos that is developing throughout the Dominion," echoing the remarks the prime minister made to cabinet in January. In effect, Skelton was telling King that his concerns were warranted. Skelton described at length the reasons for his pessimism:

The disintegration of Canada is proceeding fast. Extreme assertions of provincial power, tendencies in several provinces of the Governments to adopt an arbitrary and semi-Fascist attitude, the increasing distrust of the East on the part of the Western provinces, the bitterness and recklessness developing from the continued unemployment in spite of the spotty prosperity that has come to some sections of the population; these and many other manifestations of unrest make the situation in Canada today the most disturbing in my recollection.[72]

This outburst was alarmist if not shocking. It was written by the country's senior public servant, a person expected to contain rather than to magnify issues. If Skelton was this concerned, then there were severe problems. King seemed to agree with the prognosis. He, too, saw signs of "disintegration & rupture" and admitted that "Skelton sees it clearly throughout Canada."[73]

The cabinet decision to create a royal commission into dominion-provincial relations had been made quickly. Then for months almost nothing happened. An inquiry had been promised but none was created. Meanwhile, Canada's economic and political problems, including the problems of fiscal federalism, continued to spiral in the ways that so disturbed Oscar Skelton and Mackenzie King.

3

Organizing the Commission
Summer 1937

The necessity of long years of service on the part of a leader requires dependence on every possible device. A Royal Commission strengthens the hands of a leader with a large as well as a small minority.

– Harold Innis, 1940[1]

If you're pestered by critics and hounded by faction
To take some precipitate, positive action
The proper procedure, to take my advice, is
Appoint a Commission and stave off the crisis.

– Geoffrey Parsons, 1955[2]

A lag of six months ensued between the federal government's announcement and the passage of Order-in-Council P.C. 1908 on 14 August 1937, which established the Royal Commission on Dominion-Provincial Relations. In the meantime, the provinces were made aware of what was coming and their support was obtained. The need for a commission had emerged primarily from the financial disaster facing the western provinces and, not surprisingly, they were the most anxious to proceed. The desperate governments of Manitoba and Saskatchewan could do little but wait while Ottawa's promise of a commission of inquiry and interim aid helped fend off relentless creditors. Despite valid concerns that the province was subject

Newton Rowell. *National Portrait Gallery, London, 157999*

to federal discrimination, Alberta faced its own serious debt burdens and supported the proposed inquiry. British Columbia, meanwhile, ever alert to press its grievances and ease its own fiscal problems, was quick to support the commission but questioned how it would proceed. The federal government responded: "The Commission is to investigate the whole question of the financial position of the provinces, particularly in the light of the financial powers assigned to them in relation to the governmental responsibilities which they are required to assume."[3] In other words, a commission would chiefly focus on the problems of the provinces rather than the federal system. Premier Duff Pattullo continued to press Ottawa for more details throughout the summer, arguing that he expected sufficiently broad terms for the commission to enable his province to show how national policies, particularly the tariff, had affected British Columbia. Responding for the federal government, Finance Minister Charles Dunning relented somewhat, assuring Pattullo that the commission's instructions "will be broad enough to enable you to make any representations ... which you may desire."[4] The other provinces were quiet, at least in public.

During the spring and early summer of 1937 desultory meetings occurred within the senior bureaucracy. These were summarized in a series
of brief memos, mostly undated and handwritten, for the prime minister.
As befitting his role as the unofficial head of the federal civil service, O.D.
Skelton was the conduit and compiler of these memos. The subjects ranged
from clarifying the terms of reference to identifying possible commissioners.[5] In the first of the memos, Skelton explained that Ontario chief
justice Newton Rowell (who had already been contemplated for the commission) identified several vagaries in the draft terms but emphasized
"the necessity of preserving the essential federal basis of the constitution."
Skelton pressed for broad national representation to include all regions
of the country. He also advised that the dominion should consider preparing its own case to the commission or retain the option of doing so, lest
the provinces carry the arguments by default in their own presentations.[6]

By July, Skelton had compiled a long list of potential commissioners
arranged carefully by region, occupation, and age. The list included Newton
Rowell (despite his advanced age of seventy), National Trust Company
executive J.M. Macdonnell, several other business leaders, and such unlikely figures as the University of Toronto historians Frank Underhill and
George Brown. Even Bank of Canada governor Graham Towers was on
the list. Skelton also identified a few prospective members from outside
Canada. These included British public servants and economists such as
Josiah Stamp and F.W. Leith-Ross, the Australian economist Lyndhurst
B. Giblin (one of the architects of Australian fiscal federalism in the 1920s
and 1930s), and several Americans, including University of Chicago economist Jacob Viner and Harvard legal scholar Roscoe Pound. Skelton emphasized the importance of a Maritime representative given the depth of
regional grievances. If the Maritimes were represented, then British Columbia "would have to be brought in." Skelton warned against individuals
who might be seen as too prone to either a "sectional" or a "federal" bias.[7]

Over the summer the names of potential commissioners from English
Canada emerged: Newton Rowell for Ontario, J.W. Dafoe of the *Winnipeg
Free Press* for the Prairies, and at the insistence of Charles Dunning,
Howard Robinson, an influential New Brunswick businessman, for the
Maritimes. When it came to Quebec representation, Skelton was slightly
out of his element but he had a few people in mind. He suggested the

Montreal banker Beaudry Leman, a member of the Macmillan Commissions of 1933, which had recommended the formation of the Bank of Canada (which Leman had opposed); the prominent Université de Montréal economist Edouard Montpetit; another Montreal banker and financier, Aimee Geoffrion; the Quebec City corporation lawyer Louis St-Laurent; and McGill University law professor Frank Scott. But none of Skelton's suggestions went very far because Mackenzie King's Quebec lieutenant, Ernest Lapointe, had the final say on Quebec.[8]

In the meantime, speculation and discussion went on elsewhere. In Winnipeg, John Dafoe was involved in early discussions about a possible royal commission through his long-time friend and Liberal cabinet minister T.A. Crerar. Both were members of a coterie in Winnipeg, the self-styled "Sanhedrin" (an allusion to a rabbinical council), which included James Coyne, Frank Fowler, Albert Hudson, Herbert Symington, and Edgar Tarr. This elite group possessed a strong interest in public affairs and was active in political life and internationalist organizations such as the League of Nations Society and the Canadian Institute of International Affairs. They often met at the exclusive Manitoba Club to discuss provincial and national political issues. They wielded considerable influence with Crerar.[9]

As far back as January 1937, Crerar had informed Dafoe about Premier Bracken's proposal for a commission of inquiry. "I may tell you privately," Crerar wrote in defiance of all conventions of cabinet confidentiality, "that what Bracken asked for was a Commission to enquire into the relative fields of taxation and services occupied by the Federal Government and the Provincial Governments on the ground that conditions had wholly changed since the British North America Act was passed." In mid-April Crerar reiterated his distress over the fiscal crisis of the Prairie provinces and noted the increasing animosity between central Canada and the West. "The closer you get to this thing," he complained, "the more the complexities of it appear."[10] He asked Dafoe for his thoughts on the royal commission idea.

The veteran editor, never one to shy away from offering his opinions on Canadian affairs, set down a four-page letter exploring several options relating both to the commission and to the problems it should address. Initially, he suggested that a commission should be composed of exclusively British authorities. As Dafoe went over potential British academic experts, however, he systematically dismissed each one. The people he considered – Arthur Salter, Walter Layton, and Josiah Stamp – were not really suited to undertake an examination of Canadian federalism due to "the difficulty which a person brought up under English conditions has in adjusting himself to the atmosphere ... of a federal combination."[11] Dafoe, who was plugged into the Anglo-American and Commonwealth networks of experts, turned to the United States and Australia, where potential commissioners knowledgeable about a federal system might be found. He could not think of anyone in Australia who overly impressed him. Among the American experts he knew, only two met his criteria and they were Canadian by origin. The Montreal-born and McGill-educated Jacob Viner, professor of economics at the University of Chicago and a renowned international trade expert, had the competency and experience Dafoe thought necessary to chair the commission. He admitted, however, that Viner might not be a politically acceptable choice due to some unmentioned factor, almost certainly anti-Semitism. If Viner was out, another Canadian might be a good second choice. James T. Shotwell, an Ontario-born historian and a graduate of the University of Toronto and Columbia University, was known for his work in contemporary international relations, particularly the multi-volume Carnegie Endowment for International Peace study of Canadian-American relations. But Dafoe did not think Shotwell was as impressive intellectually as the accomplished professorial economist, Jacob Viner.[12]

Dafoe originally thought that a commission composed of Canadians would be vulnerable to the charge of regional bias. By the time he had gone over British, Australian, and American participants, he decided that a Canadian chair and even an all-Canadian commission were feasible. The one Canadian who possessed the "practical knowledge" of the difficulties of federalism, Dafoe concluded, was Newton Rowell, who had been recently appointed chief justice of the Superior Court of Ontario. Dafoe also noted that any credible commission must have at least "one French-Canadian."[13] He did not speculate much about who would best fit that bill, having opined that the "best" French-Canadian candidate by sheer ability was W.F.A. Turgeon, a Saskatchewan Court of Appeal justice. But Dafoe realized that a New Brunswick-born Saskatchewan judge would not impress Quebec.

In mid-July the cabinet decided upon the core membership of the commission. There had been much discussion about the number and selection of the commissioners. Ultimately King, and most of the cabinet, opposed any non-Canadian representation. Despite Skelton's suggestion of a larger number, King decided that "three good men would be better than five" and joined in the chorus by proposing Newton Rowell and John Dafoe for starters. Rowell was born and raised on a farm near London, Ontario. He took up law and became one of the most skilled corporate and constitutional lawyers of his time. He spent the years between 1911 and 1917 as Ontario Liberal leader and was a cabinet minister in Robert Borden's Great War Unionist government. Dafoe, raised on a farm in the Ottawa Valley, acquired his formidable knowledge of Canadian politics, economics, and government from five decades of journalism in Montreal, Ottawa, and Winnipeg, principally as editor of the *Manitoba Free Press*, which in 1931 became the *Winnipeg Free Press*. Following Lapointe's advice, King identified Supreme Court of Canada justice Thibaudeau Rinfret as the third "good man." Rinfret studied law at Laval and McGill Universities, and practised for some time while establishing connections to the Liberal Party under Laurier. In 1922 he moved to the Quebec Superior Court and then, in 1924, to the Supreme Court of Canada. His brother, Fernand, was a cabinet minister in the King government.

Dunning put up resistance to Dafoe even though the finance minister had initially suggested his name. But the prime minister favoured Rowell and Dafoe "as the right and obvious men," and he personally telephoned them on 23 July. He half expected both to demur due to their ages and other obligations but was pleasantly surprised when they agreed. King claimed they realized the "Commission was the most important opportunity & duty in Canada today. They see the need of it, and what it may mean historically to them to play the part they will have opportunity to play." Dafoe and Rowell enthusiastically supported each other's selection. Dafoe told King that "Rowell was the man for Chairman" while Rowell "was strong for Dafoe." Lapointe, aware of Dafoe's and Rowell's assent, contacted Rinfret, who was travelling in France, through the Canadian High Commission in Paris. Lapointe applied pressure on Rinfret by indicating, misleadingly, that Dafoe and Rowell would only serve if Rinfret also consented: "My colleagues and myself are agreed that no other person could represent our section of the population adequately." Rinfret agreed, and the core of the commission was in place.[14]

The matter of the commission's organization was mulled over for several more weeks. Mackenzie King and the cabinet remained unsettled and the three-man commission had worried O.D. Skelton. He believed it provided insufficient regional representation, an issue that was sure to come up once it became public. Skelton shared his misgivings with Rowell, who agreed. Personnel issues aside, Skelton also wanted to ensure that the commissioners possessed broad knowledge of Canada's political and economic situation. He pressed the issue with Mackenzie King who admitted to himself the benefits of "younger men" and better regional perspectives.[15]

Newton Rowell and John Dafoe came to Ottawa on 4 August for discussions with the prime minister and others. Rinfret remained in France until the end of the month. Oscar Skelton entertained Dafoe and Rowell at dinner along with Clark, Towers, and Alex Skelton. As senior economist at the Bank of Canada, Alex Skelton had been closely assessing the ramifications arising from either debt repudiation or insolvency from the Prairie provinces. He supported the commission but was concerned about the personnel and mandate, both of which he feared would be defined too narrowly.[16]

In mid-August, the government made the decision to add two more commissioners to represent BC and the Maritimes. King informed Rowell, emphasizing the importance of west and east coast representation. "We should add younger men," King observed to himself, "who should be able to recall what had been the arguments in discussion – men who would give the next generation help in its problems, & who wd. themselves profit by what they wd. learn and accomplish." While "the real Commission" would consist of Rowell, Dafoe, and Rinfret, others might have to be added. The advanced ages of Rowell and Dafoe had to be considered. "The chances of the lives of any of the three lasting more than five years was problematical," King mused bluntly but presciently. It was true that Rowell and Dafoe were not in the prime of life. Rowell was about to turn seventy while Dafoe was already seventy-one. At age fifty-eight, Rinfret seemed more resilient.[17]

When news of the initial three appointments had been bruited about, Premier Pattullo telegraphed King venting his concern over the absence of British Columbian representation. The prime minister assuaged Pattullo even before anyone from the West Coast was identified as a potential commissioner.[18] The omission of Maritime representation, meanwhile, was also seen as a problem. As a result, Dunning's ally, Howard Robinson, was recruited and all but appointed when he backed out due to ill-health. He was an odd pick in many ways. Already in his mid-sixties and suffering from periodic bouts of illness, Robinson was known as a reactionary Conservative with few connections outside the eastern Canadian business world, where he was a formidable figure. O.D. Skelton had already warned that Robinson was "somewhat obstinate and erratic." It was infirmity rather than character that took him out of the running. Two Dalhousie University professors, lawyer Vincent Macdonald and political scientist Robert MacKay, became possibilities. Rowell and Skelton pushed for James M. Stewart, a Halifax corporate lawyer. Stewart's affiliation with the Conservatives, however, made his selection difficult and he was passed over.[19]

Robert MacKay became the representative from the Maritimes. He was a good choice as far as the prime minister was concerned because, among other things, the Ontario-born MacKay had written a sympathetic academic study of King's grandfather, William Lyon Mackenzie, the Upper-Canadian reformer. And he had Nova Scotia premier Angus L. Macdonald's approval. Through the influence of Vancouver Liberal MP and cabinet minister Ian Mackenzie, the British Columbia-born Henry Angus, an economist at UBC, became the far West's commissioner.[20] Both MacKay and Angus were active scholars in the emerging social sciences in Canada. MacKay was a graduate of the University of Toronto and, after wartime service, earned a PhD in political science from Princeton University before taking a position at Dalhousie. Angus studied economics at McGill University and then went on to Balliol College. At Oxford, he took degrees in political economy and law. Both scholars were heavily involved in public policy issues, particularly through participation in the close-knit national community that had formed around the Canadian Institute for International Affairs, an organization supported by Dafoe and Rowell.

The commission now consisted of five men representing the country's major political-economic regions: Newton W. Rowell, chief justice of the Superior Court of Ontario; J.W. Dafoe, editor of the *Winnipeg Free Press;*

Thibaudeau Rinfret, puisne justice of the Supreme Court of Canada; Henry F. Angus, professor of economics at UBC; and Robert A. MacKay, professor of government at Dalhousie University.

When the request came to serve as commission chairman, Newton Rowell had been sitting on the Ontario bench as its chief justice for less than a year.[21] The appointment did not require his resignation. Senior judges often chaired commissions of inquiry. But Rowell worried about the heavy demands on his time required by the new commission. He was particularly concerned that his work in reorganizing the Court (for example, in promoting legislation that would require the retirement of Supreme Court justices at the age of seventy-five) would fall by the way-side. The prime minister assured him that his concerns would be dealt with. According to Rowell's biographer Margaret Prang: "[his knowledge] that J.W. Dafoe was willing to serve on the commission and French Canada was to be represented by the able Justice Thibaudeau Rinfret of the Supreme Court of Canada were considerable inducements in Rowell's mind and made the prospects of constructive work seem excellent." Rowell's respect for Dafoe was reciprocated. The venerable editor concluded that "Rowell ha[d] qualifications beyond those possessed by anyone else."[22] For his part, Rowell appreciated the importance of the task at hand. He explained the enterprise in a letter to his sister, noting that the commission would "investigate the whole financial basis of Confederation" in order to recommend wholesale changes to the federal system. He concluded: "it is the most important and difficult task I have ever been asked to undertake." Rowell foresaw the commission as primarily a legal-constitutional undertaking and he blithely concluded that it could be wrapped up in a year.[23]

When Dafoe received the invitation to serve on the commission, he did not hesitate for long. In truth, the editor was as intellectually engaged in matters of Canadian federalism as anyone on the government's short list. He had been writing on the topic for decades. He was, for example, highly critical of the Judicial Committee of the Privy Council in London and its pattern of supporting the provinces against the dominion. Writing in 1935, Dafoe described the situation as a "state of topsy-turvydom in Canada" in which the Privy Council was stuck with an outmoded attitude "which it [had taken] up some fifty years ago and in which it [had] persisted until a very recent date." The highest court "refused to see in the British North America Act anything but a British statute; it interpreted it by arbitrary rules of construction which excluded consideration being given to its historical origins." The provincial powers "swallowed up" the reserve powers of the federal government and "limited the powers conferred upon the central authority." The result "completely destroyed the balance between the Dominion and the provinces which the makers of the Constitution planned." According to Dafoe, "the damage had been done."[24] It was now time to repair that damage.

Canada, Dafoe argued, was already in a constitutional crisis. Only an amendment to the BNA Act could redistribute powers so "as to give the Dominion the powers that a central government requires and will require in increasing measure as time goes on." There was already "a loud clamor for the immediate modernization of the British North America Act." But an "awkward situation" had emerged whereby there was no democratic machinery for amending the Constitution, and even the amending procedure by the British Parliament was not known: "In view of the fact that the Constitution has been amended at least a dozen times, this statement sounds absurd. Yet it is the literal truth." Canada had the opportunity to adopt the American model or the Australian model, whereby amendments were possible through the support of a sufficient proportion of the provinces or by the direct vote of the populace. But the question could not be raised in Canada because it "touched sensibilities of race and religion." Instead, according to Dafoe, the "compact theory" of Confederation – the idea that Confederation was a treaty among provinces – had gained strength. And so, it was argued, amendment could only occur with the consensus of the nine provinces and the dominion:

> We are therefore a country bound by an unchangeable constitution at a time when the Canadian people – like the people of other lands – are avid for change and impatient at restrictions embodying bygone ideas. Practical statesmanship is seeking to lessen the pressure, meanwhile, by working out agreed policies where powers are divided between the Dominion and the provinces and making them operative by conjoint legislation.[25]

Dafoe assumed from the beginning that a commission on federalism would have to offer more than glib recommendations. It would be necessary to change and not just tinker with the mechanics of the federation. Only a commission with a broad mandate could produce results. He questioned the national allocation of fiscal resources among the provinces and was critical of Mackenzie King's fiscally orthodox view that the crisis lay in the "fixing up" of provincial taxation and jurisdiction so the provinces could "plow their own furrow." The prime minister's oft-repeated claim that "it is not wise for one government to raise revenue and for others to spend it" simply could not work in modern Canada. Dafoe was less concerned about the concentration of wealth in central Canada than about the tax revenues open to the provinces of Ontario and Quebec: "The taxable part of the national income to which the whole of Canada contributes is most easily reached in Ontario and Quebec, and if they are given enlarged taxation powers their preferred position as against the outlying provinces will be accentuated." To Dafoe, all parts of Canada contributed to the "national income" and no part should have a disproportionate share: "The great sources of revenue derived from taxation ought to be controlled by the Dominion and redistributed under some formula which will perhaps, under an appearance of inequality, establish a condition of actual equality instead of our present system where, behind a façade of equality, there are impossible conditions of inequality."[26]

Dafoe had often thought and written about solutions to Canada's many political and economic problems, including the crises of the 1930s. He had advised Crerar that the Canadian government should guarantee "minimal conditions of living to residents of Canada, irrespective of where they happened to reside." A redistribution of dominion income to the provinces was crucial. "A catastrophe such as has overtaken western Canada in the last few years," he wrote, "... would call for special consideration on the basis of minimum requirements for educational, social, and living conditions."[27] He was exploring, in effect, a formula of federal-provincial tax sharing based on differential provincial need rather than uniformity of treatment.

The main problems between the dominion and the provinces, Dafoe believed, were more economic and regional than strictly constitutional. "It is obvious," he explained, that the solution "could not be a purely mathematical one based on population. Population and area must be considered together." It was this essential point that politicians from central Canada did not seem to grasp: "It is the problems created by area which are so baffling." This position was based on a historical criticism of the basis of Confederation, particularly as it affected the Prairie West. It was John A. Macdonald's National Policy of 1879 that created these "impossible conditions of inequality." To Dafoe the tariff, the construction of the transcontinental railway, and the settlement policies of the West, when joined with freight-rate policy and the withholding of the natural resources from the Prairie provinces, had created a "diabolical" situation over many decades, "the consequences of which are with us today." He claimed that the entire structure of post-Confederation national policies created "evils" that bedeviled dominion-provincial relations, and he warned that a royal commission would only be effective if it could examine "the connection between past national policies and the current crisis." But these historical problems could not be solved by a return to the centralist goals and tactics that lay behind the National Policy. Any restructuring of Confederation would be resisted by some of the provinces as well as the federal government itself. Dafoe was convinced that Confederation was "on the rocks." There could be no avoiding these issues or providing short-term expedient solutions. There was a need to rethink the entire basis of Confederation and, in essence, to re-federate Canada.[28]

At the time he was writing to Crerar in April 1937, Dafoe did not see himself as a serious candidate for membership on the commission. He knew that he was widely viewed as an outspoken partisan and a regional champion. When the prime minister called on 23 July, Dafoe's response indicated a modicum of self-deprecation but a strong expression of interest:

> Nothing would deter me from giving my services if I could convince myself that I could make a contribution of real value to a task of immense importance, nothing less than the re-modelling of our whole national structure, which is beginning to have a jerry-built appearance. On this point I must say, I am more than a bit sceptical. The journalistic method of rapid & confident generalization from a few related facts has its uses: but I do not know that – particularly in view of my years – I am fitted

for the prolonged intellectual assault upon a most complex problem that is called for here.[29]

Dafoe was also concerned that, as a journalist, accepting the position would jeopardize his ability to criticize the government. He considered accepting the offer only because he recognized the seriousness of the task and the challenges facing the federation.[30] In particular, the crisis facing his beloved Manitoba and the opportunity to re-examine the entire basis of Confederation helped Dafoe overcome any hesitancy.

When the prime minister sent a personal plea, Dafoe accepted "with great reluctance." He wrote *Winnipeg Free Press* Ottawa reporter Grant Dexter: "I have got myself into a jam and must now go through with it ... Once I made a decision I put all these doubts and hesitation aside and am now all set to do the job as well as I can."[31] Dafoe had no illusions about the task he was undertaking and referred to it as being asked "to find foundations for a bridge in a bottomless bog."[32] But his selection would generate controversy. Ontario, Quebec, and Alberta would pose the most formidable opposition to the commission, and as George Ferguson noted, "the three premiers involved had all been targets of Dafoe's ranging fire. It would not be unnatural if all three of them, surveying the figure of Dafoe among the commissioners, came to the conclusion that the report that would be brought was already *chose jugée.*" In the view of his editorial director and biographer, G.V. Ferguson, this conclusion was wrong. Dafoe was not merely strongly opinionated but also quite capable of careful consideration of issues.[33] The work of the commission would test that capacity.

As expected, the choice of commissioners stirred up partisan opposition. Thibaudeau Rinfret had run as a Laurier Liberal candidate in 1908, and his brother, Fernand, was a Liberal cabinet minister. Rinfret was the least controversial of the appointments. He had training in both civil and common law and a judicial reputation as sympathetic to provincial constitutional claims. Rowell was another matter. Despite being well-respected and reserved in his public demeanour, and an extremely successful corporate lawyer, he was not a bland figure. A partisan Liberal for some years, including six years as Ontario Liberal leader from 1911 to 1917, he was recruited into Robert Borden's Union government cabinet from 1917 to

1920. As a result, he was forever after suspect among Laurier Liberals and anti-conscriptionists alike, with a heavy emphasis on Quebec in both cases. In addition, his devotion to prohibition did not endear him to many, including Ontario's Liberal premier Mitch Hepburn. Rowell took on many appeals to the Supreme Court of Canada and the Judicial Committee of the Privy Council, including the "Persons Case" of 1929 which determined that women had extensive political rights including appointment to the Senate of Canada.

Dafoe was another matter entirely. He was not only the editor of the most powerful newspaper in the Prairie West (owned until his death in 1930 by the highly contentious and polarizing Clifford Sifton, whose sons thereafter controlled it and a chain of papers in the West), he was the most influential newspaper man in Canada. He was also the most outspoken, as his editorials in the *Winnipeg Free Press* demonstrated. As an enthusiastic free-trade advocate, a critic of the CPR, a vociferous conscriptionist in 1917, a strong anti-imperialist, and decidedly unsympathetic to Roman Catholic and French-language rights in Manitoba, he had many enemies. Dafoe was a Prairie champion who had tilted against the Tories and the Grits alike, but particularly the former through his advocacy for the Progressive Party during the 1920s. He never held back from criticizing politicians or governments and was a vocal critic of Mackenzie King's leadership as far back as 1919. His criticism of federal leaders was redirected towards Conservative prime minister R.B. Bennett between 1930 and 1935. Dafoe's relentless assaults on the Bennett government led Tory pundits across the nation to see him as ardently Liberal. While by 1937 Dafoe was coming to "balance the ledger" in terms of his opinions of King, he remained highly critical, particularly when it came to Liberal foreign policy.[34] The prime minister was well aware of Dafoe's barbs, and he had even tried to neutralize the influential editor by offering him a cabinet post in 1935. The offer was a mere formality, however, as King knew Dafoe would refuse.

MacKay and Angus were less obvious choices, but, as academics, they were also less likely to face the same level of partisan opposition. They were each veterans of the Great War. MacKay was an artillery sergeant in the Canadian Expeditionary Force in France while Angus was a junior infantry officer in the British army in Mesopotamia. They were active and outspoken scholars in their fields of political science and economics, which put them under potential scrutiny. MacKay had reworked his PhD into a study of the "unreformed" Canadian Senate that was critical of its role as a regional voice and sceptical about the prospect of Senate reform. In 1931, he was nearly dismissed from Dalhousie University over his public criticisms of excessive corporate financing of the federal Liberals and Conservatives. MacKay had experience advising governments and did some work for the activist and reformist provincial Liberals in Nova Scotia.[35] In the 1930s, Angus had emerged as a vocal critic of Canadian government policies on Asian immigration and Asian residents of British Columbia. He called for the right of Asian Canadians to acquire Canadian nationality. Like MacKay, Angus had faced the threat of dismissal from his academic position in the early 1930s, in his case over public criticisms of a provincial government report that advocated massive cuts to UBC.[36] Although the two men were selected as regional representatives, neither was particularly regional in outlook.

It did not take long for accusations of partisanship to emerge. In Parliament, the Opposition charged that the proposed commissioners demonstrated biases towards the West and the Liberal Party. Conservative leader R.B. Bennett criticized them as a "pack of Grits."[37] He approved of Rowell but claimed that MacKay was a bitter partisan, likely due to his running afoul of some of Bennett's Maritime associates. Bennett's sharpest barbs, however, were directed at Dafoe. The Conservative leader did not easily forgive or forget, and Dafoe had provided him with many opportunities to feel upbraided by *Winnipeg Free Press* criticisms. Dafoe, he later told the Commons, "is a man who has managed by one means or another to insult all those who do not agree with his political opinions."[38] The leader of the Co-operative Commonwealth Federation (CCF), J.S. Woodsworth, focused his criticism on the commission's mandate. He believed it was a delaying tactic. The inquiry would "make a leisurely and exhaustive study of things we already know about," Woodsworth charged, "and amass a lot of facts which the government already has. It probably will consume a year, at least, before it gives its report to the government, and it may be two years before the House of Commons gets it." Woodsworth had earlier called for a non-partisan parliamentary committee, in conjunction with provincial representatives, to carry out a quick and effective study.[39]

One of the loudest and most critical voices came from Alberta. The creation of the commission in August coincided with the federal government's decision to disallow three provincial laws, so the province was in no mood for cooperation. Premier William Aberhart now strongly criticized an inquiry he had previously welcomed because the provinces had not been consulted about the selection of the personnel and there were no representatives from Alberta or Saskatchewan. Aberhart also criticized the mandate and what he perceived as the commission's "almost absolute powers" in recommending changes to the Constitution. The premier accused the King government of harbouring hostility to Alberta and its Social Credit government. It was impossible, Aberhart claimed, not to see a direct correlation between the federal disallowance of Alberta legislation and the appointment of the commission. It was not enough to have Dafoe serve as the representative of the entire Prairie region. Aberhart charged, and not without reason, that Dafoe was "constantly bitter" about the Social Credit government. Aberhart also objected to the "politically biased" Henry Angus, who had been involved in a campaign financed by Calgary business interests to report on and expose egregious Social Credit policies during the 1935 election campaign. Angus saw his work as fact-gathering, but Aberhart viewed it otherwise. Rowell drew less criticism except for the fact he was president of a Toronto-based trust company, one of the diabolical agencies of big finance. Howard Robinson, who Aberhart thought was an appointee, was "biased and unprogressive." Alberta's cooperation thereafter waned steadily.[40]

The Hepburn government in Ontario had the most vitriolic response. The Liberal premier had at first approved of the commission and promised "to co-operate in every possible way." He even attempted to influence the selection of the Ontario representative. The deputy treasurer of the province, Chester Walters, was put forward as the "foremost authority on public finance in the Dominion." But King and his associates demurred.[41] Once Hepburn sensed that the western and Maritime provinces would demand fiscal compensation for the alleged injustices of the tariff, he turned against the commission. Hepburn realized that he would find an ally in Quebec. In early June, during an after-dinner speech, the Ontario premier "praised his new friend" Maurice Duplessis as a "great national character" and claimed that Ontario and Quebec should have "a greater voice in national public policy." Hepburn used the opportunity to break openly with King and the federal Liberals. "And now I am going to make a statement that will probably make headlines," he announced. "I am a Reformer – but I am not a Mackenzie King Liberal any more. I will tell the world that and I hope he hears me." Any hopes that it was the whisky talking were shattered when the premier reiterated his position the following day.[42] The prime minister and many others assumed that the response was part of an emerging Hepburn-Duplessis alliance against Ottawa. Hepburn was hopeful that he could gain additional support from other provinces, particularly British Columbia. In a letter to Premier Pattullo, Hepburn described the record of the King government as "one of studied insults, one heaped upon another ... in brief I am sick and disgusted with King and his whole outfit and want nothing more to do with them, politically or otherwise." Pattullo, who had an amicable if occasionally tense relationship with King and the federal government, was non-committal in reply.[43]

Duff Pattullo was in Ottawa at the time and met King in October, on the eve of the 1937 Ontario provincial election. While the BC premier was frustrated with the state of financial relations between his province and Ottawa, he generally downplayed his conflicts with the federal government. Pattullo, for example, had refused Aberhart's requests to hold a conference of the premiers without dominion representation. He refused to become involved in the Hepburn-King feud. The premier "placed a lot of hope" in the newly appointed royal commission. He was less than thrilled with the choice of Rowell, whom Pattullo believed lacked "political sagacity." Upon receiving word of the commission's formation, Pattullo immediately telegraphed the prime minister to urge the addition of a British Columbian. Yet when Henry Angus was chosen as an additional commissioner, Pattullo again complained. He believed Angus "to be predisposed against the provincial-rights position of the British Columbia government."[44]

John Bracken was delighted by the news of the royal commission. Along with the Bank of Canada's report, the premier saw the federal initiative as vindicating the position of Manitoba and the Prairie region in general. Indeed, he believed that such an inquiry into the state of dominion-provincial relations was long overdue. By 1937, Bracken was the longest-serving premier in the country, having first been elected in 1922. He saw hope for the first time in a long time. The appointment of the commission was not officially announced until August, but, in the meantime, Manitoba was already planning its position and trying to coordinate efforts with the other Prairie governments.[45]

The official appointments for the Royal Commission on Dominion-Provincial Relations were made on 14 August 1937. The terms of reference referred to serious problems that threatened to paralyze the federal system. Governmental "responsibilities" now extended far beyond those envisioned at Confederation, but the discharge of those duties led to expenditures that overwhelmed "revenue-raising powers." The federal system was facing "undue strains and stresses." The sense of intractable crisis was clear. As if to underline this concern, the order-in-council stated that the prime minister, with the concurrence of the minister of finance and the minister of justice, charged the commission with the task of re-examining the fiscal "basis of Confederation" by examining and investigating the "allocation of revenue sources," the "character and amount of taxes," and determining "whether the present division of the burden of government [was] equitable and conducive to efficient administration." The final proviso was that the commissioners were to "report upon the facts disclosed by their investigations" and then pronounce on the "distribution of legislative powers," including the "financial powers and ... functions" of each level of government, all the while finding solutions that would lead to a system that worked "in harmony with national needs and the promotion of national unity."[46]

Thus charged, the commissioners set to work. Clifford Clark and Graham Towers recommended Alex Skelton as commission secretary, and Mackenzie King agreed. It was a crucial appointment for both good and ill. The son of O.D. Skelton, one of the country's most prominent academics and bureaucrats, Sandy Skelton (as he was usually called) was a member of the new elite of academic and policy-making economists in Canada. He had been an outstanding student at Queen's University in the mid-1920s, where he was an Ontario Rhodes Scholar in 1927. At University College, Oxford, Skelton combined an active sporting and extracurricular life with studies in economics, and as a result he floundered academically. Nonetheless he returned to Canada degree in hand. After teaching for a year at the University of Saskatchewan and then working as an economist for the Beauharnois Light, Heat and Power Company, he found his feet at age thirty in the new Bank of Canada as its research director. He was often described with phrases like "brilliant but mercurial."[47] Both of those traits were fully revealed during his work for the commission. Adjutor Savard, a veteran Quebec journalist and author, was selected as French-language secretary. He had very good relations with the press, particularly in Quebec. Uninterested in the policy side of the work, Savard adeptly soothed the press, reported on Quebec political gossip, and executed administrative decisions that sustained the commission's organizational life through its many crises.

The first official meetings of the royal commission were held in Ottawa from 8 to 10 September. It began by attending to such details as compensation and staffing. Royal commissioners were not usually paid a fee, although they were paid expenses. The senior trio of Rowell, Rinfret, and Dafoe would receive only living and travel expenses. The contracts for both Rowell and Rinfret stipulated a living allowance of twenty-five dollars per day, while Dafoe received only "actual" living expenses. The younger commissioners, MacKay and Angus, were granted higher compensation: they were paid a stipend of twenty-five dollars per day plus living and travel expenses. The Bank of Canada would continue to pay Skelton's salary, although his expenses of $200 to $250 per month would come from the commission's budget. None of the commissioners were provided with expenses or fees out of line with recent federal commissions, and they were in general less than those the Bennett government had paid to legal luminaries and policy experts on such commissions as Maritime claims, price spreads, railways and transportation, banking, and others.[48]

Beyond the two official secretaries, the administrative staff was limited. Rowell's personal secretary was put on the payroll, but she worked out of his law office in Toronto. Skelton brought two assistants from the Bank of Canada. The bank's librarian, Mary K. Rowland, supervised daily administration from Ottawa, providing over time a crucial organizing force. Bank of Canada research assistant John Deutsch was hired as Skelton's assistant with duties to support him in the coordination of the research studies. Deutsch later worked on several sections of the report. Two expert stenographer-secretaries were selected from the federal civil service. Rachel Fortin was hired at the outset and provided French-language services, and Mary White transferred from the House of Commons staff. Other civil servants were seconded from time to time, including official stenographers and translators for the hearings. In mid-September, Skelton arranged the appointment of an additional staffer, Wilfrid Eggleston, a former Prairie schoolteacher and later a parliamentary newspaper reporter, who served as Skelton's assistant, as press liaison, and later as a researcher and writer.

The proposal for and selection of legal advisors became a point of contention between Rowell and King, and it emphasized the advisory over the political function of the commission. Rowell was confident about his own legal knowledge and no doubt Rinfret's, and he was not enthusiastic about the need for legal counsel. He agreed due to the constitutional issues that might be raised. These appointments generated discussion at the top levels of government since they impinged on the area of legal patronage and involved large fees. King assumed the government would make the selections. Rowell, however, thought otherwise. He was "convinced that in order to avoid any possibility of misunderstanding by the provinces about the impartiality of the counsel, the commission rather than the Dominion government should choose and appoint its own counsel." Rowell's persuasive powers were successful.[49]

King pressed for the appointment of the Nova Scotia lawyer and former Liberal MP J.L. Ralston and for a junior associate in the person of Montreal attorney Arnold Heeney. Rowell rallied his associates and other names emerged. James M. Stewart's name again popped up. He was a leader in the Maritime legal profession and prominent nationally as a corporate lawyer. He was secured despite his Tory affiliations. A luminary of the Quebec and, indeed, Canadian legal world, Louis St-Laurent was also considered for a position. Chiefly upon Rinfret's urgings to Lapointe and with Rowell's support, he agreed to an appointment as co-counsel. Stewart and St-Laurent were hired at the going rate for senior legal counsel: $150 per day plus expenses. Rowell recruited Robert Fowler, a rising star in Toronto legal circles, to serve as his personal legal assistant. Fowler was officially "registrar and legal secretary to the Commission," but he turned out to be much more than merely a solicitor to the chair. As with other assistants, such as Deutsch and Eggleston, Fowler ended up as a serious contributor to the report.[50]

A final senior appointment was J.C. Thompson, an accountant with the Toronto firm of Clarkson, Gordon, Dilworth and Nash, and former provincial auditor of Alberta. Thompson was hired to organize federal and provincial fiscal data. Working entirely behind the scenes, Thompson provided the crucial financial "documentation" of the commission.[51]

Ottawa's powerful band of civil servants was instrumental in coming up with the idea and the establishment of the commission. Both O.D. Skelton and Clifford Clark were influential in advising on the list of experts. The commission ended up hiring many academics to conduct special studies. This group included several of Clark's former colleagues in political economy from Queen's University: William Mackintosh, Alex Corry, John Deutsch, Frank Knox, and W.J. Wynne. But there were others. The University of Toronto historian Donald Creighton, years before his anti-liberal animus matured, was a key consultant, serving as a research study author and then as a senior research coordinator, along with Deutsch and Corry. Another scholar, brought in at the urging of Robert MacKay, was the Maritime economic historian Stanley Saunders, who had overcome the limitation of near-blindness to achieve a graduate education. The use of academic experts constituted a major change in the traditional procedures of commissions of inquiry. While experts had been called upon on occasion in the past, the reliance on upwards of a dozen social scientists and humanists as consultants and writers signalled a new trend in government.

Alex Skelton (almost always known as Sandy within governmental circles) took responsibility for drawing up the outlines for the research studies and recruiting consultants. His imprint on these areas was far greater than that of other officials or even of the commissioners themselves. Dafoe certainly had opinions on the appointments since he was closely tied into the national network of public policy experts through his role in the Canadian Political Science Association, the Canadian Institute of International Affairs, and the League of Nations Society of Canada, but he deferred to Skelton. When subsidiary staff was being considered in the autumn of 1937, Dafoe urged Rowell and Skelton to make sure that a western economist was hired. He admitted to being "a little disturbed" over the matter and endorsed Robert McQueen of Manitoba for an appointment. He also indicated that anyone who was acceptable to Mackintosh would be fine. In the end, another Manitoba economist, the equally capable W.J. Waines, was hired since McQueen was already on the

board of the Bank of Canada.[52] Deutsch, Corry, and Creighton were credited with coordinating research material, while Mackintosh was identified
as the head of economic research, supported by Donald MacGregor of the
University of Toronto and Henri Laureys of the Université de Montréal.
All were notable, well-trained academics. But it was Sandy Skelton who
was charged with holding everything together as the only full-time appointment working on research studies. It took weeks for all of this hiring
to be done, and some were not approved until the late autumn of 1937.[53]

The impressive research program was a first in the history of royal
commissions in Canada. By the time it was completed, twenty-seven
people were named in the report as participants in research on economic
matters and nine on constitutional and legal issues. Robert Fowler recalled
some years later that the commission "broke new ground in the scope and
detail of its research program, and much of this was necessary because
needed information on the Canadian economy was simply not available
at that time."[54]

As he contemplated his newest creation in the late summer of 1937,
Mackenzie King was aware that the Pandora's box of dominion-provincial
relations was about to be opened. Clashes between the federal and Ontario
Liberals had become incessant; the cabinet had decided to drop the hammer
of disallowance upon Social Credit legislation in Alberta. The prime minister took comfort from the fact that he was early in his mandate and a
federal election would not be held for three years. But it was going to be
a "gruelling" time "with all the demagogues working together to overthrow
the federal administration – possibly Hepburn, Duplessis & Aberhart – not
forgetting Pattullo should we encounter difficulties & McNair in New
Brunswick." Amidst this troubling atmosphere, the Royal Commission on
Dominion-Provincial Relations would be seeking to carry out its work. "It
will be a stormy world to live in for a while," King recorded in his diary
from his Laurentians country home, Kingsmere, that August, two days
after the commission was established:

> With thoughts like these I sat alone on the verandah with little Pat and
> looked out at the skies, which seemed to be symbolical of the whole
> situation. A thunder storm was raging in the far west; lightning lighting
> the heavens with its flashes, darker clouds to the North, to the South &

West the skies were clear, and the three-quarter moon shining brightly. It was a strange sight, a bright moonlight sky to the left, a glowing sky to the right. I looked up overhead, the stars were shining thro' bits of floating clouds, I felt our country was escaping, yet not altogether escaping the storms round about, but that for Canada the skies would eventually clear. The rain came on after I went to bed, the downpour helped to clear the air which was very sultry meanwhile.[55]

If the air in the Laurentians cleared for a time, the atmosphere around the royal commission would soon be gathering its own storm clouds.

4

Setbacks and Recovery
Autumn 1937

*In short, the doctors were to examine the patient's past history
and present condition, diagnose the disease, and prescribe for
its cure.*

– J.A. Corry, 1940[1]

The commission got down to work with a clear plan for the path forward.
The commissioners agreed with the King government that they must map
out a national consultative process (above all with the provinces) and a
broad research program. Each province was expected to submit a detailed
submission based on a common set of questions. The commissioners
realized that these briefs would end up being as uneven as the state of
provincial finances. Moreover, the commission had to brace for several
days of public consultation with each province. The obstacles that emerged
in the first few months of work, however, threw into doubt hopes for a
quick path to completion.

At their first meetings in Ottawa held in early September, the commissioners endorsed this dual-track approach of conducting hearings and
commissioning research. But despite seeming consensus with the federal
government, these organizational and administrative discussions immediately set the inquiry on a more ambitious path than that desired by the
prime minister. It would not be a quick review based on summary arguments or limited consultations. On the contrary, from its inception, the
commission set out to create a thorough and detailed inquiry. Still, the

Joseph Sirois. *Bibliothèque et Archives nationales du Québec 650116*

time frame for the anticipated work reflected the ambitions of the commissioners. On the eve of the public hearings, the commissioners stated that they expected to complete them and assess the submissions "by next July 1, if given the cooperation provided" and "to have its report in the hands of the Government by the end of 1938." Rowell confessed to his sister, University of Toronto professor Mary Rowell, that the "task" was "the most important and difficult" he had ever undertaken.[2]

The commission was subject to oversight if not interference from the prime minister and cabinet. Legally, royal commissions are agencies of government. Previous inquiries, notably the recent Purvis Commission on Unemployment, demonstrated that Mackenzie King was not about to sit idly by while a body created as a temporary agency of government offered undesirable or even embarrassing advice. The commissioners were aware of the possibility of interference and they insisted from the outset on the autonomy of their enterprise. They realized that they had an obligation to consult with senior cabinet ministers and bureaucrats on their instructions, procedures, and staff appointments. The Royal Commission on Dominion-Provincial Relations sought to advance its study in line with but separate from the federal government's agenda.

In order to appease the government's concerns, Rowell invited the prime minister to the first organizational meeting. Astutely, King declined. He worried that "some of the Provinces" would think he was "directing the Commission."[3] The commissioners asked Finance Minister Charles Dunning and his deputy, Clifford Clark, to express an opinion "on the interpretation and intention of certain phrases of P.C. 1908" (the order-in-council appointing the commission), particularly surrounding staff appointments. The commission (other than Rinfret) was of the opinion that it should make its own staff appointments. Sandy Skelton explained to the finance department that the commission was concerned that its "independence and impartiality" would be open to "criticism from some of the provinces" if this autonomous power of appointment was not conceded.[4]

Rinfret made a crucial intervention by insisting upon a French-language secretary and a Quebec legal co-counsel. He convinced the commissioners over Dafoe's objection and Rowell convinced Mackenzie King. Savard and St-Laurent were recruited.[5]

The appointment of legal counsel was an important test of the commission's administrative autonomy. Rowell did not see the need for any reliance on legal counsel, but he acceded to the appointment of advisors. The question was whether the cabinet or the commission would make the selections. Spurred by Rowell, the commissioners insisted they should act on their own, including both civil and common law experts, or again risk their credibility in the eyes of the provinces. When it came to technical staff, there was more flexibility. The commissioners were prepared to consult with, but not submit to, Minister of Justice Ernest Lapointe in certain instances. They were aware of Lapointe's iron grip on any order-in-council appointments pertaining to Quebec.[6]

At the conclusion of this first set of meetings, Angus and MacKay drew up a list of background readings. The list contained academic works on Canadian economic history by contemporary scholars, including Harold Innis and W.A. Mackintosh, as well as a number of government inquiries, including J.R. Duncan's report on Maritime claims (1927), Thomas White's brief review of Maritimes-dominion fiscal relations (1935), and Jones's report on Nova Scotia's economic situation (1934). The most notable other work was J.A. Maxwell's exhaustive tome, *Federal Subsidies to Provincial*

Governments in Canada. While the advice was likely appreciated, it was probably not required. The commissioners were avid students of the issues even without professorial guidance.[7]

Administrative details could be burdensome, but it was the consultation process that would prove most arduous. Educating the public is the most basic objective of a royal commission, but this purportedly open process brings stakeholders with very different interests to the table.[8] Planning was under way immediately to organize public hearings in each provincial capital. The commissioners did not, however, intend to listen to anyone who happened to have an opinion. It was decided that the inquiry would not hear from individual witnesses unless they were invited or represented a "recognized" organization. Despite the desire for relatively open consultation, the most significant presentations would come from the most important stakeholders – the provincial governments. In the meantime, the research studies were to commence in order to provide background and context for the commissioners.

Drawing upon the order-in-council, the commissioners decided that their basic purpose was "to examine the economic and financial basis of Confederation and the distribution of legislative powers." Skelton's outline for the research program emphasized fiscal and economic issues, and it was adopted without reservations. It consisted of four themes: economic background, taxation, public finance, and constitutional ramifications. Each theme was conceived as a historical treatment from the time of Confederation to the late 1930s as well as a review of current conditions. But the bedrock approach was economic history and most of the research studies were written from this foundation. Constitutional issues did not receive major attention. What a later generation would describe as political economy (as opposed to narrow economics or political science) was the central approach of Canadian scholars and public servants. This analytical mode focused on macro-economics with fairly limited quantitative evidence (mostly serial data) or narrowly administrative/jurisdictional evidence. It was based upon broad political and economic perspectives often using historical data.[9]

The commissioners paid serious attention to the matter of press and public information. This attention to reportage might be expected from an inquiry that included the experienced newspaper editor J.W. Dafoe, but it was a new approach among public inquiries of the time. The commission went out of its way to ensure an effective relationship with the press while it conducted its hearings. Adjutor Savard, the French-language secretary, was hired partly due to his credentials in journalism and his ability to keep the Quebec press informed. The appointment of veteran parliamentary reporter Wilfrid Eggleston as one of Skelton's assistants was justified on the basis that he would cultivate ties with the English-language press during the cross-Canada hearings. The Canadian Press – the wire service providing news for virtually all English-Canadian newspapers – assigned a reporter, Carl Reinke, to cover the public sessions. Major newspapers such as the *Toronto Star* and *Globe and Mail* dispatched their own reporters to hearings in Ontario, but they usually relied on Reinke's dispatches in the rest of the country. The *Winnipeg Free Press* sent one of its top reporters, J.B. McGeachy, to follow the commission throughout its work. McGeachy wrote a full series of columns that wittily summarized the usually dull sessions. These columns were entitled "Confederation Clinic" and were often illustrated by Arch Dale, the celebrated *Free Press* cartoonist. Throughout its hearings, the commission received detailed coverage. Even outside Ottawa, hearings in the provincial capitals were accorded front-page

Four key staffers, 1937: Adjutor Savard, Alex (Sandy) Skelton, Robert Fowler, Wilfrid Eggleston. *Winnipeg Free Press*

treatment by the provincial daily newspapers. The major newspapers from Toronto, Montreal, Winnipeg, and Vancouver assigned their top reporters to the hearings and they provided stories that were picked up by most of the other daily papers across the country. The commission never lacked attention.[10]

A critical task for the commissioners was to confirm the participation of the provincial governments. The premiers had been officially informed about the inquiry by the prime minister. The commission followed up with a detailed set of questions for each province to address in preparing briefs for their meetings. The commissioners determined that they would hold public hearings in each province as well as regular consultations with all the premiers.

Prior to the official commission tour, Rowell undertook a preliminary "western trip" to meet each premier. Accompanied by Skelton, who was well connected with senior provincial civil servants across Canada, and either Dafoe or Angus, by mid-October Rowell had met with the four premiers. In each case, Rowell reported that the provinces were ready and even eager to make their submissions. In Manitoba, Rowell and Dafoe met with John Bracken and Stuart Garson, as well as R.M. Pearson and S.W. Christie, deputy treasurer and assistant deputy treasurer, respectively. The interviews were most "satisfactory," Rowell informed his wife, Nell. The Manitoba representatives also included two economists, Arthur Upgren of the University of Minnesota and Henry Grant of the University of Manitoba, who were already working on the provincial brief. Premier Bracken made it clear that Manitoba would have its submission ready by mid-November.[11]

Likewise, in Saskatchewan Rowell and Dafoe found a high level of readiness and cooperation. The receiving delegation in Regina included Premier W.A. (Billy) Patterson and cabinet ministers Tommy Davis (attorney general), Gordon Taggert (agriculture), and George Spence (public works) as well as several treasury officials plus two University of Saskatchewan faculty members, economist George Britnell and law professor Frederick Cronkite. Patterson pledged that Saskatchewan's brief would be ready by early December. Rowell commented that his trip to the province led him to realize first-hand what a "tragic" situation Saskatchewan had experienced in the past seven years of the Depression.[12]

Rowell and Dafoe expected the cooperation they received in Manitoba and Saskatchewan. After all, the commission was established largely to deal with the harrowing economic situations facing these two provinces. In Alberta, where relations between Ottawa and Edmonton had become confrontational due to federal disallowance of provincial legislation, the atmosphere was expected to be tense. But the commissioners' reception was surprisingly amicable. They met Premier William Aberhart and the new treasurer, Solon Low, as well as Deputy Treasurer J.F. Percival and provincial auditor C.M. Lang. John Brownlee, ousted as premier in 1934 but now an executive with the United Grain Growers in Calgary, was still highly influential as an advisor to the province.[13] *Edmonton Journal* editor John Imrie was also in attendance. The Albertans indicated that the province's "case" was already being prepared and would be ready by December. Two economists from the University of Minnesota, Warren Waite and E.P. Schmidt, were already hard at work. Rowell was pleased by Alberta's cooperation and Aberhart's geniality. He noted that the more northerly parkland region of Alberta was reasonably "well-off" but that the southern half was "dried out like Saskatchewan." Rowell did express concern about the strong influence of Major C.H. Douglas, the Scottish engineer, theorist, and pioneer of Social Credit, and his apparent control over his "guinea pig," Premier Aberhart.[14]

Henry Angus accompanied Rowell and Skelton to Victoria. The British Columbia delegation consisted of Premier Duff Pattullo and a team of officials, including Treasurer John Hart, Attorney General Gordon Wismer, as well as the province's legal counsel for the commission, J.W. deB. Farris, and the chair of the Economic Planning Board, W.A. Carrothers. Unlike the other western provinces, BC warned that it would not be ready to submit its brief until the early spring of 1938 and indicated a preference to await the presentations of the Maritime provinces.[15]

Rowell's western tour fulfilled its primary objective. The commissioners were confident that the western provinces, regardless of their disposition towards the federal government, were not only committed to the inquiry but also engaged in making serious, researched presentations. In each case, it was clear that a bevy of senior officials and outside experts would contribute. Meanwhile, MacKay and Rowell coaxed the other provinces to get under way, and the commission adjourned until the first public hearings could be arranged. These hearings were scheduled for the epicentres of Canada's fiscal crisis, Winnipeg and Regina, in late November and early December 1937.

The initial encounters of the commissioners with the three Maritime provinces were more varied. MacKay contacted Premiers Angus Macdonald of Nova Scotia, Thane Campbell of Prince Edward Island, and Allison Dysart of New Brunswick in early September. MacKay postponed the meetings after he realized his presence would not be helpful due to re-sentment in New Brunswick about his appointment.[16] Rowell and Skelton came to MacKay's aid in trying to drum up support in the three Maritime capitals. Nova Scotia was receptive, PEI was cooperative, but New Bruns-wick was decidedly prickly.

Premier Dysart was irritated by the failure of the federal government to appoint a New Brunswicker to the commission after Howard Robinson had demurred. MacKay's position as a Dalhousie University professor did not give him the regional credentials to serve as a Maritime representative. Dysart also complained about being "completely ignored" in the hiring of commission staff. MacKay explained that the appointment of commis-sioners was a federal government responsibility and argued that the selec-tion of expert advisors was based on "merit." Dysart was not mollified. MacKay warned Sandy Skelton that the province was "smouldering over appointments." MacKay spent some time trying to placate Dysart by pro-moting the hiring of several individuals with New Brunswick connections to research posts.[17] Rowell received positive receptions in Halifax and Charlottetown. He noted the congeniality and enthusiasm of the Nova Scotia premier and the "attractive" and "prosperous air of PEI."[18]

Quebec and Ontario presented more serious problems. Rowell was uncertain as to how the Quebec government of Maurice Duplessis was going to react.[19] Reports indicated that Ontario was fine with the com-mission despite Premier Hepburn's mercurial attitude towards the King government. In any case, the commission emerged from consultations with ministers and officials in the two powerhouse provinces assured of their cooperation.[20]

Provincial cooperation was essential, but the commission still needed to frame its objectives. When Rowell first held discussions about organiz-ation and procedures with King, Lapointe, and Dafoe, he reiterated his

"Adrift on a Stormy Sea" – editorial cartoon, 30 November 1937.
Winnipeg Free Press

view that the commission was "purely constitutional in character, although embracing the financial consequences of constitutional arrangements." Dafoe agreed that a constitutional crisis was facing Canada, and he was concerned over how the King government would deal with an amending procedure.[21] Quebec had advanced the position of a constitutional veto to the point that it was now widely accepted that provincial consent was essential for any amending formula. Dafoe vehemently opposed the compact theory of Confederation, but that theory was now being openly touted by Quebec as well as by Ontario.

For Dafoe, the inquiry was about more than the Constitution. He pressed Rowell and the others in the September meetings to ensure that the "distribution of legislative powers" would not overwhelm the crucial areas of fiscal policy, including taxation and "public expenditures." Two weeks after the official announcement of the commission, Dafoe wrote to Sandy Skelton that fiscal policy and not constitutional questions were the most germane. Regardless, these fiscal issues were "all inextricably intertwined":

> The basic problem as it seems to be at this stage of the inquiry is how to establish throughout the Dominion certain minimum standards both with regard to the individual and the provinces. There must, of course, be wide variations both in the wealth of provinces and in the opportunities for gainful pursuits afforded by the different territorial areas: and nothing can or should be done to reduce the variations to a uniformity. The rough and ready solution reached in Australia, as you know, is that the weak provinces are entitled, where the case is established, to special aid up to a minimum standard.

The "constitutional aspects" were "less urgent than the others" and would be the most contentious. This interpretation was agreeable to Skelton, who showed little interest in constitutional matters.[22]

Dafoe was assuming a role with the commission similar to that which he played at the *Winnipeg Free Press*. At the newspaper, senior staff did the bulk of the editorial work and writing but subjected it to Dafoe's review. He was the wise elder whose advice and authority were respected by younger colleagues. At the commission, Dafoe was not the chair, but he built up close working ties with the younger men, Angus, MacKay, and Fowler, and he maintained a good relationship with the sometimes erratic Skelton. Dafoe's senior editor at the *Winnipeg Free Press*, George Ferguson, commented on these relationships:

> The Commissioners found themselves surrounded by a large group of the ablest scholars the country possessed, mostly men much younger than Dafoe. He reveled in their company, for he loved youth; and in the informal sessions of the Commission and in his discussions with the experts there is endless evidence of the value, to the work, of his long experience, his own great learning and his sagacious judgment. As one of the associates remarked, it was the mere fact that he was there that counted the most.[23]

Ferguson also asserted that Dafoe, who had a well-earned reputation as a fierce partisan, was also quite capable of detached investigations of issues and he demonstrated this capacity during the commission's work. The even more detached Rowell, already guarding his waning reserves of health, guided the planning of the consultative and research programs drawn up by Skelton and Deutsch. As his eyes and ears on staff, Rowell had the capable Robert Fowler as his legal assistant.[24]

Just weeks into the preparation stage, the commission was dealt a setback. Justice Thibaudeau Rinfret missed the October meetings because he was ill and confined to his bed. The threat of Rinfret's resignation was suddenly a reality, and it took several weeks to determine whether he would continue. Rowell alerted his fellow commissioners about the problem and asked them to compose their views on whether a replacement would be needed. Apart from any personal sympathies regarding Rinfret's health, Rowell and the others realized that his resignation posed a threat to their credibility. Rowell explained that Rinfret "inspired great confidence in Quebec, notably with Premier Maurice Duplessis. Failure to find the right replacement might seriously jeopardize the whole enterprise." Dafoe agreed that Rinfret's "retirement would be an almost irreparable loss to the Commission."[25] Nonetheless, Rinfret resigned.[26]

Rowell deferred to the government in the search for a replacement, but he did not hesitate to make representations on behalf of the commission. He hoped the prime minister would look to the most prominent jurists of Quebec, such as Louis St-Laurent and Arthur Vallée. Both were influential lawyers of national standing. Not surprisingly, Mackenzie King handed the issue to Ernest Lapointe. On 2 November, King met with Rowell and Dafoe to discuss the situation. The names that emerged were Léon-Mercier Gouin, an academic lawyer then teaching at the small Université d'Ottawa, and René Morin, prominent in provincial business circles as chair of the Banque Canadienne Nationale. Dafoe had strong reservations about Gouin, likely due to his brother Paul Gouin's profile as a Quebec *nationaliste* and rival of Duplessis. The prime minister contacted Morin, who demurred due to business responsibilities that precluded a lengthy absence from the bank.[27] When approached, the chief justice of Quebec, Joseph-M. Tellier, also declined. Rowell admitted that he thought Tellier, ten years Rowell's senior, was already deceased.[28] St-Laurent was considered, but he was viewed as too expensive and as an awkward pick since he had already been retained as commission counsel.[29] The whole matter was handed back to Lapointe.

After consulting with his Quebec caucus and with St-Laurent, Lapointe determined that Quebec notary Joseph Sirois should be recruited. Sirois was a leading notary in Quebec City, a friend and colleague of St-Laurent, and a professor of constitutional and administrative law at Laval University, where he had completed a *doctorat* in law on notarial practice. He was a successful *fonctionnaire,* but he was not otherwise well known in Quebec or the rest of Canada. St-Laurent went to work convincing Sirois, who expressed little initial interest in the job. St-Laurent succeeded and Rowell, after some checking of his own, was pleased with the selection. He pointed out to Dafoe that in Quebec, notaries had greater popular standing than lawyers and judges and that Sirois possessed the rare distinction of being acceptable to both federal and provincial leaders.[30]

In late November 1937, the Royal Commission on Dominion-Provincial Relations prepared for its first public hearings. Then a conflict blew up with the federal cabinet over the commission's means of travel. Rowell assumed that the federal government would provide a private railway car for the staff. This means of transportation was customary for major commissions of inquiry, most recently the Macmillan Commission on Banking. On the eve of departure, however, Rowell was "dismayed and then angered to learn that the government claimed to know nothing of such an arrangement." The cabinet had decided against the private car (on the recommendation of Dunning in finance) due to the already mounting expenses of the commission and the questions that such an arrangement would raise in Parliament. Rowell was furious: "[I informed Dunning in] vigorous language what I thought of them and that if I could honourably retire I would."[31] Rowell reminded the prime minister that recent commissions had been provided with a private car. He argued that it was indispensable for the group to work together while travelling long distances. Mackenzie King was not impressed: "I was disgusted yesterday with a request from Rowell for a private car for the Dominion-Provincial Relations Commission. I am afraid that the Government is going to suffer heavily through expenditures made on account of Royal Commissions." Within two days, however, Rowell had his private railway car. "I understand they decided to let Rowell have a private car," King wrote, "as he had almost threatened resignation in the appeal made to Dunning this morning." The self-righteous prime minister concluded: "it is amazing what men who regard themselves as the saviours of Society come to demand through the inflated ideas which position brings with it."[32]

As the Prairie winter descended on southern Manitoba and temperatures plunged, the commission arrived in Winnipeg. Public hearings commenced in the Manitoba capital in recognition of the province's early support for the commission and its enthusiastic preparations. The commissioners and staff were accommodated in the Hotel Fort Garry, the CNR's Winnipeg flagship location, both an impressive residence and conveniently located half a mile from the site of commission activities. The hearings began on 29 November 1937 at the Provincial Law Courts Building on Broadway Avenue, a palatial structure almost as impressive as the Legislature Buildings situated across the wide boulevard. Commission staff took transcripts of the hearings and copied them each day, providing copies for the commissioners and staff as well as distributing them to each provincial government, a procedure followed throughout the public hearings. Regardless, certain premiers complained about the commission not keeping them informed.[33]

The seating arrangement of the commissioners reflected the geography of Canada. Angus of British Columbia was seated on the far left, Dafoe of Manitoba was next, Rowell of Ontario was in the centre, while Sirois of Quebec was next, and MacKay of Nova Scotia was on the far right. Louis St-Laurent accompanied the commission as counsel. The original plan was to use McGregor Stewart in the West and St-Laurent in the East. But Stewart, who had survived a serious childhood bout of polio and experienced life-long mobility limitations, broke his leg two weeks earlier and could not work or travel for some time.[34] As it turned out, St-Laurent played a more active role than expected: "Looking very much the highly-paid eastern Canadian lawyer in his well-cut conservative suit, his dark hair graying at the temples, and his salt-and-pepper moustache neatly trimmed," he "questioned witnesses closely and became involved in lengthy debates on their briefs."[35]

Manitoba was an appropriate place to commence the hearings for several reasons. First, it was hard hit by the Depression. Like the other

Prairie provinces, its agricultural economy was ravaged by the collapse of wheat markets with serious ramifications for other industries, including railways and manufacturing.[36] Second, Manitoba's public finances were gutted by the continuing economic crisis and the cumulative imbalances of public finance in Canada. The province and the municipalities (particularly Winnipeg) were almost incapable of dealing with the burdens of unemployment and impoverishment as well as the rising costs of government. Third, and more prosaically, the Bracken government was eager and ready to present a case for the reform of the federal system, including national economic policies starting with tariffs and freight rates.[37] At one point in the spring of 1937, Bracken tried to choreograph a common regional position by meeting with representatives from Alberta and Saskatchewan in Regina. For a time it looked as though the other two Prairie provinces would agree, but Aberhart thwarted the efforts and Bracken's attempts at formal coordination were abandoned.[38] Despite its enthusiastic support, the Manitoba government team was working on its material almost until the last minute. The completed brief was delivered, hot off the presses, only two days before hearings began, forcing the commissioners to scramble and read material the night before each presentation.[39]

There was a sense among the other provinces that Manitoba was being given preferential treatment. Despite this perception, the relationship between Bracken and Dafoe was never close. The premier was not, for example, part of Dafoe's inner circle, "the Sanhedrin" of leading Winnipeggers at the Manitoba Club. Dafoe's sympathy for Progressivism led him to support Bracken's United Farmers' coalition government during its two decades in office, although it did not prevent him from being critical. The two men did share a distinctly Prairie perspective about the severity of the crisis in Canadian federalism,[40] and they each suggested University of Chicago economist Jacob Viner, a relentless critic of protectionism, as a possible commissioner. Bracken had hoped that Viner's appointment would galvanize a common Prairie position. Viner did come on board as an advisor to the Manitoba team and later reiterated the province's argument about the impact of the tariff.[41]

The province's multi-volume brief, entitled *Manitoba's Case,* was an impressive and comprehensive set of studies, "a formidable affair in nine parts of about 40 pages each." Bracken was a careful, informed, and systematic administrator, while his new treasurer, Stuart Garson, was a devoted and at times brilliant policy-maker. With a team of experienced senior bureaucrats and policy advisors, they ensured that the province was well prepared for the hearings. Bracken presided but Garson took a leading role.[42]

Manitoba recruited a team of experts that matched the commission's own pool of talent. The province had created the Economic Survey Board in 1937, which provided eighteen economic studies over the following year. *Manitoba's Case* reflected that depth. The consultants included University of Manitoba economists H.C. Grant and W.J. Waines (who also conducted research for the commission itself) and the consulting economists Alvin Hansen from Harvard University, Arthur Upgren from the University of Minnesota, and Jacob Viner from the University of Chicago. James Coyne and Isaac Pitblado worked as legal advisors. The Manitoba submission was conceived not just as a report but also as a broad interpretation of the federal crisis from a provincial and regional perspective.[43]

Over the next week the provincial government presented its case.[44] The testimony provided the most extensive study produced to that time of Manitoba's (and indeed the West's) fiscal and economic history. Constitutional issues were not central, although they were the first ones addressed. Presented by Attorney General W.J. Major and aided by the prominent lawyer Isaac Pitblado, *Manitoba's Case* began with a careful if familiar overview of the transformation of the Canadian Constitution. Due to the cumulative impact of Judicial Committee decisions, the provinces had acquired greater "powers and responsibilities" without "any corresponding changes" to their sources of revenue. The result was the contemporary inability of governments at both the federal and provincial levels to address the duties and problems they faced. Throughout the systematic and even pedantic review of decades of constitutional decisions, the brief emphasized two points. One was that the provinces were "in no sense subordinate to the Dominion" and the other that there was an urgent need for legislative action in Canada to clarify the fiscal and legal roles of the two levels of government. The brief ended with the ominous declarations that Canada had a "system of government at variance with the needs of its citizens" and that "the constitution as it stands has ceased to be an effective instrument of government." Whether the remarks were too momentous to deal with, or the commission had not yet found a focus, the stinging critique was allowed to stand without challenge.[45]

The rest of *Manitoba's Case* was grounded in more concrete economic and fiscal issues. It argued that the distressed state of public finances was caused not only by the Depression but also by the development of the Manitoba economy within the broad framework of national policies. In effect, *Manitoba's Case* argued against the policy tenets of Canada's nation-building strategy – the "national policy" of railways, settlement, and tariffs. Settlement policies and railway building had proven costly in themselves, and they led to the expansion of provincial and local government services. The tariff was a more obvious problem because it imposed a continuing tax burden on westerners as buyers of manufactured goods. Using data first put together for the 1934 Nova Scotia *Provincial Economic Inquiry* by Queen's University political scientist Norman Rogers, and currently minister of labour in the federal government, Manitoba quantified its tariff burden at over $100 per family.[46]

Adding further injury to the economy, Manitoba like the rest of the West laboured under a "high-dollar" policy that favoured Canadian financial interests and central Canadian manufacturers trading into the United States while crippling agricultural exporters selling to Europe. The main argument as presented by the Minnesota economist Arthur Upgren stated that Canadian monetary policy harmed the West by not allowing Manitoba's producers and exporters to compete on an equal basis with Argentinean and Australian wheat exporters. This position would be echoed and amplified by the other western provinces in their submissions and testimony. The strong critique of monetary policy struck at the heart of Bank of Canada policy, central Canadian financial interests, and the fiscal orthodoxies of successive federal governments.[47] It did not go unchallenged.

By the 1930s, Manitoba was in desperate financial straits due to a seemingly unavoidable and unsustainable debt load. The province was on the hook for loans to finance the burdens of relief costs (the federal emergency funds that had been transferred since the early 1930s were not grants but loans) as well as the costs of borrowing for education and public works. Meanwhile, Manitoba was paying at the highest possible interest rates. Provincial taxes were as high as taxpayers could bear, including a 2 percent income tax on those earning above $480.[48]

In the area of social policy, the Manitoba government argued that its current policies were severely constrained while its ability to shoulder responsibilities was hamstrung. The province had a burden of debt as a result of the cumulative costs of building up education, local government, and other public services in the previous decades. Bracken and Garson urged Ottawa to assume the whole costs of relief and old age pensions, and half the costs of certain other services. The federal government should assume responsibility for costs that were generated by national and international circumstances (like relief and unemployment costs), while the provinces should gain access to revenues for the maintenance of social services at a level comparable with the more prosperous sections of the nation. The alternative was repudiation of debt by the Prairie provinces and the migration of their populations into the wealthier provinces, thereby overwhelming their social services. Only reconsideration of the nature and purpose of Confederation could alleviate the distress in the West and restore national well-being.[49]

Provincial leaders and their officials argued that the deleterious effects of the national policy had to be offset by some form of national standards. A commitment to fundamental "rights" for all citizens should form the basis for fiscal policy. As a result, it would likely be necessary to reallocate some powers. The federal government, for example, had to accept full responsibility for unemployment relief.[50] Garson reiterated Manitoba's "treasury problem," emphasizing that the BNA Act did not provide the provinces with adequate financial capacity for the provision of growing social services. This problem became evident when Manitoba's debt charges increased in order to borrow to pay the mounting costs of relief. At the same time, federal subsidies declined as a percentage of total current revenue from 88.08 percent in 1875 to 12.27 percent in 1936.[51]

Rowell and St-Laurent were shocked by the severity of the economic plight in the province and its people, but neither showed much sympathy for criticisms of monetary and tariff policies. Rowell conceded the point that Ottawa should assume responsibility for unemployment relief, although he "found it hard to believe that extensive unemployment could be a permanent problem in a country rich with unoccupied lands."[52] St-Laurent took to his role as legal counsel and put the Manitoba spokesmen through tough questioning.

St-Laurent deduced from Upgren's data that Manitoba had indulged in excessive borrowing in the boom years of the 1920s and was experiencing the consequences in the bad years of the 1930s. He also drew out the admission that a depreciated currency would have increased the costs of servicing foreign debt.[53] In response to the traditional Prairie critique of the tariff policy, and in particular to data provided by Manitoba that supported the tariff's effects on the West, St-Laurent claimed that the evidence failed to take into account sales taxes and customs duties that benefitted the western provinces. St-Laurent pointedly asked Manitoba's economic expert why the province supported the tariff in the three key dominion elections of 1891, 1911, and 1930, in which the issue was paramount.[54]

The Manitobans jumped at the opportunity to inform the commission that the golden days of the pioneer era were over. Garson assured Rowell that the "days of the heroic frontier when hard work would yield a living to anyone were gone forever and that some degree of unemployment was here to stay."[55] The criticisms of national policies were not new in the West, but they were now being expressed in a way that emphasized the outmoded policies in the context of the crash of the 1930s. A new direction and a new orientation were needed. Governments had to rethink how they calculated fiscal needs on the basis of "reasonable minimum national standards."[56]

The hearings in Winnipeg established an effective working style among commissioners and their staff. Presiding over events and in delicate health, Rowell found Sirois to be an excellent addition, "agreeable, likeable, knowledgeable about constitutional affairs," although he seldom spoke. The hearings also revealed a pattern of socializing that would be repeated in each provincial capital. In Winnipeg, the premier and his colleagues hosted the delegation at an official dinner. Rowell assured his wife that he left by mid-evening when the party turned to rounds of bridge. On another evening the commissioners dined at the Manitoba Club, hosted by Victor Sifton, Dafoe's newspaper boss. Rowell faithfully recorded his attendance at Sunday church services, unsurprising from one of the leading laymen in the United Church of Canada.[57] Like Dafoe (and presumably Sirois, who did not participate in most extracurricular events), Rowell conserved his energies.

MacKay and Angus took time to liaise with local academics, commencing a pattern that the two would follow throughout their cross-country trek. MacKay wrote frequent letters to his wife Kathleen, who remained in Halifax with their four young children. In addition to commentary on their social lives, he reported at length on commission labours. The two professors previewed material before each session and then worked up summaries for the other commissioners as well as the legal counsel. MacKay claimed that St-Laurent had to be "coached a bit for his questioning," and while he was "not doing a bad job," he was clearly a "lawyer and not an economist."[58] Commission assistant Wilfrid Eggleston reported that the social gatherings provided many distractions since Winnipeg was "a great town for hard liquor." He reported that Sandy Skelton lived up to his reputation for burning his life's candle at both ends by hosting late evening staff get-togethers at the Hotel Fort Garry.[59]

The hearings in Winnipeg provided the opportunity for a wide range of organizations to make presentations. The Catholic minority in the province, for example, presented a brief that raised the ghosts of an old issue: the Manitoba Schools Question. The delegation argued that Catholics were facing double taxation to maintain schools since no one was exempt from public school taxes and no help was given to parochial schools. The community was only too aware that it was Dafoe and his long-time boss, Clifford Sifton, who supported the present system.[60] The City of Winnipeg, meanwhile, complained that it was not receiving enough aid with the high numbers of the "employable unemployed." After reading through the Manitoba briefs, Dafoe wrote: "if they are a sample of those to come later, the combined briefs for Canada will leave no difficulty unstated, no state of friction unreported and no conceivable suggestion not advanced." J.B. McGeachy reported in the *Winnipeg Free Press* that "the keynote is unanimous and enthusiastic lamentation ... local councils, school boards, teachers, the University and even the youth of Manitoba (represented by the Youth Council) say with one voice that the outlook is black. As yesterday wore on, members of the audience began to drift away unable to bear it any longer."[61] Business, political, and social advocacy groups also made presentations, most of them bleak.[62]

While the spotlight was on Manitoba, Premier Hepburn of Ontario monitored the proceedings. Toronto lawyer Daniel Lang attended the hearings in his role as Ontario's legal counsel. He reported that Manitoba was proposing compensation for the cost of the tariff through federal assumption of responsibility for provincial debts and relief. In return, the provinces would surrender their succession duties. Lang urged Ontario to prepare its defences by "developing an attack of our own on this basis."[63] Hepburn concluded that there was a western bias by the fact that the commission commenced with hearings in Winnipeg and then Regina. When he heard about this charge, Dafoe reacted immediately: "It was a matter of general knowledge that the Commission opened when + where it did because first Manitoba + Saskatchewan were ready and the other provinces were not."[64] In the meantime, T.A. Crerar reported on rumours of a united front being prepared on behalf of Ontario and Quebec against the West, with an attempt to gain Maritime support. He accused Premiers Duplessis and Hepburn, pun no doubt intended, of being "drunk with power."[65]

On 9 December the royal commission left Winnipeg for Regina and eight days of hearings. The commission received the Saskatchewan brief just prior to their departure, resulting in a scramble to read through what MacKay called a "formidable" document of four hundred pages.[66] If the commissioners were struck by the gloomy portrayal of the impact of national policy and depression offered by the Manitoba government, it proved to be the assessment of "pollyannas" in comparison with the Saskatchewan report.[67]

In Regina the commission was greeted by even colder weather than in Winnipeg. The reception, however, was just as warm.[68] Like Manitoba, Saskatchewan welcomed the appointment of the commission and gave every indication that it would cooperate fully. Like Manitoba, Saskatchewan also took its presentation seriously and put together an impressive submission. It was credited chiefly to two University of Saskatchewan professors, Frederick Cronkite, dean of law, and George Britnell, professor of economics, with assistance from many consultants, notably economist Vernon Fowke (on monetary policy) and the agronomist William Allen (on agricultural conditions). Attorney General Tommy Davis later admitted to being pleasantly surprised that there were "a multitude of highly trained, efficient and brilliant men to whom the Government could look for aid in the preparation of its case."[69] Despite the influential role of experts, the Saskatchewan government prepared its brief in the name of "the citizens of the Province." Liberal premier William Patterson, who was also provincial treasurer, maintained a benign role in the preparation and presentation.[70]

Once again, the commission staff was set up in the finest hotel in town, the CPR's Hotel Saskatchewan. It was, MacKay recorded, quite satisfactory but not at the level of the Fort Garry.[71] The hearings were held in the Saskatchewan Legislature Building at a table from the Quebec Conference of 1864 that had found its way to Regina via Battleford when the Territorial Government was formed. The table was not large, and an amused MacKay noted that he and Angus were not even at the main table but seated to one side.[72]

After the ceremonial opening, Premier Patterson began the presentation of Saskatchewan's case. It was entitled *Submission by the Government of Saskatchewan*, but there was no surrender from the province. Patterson emphasized the need "to equalize" relations between the dominion and the provinces. Both the "possibilities" and the "handicaps" of Saskatchewan had to be examined. Patterson then turned the presentation over to Tommy Davis, who read aloud lengthy portions of the written case. Saskatchewan's perilous economic and governmental condition was laid bare. The submission began, however, by setting out a remarkably clear list of "fundamental concepts" that called for equitable treatment for all citizens regardless of their province of residence. In a clear statement about the positive state, Saskatchewan affirmed that governments had a basic obligation to provide equitable treatment, particularly in the form of social services, but it was the responsibility of the dominion to ensure such treatment was guaranteed. As with Manitoba, Saskatchewan's position focused on "the effect of national policies upon the economy of the western provinces."[73] Constitutional issues were addressed only briefly. Saskatchewan's argument highlighted the friction between a unitary form of federalism (exemplified by John A. Macdonald) and a decentralized "compact" of provinces. The province had to be put into a position "to perform the duties assigned by the constitution."[74] Saskatchewan did not oppose constitutional change and increased federal responsibilities (unemployment insurance, pensions, and social services), but it was not in favour of weakening provincial authority in crucial areas.

Saskatchewan had suffered the most from the collapse of the wheat economy and had endured the worst impact of a climate shift that created years of crop failure in the grassland plains south of the treed parkland.[75] The objective of the presentation was to demonstrate that "the very great contribution that this Province makes to the welfare of all Canada, and, on the other hand, the peculiar handicaps under which the people of this Province labour and the absolute necessity, that, insofar as possible and practicable, those handicaps should be removed." Its tone was more desperate and pointed than the Manitoba brief, claiming that Saskatchewan's fiscal situation was "well-nigh insupportable."[76] The brief emphasized "the unequal position of Saskatchewan in Confederation, and the necessity of equalizing that position with the position of other provinces in Canada." It warned that "no province [could] be expected to accept the position of a colony to be exploited, nor to accept, except in the last resort, the migration or transfer of its people to the other provinces."[77]

Davis assured the commissioners that the argument was not being put forward out of "bitterness or in a sectional spirit." He recognized that, once the commission had completed its work, the next step would be the difficult process of implementing the recommendations. This warning was a reference to Ontario and Quebec, who would ultimately decide "what would be done to equalize conditions." Saskatchewan was not "asking for the carrying out of any 'share-the-Wealth' programme," Davis asserted, "whereby the wealth of one section of Canada should be transferred to another section." The province was simply seeking the ability to generate sufficient fiscal resources to meet its obligations. The national economy was built on the export of wheat. Without the West, he argued, "the national life of Canada would collapse." The people of Saskatchewan deserved equal opportunity "to exist and continue to live and enjoy a similar standard of life as [was] enjoyed by [their] fellow citizens." Davis alluded to hostility coming from the premiers of Ontario and Quebec but argued that this attitude did not "represent the actual feelings of their people." He recognized that constitutional change would be necessary but remained hopeful that when it came to writing the history of the period, the Rowell Commission would "stand on an equal basis" with Confederation itself.[78]

At the root of Saskatchewan's case was the Depression. The population dealt with a "terrible plight," struggling under drought conditions and disadvantaged by geography. "There is no place in Canada," Davis asserted, "with the variability of income to be found in Saskatchewan." The economy was agriculture. An examination of the financial position "clearly indicated the utter impossibility of the Province being able to balance its budget and meet existing obligations from present revenues." Even under prosperous conditions, it was now impossible. The people were taxed to the limit. Lowering the costs of government was meaningless, and refunding the debt was essential but not enough to raise income levels. The revenues of the federal government had to be increased so they could then be turned back to the provinces. Saskatchewan had always received subsidies from Ottawa, but they were distributed on the basis of population and bore no relationship to the needs of the province: "We urge that subsidies, hereafter, must be based on fiscal need and not upon a flat population rate." Saskatchewan called for a move from financial subsidies to assured fiscal grants. As the brief emphasized, a new system had to be based on the "fiscal need of each province ... to perform its constitutional obligations" and, therefore, to allow services to work towards "the Canadian standard of living." The Saskatchewan government indicated a willingness to accept a grants commission along the lines of the Australian model, a body that distributed subsidies based on need. But, above all, it sought a new needs-based fiscal regime.[79]

The submission made the chilling point that nearly half the population was already on relief: "There were neither funds to continue aid to the unemployed nor prospects of jobs to enable them to look after themselves." To make matters worse, the situation was expected to deteriorate in 1938. Saskatchewan called for federal regulation of labour conditions and unemployment insurance as well as old age pensions. While calling for more intervention from Ottawa, it did not cede policy leadership or fiscal initiative.[80]

The experience in Regina left the commissioners with no doubt as to the province's grim circumstances. As Rowell told his wife, "the picture this province presents is most distressing and depressing." Nearly half of the population was "on relief" and the numbers would probably rise. He realized that the province and municipalities faced a "total inability to carry on without help on a large and generous scale" and that a "break in the morale of the people" was looming. St-Laurent was equally taken aback by the "saga of personal tragedy, loss of morale in whole communities, and public bankruptcy wrought by the Depression on the Prairies."[81]

Away from the hearings, the commissioners and staff enjoyed a busy social life. MacKay was able to visit Saskatoon one weekend to meet academic colleagues at the University of Saskatchewan and enjoy a five-mile walk along the South Saskatchewan River.[82] Eggleston reported on the late evenings of dinners, bridge, and beer, usually with Skelton and others in the federal retinue, and often in the company of Henry Angus and Robert MacKay.[83]

After the hearings in Saskatchewan, the commission took a one-month break for the Christmas-New Year season. The commissioners were satisfied with the first two provincial visits as well as with the degree of public interest in the hearings. Among other things, Rowell was delighted to report that Sirois had proven to be a great addition. He was knowledgeable about constitutional law, as well as business and financial matters, and had "won the confidence and high regard" of the commission.[84]

The reporters sent to cover the hearings, in particular J.B. McGeachy of the *Winnipeg Free Press;* Wellington Jeffers, financial editor of the *Globe and Mail;* Norman White of the *Financial Post;* and D.A. McGregor of the Vancouver *Province,* seemed equally impressed by the commissioners. Rowell did not come across as the austere and aloof character they had presumed. They were pleasantly surprised when he "turned a blind eye" to the "drinking habits" of certain members of the commission staff, notably Sandy Skelton and the press corps. But Rowell was in fragile health. He "stood up well," but only by "rigid disciplining" of his time and energy. He attended few evening social functions and always left early. The more vigorous J.W. Dafoe, like Rowell a non-drinker, followed much the same path of conserving his considerable energies for work and not frittering them away on socializing.[85]

The hearings had gone well, but the material presented and the cases made by the two provinces had struck a warning note in central Canada. As the commission prepared for its break, T.A. Crerar alerted Dafoe that Premiers Hepburn and Duplessis were scheming against substantive reform of the federal order. Crerar claimed that the two leaders were now intent on undermining the federal government of Mackenzie King. The reactions in Toronto and Quebec City to the Manitoba and Saskatchewan cases were derisive, and Crerar reported, the two premiers were often inebriated in talks to the press. Hepburn and Duplessis espoused the view "that the West ha[d] spent its substance in riotous living and, to escape the consequences, [was] asking the rest of Canada to make good its own de- linquencies." While emphasizing that the federal government did not share this view, Crerar warned Dafoe that opposition to the cases made by Manitoba and Saskatchewan was being stirred up by the Ontario and Quebec premiers and that they were sure to make trouble.[86]

5

Winter of Discontent
January–March 1938

*A royal commission is an arm of government and should not
be used to destroy the body that has created it.*

– *Mackenzie King, 21 December 1937*[1]

BC hearings, March 1938. *Dafoe Papers, University of Manitoba Archives*

Despite the grim evidence, the commissioners were confident that their engagement with Manitoba and Saskatchewan had been successful. The two Prairie provinces were supportive and cooperative: they took the task at hand seriously, and most important, they offered impressive policy innovations. But as the Royal Commission on Dominion-Provincial Relations paused for the holiday season of 1937, and while the other provinces prepared their briefs, problems emerged. The public and covert sniping of Premiers Duplessis and Hepburn was becoming a threat to the inquiry. A more immediate issue, however, involved the federal government and focused on the recommendations of another inquiry – the National Employment Commission studying the unemployment crisis.

Since its election in 1935, the Liberal government had made a general commitment to unemployment insurance. The provincial responses ranged from lukewarm interest to full support.[2] Yet Mackenzie King and much of the cabinet remained wary of adopting the measure. The move required a constitutional amendment, but it also signalled a shift in responsibilities for the dominion government with the accompanying drain on federal coffers. It would also involve a complicated definition of coverage since a large proportion of the labour force was employed in agriculture. The Purvis Commission was expected to resolve the latter question, but its interim reports and leaks about its final recommendations irritated the prime minister and led him to try to shape aspects of the final report. King applied pressure through Labour Minister Norman Rogers. In January 1938, the Purvis Report came out in favour of unemployment insurance, a revitalized national employment service, investment in residential housing, training for young adult and female workers, and the replacement of conditional grants with unconditional grants-in-aid to the provinces for the unemployable unemployed – that is, "relief" payments. According to Commissioner Bill Mackintosh, "the more important recommendations of the Commission were directed to an attempt to disentangle financial assistance to the provinces from functional aid in dealing with the problem of unemployment."[3]

The recommendations went too far for the cautious Mackenzie King. The prime minister was becoming increasingly concerned with the influence wielded by the new coterie of policy advisors emerging from Canada's universities. The Purvis Commission seemed to demonstrate that these politically naïve academics would use their influence to push the government into politically dangerous territory. In particular, King noted the influence of the Department of Political Economy at Queen's University, including Norman Rogers in cabinet, O.D. Skelton and Clifford Clark in the public service, and Sandy Skelton, Bill Mackintosh, and others working with the Rowell Commission. Together, they advocated what King viewed as a push towards centralization and intervention.[4] He was "incensed" by the dangers posed by an "invasion" of provincial authority proposed by the Purvis Commission. As a way out of the issue, Ottawa announced that any further policy initiatives in the area of unemployment insurance would have to await the deliberations of the Rowell Commission.[5]

Hearings for the Rowell Commission, meanwhile, reconvened in Ottawa in mid-January 1938. For the commissioners, these sessions were less stressful. Spouses were able to accompany their husbands to Ottawa. Rowell was particularly "delighted" and rejuvenated by the social spark the gathering provided. Angus and MacKay were parents of young children and residents of the farthest reaches of Canada. Separation from family was and would remain particularly taxing for the two professors. The Ottawa meetings proved a respite.[6]

The discussions in these hearings were also less intense than those with the provinces. They did not attract more than a handful of people, despite the comfortable surroundings of the ornate Railway Committee Room in the Parliament Buildings.[7] For ten days, the commission heard presentations from senior officials in federal government departments and representatives of national businesses. These Ottawa hearings were continued later in February and May. By the time they ended, the commission heard from over two dozen federal officials, including deputy ministers and heads of agencies. The group did not include the most powerful federal civil servants, O.D. Skelton and Clifford Clark. Unlike the phalanxes of provincial bureaucrats who appeared before the commission when it heard provincial presentations, the federal bureaucrats who did appear were not there to defend a departmental brief; rather, their roles were to dilate upon particular issues and to describe fiscal and administrative aspects, not to explicitly advocate policy directions. For the most part, the presentations and discussions were descriptive.[8]

Despite their mundane technical tone, the federal departmental officials raised some serious issues. One example was the subject of Indigenous health policy. The commissioners learned of the health crisis facing the Indigenous population in Canada, in particular the scourge of tuberculosis. The death rates were reported to be between "13 to 15 times greater than [that of] whites." This severe death rate was explained away as a sign of pre-existing poor health and a result of limited treatment facilities. The contrast with provincial approaches to treatment was left hanging over the proceedings. Federal officials admitted that the problems were caused by a lack of government funding.[9] Most of the provinces also recognized the crisis and indicated a willingness to extend care to the Indigenous population but only if federal funding was available. Saskatchewan, which had the worst overall rates of tuberculosis in Canada, argued that joint funding was essential to curb the "menace" of venereal diseases and, more tellingly, the plague of tuberculosis, each of which was ravaging First Nation communities. But the issues received no further attention. "Indian health [sic]" was mostly a federal responsibility and, as far as they were concerned, outside the purview of the commission.[10]

The Ottawa sessions called on a number of the national associations that the commission approved for presentations. These organizations included the Canadian Manufacturer's Association, two national life insurance organizations, the Trades and Labour Congress, the Chartered Banks of Canada, the Canadian Electrical Association, the Canadian Welfare Council, the National Council of Women, the Board of Evangelism of the United Church of Canada, the Victorian Order of Nurses, and the Canadian Chamber of Commerce.[11] While a wide variety of organizations were invited to appear before the inquiry, the commissioners served as the gatekeepers regarding who had the "authority" and "relevance" to make presentations. Aside from the provincial governments, the commission was prepared to hear from "recognized" public organizations but reserved the right to determine whether to invite or hear from specific individuals. The private groups that were invited were predominantly mainstream business and professional lobbyists, but also invited were national and provincial teachers' organizations, social workers associations, religious and fraternal social service groups (the United Church being particularly well represented), and an array of local government boards.

Individual invitees were few and were confined to acclaimed economic or political experts, usually from outside Canada. They included Gunnar

Myrdal from Sweden, Lyndhurst F. Giblin from Australia, and Heinrich Bruning from Germany as well as several American policy experts. Myrdal and Giblin were prominent economists who had been involved in politics, while Bruning was an academic, bureaucrat, and politician until the advent of Hitler. As historian Jessica Squires has observed, expert witnesses represented a shift towards an increasing public reliance on prominent practitioners to explain and solve problems. Squires also argues that the commissioners "used the yardsticks of scientific and professional respectability to exclude groups with alternative perspectives not easily adapted to forming consensus."[12] This is true to an extent, but despite tight control on the presenters, the hearings did include dissenting groups such as the Communist Party of Canada, the Quebec League of Women Voters, and the League for Economic Democracy. It also heard conservative voices, including a plethora of taxpayers' organizations, "sound money" groups, and temperance societies.[13]

In his colourful "Confederation Clinic" columns, J.B. McGeachy described the national business organizations as represented by "twelve cylinder K.C's from Montreal and Toronto" who "sounded off for the big financial interests." The presenters were "able but stuffy." McGeachy noted that these national organizations were particularly critical of provincial obstructionism and "the Duplessis-Hepburn league for the defence of provincial rights."[14] The lengthy presentation by the Canadian Manufacturers' Association epitomized the message the commission would hear repeatedly from business lobbies across the country: cut taxes but defend the tariff, and reduce government expenditures while expanding federal services. The commissioners were not impressed by these solutions to everything from taxation to efficiency in government and the simplistic call for increased federal action.[15]

Some organizations reflected the complexity of and confusion over federalism by advocating both provincial and federal regulation. The Canadian Life Insurance Officers Association presented a brief proposing that the provincial legislatures should have exclusive jurisdiction to prescribe the statutory conditions and incidents of insurance contracts, and exclusive jurisdiction to license insurance agents, brokers, and adjusters. It also recommended that the provinces be able to supervise the financial affairs of insurance companies incorporated and operating solely within the province of incorporation. At the same time, the association wanted Ottawa to wield exclusive jurisdiction and responsibility for licensing all other companies, requiring deposits, prescribing annual and statistical insurance returns, conducting financial inspections and supervision, and publishing annual reports concerning such companies.[16] Years later, J.A. Corry remarked upon the inconsistency in their position. For decades insurance companies had been urging the courts to rule that the federal government had no constitutional power to regulate the business of insurance. In tough economic times, they had become firm supporters of stabilizing public finance and restoring confidence and credit through increased action by the federal government.[17]

Rowell, MacKay, and Dafoe were much engaged by the brief from the League of Nations Society. The presentation was by legal scholar N.A.M. Mackenzie (also a member of the Canadian Institute of International Affairs along with most of the commissioners), and he examined one of the major causes of constitutional reform in the 1930s. The society advocated a clearer demarcation of Canada's right to conduct international relations, specifically through a clearer definition of the "treaty-making power," which it argued had become weaker due to Judicial Committee of the Privy Council decisions in recent years. Mackenzie pointedly denied that granting clear federal authority for treaty-making would affect provincial rights.[18]

The commissioners also enjoyed the presentation, if not the message, of F.R. Scott and Leonard Marsh of McGill University on behalf of the social democratic League for Social Reconstruction (LSR).[19] Entitled *Canada – One or Nine? The Purpose of Confederation*, the brief pointed to the constitutional mess in Canada, the dangers of spiralling public debt, increasing monopolistic economic power, and the debilitating cycles of boom and bust. The law professor Frank Scott presented on legal-constitutional aspects. He was on familiar ground, arguing that the JCPC had forced Canadian federalism into the confines of a looser, inefficient English model, thereby encouraging sectionalism and allowing a "parallel government" of monopoly capitalism to emerge. The federal government possessed an inherent responsibility for the basic social security of every citizen. In addition, Ottawa was responsible for the economic stability of every part of the nation through the development of natural resources.

While the Fathers of Confederation could not have planned for these specific contingencies in 1867, the structure as presented in the BNA Act laid out the basis. The ability to amend the Constitution would provide the remedy.[20]

Leonard Marsh, English-born, London-School-of-Economics educated, and a professor of social science, proposed social and fiscal policy recommendations, including the creation of a national welfare code and a department of national welfare: "Taxes should be based on wealth, not consumption, and revenues should be used more creatively as an instrument of economic social policy." The national debt should be reduced by "a profits tax, a debt redemption levy, and the nationalization of profitable industries."[21] A bemused McGeachy reported that the LSR was no less "centralizing" than the Canadian Manufacturers' Association. He might also have explained that the league's academic leaders, including Scott and Marsh, had been responsible for a book entitled *Social Planning for Canada*, one of the few serious critiques of the Canadian economic and political order in the 1930s and a paean for centralization.[22]

Like the LSR, the Trades and Labour Congress (TLC) called for an increase in the role of the state and centralization of power in specific areas, such as unemployment insurance and labour legislation. The Depression had made clear the need for an expanded welfare state to provide aid to those most vulnerable to the market economy and greater organizational rights for labour. The TLC, in the person of its leader, Paddy Draper, emphasized the urgency of greater state intervention in labour relations and the provision of social minima. Its advocacy for "re-centralization" was similar to that of the LSR and, as noted, common to many "national" organizations. By failing to provide strategies to deal with existing constitutional and institutional barriers, the support for state action elicited pointed questions from Rowell.[23]

A much-anticipated presentation during the January hearings was from Heinrich Bruning, former chancellor of Germany and now exiled to the United States, where he taught political science at Harvard University. McGeachy noted that Bruning was afforded the singular indulgence of smoking cigarettes during his presentation. He told the commission that, like Canada, the German federation had experienced problems of divided jurisdiction and strained fiscal relations. But he concluded that it was not federalism or the specifics of the German federation but rather the weak traditions of democracy that led Germany on its path towards fascism after 1932.[24]

After the Ottawa respite, the commission resumed its main task of engaging with the provincial governments. Alberta had proven elusive about submitting its brief, but the Maritime provinces and British Columbia had agreed to submit their studies and host the inquiry before winter was over. Accordingly, the commissioners reconvened and headed east in February 1938. They started in Halifax since the Nova Scotia government was ready and waiting.

There was unease within the commission about the approach to be taken in the Maritimes. MacKay, in particular, was worried that the commission would be used by the three eastern provinces as a "court of review" for Maritime grievances. He was particularly concerned they would be subject to the rehashing of the many complaints expressed in previous commissions of inquiry, including the 1926 federal Royal Commission on the Claims of the Maritime Provinces (the Duncan Commission); Nova Scotia's own 1934 commission into its economic problems, the *Provincial Economic Inquiry* (the Jones Commission); and a 1935 federal inquiry into Maritime provincial fiscal relations with Ottawa headed by former finance minister Thomas White.

When the Liberal government of Angus Macdonald came into office in Nova Scotia in 1933, it immediately appointed an inquiry into the province's economy. The objective was to recommend new economic policies to deal with the Depression and to "provide an intellectual foundation for future constitutional and fiscal negotiations with Ottawa."[25] Its chair, J.H. Jones, was a professor of economics at the University of Leeds, but he was joined by Harold Innis, already a prominent political economist at the University of Toronto, and a Nova Scotian, Alexander Johnston, a former federal deputy minister of marine and fisheries. The report, though terse, was supported by a number of research studies by prominent political economy professors, including Robert MacKay and Norman Rogers. MacKay reported on the serious limitations of the existing system of federal transfers, which was irregular and inadequate for the Maritimes. Rogers calculated the tariff burdens of each of the hinterland provinces of Canada and the effects on Nova Scotia's industrial and transportation systems. The

Jones Commission concluded that "constitutional changes are essential to the maintenance of national standards." It was Ottawa's task to "establish equity" among the provinces because federal economic policies helped create regional imbalances within the nation, including measurable high costs on each Maritime resident due to the federal tariff. To this end, the Jones Commission called on the federal government to assume responsibility for some social services within provincial control and to move into other services, such as health and employment insurance, which could be established in the future. Ottawa could also create "a fund for allocation among the different Provinces in accordance with their needs."[26] The Jones Commission, historian Stephen Henderson has argued, with its policy criticisms and supporting research studies, can be read as an "influential forerunner of the Rowell-Sirois Commission."[27] Above all, the search for adequate federal aid to the provinces based on the new concept of "fiscal need" became central to Angus L. Macdonald's thinking on constitutional reform.

A federal inquiry followed in 1935, appointed by the Bennett government to provide an update to the 1926 Duncan Commission. Chaired by former federal finance minister Thomas White, the terse twenty-four-page *Inquiry into the Readjustment of the Financial Arrangement between the Maritimes Provinces and the Dominion of Canada* undertook no bold initiatives. It acknowledged the provinces' deficient fiscal resources and urgent need, and recommended limited increases in regional subsidies, but shied away from identifying any principles for fundamental revisions to the system. The conclusion elicited dissent from the only Maritimer on the commission, Justice John A. Mathieson of Prince Edward Island, who pleaded for a new principle of fiscal need to recalibrate federal grants.[28] According to Henderson, "[Premier] Macdonald received this [report] as a mixed blessing; his government got badly needed revenue, but the new money became part of a fixed subsidy, not tied to the province's relative economic position."[29] Like the Prairie provinces, Nova Scotia understood that a subsidy for the costs of government from Ottawa was a poor alternative to the award of grants for the full cost of government services in specific areas.

Nova Scotia was well known for its long campaign for "better terms" within Confederation, and the Rowell Commission was welcomed by

Macdonald's Liberal government. The inquiry was "hailed as the salvation of provincial autonomy." MacKay, however, remained concerned. While accepting that the Maritime provinces could recycle the Duncan and Jones material, he wanted the provinces to know that their work was "not a claims commission nor a court of revision."[30] When the Nova Scotia brief was delivered, MacKay was relieved that it was a critical but forward-looking analysis of Nova Scotia in the Canadian federation. Even Rowell, who was at times impatient with Maritime grievances, was impressed by the Nova Scotia submission.[31]

The commission arrived in Halifax and held hearings in Province House from 3 to 8 February 1938. In attendance were the five commissioners, legal counsels St-Laurent and Stewart, as well as Sandy Skelton and other senior staff. Premier Macdonald was a person of considerable analytical and political skill, and his presentation engaged the close attention of the commission. In his "Confederation Clinic," McGeachy described Macdonald as a "slight frail, greying man of maybe 45 who might be a bookkeeper with poetic aspirations." The surroundings were apparently just as uninspiring. McGeachy commented on the "welter of ruins and traditions," the crowded chamber, the run-down legislative building, and the shabby main thorough-fare of Halifax.[32]

The surroundings may not have impressed the commissioners but the Nova Scotia premier certainly did. Macdonald dominated the provincial testimony, aided by Attorney General Josiah MacQuarrie. The premier delivered the Nova Scotia *Submission* with "astonishing" skill.[33] The document was far shorter than the Manitoba and Saskatchewan briefs at 141 pages and offered a "well-crafted legal argument rather than a statistical analysis of Nova Scotia's place in Confederation." McGeachy was impressed, noting that Macdonald was the "first witness to testify with utter self-confidence, no fumbling words or ideas, and something like a prose style."[34]

The Nova Scotia premier argued that Confederation, Canada's so-called nation-building event, was certainly not unifying. He cited the statement of the Privy Council in 1892 that the BNA Act did not create a unified federal system. In Nova Scotia, a "double loyalty" to province and country reflected its political life and goals since the early eighteenth century. Macdonald wished to go beyond the traditional arguments about the problems of regional imbalances and was "willing to sacrifice some provincial prerogatives to achieve a better distribution of powers and resources, with an eye to strengthening the Canadian federation."[35]

The siren call of constitutional issues was irresistible in the 1930s and the Nova Scotia *Submission* proposed no fewer than nine constitutional amendments based on the contemporary demands of government and judicial interpretation. This attention to constitutional detail contrasted with the Manitoba and Saskatchewan briefs, which acknowledged the problems created by changing constitutional roles and judicial interpretation but offered only cautious support for constitutional change.[36] The details of the Nova Scotia position were set out as nine "propositions" that elaborated both the amendments and the principles behind them. In setting out this agenda, Nova Scotia was actually breaking away from past grievances or constitutional nostalgia, marking a shift from the traditional Maritime Rights stance. As the *Submission* stated, change was urgent and it should be based on the governmental situation "as it exist[ed] and not as it might have existed." Nova Scotia's list included the power of constitutional amendment and the mutual right to delegate legislation. Several amendments related to fiscal policy and the areas of taxation that had to be rationalized to give each level of government exclusive fields and necessary revenues. Macdonald conceded that if Ottawa accepted responsibility for old age pensions, unemployment insurance, and mothers' allowances, the federal government would require more sources of revenue. The provinces could then vacate income tax and succession duties. In return, the provinces should gain exclusive control over "sales tax" areas, such as gasoline and electricity taxes. In sum, each level of government required the constitutional guarantee of "sufficient revenue" to meet its responsibilities.[37]

The Nova Scotia case called for a federalism in which "the identity of the component parts" was recognized. Only the central government could offer this recognition. This necessitated a restructuring of governmental finance in Canada based on a policy of "fiscal need." This new principle meant a major transfer of revenue from Ottawa to the provinces and meant the calculation of a "national minimum" of services that each province should be capable of delivering as it saw fit. Macdonald and MacQuarrie argued that intergovernmental transfers based on provincial fiscal need had been at the heart of post-Confederation federal-provincial relations. If the argument was familiar to the commission or some of its members, this was partly because it had been made by Robert MacKay in the Jones Report.[38]

As the Nova Scotia government explained, the problem was that the original system of per capita grants was inadequate even by the standards of 1867. The calculation of federal transfers on a "population basis," even when revised, as it was from time to time, had never provided adequate resources for the provinces, particularly when their responsibilities increased to provide social services. The use, misuse, and, at times, rejection of the approach in the past only showed that it was the recurring motif that could and should become the principle for federal aid to the provinces. The previous inquiries led by Duncan, Jones, and White all made the same point: the Maritime provinces simply did not have sufficient fiscal resources to meet provincial need. But only the Jones Report argued in favour of a thorough calculation of, and permanent provisions for, provincial financial need. Taking a swipe at Ontario and Quebec, as well as Nova Scotia's history of inquiries, the premier noted sarcastically: "we do not fear Commissions down here."

Previous inquiries highlighted the harm done by federal transportation and, above all, tariff policies. Nova Scotia may have benefitted from industrial development based on protection, but, like all the peripheral provinces, it relied on subsidized protective tariff-based industry and suffered a net loss of income that could be calculated on a per capita basis.[39] Nova Scotia now ranked last in per capita income, which illustrated the inadequacies of the current dispensation. This diagnosis returned to the concept of fiscal need, or, as Macdonald explained, "the requirements of the people as distinguished from the government of a province." Due to the premier's persuasive style, Nova Scotia became the most articulate exponent for the new policy of fiscal need. It was not, of course, the first to express this innovative position. Like those of Manitoba and Saskatchewan, Nova Scotia's proposal was based on the two principles of national standards for basic social services and unconditional grants from Ottawa to the provinces.[40]

The mechanism to bring about this redistribution, Macdonald proposed, was a federal-provincial grants commission on the Australian model.

The Australian experience provided ample evidence that the determination of appropriate levels of transfers was feasible. Rowell challenged Macdonald, pointing out that a state agency meting out grants based on fiscal need could decrease just as easily as increase them. Macdonald responded that the existing programs of subsidies were so inadequate and unreliable that change was essential regardless. The federal government should serve "as the distributing agent for the wealth of other provinces." He continued: "it was only reasonable that some of that wealth should be distributed on what we think is a more equitable basis." The old ways of conducting business between Ottawa and the provinces (if not the BNA Act itself) were in desperate need of modernizing. Commerce had become corporate and centralized in Toronto and Montreal. As a result, the large sources of direct taxation (succession and corporate incomes) had escaped the grasp of the smaller provinces. Since 1917, the dominion had pushed (with constitutional legitimacy) into the direct taxation field of personal incomes. Yet provincial responsibilities had only grown in education, social welfare, and unemployment relief. Clearly a new deal was needed. The fiscal need of the provinces through the requirements of its citizens had to become the basis of a redistribution of tax revenues from the dominion to the provinces.[41]

Despite Macdonald's attempts to rise above mere regional grievances, the commission heard the deeply rooted and historical appeal of a province wronged by Confederation. The case was presented with such clarity, however, that the commissioners, particularly Rowell, were satisfied that Nova Scotia was at least pointing towards positive solutions to current problems rather than dwelling on past grievances.[42] McGeachy was more flippant. While Nova Scotia was prepared to live with Confederation, it was still not about to celebrate it. The province remained "disillusioned and disappointed" with national policies.[43]

Outside the formal sessions, the commissioners enjoyed their now habitual round of social activities. Legal counsel J.M. Stewart hosted a dinner at his impressive home, while staffers engaged in the usual diversions, such as playing bridge. Wilfrid Eggleston reported that they continued to work on a parlour game begun in Winnipeg using the Duke University "telepathy" card tests at which Savard and Skelton had shown "uncanny" skills. More serious activities included meetings with local social scientists arranged by Mackay, and speaking engagements with local Canadian Institute of International Affairs colleagues for Angus and Dafoe.[44]

On 9 February, the commissioners and their entourage (minus Skelton who had returned to Ottawa) travelled to Charlottetown, Prince Edward Island. The ferry crossing had been rough, and a blinding snowstorm made it difficult to find taxis to take them to the CNR's Charlottetown Hotel. While the rest of the group waited in the station until the road was cleared, Dafoe showed his Winnipeg grit and struck out on foot with a few companions "to fight his way successfully against the wind and snow to the [hotel]. The old man thoroughly enjoyed the struggle against the elements."[45] The weather remained stormy throughout their stay. Although the social environment was amiable, with the usual succession of dinners and luncheons, the atmosphere of the hearings was somewhat less engaging.[46] The commission excited little public attention in PEI. As historian Ed Macdonald points out, "in the late 1930s, the questioning attitude of the commissioners put bread in no one's mouth, and their sojourn in Charlottetown caused only a ripple of interest." The provincial submission was only delivered to the commissioners the day before they left Halifax for Charlottetown.[47]

The premier, Thane Campbell, who led a Liberal government that had won every seat in the 1935 election, carried the provincial case over two days assisted by two officials. The Campbell government used the hearings, held at the newly renovated Provincial Law Courts Building, to list "the disabilities under which they labored, and rehearsed once more the old arguments about how Confederation's workings had cost the provincial economy." The introductory paragraphs of the brief warned of the "extreme caution" in the province about the inquiry. This caution was rooted in the long-standing assessment that PEI had never received "fair or adequate" revenues or aid from Ottawa and that the National Policy had always worked to its "detriment."[48] Campbell asserted that the grievances and suspicion against Canada ran deep and that PEI laboured under fiscal and economic burdens. The commissioners detected a sense of resignation.

Prince Edward Island's current economic situation was not dire, but it was dreary. Due to its agricultural economy, characterized by a high degree of self-sufficiency, the small province did not experience mass unemployment. Its economy was affected but not devastated by the slumping markets. Moreover, it had not undergone expanding public works or services in the previous decades. There were much lower unemployment and relief costs than elsewhere in Canada. Relief work was used largely for public works projects, but the traditional patronage system diverted much of the funding into the pockets of friends of the ruling party. Campbell and his associates argued that new government responsibilities were emerging in all areas of social services and that they compounded the post-Confederation problem of weak fiscal resources and economic opportunities. The province volunteered to transfer public welfare services to the federal government and to share others. Ottawa, for example, could collect the province's income taxes. PEI was willing to accept the mechanisms of either a grants commission or a loan council.[49]

The provincial submission was concise at fifty-four pages. It was critical but not threatening, just as the premier's testimony was assertive but not confrontational. *The Case of Prince Edward Island* was uneven, with more space devoted to explaining historical grievances over Confederation and the National Policy than to specific remedies. This injustice was rooted in the colonial history of the province: PEI was still paying debts incurred in 1869 to buy out the absentee landowners in Britain who, in 1767, had acquired most public land and ultimately left Island settlers as virtual tenants. The colony had been "partly cajoled and partly forced" into Confederation and remained dissatisfied by the terms of entry. Since then, the province had experienced an almost perpetual gap between revenues and expenses. The brief did reserve ten pages for demands for financial aid because it "had not been and [was] not receiving a fair or adequate share of assistance" from the dominion. In preparing its submission, the government relied on the eminent Indian theorist of fiscal federalism B.P. Adarkar, an advocate of the concept of fiscal transfers and fiscal need as practised in Australia and proposed by Nova Scotia.[50]

The conclusion to the brief focused on relieving provincial treasuries of their burden of debt and uncertain revenues through some sort of reallocation of governmental responsibilities. But the tone was not hopeful that systematic changes would actually be made. The Charlottetown meetings struck a different note from previous hearings. The province seemed guarded about making change and proud of its limited goals for government. It seemed willing to live frugally, just as its citizens did.[51] Rather than feeling much sympathy, Rowell in private thought the emphasis on "what Prince Edward Island had suffered by entering Confederation" tended to "irritate" the rest of Canada. PEI, he joked to his wife, was like a spouse who never tired of reminding his partner that he had made a mistake by marrying her.[52]

The commission had hoped to travel next to Fredericton, but the New Brunswick brief was not ready. The provincial government, although a Liberal administration headed by A.A. Dysart, was critical from the outset regarding the commission's work. In part, this was because the province, like Prince Edward Island, was not in acute fiscal distress. The Depression had reinforced the subsistence way of life in parts of New Brunswick, and the province bucked the national urbanization trend and became even more rural in the 1930s.[53] Agriculture, lumbering, and pulp and paper dominated the economy, but the other pillar was the government itself. A traditional system of patronage rooted in primary-sector clientele networks existed, and it focused on infrastructure spending, such as road works. After 1935, the Dysart government undertook a relatively robust public works program and New Brunswick had the largest per capita program of any province. Problems were, however, looming on the horizon. Provincial bonded debt was rapidly increasing. But the provincial government was sulking and had refused to engage with the agenda after its snit over commission appointments.

Rowell was not impressed. New Brunswick's lack of preparedness compounded his overall impatience with what he encountered in the Maritimes. He complained to his wife that he could not "understand the psychology of the Maritimers who [were] constantly talking about what they [had] lost by Confederation as if they [thought] that [would] make it easier to get the other provinces to recognize their present needs." The region, he wrote to his son, should concentrate on "stating the present position with a view to a general adjustment which it is our duty to consider." While he was impressed by the fiscal and economic problems, the drone of historical grievances was a worn and repetitive refrain that he had already heard enough of from the western provinces.[54] Rowell did not seem to absorb the positive alternatives presented by Nova Scotia.

Since New Brunswick's brief was not ready, the commission returned to Ottawa. After two days it adjourned for a month before resuming hearings in British Columbia. It would then move on to Alberta. Both provinces had completed their submissions, but Alberta's brief was withheld from circulation amidst the increasingly fraught relations between the dominion and the province. The adjournment provided Rowell, fatigued from the strain of travel and the hearings, with the opportunity to holiday with his wife in Georgia, where he rested and golfed at Augusta in the salubrious Georgia hills.[55] Robert MacKay, meanwhile, was also feeling the strain of the schedule and work. In particular, he was finding it increasingly difficult to be away from his family in Halifax for such long stretches of time. Apart from his own exertions, he was aware he was leaving the responsibility for his young family of four children solely to his wife, Kathleen. The new private railway car assigned to the commission was impressive and at least made their road trips more palatable.[56]

By mid-March 1938, the commission had made its way to Victoria, British Columbia. The commissioners and their staff were entranced by the surroundings. They were cheered by the temperate climate and verdant scenery. Despite the west coast spring conditions, the commissioners experienced a frostier reception than on the Prairies or in the Maritimes. According to Dafoe's biographer Murray Donnelly, "there was a note of incongruity in the lengthy discussion of Canadian problems that took place down beyond the mountains."[57] The BC government was well prepared and produced a strong brief, but its outlook differed from that of the beleaguered Maritimes or desperate Prairies. British Columbia shared with Nova Scotia and Manitoba a similar history of defending provincial rights, but it did not share the same economic experience. BC possessed a strong economy with extraordinary prospects even as parts of it had been battered by the worldwide depression. The province had a history of demanding more money from Ottawa, but it came from a position of economic strength rather than need.

The Liberal provincial government of Duff Pattullo began preparations for its brief as soon as the commission had been announced. Under the direction of former economics professor and head of the Economic Council of BC, W.A. Carrothers, and its coterie of well-educated and skilled economic policy advisors like Neil Perry and Harry Cassidy and confident political leaders, including Provincial Secretary George Weir and Finance Minister John Hart, the province drew up a comprehensive outline of its economic and fiscal circumstances and concerns. The research was rooted in a historical approach starting with BC's entry into Confederation and emphasizing the province's lengthy pursuit of better terms and demands for financial compensation for lost revenues over the decades.[58] Like the Maritimes and the Prairies, British Columbia had a strong sense of a separate history with distinct grievances.

The very title of the submission, *British Columbia in the Canadian Confederation*, hinted at a distant relationship with Canada. In the view of Pattullo's biographer, Robin Fisher, it seemed at times that, in BC, the federal government "was hardly seen at all." While the province was often lumped into the larger region of western Canada, the submission attempted to make it clear that BC and the Prairies were distinct. Pattullo had rejected proposals that the western provinces put together a joint presentation. Yet the brief showed that BC shared a great deal with the Prairie provinces in its critical analysis of federal economic, fiscal, and monetary policies, particularly the National Policy. But even as it identified similar problems, BC did not embrace the same vision of federalism expressed by Manitoba and Saskatchewan or even Nova Scotia. The province did not express the need for a search for a better federation but, rather, for a better deal.[59]

When the hearings opened, Premier Pattullo wasted no time on pleasantries. He introduced the provincial case with his "customary directness." He summarized the substance of the provincial case, which was lengthy and critical. Much of it, the premier pointed out, had already been presented to the federal government in various forms over many decades. British Columbia was unhappy with its lot in Confederation, but the province's position was not the same as that of the other discontented provinces. With its 354 pages of text and 192 data tables, the submission was as technically sophisticated and carefully researched as the Prairie briefs. It lacked, however, the broad synthesis of the Manitoba, Saskatchewan, and Nova Scotia submissions.[60]

For British Columbia, the dominion government had consistently made the challenges of effective government worse by unfulfilled promises regarding railways and public lands, and, above all, inadequate federal subsidies. In tandem, the inadequate "subsidies" starting in 1870 combined with the weak sources of revenues due to federal takeover of public lands (the Railway Belt through central BC for the CPR project and the Peace River Bloc in the northeast under the Dominion Lands Act) meant that BC had not received "equality of treatment" with the other provinces. Until it received equal treatment, mere revisions to dominion-provincial fiscal relations were irrelevant.[61]

British Columbia's geography meant that per capita costs of providing government services were very high, a factor the province had argued ad nauseam to the dominion. The Depression made the situation worse by raising people's expectations and increasing governmental responsibilities. BC was now requesting "equitable treatment," and its position should not be interpreted as a "plea of poverty." In fact, the crucial factor behind the BC case was that the province, however fiscally challenged by debt charges, by lack of tax revenue, and by irritating national policies, was actually quite prosperous. Income levels were high, the resource and transportation sectors were growing rapidly, and the government wanted to ensure both continued economic growth and the delivery of a generous array of social services in health and education. Pattullo hoped that the commission would recommend changes to the dominion-provincial relationship that would allow the provinces to be "autonomous within their own spheres" without having to beg Ottawa for financial aid. The province wanted assured grants so it could pursue its social policy agenda, while unemployment, pensions, and labour regulation were transferred to Ottawa.[62]

The premier was counting on more than the force of his argument: "In the theatrical atmosphere of the commission's hearings, the tone of the presentation was probably more important than the substance." British Columbia was the first province to place its case in the hands of its legal counsel. J.W. deB. Farris, a prominent corporate lawyer in Vancouver who had recently been appointed to the Senate, was consulted from the start. It was his job to demonstrate that the fiscal relationship had "broken down" and that BC had a case for "special consideration" from Ottawa.[63] Farris was aggressive and adversarial, and treated the hearings as a courtroom.[64]

Farris's "high-powered style" did not endear him to either the commissioners or the press. McGeachy described Farris as a "50 horse-power counsel," orotund but imprecise, who "turned the inquiry into a lawsuit." At the hearings, Rowell was annoyed and reminded Farris that he was not conducting a court of claims. Rowell took some solace when the province was almost universally chastised in the local press for being "extreme in its demands" and "ultra-provincial" in its attitudes. Rowell was assuaged by presentations made by public organizations that stressed "the national point of view and urged the strengthening of the central authority whereas the Provincial brief ha[d] stressed little but BC grievances."[65] The adversarial atmosphere became even more tense when Farris faced the cross-examination of commission co-counsel J.M. Stewart. Their dialogue was a querulous if mercifully brief battle over legalistic and factual points. Farris came at considerable expense. In addition to irritating the commission he irked the BC government by submitting a fee for over $32,000 for his work.[66]

As much as the commissioners wanted to attribute the adversarial atmosphere to the leading personalities making the province's case, they realized that federal-provincial relations were poorly structured. In Pattullo's mind, the commissioners were not open to hearing or appreciating the provincial situation or its history. Instead, they were more interested "in scoring minor points off the silly provincials than in putting their minds to the fact that the Pattullo government was proposing an alternative view of Confederation that acknowledged Canada's regional realities." For Pattullo, it was clear "that the fix was in." The commission "was not a device to negotiate with the government of British Columbia but rather a means of imposing the federal point of view." The premier was exasperated and felt he was being backed into a corner. "The centralizers," he explained, "almost force one to appear in the light of a provincialist."[67] Criticized by the provinces' newspapers and scrutinized by the commissioners, Pattullo's presentation was even more aggressive than the provincial brief. Rowell came away convinced that the BC government realized it had "made a mistake" in its aggressive presentation and vague demands. Similarly, MacKay observed to his wife that Pattullo and Farris

"Paper Blizzard" – editorial cartoon, 18 December
1937. *Winnipeg Tribune*

had weakened "an otherwise good case" by their aggressive tones and their
failure to make "concrete proposals except for a larger hand out." Eggleston
captured the mood of the commission staff by describing the BC case as
"grousing about the terms of Confederation" and the hearings as a "tribunal
for hearing its claims for more money."[68]

In the meantime, MacKay and Angus met privately with senior government officials in an attempt to gain a more balanced sense of the province's situation and cultivate more amicable relations. They heard complaints
about wasteful provincial forestry policies and practices, and the administrative and fiscal problems facing BC's extensive if ill-coordinated social
policies. MacKay thought Rowell now recognized that their inquiry must
shift from legal and constitutional questions to administrative and fiscal
questions. Rowell seemed rested after his recent trip to Georgia and took
some time in Victoria to play golf. The others, led by Angus in his childhood home town, enjoyed the mild temperatures and scenery, including

motoring around Victoria, while Angus and MacKay continued their practice of lengthy walking when time permitted. Dafoe spoke about Canada's international relations to the Victoria branch of the Canadian Institute of International Affairs. It was a sombre warning delivered as Germany took over Austria.[69]

After two busy weeks in Victoria and a day of meetings in Vancouver (where MacKay also met for a reunion with old regimental mates and Angus returned briefly to his family), the commission headed off to Alberta at the end of March. It arrived at a low point in Alberta-Canada relations. The government's attitude towards the commission was made apparent when only the press greeted its arrival in Edmonton: "It seemed that in the strange land of Social Credit," noted MacKay, "the government's attitude would be as chilly as the tag end of the Alberta winter."

The Alberta government had supported the idea of the royal commission at the December 1936 meeting of the National Finance Committee, but that support diminished in the months that followed. The quarrel between Premier Aberhart and the federal finance department over the Loan Council in 1936 was followed by more severe conflict in 1937 after Ottawa decided to allow Alberta to default on provincial debt while saving Manitoba and Saskatchewan from a similar fate. Mackenzie King had assured Aberhart that press reports alleging discrimination were wholly unfounded: "There has been and there is now no desire to discriminate between Alberta and other provinces." Privately, however, King noted proudly that he had manoeuvred Aberhart "into a cleft stick" by gaining his agreement to the Bank of Canada's investigation into the province's finances. "This," the prime minister crowed, "will enable us to show wherein his methods have been different from those of the other two Provinces."[70]

The battles between King and Aberhart intensified in 1937 and 1938 over Alberta's enactment of "Social Credit" legislation. The Credit of Alberta Regulation Act placed the federally chartered banks under directorates appointed by a provincial board. The Bank Employees Civil Rights Act made it illegal for the banks to take civil action against the province. An amendment to the Judicature Act made it illegal to challenge the validity of provincial laws in court. "[Alberta's action] was certainly legislation which not only pressed the theory of provincial rights to its utmost extremity," constitutional expert J.R. Mallory explained, "but challenged the

Dominion to interfere with the programme of a provincial government aggressively attempting to modify fundamental national policy." Ottawa disallowed the legislation as an invasion of federal powers. Alberta reintroduced it along with the Accurate News and Information Act, which provided several means of provincial government control over newspaper reporting. The legislation was reserved and then reviewed by the Supreme Court of Canada, which declared it *ultra vires*, a decision supported by the JCPC. While hailed by some in English Canada at the time as "a revival of Dominion control over the provinces," the disallowances were among the last ever used.[71]

These disputes undercut Alberta's support for the royal commission. Ottawa, which had usurped the province's constitutional power, was now perceived as seeking to increase federal control. The inquiry's sweeping mandate to recommend major changes to the federal system was interpreted as one more example of federal financial domination. "Both the personnel and terms of reference of the Commission," Aberhart had argued in August 1937, "rendered it useless for all practical purposes." Changes to Canadian federalism should come through consultation with the provinces. "I may say," King responded, "that there is no ground whatever for your implication of a connection between the announcement of the Commission's appointment and the disallowance of your recent legislation."[72] Despite the protest, more federal actions were to come. Shortly before the commission was scheduled to appear in Edmonton, the Supreme Court delivered its decision on Alberta's legislative efforts to hobble national financial institutions.

The Social Credit "phenomenon" in Alberta had led to considerable dominion-provincial conflict, but the party's "philosophy" was not based specifically on a regional sense of western alienation. Aberhart was himself a conservative who had never opposed such traditionally decried national policies on the Prairies, such as the tariff, freight rates, or control of natural resources. Social Creditors were not opposed to Ottawa's role in Confederation per se; they were, however, fiercely opposed to aspects of the orthodox international system of finance in the forms of monetary and fiscal policy.[73]

The morning after arriving in Edmonton, a wary Rowell (who confessed to his wife that he now always seemed to look "tired or bored" in newspaper photos) spent an hour with the premier and cabinet. Aberhart informed Rowell that the Alberta brief was at the printer. He professed the cabinet's willingness to present a submission but warned that the legislature seemed dead set against it. The legislature, or at least its Social Credit majority, promptly voted against either submission of the brief or participation in the hearings. Aberhart admitted that the Social Credit theorist from the United Kingdom, Major Douglas, had urged Alberta not to submit a brief. "This is a new form of government in Canada," Rowell observed incredulously. "Instead of government from Downing Street as the cry was a century ago," he remarked, "it is government from the Social Credit head-quarters in London." He offered Aberhart the alternative of subpoenaing Alberta government witnesses as a commission has the right to do, but the premier stated he would not like to see this loophole used against the legislature's decision. Rowell made it clear to Aberhart that any "informal" presentation of the Alberta case was not acceptable.[74]

MacKay sensed more devious currents. He discerned that Aberhart was more the master of the situation than he let on and was "as astute a dema-gogue as Mitch Hepburn." He also noted that "in this province democracy rules through the caucus" and that the government and the caucus, in turn, was run by the Social Credit Board and its "advisors." It all led MacKay to worry that "Alberta ha[d] the beginnings at least of a real fascist move-ment" and that Social Credit was, at its roots, "totalitarian." MacKay had the impression that Social Credit politics were expressed in "religious terms," a view he repeated after a reunion with his Edmonton-area family members.[75]

Despite the lack of official government cooperation or a provincial brief, the hearings went ahead. When Rowell opened the proceedings, he mentioned the province but not the government. According to Rowell's biographer, "the people of Alberta were interested in the commission, for they turned out in larger numbers than in any centre to date, filling a dis-mal courtroom, the poorest accommodation provided by any province." The drama surrounding Alberta's boycott of the commission brought out the crowds. J.B. McGeachy reported that the opening session was the best attended thus far, with seventy-five people sitting in, while MacKay thought there were more than one hundred.[76] The aloofness of the government did provide the commissioners with a less busy schedule. There were few social events or dinners to attend, and the lieutenant-governor did not host a dinner because he was in the process of being ejected in retaliation for refusing to give assent to several Social Credit bills. Rowell found the presentations by the United Farmers and Co-operative Commonwealth Federation interesting if impractical.[77]

The Alberta brief was entitled *The Case for Alberta*. It was addressed to "The Sovereign People of Canada." In the fall of 1938, Alberta's *Case* was distributed to governments throughout the country as well as to the commission.[78] On its own, it was an impressive study, based on skilled economic analysis from the two Minnesota economists who wrote it, although no credit for this expert input was given in print.[79] The historical case differed little from its Manitoba, Saskatchewan, or BC counterparts. In 377 pages *The Case for Alberta* examined the material resources and economic history of the province. It devoted several chapters to the harmful impact of national tariffs as well as settlement, railway, and monetary policies. The brief focused on the problems of public finance in areas from education to municipal government to provincial budgets. It made the same points about the outmoded fiscal framework, including taxation and monetary policy, as did the dominion.[80] Alberta sought the transfer of responsibility over unemployment and labour regulation to Ottawa, the creation of an "economic restoration" program of federal highways, irrigation, and other projects; the revision of credit and monetary policy towards lower interest rates and a depreciated foreign exchange rate; and, above all, the shift to the grants-in-aid approach to federal fiscal support, which would ensure adequate and effective funding for vital provincial social services like public health, education, and social welfare.[81]

The Alberta study departed from the western consensus in its second section, almost certainly not written by the expert consultants. This part consisted of a fifty-five-page prescription for the implementation of a national Social Credit program. It attempted to explain the schism between conventional and Social Credit political economy, and between the incremental adjustments that the "orthodox" approach recommended and the transformative change Social Credit promised. Through a mixture of appealing to the wisdom of the Canadian people, and tapping the unused wealth of the country lying wasted due to the monetary system, the allure of escaping the curse of "poverty amidst the wealth" was given full rein.[82]

The commission never formally acknowledged the existence of *The Case for Alberta*. In September 1938, the commissioners received copies and considered whether or how to use them, but they backed away from doing so. Dafoe petulantly admitted that the *Case* was on his desk but that he had "no present intention of reading it." When federal finance minister Charles Dunning belatedly revealed that Alberta had insisted that the brief not be taken as *the* provincial position, the commissioners decided that they could not even formally consider it. This pretense of ignorance extended not only to excising any mention of the submission itself (implying that Alberta's boycott of the hearings extended to the tabling of exhibits) but also to any reference to it whatsoever in their report.[83] The commissioners ignored what was in the main a well-prepared study.

The commission did hear the presentation by the Edmonton Chamber of Commerce, which had been prepared as a stand-in for the Alberta brief as soon as the province threatened its boycott in October 1937. The chamber's sixty-four-page *Submission* had the imprimatur of *Edmonton Journal* editor John Imrie, with expert contributions by the influential accountant Francis Winspear and the prominent lawyer (and later Supreme Court of Canada justice) Ronald Martland. It began with a statement about the "fundamental rights of Canadians," conceived in terms of both basic political and legal rights as well as of the equality of the provinces. There was an underlying tone critical of Alberta for suspending certain rights and of Canada for overriding the provinces via disallowance. It proceeded to examine many of the same themes as the Alberta case relating to the severe fiscal crunch and the cumulative burdens of national policies. These problems included the many "disabilities arising" from land policy, tariffs, transportation policies, interest rates, and monetary policies. It advocated a new fiscal deal through permanent joint agencies and recommended not only a limited reallocation of responsibilities (in the area of unemployment insurance and pensions) but also a return to the stricter respect for mutual autonomy, particularly to aid the province in resolving its long-standing debt problems, as found in the original 1867 agreement. Although briefly exploring the idea of citizens' rights as the basis for governmental policy, it did not elaborate on this theme.[84]

The remainder of the hearings in Edmonton, which lasted a week, continued to draw respectable audiences. Rowell admitted that he was impatient with the lengthy presentations of several organizations, ranging from the CCF and the UFA to social service organizations and the usual parade of municipal governments.[85] The commissioners and staff boarded their railway car to travel to Ottawa with plans to complete the hearings in late April.

The trips across Canada in 1937–38 had drawn well-argued briefs and testimony, with the exceptions of dissident Alberta and dilatory New Brunswick. By mid-April, the New Brunswick government reported that it was now ready to testify, but Rowell fell ill and requested a postponement. Although cautioned by Rowell not to reach any premature conclusions, the commissioners had heard vivid accounts of the problems of government that pointed towards common themes and goals. In the East, it was the matter of subsidies versus grants and the burdens of the national policy; in the West, it was the entire package of national economic, monetary, and fiscal policy. The common theme, however, was that Confederation had failed to provide widespread economic or social benefits and that federalism in Canada had become almost unworkable. The themes that emerged pointed to a need to recast the regional effects of national economic development policies and even to reconsider national policies; to reconsider the basic roles and allocation of state duties; and to reshape monetary policies and the fiscal structure of dominion-provincial relations. The tone may have changed between December 1937 and March 1938, but even with Alberta's attenuated stance, there seemed enough willingness on the part of the six provinces consulted to address the issues. Amid the discontent, cautious hopes were still alive. But the two largest and most influential provinces – Ontario and Quebec – had yet to weigh in, and their leaders were seething with hostility and intrigue.

6

Stormy Spring
April–June 1938

I am proud to say that Quebec and Ontario have got together to get justice for themselves in the belief that charity begins at home. It's not a matter of ganging up but to stop a raid against Confederation.

– *Maurice Duplessis, 15 December 1937*[1]

Equality between provinces is impossible. The provinces are fiscal entities and governments, like individuals, must learn to manage within their means.

– *Mitchell Hepburn, 4 May 1937*[2]

The chances of the Rowell-Sirois Commission achieving consensus among the provinces were diminishing. The inquiry had yet to make an appearance in either of Canada's most populous provinces, and the commissioners were concerned that the governments of Ontario and Quebec would derail the entire process. Neither province had yet indicated what form, if any, their participation would take. Whereas the other provinces had indicated intentions to prepare briefs, Ontario and Quebec left their situations purposefully ambiguous. The commissioners expected the same indifferent contribution and possibly an even more hostile reception than they had received in Alberta. Ontario's Liberal premier, Mitch Hepburn, insisted that the commission delay its appearance in Toronto until late

"Reckless" – editorial cartoon, 4 May 1938. *Toronto Star*

April when the session of the provincial legislature ended. The delay was welcome news for the commissioners, who feared a spectacle awaiting their arrival. Quebec's Union Nationale premier, Maurice Duplessis, had given no clear signals as to how his province would respond to the commission. In the meantime, the inquiry faced problems of its own.

Premier Hepburn responded positively to the initial announcement of the royal commission. "This government will co-operate in every possible way," the Ontario premier proclaimed. "We are entirely satisfied with the personnel of the Federal commission and we feel that an amendment of the BNA Act is long overdue. The Act was made for the people, not the people for the Act, and it is generally recognized that the Act is now out of date."[3] But those expressions papered over Hepburn's visceral animosity towards Newton Rowell and John W. Dafoe, not to mention Mackenzie

King. It also disguised what Hepburn perceived as an opportunity to make political gains.

Hepburn and Rowell did not like each other. They had incompatible personal habits, as well as political and social outlooks, but the differences went deeper. When Rowell was sworn in as chief justice of Ontario in 1937, Hepburn was not present due to illness. It was an "agreeable coincidence," explained his biographer, Margaret Prang, since "Rowell was no admirer of Hepburn, whose vulgar flamboyance and demagoguery he believed did no credit to Liberalism."[4] Likewise, the Ontario premier had only contempt for Dafoe, and the feeling was mutual: "Dafoe detested Hepburn as a politician of the cheapest kind," opined Dafoe biographer Murray Donnelly, "and the fact that the people of Ontario could elect such a man left him, as he had said in many editorials, profoundly pessimistic about the future of democracy."[5]

Hepburn's hostility to the commission grew alongside his acrimonious feud with fellow Liberal Mackenzie King. While personal relations could not be worse, Ontario's opposition was inevitable based on traditional provincial rights grounds. A federal inquiry established to study dominion-provincial relations was sure to raise the ire of the most powerful provinces. Ontario's rhetoric against the federal government was ramped up over the months following the commission's creation. To Hepburn, even the manner in which the commission was conceived and established demonstrated ill-intent. It was sweeping in scope and set to investigate the history of federalism in Canada, yet there had been no consultation with the provinces. "I have always regarded Confederation as the outcome of a conference," Hepburn argued. If there was to be a change in Confederation, "it can be brought about only by a renewed conference of the representatives of the people and with unanimity of approval." Even though he was informed that the idea of the commission was being discussed in late 1936 and early 1937, the Ontario premier claimed ignorance as to its creation. "I was perplexed," he commented somewhat misleadingly, "after first hearing of the Commission's appointment while eating breakfast one morning."[6] The western provinces, Hepburn claimed, were given advance notice when they had met in Regina in June 1937 and agreed to demand $58 million per year in additional grants. Hepburn's claim was questionable since the commission proposal was announced in Parliament in April. But Hepburn was a creature of the moment. The commission should have been created by Parliament, not cabinet, he now asserted. The situation "went deeper than discourtesy," and Canada's most powerful province was unlikely to appear before an "illegitimate body" as either an "applicant or as a defendant."[7] He argued that the commission was created only to increase the powers of the federal government, and that Ontario "was not here to bargain away functions with which we have been charged, not here to trade off the resources we are sworn to preserve."[8] The premier made it clear that he would not be "pushed" into any "new scheme of government financing" that would work to the detriment of his province.[9]

Political theatre aside, behind Hepburn's opposition there were serious practical and theoretical concerns. Ontario worried that its revenue sources and tariff-backed industries might well be affected by national policies that aimed to overcome provincial fiscal weaknesses and regional disparities. Ontario politicians, the premier noted, "have always valued autonomy more than equality."[10] The province would be reluctant "to agree to the principle of provincial equalization involved in a national plan of this kind." Ontario, Hepburn declared, "should not be forced to subsidize the rest of Canada."[11]

Hepburn found an ally in the premier of Quebec, who also complained about not being consulted about the commission's creation and its implicit threat to the existing fiscal order. When the two premiers met in Montreal in December 1937, Hepburn groused to Maurice Duplessis in public about the commission. He suggested an "economic alliance" between Ontario and Quebec to withstand western demands.[12] With the Prairie provinces virtually bankrupt, there was little doubt where Ottawa would look for financial help. When a report of the meeting between Hepburn and Duplessis reached the prime minister vacationing in Florida, Mackenzie King responded that it was "just as well to have these two incipient dictators out in the open linked together." He reflected further that "it is an outrage that this young upstart [Hepburn] should seek to array central provinces against West & East, as he is in attacking representations before Rowell Commission."[13]

Duplessis announced two days after meeting Hepburn that Quebec, Ontario, and the Maritimes would not be dominated by Ottawa and the western provinces. The statement ignited a flood of criticism in the national press. Duplessis responded to those charging him with damaging national unity: "I am proud to say that Quebec and Ontario have got together to get justice for themselves in the belief that charity begins at home. It's not a matter of ganging up but to stop a raid against Confederation." Hepburn agreed that a common front was essential:

> The more I read of the representations made by the other provinces the more convinced I am of the necessity of Ontario and Quebec resisting together, and in no uncertain way, the ever increasing, unreasonable and impossible demand ... I can readily understand the advantage it would be to the other provinces for them to raid the Federal Treasury, particularly when Ontario and Quebec contribute 80% of the revenue. I have further information to the effect that the King Government is determined to take over the collection of succession duties. This would deprive us of our greatest source of revenue.[14]

This "common front" was already resisting the establishment of a federal unemployment insurance program. Ontario and Quebec wanted a system financed by Ottawa but administered by the provinces. In November, Hepburn blithely told King that Ontario would not object to a constitutional amendment enabling Ottawa to introduce unemployment insurance. When the Ontario premier received a draft amendment in January 1938, he told Duplessis that King was "simply asking for a blank cheque insofar as amending the British North America Act is concerned and is using unemployment insurance as the thin edge of the wedge." Hepburn remained "solidly behind" the principle of a national unemployment scheme "but not at the expense of Confederation."[15] While Hepburn refused to agree until he had seen the details of the proposed measure, King refused to discuss the details until the amendment was passed.[16] The prime minister "wants us to consent to the revision of the B.N.A. Act without telling us exactly what he proposes to do," Hepburn told Duplessis. "We agree in principle but we want the details, and if we consider the measure does not meet the needs of Ontario we reserve the right to object. Our consent to a revision of the B.N.A. Act is predicated on the condition that we will be able to study the bill which the Federal Government proposes."[17]

The Quebec premier was in full agreement. King was asking the provinces to "exchange our birth right for a mess of pottage" and using unemployment insurance "as a smoke screen to be able to tamper with the Constitution and open the door to numerous and important changes with regards to the British North America Act."[18] On 14 February, Hepburn informed Duplessis that he regretted ever endorsing the national unemployment scheme: "If this means we have to sacrifice Confederation I am quite prepared to withdraw any support whatsoever. It is clear to me that with the Western provinces hopelessly bankrupt, any national scheme of unemployment insurance will have to be borne by the two central provinces, and if unemployment insurance is necessary it probably will be better to run our own show."[19] Now the two largest provinces intended to resist attempts by the federal government to regulate their spending and borrowing. They "declared war" on the Rowell-Sirois Commission, arguing that the federal government "had no right to conduct an inquiry into provincial affairs and no power to amend the constitution without their consent."[20]

Hepburn rejected the claim that there was a crisis in public finance that required major reform. The Depression highlighted serious waste in public administration, but this did not equate to a crisis. There was no need to revamp the entire system. Economy, he argued, was still possible under the existing political framework: "The overlapping of functions between the central and provincial bodies could surely be corrected without destroying the balance which had originally been set up for the insurance of self-government. In other words, a satisfactory solution was quite possible without changing the constitution." As far as Hepburn was concerned, Ontario had weathered the Depression by careful budgeting and cutting government expenditures: "Now the principle of equalization threatened to penalize her for having achieved such a status." The premier recognized that conditions had changed since 1867. New services were required to respond to twentieth-century conditions. The question was which level of government should take on these new services: "Hepburn's answer was simple and straightforward: give the provinces responsibility of administering services and give them the fiscal means to make this possible."[21]

While the storm clouds were gathering in Ontario and Quebec, the Rowell-Sirois Commission reconvened for a strategy session in Ottawa in mid-April 1938. Rowell was unable to attend due to illness. MacKay reported to his fellow commissioners that Duplessis had recently spent his forty-eighth birthday in Toronto with Hepburn. The gathering, "with everyone smiling and saying nothing for publication, seems to have greased the 'axis.'" MacKay feared that both Duplessis and Hepburn would boycott the commission hearings. "The real bond between Maurice & Mitch," he explained to his wife, "is a common hatred of WLMK and Lapointe." He fretted to her over the frailty of Rowell, the apparent weakening of Dafoe, and the fatigue of Sirois, altogether somewhat disheartening circumstances.[22]

The commissioners proceeded to Toronto, welcomed by fierce thunderstorms. They set up in the brand-new Park Plaza Hotel. Dafoe and MacKay were impressed with its "modernistic" and comfortable appurtenances. The commissioners could not review Ontario's submission, however, since the documents were still being printed. Dafoe found time to meet with his Sifton newspaper partners while MacKay and Angus took advantage of a change in the weather to spend a day golfing. The warm spell lent ease to the surroundings but not to what was to come.[23]

On 25 April, the government of Ontario met the royal commission in the Ontario legislative chamber. Attorney General Gordon Conant extended a welcome that McGeachy described as the kind offered when "a man welcomes poor relations with cautious warmth and few words."[24] Hepburn refused to return from his farm near St. Thomas in time for the commission's arrival. Just three days before, Conant had learned that he was to greet the commission in the absence of the premier. He sent Hepburn a draft of his opening comments and indicated that, on their previous stops, the commissioners had been "entertained" by the province. "Apparently this has taken the form of an informal dinner," Conant noted, "with even more informal speeches."[25] In his opening remarks, Conant needled the commission for leaving Ontario until near the end of its travels: "Although one of the last in which sittings are to be held," he said, "Ontario is by no means the least of the Provinces that go to make up the Dominion of Canada." While Confederation itself had come about from "conference and agreement," Conant noted sarcastically, the inquiry format marked a notable "departure from our practice" of federal-provincial meetings.[26]

While Ontario was preparing its brief for distribution, the first week consisted of presentations and reports from a wide range of business, social service, and trade and professional organizations. In his "Confederation Clinic," McGeachy observed that "witnesses who speak for local governments or occupational groups are nearly all federalists," by which he meant advocates of overriding dominion authority.[27] An example was the brief of the Canadian Chambers of Commerce, which favoured the Loan Council approach to federal-provincial finances.[28]

Robert Fowler, increasingly active on the commission, hosted a cocktail party that amused John Dafoe since it gave him the chance to observe the Toronto professional and academic elites at close quarters. Since the hearings took place on his home turf, a refreshed Newton Rowell entertained his colleagues on several occasions. On the weekend, he showed the commissioners around his three-hundred-acre farm at Kleinburg, a picturesque town on the Humber River, north of Toronto. Dafoe was pleased with the guided tour by "squire Rowell." The reprieve did allow the commissioners time to prepare for the appearance of the wrathful premier of Ontario. They reminded each other to avoid falling into the premier's traps by not reacting to what they knew would be an incendiary presentation.[29]

Mitch Hepburn appeared on the afternoon of Monday 2 May, flanked by seventeen ministers and civil servants. MacKay remarked to his wife: "[Hepburn] is out apparently to damn the Dominion Government and the West. We haven't seen the brief yet. It has been held back to the last minute, but we've got an inkling of the tenor."[30] And Hepburn met all expectations. The Ontario premier was armed with his own proposals, consisting of a personal statement drafted with the aid of W.H. Moore, a maverick Liberal member of Parliament. His statement was barely aligned with the rest of Ontario's brief.

The premier began with a terse welcome but turned to what he warned was "a long deep note of discontent." This "note" consisted of a critique of the commission, a dismissal of the concerns raised by the Prairie provinces (particularly Manitoba), and complaints about how Ontario had been overtaxed to support other provinces. Hepburn airily praised individualism as the foundation of freedom. "We are a stupid people," he warned, "if we imagine ourselves immune from the consequences of concentrating power

in a few hands. The accumulation of power leads to autocracy; its distribution is the safety-zone of democracy."[31]

The premier spent considerable time refuting western concerns and
issues. He claimed that the goal of the West was a diversion of money "from
the sorely pressed provinces of Ontario and Quebec." The Prairie provinces
had presented their accounting based on the alleged costs of national
tariff and monetary policies. Hepburn attacked Manitoba's "weak case,"
written by "American professors" and consisting of "an unashamed raid
by the orphans of Confederation on the pockets of central Canada." The
West, he asserted, was responsible for its own problems: "I have every
sympathy for those 99 thousand farmers whose main source of revenue
has declined; but really I do not see that it is necessary to upset
Confederation on their behalf." Westerners were "the makers of their own
(and other people's) misfortunes ... if the millions of state funds (provincial
and federal) expended on wheat seed that blew away had been put into
mills and factories, the west would have been able to clothe itself and
provide most of the goods in life." Regardless, Hepburn claimed, the industrial worker suffered more in the Depression than the farmer. If the
western provinces could not "manage within their means" and finance an
adequate level of social services out of their own resources, they should
amalgamate rather than raid the treasuries of other provinces.[32]

Hepburn blustered that Ontario had grown tired of western whining
about the injustices of Confederation focused around tariff and industrial
exploitation. Provincial economists had worked through the claims against
the tariff and found them "a combination of hopeless economics, flawed
methodology, and bad arithmetic." If the West wanted to balance accounts,
Ontario had a few items to add to the ledger. These included the debt and
expenditures on western railways, low freight rates for western wheat, the
tariff that limited Ontario's use of imported coal, the cost of special grants
to the West for export subsidies, the wheat pools, and state aid in the
marketing of wheat. Despite tumultuous changes in the world economy,
the Canadian federal system could prosper while preserving its "political
heritage."[33]

Hepburn concluded his remarks by opposing the growing need for
social services in general and a uniform standard through federal programs
in particular. Social services should only exist on a contributory basis.[34]

In such a diverse country as Canada, the costs of social programs had to be charged against the incomes arising in each province: "Equity between the provinces is impossible. Prince Edward Island can never be like Manitoba; Ontario may not have the coal and petroleum with which Alberta is so richly endowed; and yet somehow, we must get along together."[35]

According to Hepburn's biographer John Saywell, the premier gave "a ninety-minute political harangue of the kind that had got him elected. Failing to get the cheers and wisecracks usually forthcoming from his audiences, and finding his jokes falling 'like a pancake in a puddle,' Hepburn continued to read his speech at breakneck pace." As he read his script, he sometimes stumbled over words and phrases. Fowler noted in his summary for the commissioners that Hepburn spoke with a "hesitancy and uncertainty" that suggested a lack of familiarity with the text.[36]

The commissioners listened in "grim silence." Dafoe found Hepburn's statement "at best, superficial sarcasm; at worst, stupidity." Calling the presentation "a dud," and the effect "grotesque," Dafoe concluded that the whole event showed that Hepburn's feud with King was "becoming an obsession." MacKay reported that Hepburn's performance was "cheap" and rude, and "fell terribly flat" with the audience, not to mention the commissioners. Rowell had been advised by his colleagues not to allow himself to be baited by Hepburn into an exchange, and so the weary chairman held back.[37] He did offer a few mild words in response. Rowell indicated that the commission was not set up to revise the Constitution: "We are a fact-finding body ... If on the facts as we find them it appears that there should be some change in the financial relations between the Dominion and the provinces, it is our duty to recommend what those changes should be, but our recommendations must be within the strict limits of a federal constitution." Any recommendations, he assured Hepburn, would have to be considered by a dominion-provincial conference.[38]

Just as Ontario had sent a representative to monitor and report on the Manitoba and Saskatchewan hearings, Manitoba's treasurer, Stuart Garson, attended the Ontario presentation. He was accompanied by Saskatchewan's policy advisor, Fred Cronkite, and BC's legal counsel, J.W. deB. Farris. Not surprisingly, Garson was annoyed by Hepburn's dismissal of the Manitoba case as "a bit of political arithmetic awry with reality."[39]

The press was not as restrained. McGeachy observed that "the great Hepburn, defender of hard-pressed Ontario, against the idle rich of Saskatchewan and Manitoba, took the stand today." He described the speech as "full of half-baked economics, appeals to prejudice, jumbled logic and parish politics."[40] The *Globe and Mail* referred to it as "an instrument of destruction from the standpoint of national unity." Federal Liberals called it a mixture of "insolence and insularity."[41] But however offensive in tone, Hepburn revealed much about the Ontario government's position on federal-provincial relations.

If Hepburn ranted, the Ontario submission was not nearly as incendiary and the rest of the Ontario delegation was ready with a much more serious set of views. The next four days were spent working through the document entitled *Statement by the Government of Ontario to the Royal Commission on Dominion-Provincial Relations*. The three-volume brief was written by Deputy Minister of the Treasury Chester Walters and McMaster University economics professor Kenneth Taylor. They were both very capable, and they drew upon a civil service that was at its top levels highly competent. They prepared an impressive analytical statement of the Ontario government's position. It provided an overview of the province's interpretation of the federal system, its specific economic and social policy needs, and its fiscal and revenue requirements. At eighty-five pages, it was less extensive than any of the Prairie submissions or those of BC and Nova Scotia.[42] The *Statement* approached the commission not through a federal/constitutional lens but, rather, through an overview of Ontario's economic and fiscal circumstances. It was a formidable analysis on every issue from taxation levels to the impact of the tariff.

Walters and Taylor presented the Ontario case in the absence of the premier, who held the positions of provincial treasurer and minister of economics. The ebullient Chester Walters, trained as a public accountant, had risen in the Ottawa civil service from an auditor in the department of finance to federal commissioner of income before moving to Toronto in 1933 as deputy minister of public works and then as controller of finance. He was effectively deputy treasurer under Hepburn. He was also prominent in the circles of public administration in Canada. The scholarly Kenneth Taylor was one of Canada's leading economists and, some years later, became a senior official in the federal Department of Finance. They were an effective team with contrasting styles, but both demonstrated an impressive command over details. Other members of the provincial cabinet, notably Eric Cross, Thomas McQuesten, and Gordon Conant, as well as senior officials including legal counsel Daniel Lang, reviewed parts of the case. Hepburn's absence helped ease tensions considerably, although he appeared briefly to describe one of his proudest achievements, Ontario's expansion of medical and hospital care.[43]

Taylor began by examining the details regarding the growing inequities of the fiscal system as experienced by Ontario. The province contributed increasing tax revenues yet was unable to raise sufficient revenues for infrastructure spending. Walters claimed that the problems with government revenue went back to Confederation. The agrarian and rural societies in the Prairies and Maritimes were to a high degree self-reliant while industrial and urban societies like Ontario made heavier demands on the state in areas such as transportation, education, and public health. Federal outlays had quadrupled since 1900, but Ontario was spending thirteen times as much in 1937 as it had at the turn of the century.[44]

Ontario had faced growing pressures to deliver social services, education, and highways. The sharp growth of these services required increased provincial revenues rather than limitations. But Ontario opposed increased federal subsidies to the provinces and instead called for a reallocation of tax fields. The solution lay in giving the provinces exclusive control over income taxes by returning to the system prior to 1917. Taylor pointed out that over 45 percent of federal taxes were collected in Ontario while the province received only 28 percent of federal expenditures: "We feel in Ontario we have borne a reasonable share, a full share, perhaps some of us think a little more than our full share, of the burden of taxation."[45] Ontario had been transferring a sum of $75 million to $80 million per year for the benefit of the Maritimes and the Prairies. While admitting that "income tends to be somewhat concentrated in the central areas," he claimed that "it is disbursed in the opposite direction by the normal operation of the Dominion public finance."[46]

The Ontario *Statement* was intended to highlight the role played by the province in "building up Canada" and to demonstrate that: "with our share of the national income and with the financial burden that we have undertaken, the taxpaying capacity of the people of Ontario has been burdened almost to its limit." If Ottawa recognized the province's "moral and equitable right to priority in income taxes and all other direct taxes," then Ontario would take over total responsibility for aid to the unemployed and for municipal tax relief. When Rowell suggested that the income tax was essential to federal coffers for national programs such as war debts, Walters responded: "it is not for the people of Czechoslovakia to tell Herr Hitler where he is to get a further outlet." Rowell replied that he trusted the relations between Ontario and the federal government were not similar to those between Hitler and the Czechs.[47]

The regionalist arguments led to flare-ups between the Ontario delegation and the commissioners. Dafoe, for example, disagreed vehemently with Taylor's claim that the Prairie grain trade was more of a burden than a source of profit to the rest of Canada. Taylor's concern about Ontario's corporate tax burdens drew close scrutiny from Rowell, who proposed that national business income was concentrated in central Canada and could only be taxed there. It all led Rowell to remark that the other parts of Canada had "illusions" about the wealth and sources of wealth in Ontario and Quebec and vice versa but that he hoped "one result of this investigation will be to clear up some of the delusions."[48]

On the subsequent Monday evening, the commission hosted a dinner for the Ontarians at the exclusive York Club. Rowell, "no doubt with secret amusement, arranged the seating plan to have Hepburn next to Dafoe." But the premier failed to show up, and Dafoe was "considerably relieved." The evening passed uneventfully.[49] Later in the week, on Thursday evening, Hepburn hosted the commission, the staff, the lieutenant-governor, and the Ontario cabinet to a lavish dinner at the King Edward Hotel. Rowell attended, apparently out of a sense of duty, and left almost immediately after the meal was over. Dafoe soon followed. It was a weeknight and they still had the last day of Ontario's presentation.

After their departure the evening grew more boisterous. "The evening began quietly," MacKay reported to his wife, "but after the departure of Rowell, a staunch teetotaler, the party began." Chester Walters and Gordon Conant apparently orchestrated the shift from a formal dinner into a party involving heavy drinking and exuberant singing. "Seeing what was coming," MacKay confessed, "I had a good drink of Scotch to remove my inhibitions – I can't quite play the fool when completely sober." He went on to describe the highlights of the night:

A little later there were demands for something from "Mitch," he proceeded to oblige by leading a chorus with his arm around Cronkite, Dean of Sask. Law School who has been representing Sask. He and "Cronk" then sang a duet. I've forgotten the song, but as I recall it wasn't quite printable. At the close of which he or Cronk announced an "Ontario-Saskatchewan" axis. After which choruses again, then a demand for the recitation of a famous ballad – again unprintable – from Mitch, which he did superbly, again more choruses and stories. In some of the choruses Mitch insisted on my joining in – which I did to the best of my ability, one arm around Mitch or Cronk. And there were French songs, and of course, "Allouette" (how do you spell it) from Leduc, Savard, and Chester Walters who sings a superb tenor. And a couple of Irish songs from Peter Heenan. The party broke up about 11:30 with a rousing chorus of "O Canada" after which "Mitch" presented me with his rose, and I him with mine, and Mitch and "Cronk" finished each other's glass. All of this sounds as if it was a drunken ordeal. It really wasn't ... And it wasn't all merely fun ... on one occasion, just when a song was at its height, Mitch quit singing and remarked in my ear to the effect that after all Ontario wasn't so damned provincially minded and that we were all Canadians anyway.

The informal and relaxed atmosphere, with inhibitions loosened through drink, seemed to provide a bonding experience for those involved. MacKay reported that "two different Cabinet ministers and Chester Walters as well as [Daniel] Lang more or less apologized to me during the evening" for Hepburn's speech and tone. The Ontarians reported that the premier felt "he more or less had to do it (no doubt his bargain with Duplessis) though he thoroughly disliked it." The upshot of the party was twofold: the tone of the remainder of the hearings improved, and Hepburn apparently called Duplessis to urge him to appear before the commission.[50] MacKay had to admit that Hepburn, while a polarizing figure, had his charm: "We all – that is those of the Commission who stayed and the staff – came home more or less under the undeniable spell of Hepburn's personality. One can't help liking him, even though he might thoroughly disagree with him."[51]

The final day of Ontario's presentation turned to constitutional questions. Ontario's legal counsel Daniel Lang argued that Canada required a strict federal constitution. He defended the Ontario *Statement* and its argument that Confederation was intended as "a balance between centralization and decentralization." This balance meant adhering to the autonomy and indeed sovereignty of each level of government. Lang sparred with Rowell about the appropriate "balance" between the two levels but demurred at Rowell's assertion that such powers as disallowance suggested a certain federal governmental priority.[52]

Attorney General Gordon Conant closed the testimony in the same reserved tone that had opened it. He noted that the heart of the problem was that, after seventy years as a nation, "all the Provinces are not in the same economic condition." The blame should not be placed upon Ontario. Nor should the federal government seek to alter taxing powers. Instead, it should restore direct taxation solely to the provinces. "The power to tax," Conant warned, "has the power to destroy." Ontario was no "Midas, as it were, the villain at the feast sitting back without obligations but with unbounded wealth."[53] In closing, he echoed Lang, who had cited the dictum about the sovereign nature of provincial as well as federal legislatures.[54]

The Ontario presentation was subjected to an outpouring of criticism from across the country for damaging national unity. But despite the confrontational arguments, Ontario's position was based on the province's long-standing view of the federal system and the province's role within it: "The emphasis," according to historian Christopher Armstrong, "was squarely on autonomy rather than on equalization." The Ontario position seemed unfairly critical of western Canada, but it could be suggested that the West was just as guilty in vilifying central Canada. Despite Hepburn's antics, most of the commissioners realized that they had to be openminded. But a dour Dafoe was not in the mood to show Ontario any quarter. The briefs were "pretty controversial," he wrote. He had difficulty sitting quietly and listening, and admitted to being "a bit more talkative than [he] normally [was]. [He] couldn't let them get away with some of the things they tried to put over."[55]

There was, however, room for optimism about the hearings. Despite Ontario's posturing and the fatuous remarks of the premier, the provincial spokesmen had shown flexibility on key issues. They had abandoned the doctrine that Confederation was a compact in which Ottawa was a junior partner or delegate. They accepted that interregional and dominion-provincial transfers were a fact of fiscal life, as evidenced by the acceptance of federal takeover of unemployment insurance. But there was no mistaking Ontario's intention to defend its jurisdiction and its tax base. The province took a particularly aggressive position regarding the claims of the other regions to larger transfers of the wealth derived in Ontario. In sum, despite Hepburn's excesses, Ontario presented a tough yet rational case that could form the basis for negotiation. There were political and personal quarrels, and legitimate differences between Ontario, some other provinces, and Canada, but the fundamental positions were shifting.[56]

Back in Ottawa, the federal government was closely monitoring the Ontario presentations. The cabinet meeting on the day after Hepburn spoke was dominated by what Prime Minister King described as the "fresh blast from Hepburn before the Rowell Commission." In orchestrating a strategy as to how to respond, Ernest Lapointe supported "some immediate attack." King agreed but wanted to be sure he had the full support of his colleagues. He also thought it best to wait until a federal election "and then go at it without reserve." That afternoon, King intended to go into the House and answer Hepburn's charges that the federal government had shown favouritism towards the western provinces. Norman Rogers, Charles Dunning, and Ian Mackenzie were ready to go to battle with Hepburn, but the others, many of whom held seats in Ontario, were more cautious. King also worried about Quebec and Duplessis. When the time came, the Quebec cabinet ministers – Lapointe, Cardin, Rinfret, and Power – would have to "exert themselves" against the provincial government in Quebec. The prime minister announced that he intended to go on a tour of the West in the autumn in order to lay the groundwork for the next election. The direction would be "against centralization" but for "national unity." Personally, he recorded: "I intend to resist absolutely anything in the nature of coercion of provinces, but intend to let matters get to the point where they will come to beg of us to take over some of the obligations that they today pretend they are ready to assume. What they are really after is getting more sources of revenue into their hands."[57]

Ontario and Quebec posed serious obstacles to the Rowell-Sirois Commission as well as to the King government in Ottawa. But the two provinces had to be handled differently. The prime minister ordered his staff to compile a detailed dossier of Hepburn's relationship with the federal government throughout 1938. The Ontario premier would be confronted openly and directly. The situation with Duplessis had to be handled more deftly. The federal government could not be seen to confront Quebec without stirring up a nationalistic reaction in the province. When the commission was still in Toronto, King insisted on speaking with Rowell on the phone. The prime minister urged him to advise Duplessis that the commission was simply "a fact-finding body" that had no specific agenda.[58]

The civil servants in Ottawa were also concerned. At the Bank of Canada, Graham Towers wondered whether the commission was now in jeopardy. If provincial opposition prevented "major changes in tax sources or responsibilities," the result would be a series of defaults and interest reductions: "It would disappoint all the hopes that the Rowell Commission would produce something which would enable an orderly rearrangement to take place." Towers opined that, if certain provinces obstructed the commission, "the Dominion is fully entitled to do something special for the distressed provinces. They should not be penalized by the intransigence of other sections of the country." He suggested that the commissioners should not be informed that the dominion was contemplating such action. If this occurred, the Prairie provinces should be asked to surrender all claims to their subsidies and instead receive dominion bonds in exchange for total provincial debt. The provinces would no longer be allowed to borrow in foreign currency. Towers made it clear that he was talking solely about the Prairie provinces: "The British Columbia problem – if it is really a financial rather than a political problem – seems to require separate consideration."[59] Towers was proposing an astounding course of action in which the federal government would pursue the very collapse of three provinces that the commission had been called into existence to prevent.

Near the end of the hearings in Toronto, Rowell was bedridden with an attack of what was described in public as pleurisy, a lung infection causing chest pains. For several weeks, Dafoe had remarked in letters to his wife about Rowell's shaky health. In mid-April, Rowell had been forced to delay the commission's trip to New Brunswick. A week later, Dafoe reported on Rowell's pallor and weariness, noting he was "very white & frail." He returned to lead the hearings at Queen's Park on 25 April. He worked for several days, but on 7 May, the day after the review of Ontario's *Statement*, Rowell suffered a severe heart attack, followed by a paralyzing stroke that deprived him of the power of speech. His condition was dire.[60]

Despite worries over Rowell's health, the commission's activities continued. The Ontario meetings ended with a Saturday motor trip, led by Minister of Highways Thomas McQuesten, to the Niagara Peninsula along Ontario's unique and impressive new motorway, soon dubbed the Queen Elizabeth Way, connecting Toronto and Fort Erie. These amicable relations were sustained when Daniel Lang, the Ontario legal counsel, and his law partner, Roland Michener, spent all day Sunday golfing with Angus and MacKay.[61] Dafoe did not attend the weekend festivities; instead, he connected with colleagues from the Canadian Institute of International Affairs and met the notable British journalist and anti-appeasement advocate John Wheeler-Bennett, who was lecturing throughout North America. Previously Dafoe had dined at Rowell's home with the exiled German novelist Thomas Mann, who was also on a lecture tour. Both encounters reinforced Dafoe's deep pessimism over the international situation.[62]

From Toronto, the four healthy commissioners travelled to Quebec City and checked into the Chateau Frontenac, the grandest of Canada's railway hotels. They remained unsure as to what to expect from the government of Maurice Duplessis. Rinfret's earlier withdrawal from the commission removed the only person who had some rapport with the premier. Sirois did not fill this same role. In many ways, Quebec was on a collision path with the federal government. The Depression exposed the issues of provincial autonomy and cultural survival in Quebec, thereby exacerbating French-Canadian nationalism. The Duplessis government "sensed a new and greater menace" in the King administration and believed that the forces of centralization were gathering in Ottawa. When the commission was officially formed, Duplessis immediately objected on the grounds that it was "appointed without prior consultation with the provinces and unilaterally investigated matters that were crucially important to them." Quebec opposed "any abridgement of provincial rights, or any significant change in the federal pact unless accepted by all the provinces."[63] In December 1937, Duplessis had warned that central and eastern Canada should make clear that Quebec would "not be run for the western provinces or Ottawa." In 1938, Duplessis endorsed Hepburn's apparent reversal on unemployment insurance. He told the Ontario premier: "I am sure that the Federal authorities are using unemployment insurance as a smoke-screen to be able to temper [sic] with the constitution."[64]

The two Quebec members of the commission, Joseph Sirois and Louis St-Laurent, were wary about the reaction they would receive in their home province. While Duplessis's opposition would be cast as mere provincial obstructionism and narrow parochial selfishness in the rest of Canada, Sirois and St-Laurent were well aware that the issues went much deeper and touched the nerve of Quebec nationalism and Quebec's way of conducting public policy. How could the changes demanded in the West (which were tantamount to remaking the federal system in a number of ways) be reconciled with the responsibility of the Quebec government to protect its inherited constitutional rights as well as the social and administrative system that shielded French Canadians? When the commission reached Quebec, "the role of St-Laurent took on added importance in the delicate situation." As his biographer, Dale Thomson, explained, "besides trying to obtain the co-operation of the Union Nationale government, [St-Laurent] had to bolster the spirits of his friend Sirois, who was horrified at being thrown into the centre of the controversy, and concerned over finding himself at odds with an important segment of Quebec opinion."[65]

Sirois served as acting chair when the hearings opened in Quebec City on 12 May. St-Laurent was present as legal counsel. It was notable that the commission was given a meeting room in the Palais de Justice since the nearby Hôtel du Parlement committee rooms were occupied by the Quebec Tax Commission, whose sessions opened at the same time. The Palais was more than adequate but the symbolism was obvious. Symbolism turned to reality when Premier Duplessis refused to appear before the commission.

Instead, the provincial brief was presented and read by chief counsel for the Union Nationale government, L. Emery Beaulieu. In the words of Duplessis' biographer, Conrad Black, "the substance of Quebec's view was that the federal government possessed no right even to constitute such a commission, but that out of 'pure courtesy' Quebec would consent to be heard."[66] Regardless, it was little more than a "terse ten-page submission" announcing that the federal government had no constitutional power to act unilaterally let alone to investigate the financial or constitutional affairs of a province. At the time of Confederation, the provinces were provided sovereignty in their own domains, including a right of absolute veto over any alterations to the original pact. Moreover, the federal government derived its powers from the provinces: "From that there follows a primordial consequence. Participating in the nature of these conventions the federative pact cannot be amended or modified without the consent of all the parties, that is all of the provinces." This stance was a strongly provincialist stance, based on Quebec's "compact" interpretation of Confederation as a constitutional agreement among the colonies that created and delegated certain powers to the new country.[67] Quebec's position was tough and aggressive, but Sirois and St-Laurent realized that it had a basis in certain traditional guarantees of legal, religious, and language rights that went back to the days of the 1774 Quebec Act and the 1791 Constitutional Act. Robert Fowler could not help but see the similarities between the Quebec and Ontario positions as "a claim for provincial autonomy and opposed to centralization" and not merely a political stance.[68]

The Quebec government refused to participate any further, even to the point of not supplying statistical information, although it later relented on the matter. Some organizations presented briefs, including the influential nationalist group known as the Société de St. Jean de Baptiste (SSJB). Dafoe described the presentation:

> We had quite a rigmarole about Canada being a bilingual country in every respect and how Quebec must recover her old civilization of the family and the peasant in an economy controlled by the church. It was presented by the St. Jean Baptiste Society but was prepared by a professor in Montreal University [constitutional scholar P.B. Mignault] who is on the Commission payroll for some special work which he is expected to do; a fact which moved Alex Skelton to wrath.

It was Dafoe's turn to be "moved to wrath" as he recounted the substance of Mignault's remarks:

We had heard what a paradise Quebec has been and will be again when it is reorganized on clerical-fascist-authoritarian lines [after which] two ladies [Thérèse Casgrain and Idola Saint-Jean] told a very different story. They spoke for the Women's League which is fighting for the franchise for the women in the province and they told a shocking story of the exploitation of women in Quebec.[69]

The presentation led to a debate between the SSJB lawyer Hector Lalonde and Henry Angus (conducted in French since Angus was fluently bilingual) that was commented upon in the Quebec press. The discussion focused on whether the Canadian federation was a compact among existing colonies built upon previous constitutional agreements such as the Quebec Act, or a new country with two levels of government brought into existence by the citizens of the colonies. Lalonde defended the entrenched Quebec argument, while Angus argued a position reflecting an interpretation of the federation based on rulings by the Judicial Committee of the Privy Council.[70] As for women's rights, Dafoe recounted that the advocates of full political and legal rights for women were received sympathetically enough by the commissioners. However, commission counsel, Louis St-Laurent, subjected the two women to a chilling cross-examination about whether the majority of women or men in Quebec supported female suffrage and other legal rights for women.[71]

A luncheon tendered by the lieutenant-governor was held during the first day of hearings. This engagement was followed by a cocktail party in the Quebec Speaker's Chambers. There the commissioners were handed an invitation to join Premier Duplessis for dinner at the Chateau Frontenac. Not to be outdone by Hepburn, Duplessis ensured the occasion was a rowdy affair. Only this time, there was none of the sentimentality of the Toronto soiree, and the evening ended on a particularly sour note: "The dinner was called for eight and the guests were punctual," MacKay reported, "but the Premier let them wait for some time before he received them, and when he did so he was drunk. His remarks at dinner were most provocative, and much of the abuse he poured forth was directed at Dafoe, who seemed to symbolize all that Duplessis found wrong with Confederation."[72] After "considerable welkin-ringing," the Quebec premier began to embarrass his guests with "a good deal of vulgar banter." MacKay recorded that Duplessis had arrived "late and drunk" and that he was "thoroughly insulting" to everyone, including his own cabinet ministers, the commissioners, and even the chief justice of Quebec. MacKay remarked that, unlike Hepburn, Duplessis "wasn't even funny."[73] Rather than ending with communal songs, revelry, and alcohol-induced bonding, the night concluded, in the recollection of commission-staffer Donald Creighton, with "Duplessis hurling champagne glasses at the chandeliers with such accuracy that the restaurant was soon in semi-darkness and the floor and tables littered with broken glass."[74] It was an embarrassing evening that left even a veteran partier like Sandy Skelton skulking away from the mess.

The commissioners found their time away from the Quebec meetings to be more enjoyable. Acting as tour guide, St-Laurent took his colleagues on a visit to the Plains of Abraham. He hosted the avid golfers Angus and MacKay for a round at the Montmorency Club. Sirois, meanwhile, hosted Dafoe on a drive to the scenic Cap Rouge and Ile d'Orleans as well as a Sunday dinner at his family home on the picturesque island.[75] Despite the worrying absence of Rowell, the commissioners grew closer due to the dramatic experiences of Queen's Park and the Chateau Frontenac.

From Quebec City, the commission moved on to Fredericton, New Brunswick. While the provincial response was not likely to get worse, the commissioners braced for hostility. Conditions for engagement with New Brunswick were not favourable in light of the province's initial protest about a lack of representation on the commission and then the questionable delays in having its brief ready. The Liberal premier, A.A. Dysart, had been stung by a Dafoe editorial in the *Winnipeg Free Press* in December 1937, which suggested that New Brunswick was not open to constitutional discussions. Dysart complained vociferously to the prime minister, claiming that the comment constituted a "grave danger" to the impartiality and effectiveness of the commission. The matter passed after Mackenzie King assuaged the premier and heard from Dafoe that he would resign rather than muzzle the *Winnipeg Free Press*.[76] In the months that followed, the provincial government of New Brunswick repeatedly asked to be last to make its presentation to the commission while it struggled to complete what turned out to be a narrow and rather insubstantial submission.[77]

The New Brunswick hearings got off to an awkward start. The commissioners arrived in the Fredericton railway station earlier than scheduled, and, as a result, the provincial delegation was not present to greet them. But after what the commissioners had just experienced in Ontario and Quebec, the lacklustre welcome caused little stir. As it turned out, the New Brunswick experience was civil and even pleasant. The social gatherings ranged from afternoon teas to the usual dinner parties, a midnight lobster feast, and a Sunday trip to a salmon stream. As McGeachy recorded, the entire week was "as innocent as a picnic."[78] The premier and his wife escorted Sirois and Dafoe on a sightseeing motor tour on the weekend.[79]

When New Brunswick finally made its presentation on 18 May, Premier Dysart was gracious in his welcoming address, and the atmosphere for the sessions was amicable. The provincial speakers, however, immediately focused in on a narrow set of concerns.[80] "The Act of British North America," the brief began, "was designed to accomplish the welfare of all the provinces. If, for example, the province of New Brunswick with its limited taxation possibilities is not able to provide for its people the same privileges which are enjoyed by those in other provinces, New Brunswick should be placed in such a position through assistance by the Dominion."[81] But there was little detail as to how the province hoped to see this assistance come about. One-third of the brief focused on constitutional questions and advanced a version of the compact theory of Confederation. This was a genuine view among the New Brunswick government but not popular among the commissioners. The New Brunswick position was summarized by its legal counsel, W.P. Jones, a backbench MLA. Jones emphasized the serious fiscal difficulties experienced by the province and reiterated the notion that "the rich shall help out the poor."[82] New Brunswick entered Confederation in 1867 on the basis of an agreement that had not been fully carried out: "The terms of this agreement had, in New Brunswick's opinion, committed Canada to channeling all of its trade through Maritime ports." The promise was not fulfilled and, since "this agreement had been broken, the Maritime Provinces had suffered grievously and deserved compensation."[83]

The rest of the brief relied on the familiar Maritime refrains found in the White, Jones, and Duncan inquiries. In the view of the commissioners, the case was backward-looking and aimed at compensation for past wrongs rather than concentrating on the province's current situation and future goals. It was apparent that New Brunswick faced tough fiscal prospects.

The provincial debt doubled in the decade of the 1930s, and the government was constantly bailing out local governments that lacked proper tax bases. In sum and perhaps in weariness, Dafoe described the presentation as "tedious" and even "absurd in a number of respects." He wondered whether the province's legal counsel even took his own constitutional arguments seriously, but he did not engage in sharp rejoinder. The New Brunswick government did not seize the opportunity to engage in a serious critique of federalism but, instead, criticized the outcome of previous policies without offering specific ways forward.[84] The Fredericton hearings, which wrapped up after three and half days on 21 May, marked the end of the first round of provincial consultations.

The Rowell-Sirois Commission returned to Ottawa in order to hear from groups and individuals that had not previously been able to present, such as Charlotte Whitton of the Canadian Welfare Council and Reverend J.R. Mutchmor of the United Church of Canada. Both called for an expansion of federal aid to social services but continued provincial and local administration. Other groups included the Canadian Legion, the Canadian Chambers of Commerce, and the National Council of Women.[85] A presentation by the Communist Party of Canada offered the most unabashed argument for governmental centralization. It demanded the strengthening of Ottawa at the expense of the provincial governments to deal with the Depression. Moreover, it "looked forward, as John A. Macdonald had done, to the virtual disappearance of the provincial governments." Indeed, the existence of the provincial governments could be attributed to "semi-feudal influences, seeking to preserve the powers of landlordism and feudalism in the provinces." According to Communist Party leader Tim Buck, "All forces desiring economic progress demand the completion of Canadian national unification to enable the Dominion government to meet these burning needs ... Every Canadian ... is against the blocking of national progress by the provincial dismemberment of the nation at the hands of reaction." McGeachy noted that there were only three people in attendance in the public gallery. The small audience may help to explain the generosity of Skelton and the commissioners in inviting Buck to dine at the Rideau Club.[86]

The most intriguing testimony was from two invited experts. One was Gunnar Myrdal, the prominent Swedish economist and social democratic activist. Myrdal drew the entire staff and advisors, such as Bill Mackintosh and Donald MacGregor, as well as senior officials like Clifford Clark. Myrdal, who was spending a year teaching at Harvard University, described the social and economic reorganization that Sweden had undertaken in the 1920s and 1930s to protect and develop its economy. He noted that Canada and Sweden had similar open, resource-based economies, large agricultural sectors, recent histories of industrialization, and a reliance on foreign investment. Sweden, however, had developed within a distinctive social framework different from Canada. Myrdal's interpretation swept away centuries of divergent experience when he argued that Sweden had been relatively poor and, in effect, a "new" country of the nineteenth century but that it had used a strong public sector, a high level of trade union membership, a central bank, and strong state regulation to ensure stability and employment once the Depression's impact became clear. He pointed out that Sweden had been unafraid of deficit financing but distinguished between ordinary fiscal policy based on "sound finances" and crisis "investment" budgets based on deficits and debt. Sweden had moved quickly away from the gold standard in 1931 and therefore had benefitted from currency depreciation to boost foreign trade. The panacea of unemployment insurance was adopted in 1934, but it was fairly limited. Labour unions were active agents, but they had emphasized the maintenance of high levels of employment rather than wage increases – so much so that Sweden remained a relatively low-wage economy. Myrdal also emphasized that many social programs were administered and financed at the community or cantonal level through loans and local income taxes levied by the central government. Sweden had weathered and even improved its position during the Depression. Myrdal was careful to emphasize the uniqueness of Sweden, but he sketched out an intriguing mix of policy alternatives that Canada might consider.[87]

If Myrdal attracted an audience, Graham Towers, who appeared in the afternoon of Friday 2 June, drew a rapt circle of attention for his private testimony. The performance by the governor of the Bank of Canada was described by McGeachy as revealing "the serene consciousness of effortless superiority said to be confined to England." Towers was a man who "move[d] in a rarified Empyrean far from the turmoil of politics." Neither ideas nor interests seemed to matter relative to "efficiency and savings."[88]

But, despite Towers's haughty air and artful caution, the testimony was remarkable for what it conceded about economic policy. Skelton, Fowler, and Angus pressed Towers to indicate his policy preferences. Towers repeatedly stated that, due to his position as bank governor, he could not make specific policy recommendations. But at times he was cornered and forced to provide revealing responses. He admitted, for example, that national economic policies had differential and sometimes harmful impacts on provincial conditions. He admitted that compensation to provinces experiencing fiscal deficiencies might be feasible. Last, Towers admitted that conditional grants from the dominion to the provinces were in general best avoided.[89]

Following Towers's presentation, the royal commission adjourned until early August. It had heard over four hundred written presentations and recorded over nine thousand pages of transcripts. Skelton reported that the commissioned experts were in the midst of preparing their own written studies. The only hearings still planned were a final round with all of the provinces.

The Ottawa hearings coincided with the collapse of another commissioner. On 31 May, Robert MacKay experienced acute appendicitis symptoms and ended up in Ottawa Civic Hospital for an emergency operation. In 1938 an appendectomy was a serious procedure, but fortunately MacKay was otherwise in good health. He was confined to hospital for ten days and was destined for a lengthy convalescence.[90] The fact that the youngest member of the commission, at forty-four years, was seriously ill did not bode well for keeping the work on schedule. After his hospitalization, MacKay was sent home to Halifax where he spent the months of June and July convalescing. With two of the commissioners now ill, the way forward was even more difficult to discern.

7

Hard Seasons
Summer and Fall 1938

It is held in some quarters that the Commission has dug up more grief than it can settle, and that its appointment was a mistake. There may be some force in that, though I think myself all the grief was there, and that bringing it into the open and facing it was unavoidable, and a necessary preliminary to straightening out the tangle. But whether that is so or not, the Commission has been appointed, and the Government, not the Commission, will be held responsible if it fails.

– O.D. Skelton, 16 July 1938[1]

Newton Rowell's breakdown led to serious problems for the commission. Although in fragile health from the onset of the work, Rowell was the dominant and active force in the inquiry. His fellow commissioners and staff respected his leadership, and his presence brought stability that prevented egos and personalities, particularly those of provincial antagonists, from going unchecked. Likewise, Rowell possessed an ability to communicate with and stand up to federal leaders. He also had a standing in his home province of Ontario that offered some defence against Hepburn. His collapse threw the commission into disarray, and, for the first few months after, it was difficult to see the path forward. The commissioners and senior staffers anxiously awaited news about Rowell's condition. At first there was some hope for his recovery, but it soon became

The commission group portrait, 1938. *Library and Archives Canada, 3526254*

apparent that the seventy-one-year-old would not rebound.[2] The matter of his return or replacement dragged on for six months. In the meantime, the commissioners awaited Skelton's reports on the status of the research studies. Again, they were to be disappointed. Deadlines were pushed back while the commissioners struggled to keep the work on track. As they waited and fretted, provincial opposition mounted. By mid-summer, Ontario's antics threatened to derail the entire process.

The responses of Ontario, Quebec, and Alberta had already caused considerable concern. Federal cabinet minister T.A. Crerar had long believed that the alliance between Hepburn and Duplessis "went much deeper than the scanty news reports indicated." He had warned Dafoe in December 1937 that the two premiers were plotting to bring down the King government in Ottawa: "When one looks at this it seems incomprehensible that such a thing could ever be thought of, but Hepburn and Duplessis are both drunk with power; they are both impulsive and little given to reflection." The prime minister was well aware that Hepburn had his sights set on the leadership of the federal Liberal Party. Hepburn was boasting that he could take twenty Ontario seats away from the federal Liberals and that he wanted Dunning, Rogers, Rinfret, and Howe out of cabinet. King was informed that Hepburn would not support him in the next federal election, expected for 1939, and that the Liberal premier might oppose the federal party. Duplessis was making similar noises in Quebec, claiming that he wanted Lapointe and Rinfret out of cabinet. One report indicated that Hepburn was "the only man who could influence Duplessis and that he could get Duplessis to do anything [Hepburn] wanted." For King, the causes of Hepburn's antagonism came down to a question of character: "Men of the Hepburn ... stamp are unprincipled men, fond of drinking, good fellowship, and are really uncomfortable in the presence of men of perspective, culture and integrity."[3]

The tenor of the royal commission hearings in Toronto and Quebec led the federal cabinet to consider taking a public stand against the Hepburn-Duplessis alliance. As Hepburn's biographer notes, "Mitch's bark at the royal commission hearings had raised the question of whether Ottawa could afford to slumber any longer."[4] Cabinet discussions reached the point of plotting how to take down both obstructive premiers. Lapointe did not think confronting Duplessis in Quebec was a good strategy; instead, he preferred "an immediate assault in Ontario." But King was cautious in making Ontario the dominion-provincial (and inter-party) battleground and assumed that most of the cabinet agreed: "Felt it wiser to wait and not create an open cleavage of the Party immediately, the hope being that, in the interval, some means of bringing Hepburn to his senses might be found." Unless something changed, King would have to face off against Hepburn when the federal election was called.[5]

At a meeting of the National Liberal Federation (the national party organization) on 18 May 1938, there were no representatives from the Ontario provincial party in attendance. Regardless, "Mitch's shadow hung over the proceedings." A resolution on national unity emphasized the need for harmonious relations between Ottawa and the provinces; another opposed communism, fascism, Nazism, separatism, sectionalism, and provincialism as inconsistent with Liberal principles. When addressing the meeting, King worried that he came across too forcefully and made it too obvious that he was attacking Hepburn:

When I sat down, I did not know whether I had made things better or worse ... It is pretty clear that our members are loyally behind me. Also that they are all very fearful of what the effect of Hepburn's behaviour is likely to be. My own feeling is that he, himself, will be out of the way before any general election comes. Though, if he is not, we may expect to see battles in Ontario similar to what they have been in Alberta, and in Quebec where we will have a crop of dictators of a bad breed.[6]

The wary King was right to be concerned.

Hepburn escalated the conflict in the weeks that followed. He argued that the federal government's Municipal Improvements Act and the National Housing Act, designed to offer loans to municipalities and money to local governments for housing, invaded provincial jurisdiction. When Dunning brought down the budget in June, it included a change to the gift-tax. Hepburn wrote immediately to King, indicating his "surprise and displeasure." Since the Great War and the imposition of the Income War Tax,

the invasion by the Dominion authorities of the Provincial field of taxation has been the subject of protests by practically every provincial government regardless of political stripe ... Various Provinces made strong representations before the Rowell Commission, complaining bitterly against the impoverishment of their own revenues by reason of the Dominion's invasion of the field of direct taxation, which, according to the implicit understanding of Confederation, was to be left to the Provinces.

To introduce "the change at this particular time, with the Rowell Commission Report pending," Hepburn claimed, "constitutes little short of effrontery to the Provinces that entered protests, if not a snub to the Commission itself." The chances of success for the royal commission seemed to diminish daily.[7]

On 13 July, Hepburn took direct action. He wrote to Alex Skelton, declaring that Ontario would no longer cooperate with the commission. Federal decisions in the area of taxation had made this move necessary: "Recent action of the Federal Government constitutes, in my opinion, an absolute breach of faith insofar as the Royal Commission on Dominion-Provincial Relations is concerned." The Ontario government decided to "dissociate [itself] entirely from any participation." Hepburn railed against the "invasion" of a provincial tax field and the contravention of the "implicit understanding at Confederation," which "seriously menaces" all provincial budgets. His remarks brooked little likelihood of compromise.[8]

The commission now had to await the response of the federal government. Sandy Skelton asked the prime minister for his views on how to proceed, but King did not yet want to declare a position. Skelton worried about the impact of Hepburn's threat, which imperilled a final federal-provincial plenary conference. If Ontario boycotted further proceedings, Skelton wrote: "I am afraid it would be quite an anti-climax and would add considerably to the acrimony of the situation. It would certainly strengthen the impression that the Commission is primarily designed to bail the 'have nots' out of their difficulties at the expense of the 'haves,' rather than attack crucial national problems of fundamental importance."[9]

Ontario now stood alongside Quebec and Alberta in directly thwarting the commission's work. Quebec had formally declared its refusal to recognize the validity of the commission at the hearings in mid-May, and Alberta had long since distanced itself. Duplessis claimed that Quebec's refusal was justified on legal and constitutional grounds. The commission should have been appointed by parliamentary vote rather than order-in-council. The Quebec government continued to declare that it would not provide further information or even answer questions from the commission.[10] With Ontario's "withdrawal" now public, Aberhart took it as confirmation of the rectitude of Alberta's decision to ignore the commission. He applauded Hepburn's decision to end any consultations and used the opportunity to try to heal divisions between Ontario and the West. "It has been the unwavering opinion of this government," Aberhart wrote to Hepburn in late summer, "that the personnel and terms of reference of the Commission rendered it useless for the great and responsible task with which it was entrusted. Subsequent events have merely served to strengthen this view." The Alberta premier called on the provinces to meet without the federal government to secure an adjustment in dominion-provincial relations. The enemy was the federal Liberal government and Mackenzie

King, including the Royal Commission on Dominion-Provincial Relations, and not each other.[11]

The prime minister tried to convince himself and his colleagues that Hepburn's move was of no real consequence because Ontario's position before the commission had already been ascertained: "It is not the business of the Commission to change the constitution. Its business is to find facts that will be of value to a Conference later."[12] But the realm of dominion-provincial relations was becoming increasingly difficult to manoeuvre, and the commissioners could not ignore the acrimonious setting.

Federal officials closely monitored Hepburn's actions and their implications. King was informed by O.D. Skelton in mid-July that not only were Hepburn and Duplessis "conferring" but also that the Ontario premier planned to meet with Premier Bracken of Manitoba and Premier Patterson of Saskatchewan on his way to an Arctic sightseeing expedition: "It is conceivable that an effort is on foot to arrange a Conference of all the Provinces, without the Dominion, to try to line them all up for increased federal subsidies and relief responsibility, and decreased federal powers otherwise." Skelton was worried that Hepburn's refusal to cooperate with the commission might well lead to Ontario to release an alternate set of proposals even before the commission could finish its work. "It is held in some quarters," he told King,

> that the Commission has dug up more grief than it can settle, and that its appointment was a mistake. There may be some force in that, though I think myself all the grief was there, and that bringing it into the open and facing it was unavoidable, and a necessary preliminary to straightening out the tangle. But whether that is so or not, the Commission has been appointed, and the Government, not the Commission, will be held responsible if it fails.[13]

Hepburn met with Duplessis and announced that they were going to fly across the country to meet with other premiers. The press assumed Hepburn was calling for the creation of a new federal party, which Jimmy Gardiner, the federal minister of agriculture from Saskatchewan, would lead. Hepburn did fly to Regina on 17 July, where he met with Gardiner, Premier Patterson, and the Saskatchewan cabinet. When questioned by the press about his motives, Hepburn denied that he was out to establish a new federal party. Upon his return to Ontario, he entertained Duplessis as a guest at his onion farm in St. Thomas. While the two men avoided speaking about politics to the press, Duplessis made a brief comment that the provinces "must have more autonomy or there cannot be unity in Canada. The individual members of a nation must be given their rights or there can be no nation." As the men "drank into the night," there was considerable talk of King and national politics. Duplessis was "hell-bent" on Hepburn entering the federal arena, and he promised to deliver votes from Quebec as well as French-Canadian areas across the country.[14]

Amidst the turmoil, the commissioners tried to advance their work. Reports on Rowell's condition were discouraging. "The chances of a useful report depend more on Rowell's health than upon any other consideration," Dafoe warned King. By the end of May, Dafoe admitted that they were "up in the air over Rowell's illness." Reports indicated that he was experiencing heart attacks at three- to four-day intervals. Dafoe concluded that Rowell was unlikely to ever work again. By early July, he admitted that Rowell's condition was terrible and that it was "disastrous" for the commission. Angus commented that he was "hoping against hope" that Rowell might recover after a respite of several months. By the end of July, Fowler – who served as Rowell's aide and had the closest connections to the Rowell family – delivered the bad news. He told Dafoe that he was awaiting some "definitive news" from Rowell's wife but that he had "just about given up hope" that Rowell could undertake any further work.[15] Matters were not eased by MacKay's collapse and lengthy convalescence. He was almost entirely a bystander in commission activities between late May and late July.

Rowell's condition led to an important question: Who would take his place? Among the senior mandarins in Ottawa, the issue was already being discussed. In mid-July, Oscar Skelton reported that Rowell was unable to speak or write and, further, "there seems practically no likelihood of his being able to take any part whatever in the organization and preparation of the Report and the Commission." Skelton viewed the situation as "very serious" because "Rowell was the driving force."[16] Dafoe had "knowledge and wisdom, breadth of view and power of exposition, but," Skelton argued, "it may be doubted whether he has now the physical vigor necessary to pull the work of the Commission together and produce a report that will serve as the basis of all future discussions and revision of Dominion-Provincial relations." Skelton went further, noting that "each of the other members has a contribution to make, but none of them can fill the Chief Justice's role."[17] Skelton urged that Rowell be replaced. He suggested W.A. Mackintosh for the commission, but King objected, unsurprisingly after Mackintosh's role on the nettlesome Purvis Commission. Skelton went so far as to propose that either Chief Justice Lyman Duff of the Supreme Court or R.B. Bennett should be approached to chair the commission. Duff was a viable although flawed option. He was a respected justice of the Supreme Court of Canada (appointed in 1906, he was chief justice from 1933 to 1944) but was prone to a provincial rights position and known to have a serious drinking problem.[18] Bennett was an outlandish suggestion, as Skelton must have realized. "I am aware of the widespread feeling, not confined to government circles, against his frequent partisan or personal bitterness, and also Mr. Dafoe's view," Skelton noted with remarkable understatement. He continued,

> I think, however, he would rise to the occasion and be keen to do a crowning job for his country and for his own reputation before he retires completely to private life. If he helped bring the Commission to a successful issue, the Government would get the credit for a big gesture; if the Commission failed to measure up to its need, the responsibility would be divided.[19]

Skelton's suggestion was too clever by half even for King, who had little regard for Bennett's judgment or reliability: "subject matter of memorandum discussed in Council," King wrote curtly in his diary. "Thought inadvisable to appoint anyone. Last suggestion not approved."[20] The prime minister forced the commission to gather its own resources and move forward without a representative from Canada's most powerful province.

As a result of Rowell's collapse, Sandy Skelton's position became not only more essential but also more problematic. Skelton was certainly a "key figure in both the research and the drafting of the report," but he was not the dominant force his academic and bureaucrat friends later described. Robert Bryce, who worked with Skelton in the public service, reflected that he "was a strong man, with strong opinions; he saw things as black or white with no shades of grey. He was intelligent, intuitive, and convivial to a fault. He was friendly but did not like compromisers. He was well informed, both from study and from his numerous contacts; he made up his mind quickly." But the younger Skelton had the reputation for having an active social life of after-hours drinking and carousing, a trait he shared with the amiable associate secretary, Adjutor Savard. Skelton's penchant for socializing for the most part bemused the commissioners. They were, perhaps surprisingly, amused by his devotion to the famous Hull restaurant, the Café Henry Burger, which catered to both the gourmet (Mackenzie King regularly lunched there) and the reveller (Sandy Skelton enjoyed its late hours of operation).[21] But Skelton's "work habits were irregular," Robert Bryce later admitted, "prodigious at times and suspended at others."[22] While amusing, the matter became contentious as pressure grew on the commission to complete its work. Fellow commission staffer J.A. Corry described Skelton in more measured terms than Bryce. Skelton possessed a quick, comprehending mind but a quixotic nature: "He was fearless and loved a fight, the rougher the better. Sandy was as close to being a Renaissance figure as our age provides. He was versatile, imaginative, always testing his powers in extravagant ways."[23] These were not the typical attributes of a successful bureaucrat.

Skelton's role on the commission was severely tested in the area for which he was most responsible: the research studies. The original plan of 1937 was that the research would be completed by mid-spring 1938 and distributed to the provincial governments as well as reviewed by the commissioners in preparation for a final plenary round of consultations before the report-writing began. But by early April 1938, soon after the disappointing sessions in Edmonton, Skelton informed Rowell that the original 1 May deadline for the completion of the research studies would not be met. He attributed this delay both to the failure of some of the provinces to submit statistical information and to the inability of the academic experts to get away from their university duties in order to finish their work. He claimed that the "great bulk of the material" should be ready by May "but only in crude form." Realistically, it would be best to plan for a 1 July completion date with final sittings held in September. While in Toronto on 25 April, Skelton admitted that neither the 1 May nor 1 July deadlines would be met. The commission was planning to meet in late June to review the commissioned research studies and plan for the final set of hearings.[24] In the meantime, the commissioners approved a publication and mimeographing schedule. They would publish seven of the research studies and mimeograph and distribute a further nine. The published works would be sent out in 2,500 English-language and 1,000 French-language copies, while the mimeographed works would have 350 French and one thousand English copies.[25]

Skelton had to report to the provinces on the revised schedule for the research studies and on the fallout from Hepburn's mid-July denunciation. Here Skelton's bureaucratic skills and good connections with the provincial governments came to the fore. He organized meetings with the western premiers and officials. He drew upon the assistance of Wilfrid Eggleston and Alex Corry, and between them, the three staffers ensured that a cancellation of the planned "round-table" with the provinces would not lead to further loss of support, even from Edmonton. The three staffers travelled from Victoria to Winnipeg, explaining the situation and shoring up support among the provinces. It was left to the former Albertan, Wilfrid Eggleston, to try to rebuild ties with the Alberta government. He reported that he was met with courtesy but no promise that Alberta would participate more fully. Reflecting his own conversations and those of Corry and Skelton, Eggleston also downplayed the dangers of Hepburn successfully fomenting a more general boycott of the commission's work.[26]

This news eased the concerns of both the commission and the Prime Minister's Office. Sandy Skelton then informed the premiers about a revised schedule of activities and a commitment to publish the research studies in mid-August. The research studies would be circulated to the provinces in September and a final round of hearings would be conducted in October. But the saga of missed deadlines continued, and it was not until October that Skelton was able to inform the premiers that the research studies were being sent for their review. He pointed out that these studies were "by recognized authorities" but did not represent the views of the commissioners. They were being sent out as draft studies prior to the final hearings (now being scheduled for November) so the provincial governments could offer criticism and corrections either at public hearings or by written reply. British Columbia and Manitoba responded that they would likely require more time to respond.[27]

Already anxious due to Rowell's health, the commissioners remained impatient over the delays and missed deadlines. Through the summer of 1938, they became concerned over the state of the research studies, although they were not much better informed than the premiers. On 23 June, Skelton reported that, while most of the reports were sufficiently advanced and "substantial first drafts" could soon be expected, some of them needed further work. This was particularly true for the provincial public finance spreadsheets being prepared by J.C. Thompson. Some of the reports, Skelton admitted, were delayed, some "sketchy," others in need of "condensation." Skelton admitted that "the slow progress [was] disturbing" but hoped that "dawn [was] beginning to break now on the research programme."[28] It proved to be a false dawn.

On that same day in June, after a short visit to Ottawa, Robert Fowler provided a worried report to Angus and Dafoe, who were back in their homes. The status of the research studies was much worse than Skelton had stated. Fowler admitted that he was in a "difficult personal position ... because of conflict between [his] desire to see the work of the Commission progress properly and [his] sense of loyalty to colleagues." But he was "very much distressed at the state of the work in Ottawa" and confessed that not a single expert study was even close to completion. To make matters worse, the working conditions in Ottawa were unpleasant. The city was "sweltering" and the Sovereign Building, where offices had been rented, was "hotter than the hubs of hell."[29]

The issue of the research reports was important due to the broad scope of the commission. The range of the reports was considerable, spanning such traditional areas as constitutional and administrative issues but also extending into novel areas of economic and social policy-making. All the topics were controversial. Whether it was monetary policy, social legislation, macro-economic policy, or the division of powers, scrutiny would be intense. With some of the provinces not cooperating and the quality of their briefs so uneven, the research studies were essential for the commission's credibility. Fowler wondered whether "it would be better to cut off the research sharply where it rests now – and get on with the job" of writing the report.[30] Sandy Skelton stuck to the position that the research reports were essential.

Angus advised that the commissioners should adjust their own plans and admit that delays might be lengthy. The commission should still try to reconvene by 1 August and get the research studies to the provinces two weeks later. Dafoe was of a similar mind, admitting to Angus that he was "rather impatient" to get at the economic and fiscal studies. Dafoe hoped that Fowler was "unduly pessimistic about the state of the research studies," yet noted that "Skelton's alternative optimism ha[d] produced no documents as yet." While Dafoe could "understand the inclination of our experts to seek more and more time, unless we are to be hopelessly bogged down it will be essential that they draw their conclusions together and let us have them, such as they are, without delay." The research studies were essential to their deliberations and there was no moving forward without them.[31]

Joseph Sirois was patient with and even indulgent of Skelton. There was a vast amount of work to be done in editing and revising the research, and he urged his fellow commissioners to turn to the substantive issues they must deal with when it came to writing the report. As he eased into the role of chair, Sirois was careful to encourage as much collegiality as possible among an anxious crew. In response to one of MacKay's irate complaints about Skelton's work, Sirois replied: "Mr. Skelton must stand a terrific strain and we cannot be too grateful for the manner in which he handles his work."[32] Sirois maintained a tolerance of Skelton's ways and propensity for eccentric activity that the other commissioners did not always share. In the summer of 1938, Skelton adopted a black bear cub that he discovered in Parc Laurentide on a drive back to Ottawa from consultations with Dr. Sirois in Quebec. The bear cub was housed for some weeks in his Rockcliffe home until local authorities banned it. Sirois was amused by the stunt.[33] Sirois clearly realized he had to hold together highly divergent personalities and styles of work. He did so not with the sternness of Rowell but with an empathy that was his own. With Angus and MacKay on one side and Skelton (and his assistants) on the other, the potential for conflict was ever-present.

The work dragged on as summer passed. In early August, the commission reconvened in Ottawa for a week of meetings.[34] MacKay was back in good form after recovering from his appendicitis operation. One positive aspect of the week was that the commissioners were able to fit in at very short notice a much-anticipated session with the Australian economist Lyndhurst F. Giblin, a founder if not the originator of the Australian Loan Council and the Commonwealth Grants Commission. The possibility of his testimony excited some anticipation early in 1938, when Rowell had expressed the hope that it might involve a joint session with all the provinces.[35] The session did not occur, lost amidst the Hepburn rebellion and Giblin's erratic schedule. When he did appear, Giblin was a lively and amusing witness, but the impact of his talk was negligible. He was more interested in reminiscences about Canada than commentary on current issues. In addition, the Australian approach and Giblin's own conservative and decentralist views had increasingly less appeal to the commission.[36]

The August meetings allowed the commissioners to address the consequences of the Hepburn-Duplessis boycott and the frayed state of the research program. Due to the boycott, it was clear that plans for a plenary with all the provinces and even the widespread distribution of the research studies were moot. The commissioners instructed Skelton to write to Hepburn, expressing strong regrets at the Ontario decision and inviting him to reconsider. Skelton's letter was a model of diplomacy, emphasizing that the commission would be most pleased to cooperate with Ontario should the provincial government reconsider its decision. Sirois penned a similar request to Duplessis in Quebec but both attempts were futile.[37] The effects of Skelton's diplomatic efforts with the western provinces, however, had some positive results. BC premier Duff Pattullo reiterated his "high hopes" that the commission could provide the basis for a new "understanding" between governments and expressed "regret" at the "hostile attitude" of the three provinces of Alberta, Ontario, and Quebec.[38]

The bulk of the commission's time was spent reviewing and commenting on drafts of the ten research studies already completed. The quality was uneven and some of the constitutional studies were disappointing. This disappointment was so strong that several works had already been jettisoned. A set of research memoranda on constitutional issues by Calgary lawyer Harold Crowle was set aside as irrelevant. Constitutional studies by Vincent MacDonald, dean of law at Dalhousie University, were deemed verbose, argumentative, and of marginal value. A report on the operation of other federations by University of Toronto law professor W.P.M. Kennedy was accepted and paid for (at a handsome fee) but also ignored and never printed.[39]

On the other hand, W.A. Mackintosh contributed an extremely impressive study of Canadian economic history and Frank Knox wrote a stimulating and critical report on monetary policy. Both economists had been conducting research on these subjects for years. Other notable works included Donald Creighton's examination of Confederation, W.J. Waines's sobering analysis of Prairie population futures, J.A. Corry's research into divided jurisdiction and the growth of government regulation, and A.E. Grauer's studies of social insurance, public health, labour legislation, and housing. The latter, in particular, revealed a breadth of information about social policy initiatives being undertaken in other countries, particularly Great Britain and Western Europe.[40]

Dafoe and MacKay commented on the "tedious grind" that now faced the commissioners. Several of the studies were "of inordinate length," and the commissioners were forced to work through the last weekend together prior to breaking until early October. All was not tedium and stress. O.D. Skelton hosted a dinner for the commissioners at the Ottawa Country Club, which included members of the Department of External Affairs and the Bank of Canada.[41] Sirois sustained morale by mollifying concerns over the delays. He reported to his colleagues that senior officials in the dominion government were "perfectly satisfied with what ha[d] been done."[42]

Skelton continued to have difficulties with the research reports. Several reports were being rewritten by the team of Skelton, Deutsch, Fowler, and Eggleston. The staff ensemble was a great help. Deutsch was Skelton's assistant, a capable economist, and his work was expected. On the other hand, Fowler had been hired as Rowell's legal assistant, yet he had stayed on without any assurance of compensation. Fowler had effectively become a staff member. Eggleston, demonstrably fascinated by the issues, had long since moved from press officer to researcher/writer.[43] Still, several of the research reports were returned to their authors for revision. In mid-September, Skelton admitted that a number of the studies still needed additional documentation.[44] A week later, he advised that the reports were ready for distribution. He was playing for time, however, and when the commission convened again in Ottawa in early October, the studies were still not ready. The last batch of them was not sent out for review until 1 November, six months after they had been promised.[45]

By September the commissioners and government fully realized that Newton Rowell would not return to work. Perhaps unaware of the earlier discussions in Ottawa, MacKay pushed for an Ontarian to serve as a replacement. He suggested that Dafoe meet with the prime minister "without taking other Commissioners into [his] confidence." MacKay proposed either Justice Alexander Maclean of the Exchequer Court of Canada or James M. Macdonnell of National Trust. Dafoe immediately scotched MacKay's scheme, arguing that Rowell did not need to be replaced and that Ontario did not require a designated commissioner. He then wrote to Sandy Skelton, informing him of MacKay's idea (though not his stealthy tactic) and proposed that the commissioners and their secretariat meet with senior cabinet ministers and government officials to review the operations. There was no further discussion of a replacement. Rowell was sorely missed but the work would go on.[46] On 19 October 1938, Newton Rowell submitted his resignation from the commission. It was accepted a month later. The delay annoyed Rowell's wife, who had to endure press reports suggesting that he had refused to resign.[47]

On 22 November Joseph Sirois was officially elevated to chief commissioner.[48] No Ontario replacement for Rowell was named. Sirois had by then gained the confidence of his fellow commissioners for his arm's-length approach to policy debates, his efforts to mute personnel clashes, and his skill at fending off government pressure. MacKay remained slightly wary of Sirois, however, because his political connections were chiefly derived from ties with Ernest Lapointe and Quebec. MacKay was also concerned that Sirois tended to trust and even defer to Skelton. Sirois was not a forceful personality, and he did not have broad political, economic, and constitutional interests. But his deftness at managing difficult personalities and his insightful appreciation of provincial rights arguments meant he had both tact and tactical skills that Dafoe, Angus, and MacKay came to appreciate greatly.

Upon settling in as chair in the fall of 1938, Sirois toned down the commission's reputation for rather lavish costs. He orchestrated a move in Ottawa from offices in the Sovereign Building (with accommodations at the expensive Chateau Laurier) to the Roxborough Building. The new quarters were more modest and "homelike." Each commissioner had a two-room suite available, while the commission used ground-floor office space.[49] The commissioners reconvened as scheduled in early October for two months of meetings and a final set of hearings – the promised consultations with the provinces. Although Sirois would officially head the commission, Dafoe took a more active role in pushing the work forward. It was the triumvirate of Dafoe, Angus, and MacKay that now sparked the productive efforts of the work, with a more detached Sirois ensuring smooth relations both inside and outside the commission. This entailed supervising Skelton on administrative matters and pushing ahead with summaries of the research and the outlines of the report, while also dealing with the federal government.[50]

The problems with Sandy Skelton boiled over into open conflict. There had been rumblings of trouble in the spring and summer, but October witnessed the first open confrontation. Skelton wanted to adjust the plans for reviewing material and writing the report. Dafoe had a good relationship with Skelton. He was drawn into MacKay's complaints about Skelton but responded in more measured terms of "difficulties ... mostly of procedure." MacKay was far more dramatic and confrontational. Skelton, he charged, was determined to act in disregard to the wishes and expectations of the commissioners. There was "skullduggery afoot," MacKay complained. He went further and stated that the commission's recorded decisions were not being carried out. Not only were the research studies not ready for internal review but Skelton was indicating they would not be distributed to the commissioners or provincial governments as planned.

MacKay and Angus orchestrated a "showdown" with Skelton in early October. Angus, a cooler head than MacKay, made the case that the decisions of the commissioners had to prevail. Staff members could not amend these decisions. As far as Angus was concerned, the "air h[a]s been cleared, and secretaries and whoever was behind them more or less put in their place." Both MacKay and Angus later recalled the incident as one of the most crucial moments for the survival of the commission. While MacKay was most concerned with the meddling of Skelton, he hinted that other senior officials (Clark, Towers, and O.D. Skelton) and even cabinet ministers (Dunning and Lapointe) also needed a reminder as to their roles. MacKay was concerned that Skelton was bullying his way into producing his own report.[51]

After the confrontation, Skelton sulked for several days, but the work moved forward, the research studies were made available, and plans for reviewing evidence and starting on the writing were established. In order to rebuild morale and seal their renewed commitments, Sirois proposed a staff dinner. Savard made the arrangements and they enjoyed a lavish meal in the Tudor Room of the Chateau Laurier.[52]

Sandy Skelton was under pressure, but there was little he could do about the poor quality of some of the research reports.[53] Regardless, after heavy revision and editing, they did form an impressive body of work. Creighton's "British North America at Confederation" received a favourable response, although the historian was asked to clarify the importance of pre-Confederation fiscal problems.[54] The Mackintosh work, "Economic Background of Dominion-Provincial Relations," was similarly praised for its analysis of national economic policies, particularly tariffs and railways.[55] On the other hand, Stanley Saunders's study of the economic history of the Maritimes caused further tension between Skelton and MacKay. Skelton thought the work was of poor quality and wanted to dispose of it. MacKay, who had collaborated with Saunders in the past, countered that Mackintosh had neglected the Maritimes and that the Saunders study was essential for balance. The real problem, according to MacKay, was that Saunders and Skelton did not get along and that "each consider[ed] the other a crook and a liar." While Saunders was "too honest to guess at facts, and of course work[ed] slowly," Skelton "guesse[d] at facts, or at least ... to brilliant generalizations, most of the time, then argue[d] out of it if he [found] he [was] wrong." MacKay took responsibility for the Saunders revisions.[56] He criticized Skelton for being too territorial: "Skelton feels his personal reputation [is] so much at stake over them that he has taken a great deal of time and trouble to have much of the material rewritten either by himself or someone else."[57]

The uneven research and argumentation of the research studies had already led Skelton to seek outside help. He turned to Harold Innis, the University of Toronto economist. While Innis was known for his disdain of academic consultations with government and had declined an invitation to participate in the research studies, he now agreed to Skelton's request. Despite his criticism of and scepticism about the royal commission, Innis had assisted his colleague Donald MacGregor in his work on national income and Donald Creighton in his study of Confederation. Skelton sent all the research studies to Innis just prior to Christmas of 1938. Skelton admitted that he was "very conscious of the inadequacies and vulnerabilities of several of them."[58]

Within two weeks Innis responded. The economist was both penetrating in his criticism and broad in his tolerance. While offering detailed criticisms, Innis made three general points. The reports varied widely "in caliber and content," they were "too definitely financial" and did not "wrestle with the regional problem with any great effect." Innis noted bluntly that at least the studies were finished and neither his critical comments nor any serious efforts to rework them would be of much benefit at this point.[59] The evaluation did not ease Skelton's mind. "I know that a lot of our studies are third rate," he admitted, "lamentably lacking in analysis and failing completely to grasp the main issues or, at any rate, to see them in a comprehensive way."[60] Innis urged Skelton not to worry unduly about all the criticisms. It was understandable that the research studies were uneven in quality. He did recommend that Skelton try to "publish the best and make the report a protection against criticism which would be leveled at [him] if [he] had published the weakest as well." In the end, seven studies were published, eleven were mimeographed, but all were widely available.[61]

Amid the October tumult, the federal government requested a progress report from the Rowell-Sirois Commission. As the prime minister expressed the matter to Sirois, the government appreciated the "extent and difficulties of [the commission's] task" but "wishe[ed] to know of the progress and plans." Mackenzie King reiterated the intention to circulate the report to the provinces in order to convene a conference "to increase the effective work of our federal system and the country's business." While King noted that he would be pleased to meet with the commissioners to discuss their work, the government's two top bureaucrats, O.D. Skelton and Clifford Clark, were instructed to "keep in touch with the Commission as the occasion arises."[62] Sirois was careful but optimistic in his reply. He was undoubtedly spurred on by the ever-hopeful Dafoe, who had already urged Skelton and the others to "get down to business." Sirois informed King that the commission was "reviewing the evidence and the research material" and planning to provide the provinces with the opportunity to offer critical reviews of the research studies and previous submissions. Clark and the elder Skelton were already being kept fully abreast of the work. While the commission was happy to meet with the prime minister, Sirois stated that the plan was to have the report completed by the end of March 1939.[63]

The "round-table" between the royal commission and the provinces was never held due to Ontario's boycott and the commission's own problems completing the research studies. But a final set of meetings with the more conciliatory provinces began in late November. Representatives from New Brunswick and Prince Edward Island appeared, while Nova Scotia sent a written statement. British Columbia and Manitoba appeared, while Saskatchewan was content with the case it had already made. Manitoba's expert witnesses added emphasis to provincial claims. Alvin Hansen, now at Harvard University, was the first. He defended the western provinces' position that monetary policy in the form of maintaining a strong dollar against world currencies had weakened Canada and reiterated a defence of currency inflation as a device particularly valuable for resource economies.[64] The University of Chicago economist Jacob Viner offered critical observations about Canadian commercial policy. The protective tariff once adopted was difficult to remove despite its many undesirable effects. The economic prospects for the Prairie West, Viner noted, were poor and likely involved a major depopulation of the rural economy as it was forced to consolidate farm size and agricultural methods.[65]

By the time the commissioners took up the prime minister's offer to meet, it was 2 December, the evening after the last of the hearings. The meeting brought together almost all of the core group that had been involved in proceedings from the beginning. The four commissioners and Sandy Skelton were present. Two cabinet ministers, Charles Dunning and Ernest Lapointe, were in attendance, as were the mandarins Oscar Skelton, Clifford Clark, and Graham Towers. Since he was in town on other business, Saskatchewan attorney general and King confidante Tommy Davis also attended. Proceedings began with a dinner at Laurier House and the conversations went well according to Mackenzie King. The prime minister found the proceedings enjoyable and reassuring. Sirois was "exceptionally

well informed, very able," while MacKay was an engaging conversation-
alist on the topic of the prime minister's maternal grandfather. King admitted he "felt tired" during the evening and did not follow the conversations
as closely as he would have liked. But on the vital question of when the
report would be finished, he came away convinced that it would be May
or June 1939. King was only mildly concerned by the delays. It was "most
important" to receive a report prior to the prorogation of Parliament, which
he foresaw in the autumn of 1939.[66] The commissioners realized that their
report would shape neither a legislative nor a policy agenda in the life of
the current Parliament. This realization came as a relief and reduced the
pressure to wrap up the report as quickly as possible.

The momentary sense of optimism was captured in a piece of light
verse written by Annie Angus, the wife of Henry Angus:

> Four Royal Commissioners,
> Sitting on a Fence,
> Reading and Writing,
> Spending public pence –
> Or so say their enemies, Wishing them far hence.

Noting certain propensities of each of the commissioners, Annie Angus
commented on "monsieur le docteur" Sirois's avuncular ways, "Doc"
Dafoe's love of obscure parliamentary rules, MacKay's love of Madame
Burger's rich meals, and Angus's utilitarian factuality. She alluded to the
havoc caused by Skelton's adoption of the bear cub and Savard's propensity for romantic entanglements. Her cheery verses mentioned all of the
staff, including Robert Fowler, Mary Rowland, the secretaries, Mary White
and Rachel Fortin, as well as the journalists Hamish McGeachy and Wilfrid
Eggleston. Despite all the travails of the previous year, from Rowell's collapse to Hepburn's fury and Duplessis's boycott, the commission had
survived. Now, Annie Angus concluded most hopefully, they would "mer-
rily Rowell along, Rowell along, / The end's not yet, but won't be long.[67]

8

Toil and Trouble
1939 and 1940

The "too confident assumption in which so many people indulge, that the war washed up the work," will change to a "recognition that the war may add to the timeliness and value of the report."

– J.W. Dafoe to Robert Fowler, 30 September 1939[1]

By the end of 1938 it appeared that the major problems of the inquiry phase of the Rowell-Sirois Commission's work were either solved or on their way to being solved. The public hearings were over, the uncertainty over the chairmanship was clarified, and the delays over the research studies were dealt with. It was time to write the report and make recommendations. The problems, however, were nothing compared to the dangerous situation developing in Europe: dark clouds of war were gathering on the horizon, and they threatened to overwhelm and undermine all the work of the Rowell-Sirois Commission.

Before the writing process commenced, the commissioners decided to send last-minute invitations for final appraisals of the national scene. These were sent to former Conservative prime minister R.B. Bennett and Bank of Canada governor Graham Towers. Bennett was invited to participate in an "entirely confidential" and "informal" session. He contemplated it but demurred, claiming that he was too busy wrapping up his Canadian affairs before moving to Surrey, England.[2] Towers had already made a presentation in June but appeared again in December. He consented but

Sandy Skelton. *Queen's University Archives, 2162*

only if it was a "confidential session" that left no official record. In his presentation, the bank governor was said to have defended the fiscal and monetary orthodoxies attacked by the western provinces as well as by Frank Knox in his research study on dominion monetary policy. Despite Towers's stout defence of bank policies, Sandy Skelton reported to his putative boss that the commissioners were not overly convinced.[3] Surprisingly perhaps, they were leaning towards relatively unorthodox fiscal and monetary positions while not directly confronting either the face of orthodoxy (the Bank of Canada) or the body that upheld it (the King government).

As the commissioners and senior staff prepared to begin the writing, they sought clarification on two issues posed by certain provinces. The first involved the thorny question of how to handle British Columbia's historical "special claim" for dominion compensation and subsidies. Sandy Skelton requested advice from the federal government. Clifford Clark in the Department of Finance was dismissive and reported that. if the province was "prepared to rest its case on this general argumentative ground rather than on any meticulous mathematical basis, the Dominion [would] not feel it necessary to submit any counter representation." The other issue involved Alberta's decision to present its brief to Canadians but not to the commission. Finance Minister Charles Dunning informed Joseph Sirois that he did not think the dominion could override Alberta's position. This stance reinforced the commission's determination to ignore the brief.[4] It was a decision that left Alberta voiceless when the commission prepared its report.

The commissioners and staff worked out a plan for writing the report. They agreed upon an outline and a schedule in order to complete a two-part document. The first part would offer a treatment of the fiscal and administrative history of Canada while the second would provide an examination of "alternative proposals" (presentations at the hearings), including the commission's own recommendations. It was made clear that Part 1 would be completed first by Skelton, with the assistance of Eggleston, Corry, and Deutsch (although Donald Creighton was later called upon too), while Part 2 would be "outlined" by the most active commissioners, Angus, MacKay, and Dafoe, with help from Fowler, but its final draft would likely have to await completion of Part 1.[5]

Eggleston and Skelton, with assistance from Fowler and *Winnipeg Free Press* journalist J.B. McGeachy, were charged with the preparation of summaries of the research reports and hearings.[6] These included briefs of the more contentious and important research studies, such as J.A. Corry on disallowance, Stanley Saunders on the Maritimes, Esdras Minville on Quebec's distinctive (church-based, municipally financed) social service system, and C.T. Kraft on dominion subsidies and grants. A.E. Grauer's four studies of social policy (public health, housing, social insurance, and labour legislation) contained rich comparative work on Europe, Britain, the United States, and Australia-New Zealand, but they required several careful summaries. Fowler wrote a digest of the briefs and a three-hundred-page index, which proved a vital resource. He had also written a 143-page summary of the key hearings, which concentrated on the views of the provinces.[7] The commissioners reviewed these documents between mid-October and late November. By mid-December 1938, they seemed ready to write their report.

Dafoe and Skelton exchanged ideas about how Part 1, which had been conceived of in narrow economic and administrative terms, should be broadened to include an examination of the political circumstances from which polices had emerged. Dafoe laid out his views, informed by the work of Manitoba historian Chester Martin, as to how the original Confederation of 1867 had been transformed by the acquisition of Rupert's Land and the North-Western Territory in 1868 followed by the 1870 creation of Manitoba. John A. Macdonald's efforts to implement his federal vision involved the subordination of all these jurisdictions to the Dominion. As Dafoe articulated on numerous occasions, the "minor Confederation" of 1867 was followed by the "extension of Confederation" in 1870, an act of constitutional aggression on the part of Ottawa that overwhelmed the old Constitution and that had reverberations that continued to the present. In support of his arguments, Dafoe cited books on western settlement by Chester Martin and economic studies by Bill Mackintosh as well as several volumes in the Carnegie Series on the "relations between Canada and the United States." Dafoe had "great hopes" for Part 1 because it could shape the "basic information necessary for a consideration of all the questions" they would try to answer in Part 2, which then would undoubtedly lead to controversy.[8]

Sandy Skelton conceded Dafoe's point that Part 1 must show how political movements and party politics interacted with the "underlying" economic factors to "crystallize" policy goals in law and administration. Skelton was still trying to get some of the research authors to tie their work more directly to political circumstances. This was not only a matter of thematic inclusion but also a way to explain the broad changes in the role of the state, which had emerged during the 1930s. Skelton argued that the vital framework for the commission was a new relationship between the citizenry and the state: "Both the old parties were satisfied that the proper role for government was to create the most favourable possible conditions in which Canadians could earn a living, and that responsibility stopped there." Since the onset of the Depression, however, and the rise of "left-wing parties" like the CCF, a new approach to the citizen-state relationship had arisen: "The state must now take a direct hand in the part of every individual actor, and whether there are lines enough to go round or not, the play must go on."[9]

As early as July 1938, Dafoe and Angus had thought about models for their report. For inspiration, Dafoe looked south to the United States, while Angus turned to the British Empire. Dafoe admired two American academic inquiries into the Great Depression, each of which consisted of policy discussions over New Deal legislation and proposals. One was co-ordinated by Robert MacIver, the Columbia University sociologist who taught during the 1920s at the University of Toronto. This 250-page work, *Economic Reconstruction,* had contributions from economists such as Alvin Hansen, Joseph Schumpeter, and Jacob Viner. The book was an inquest into the failures of the market economy and began with the conundrum of "poverty in the midst of plenty." The other was an unpublished (if widely circulated) memo on the United States banking system by the University of Chicago economics department. Its support for a fully regulated banking and monetary system had become a source of debate surrounding early New Deal banking reforms.[10]

Angus, meanwhile, recommended a broader work, the East Indian Constitutional Reports of 1918. His reference was to a substantial work, the *Report on Indian Constitutional Reforms*, prepared under the names of E.S. Montagu, secretary of state for India, and Lord Chelmsford, viceroy of India from 1916 to 1921.[11] The Montagu-Chelmsford Report was, much like the later Canadian commission, a survey of governmental institutions and policy based on a thorough historical examination of the constitutional, political, and fiscal structures of Indian governments. It recommended full responsible government for India and entrenchment of the federal system. Angus chose not to dwell on the fact that the enactments that followed the report fell short of the recommendations and led to deep conflict between Indian governments and British authorities.

These speculations indicated that Dafoe and Angus were thinking far beyond the narrow and practical approach of the King government, or the now-retired Newton Rowell, that the commission produce a mere "fact-finding study." As Dafoe put it: "Our business is not merely to assemble facts in a mountain of material into which economists, students, public men, etc. can dig. It is to sort out, arrange, appraise the facts that lie behind and justify our recommendations or our suggestions." Dafoe aimed for a broad examination of the Canadian federal system. Angus concurred: "The prime importance of our report is educational; it should make clear the meaning and the implications of the decisions which have to be taken and, by stating every issue in its proper context and examining its bearing on other issues, it should help to keep discussion on a high plane."[12] That said, they were not inclined to lobbying governments or cajoling the public to bring about the desired state of public education.

The writing began well into the first few weeks of 1939. Dafoe was pleased that Skelton had obtained the begrudging approval of Harold Innis for the research studies. Dafoe also applauded Skelton's decision to bring in Donald Creighton to work on sections of Part 1.[13] If Dafoe was encouraging to Skelton, however, Angus had long since grown impatient: "We have never had a single draft from Skelton without a rather hurt apology to the effect that he could and would have produced something totally different, given time." Angus continued: "[I can] not imagine [Skelton] leaving this shelter and therefore I suppose that he will wait until we demand the final version." But the criticism went beyond Skelton's delays. When the commissioners reconvened in Ottawa for an extended period between January and March 1939, Angus complained that Sirois was too defensive about potential lines of attack that could be brought against the report, particularly from Quebec.[14] MacKay, meanwhile, was also critical of Sirois, whom he felt was a cautious and even "timid" thinker. Mackay complained that Sirois was "too easy going to sit on anyone, and accepts all Skelton's alibis." He rued the loss of Rowell and his "hard, clear, unemotional analytical mind." MacKay complained that "Job never served on a Royal Commission with a mere titular chairman," although he did not even hint that Sirois should be replaced or bypassed. Dafoe had his limitations as well. The old newspaper editor began to show signs of physical decline. He suffered a severe case of bronchitis that kept him off work for some time in January, a condition that had become an annual winter affliction. The Dafoe of early 1939 was not as lively as the Dafoe of 1938. To MacKay, he was not as analytical as either Rowell or Angus and tended towards a factual and declaratory mode of thought and writing. Dafoe's reportorial skills, he admitted, would serve them well when they came to translate their plans and goals into a persuasive report.[15]

As January turned to February and then to March in 1939, it became clear that the most recent promised deadline would not be met. Internal tensions emerged over several days in early February when Angus and MacKay grew impatient with Skelton's failure to deliver on Part 1 as well as the last of the research studies that should have been ready for printing weeks earlier. The two commissioners called Skelton out for his absences for "the 'flu' or something, which ha[d] probably been brought on or encouraged at least, by really hard work on his part & at the disregard for horses & rum." Angus and MacKay were also frustrated by Sirois's aversion "to any changes in tax revenues," which then added to Skelton's hesitancy in presenting a definite plan.[16]

Dafoe was trying to push for a list of "fundamental" rights, including basic freedoms such as speech, assembly, public commentary, and an anti-discrimination declaration. This rights-based approach had been supported by Rowell and, to an extent, by Angus. The commissioners tried during the hearings to determine if the provinces were sympathetic to creating a list of "fundamental rights," but the provinces did not express a view.[17] Angus was an outspoken advocate of individual rights, notably in defence of Asian immigrants in British Columbia. MacKay was quite sceptical of constitutionally entrenched rights. He believed that bills of rights transferred too much power to the courts, with undue consequences. The United States Bill of Rights, for example, had become far more beneficial to corporate and business interests than to individuals. Sirois was concerned that any recommendation for a bill of rights would meet the ire of Quebec and its deep reliance on historical treaties since the Conquest of 1763. Dafoe continued to press the issue throughout 1939, while MacKay argued against it. In the end, Dafoe accepted the argument that such an approach would prove too difficult politically.[18]

On 9 March, after a brief celebration of Dafoe's seventy-third birthday, the commissioners returned to their writing.[19] When the federal government, under prodding from the Opposition, asked for a progress update, Sirois responded precisely and succinctly that the report required such deep research that it could not now be completed before July. The letter was not quite a brush-off but it expressed confidence that they were forging ahead. Regardless, both the commission and the government were increasingly distracted by the wretched news of further deterioration in the European situation. They worked until the end of the month and then dispersed. Angus travelled home on the second day of regular Trans-Canada Airlines flights between Montreal and Vancouver.[20]

When the commissioners reconvened in late April, they heard the news that in May Canada would host a royal visit from King George V and

Queen Elizabeth.[21] They welcomed the distraction, which involved crafty efforts to get ringside seats for the Ottawa part of the tour, which occurred in mid-May. MacKay, who had become the main organizer of the commissioners' work, had offered to stay in Ottawa over the summer to keep the work moving forward. He spent some time making arrangements for a summer cottage rental so his family could join him even as he groused about Sandy Skelton's "impossible" work habits.[22]

The commissioners realized that they were now wrestling with their central recommendations, or what Dafoe referred to as the "crux of the whole show." This "crux" was "the financial complex – debts, refunding, allocation of revenues, subsidies and so forth." Dafoe was encouraged and even excited by the innovative ideas being put forward. Angus, Skelton, and Fowler, with help from auditor J.C. Thompson, "concocted a plan which at first struck [Dafoe] as too good to be true, but it seem[ed] to be standing up pretty well to pounding." By the middle of May, just prior to the arrival of the Royals, MacKay reported that the commissioners had "just about finished" the key fiscal proposals. With evident excitement, he wrote to his wife that the plan was so innovative that it "may take the country's breath away at first."[23]

The plan called for a shift in the very nature of dominion contributions for social services, moving them away from being conditional grants (the contemporary norm in such federations as the United States and Australia) and back towards being unconditional grants (which had been in effect at the time of Confederation). Moreover, the grants would not to be based on a simple per capita award but, rather, on an amount based on fiscal need that would be reviewed every five years. In order to finance this provision of grants without strings and on a grander scale than provided by the old 1867 formula of per capita grants, the plan relied upon the transfer of all direct taxes – income, corporate, and estate taxes – to the dominion in return for a fundamentally different form of grant. This means of funding would signal a major change of practice though not of assigned powers. There were other notable aspects of this fiscal plan, including debt relief for the provinces and mechanisms to control future debt, but the central aspect was the transformation of the fiscal basis of the Canadian government.[24]

What worried MacKay and the other commissioners was the recurring concern as to "how far Sirois [would] go with [them] on finances." Both

Dafoe and MacKay knew that it would take Sirois some time to digest the proposals before he would reach a conclusion. While Dafoe was confident that Sirois would come around, he admitted that the Quebecer seemed to be in "some mental distress" over the specific matter of taxation, above all his concern that Quebec would be deprived of some powers of taxation. According to Fowler, Sirois sent him a thirty-four-page memo dissenting from what he perceived as the centralizing thrust of the fiscal plan. Fowler claimed that he tried to ease Sirois's concerns during a lengthy conversation.[25]

When the commissioners reconvened in early June, they concentrated on two issues. The first was a lengthy and complicated treatment of transportation policy. MacKay and Angus worked to counter Dafoe's western biases and arguments, which favoured subsidies for producers. The other issue was the fiscal relationship between the dominion and the provinces, including the unemployment problem, taxation, and federal transfers. The issues were significant, so much so that the two legal advisors, J. MacGregor Stewart and Louis St-Laurent, were called in to offer advice. Specifically, they were called on to persuade the cautious Sirois to accept "emotionally" what he had agreed to "rationally."[26]

The critical meetings with St-Laurent and Stewart were held in mid-June. The commissioners and senior staff went over the proposals with the two legal advisors. St-Laurent was more expansive in his comments than Stewart. He warned that the draft of the introduction "was misleading and unnecessarily provocative." He advised that "rather than suggest the recommendations would require sacrifices, it should stress the economic shift which has taken place from self-sufficiency to inter-dependence, and the necessity of recognizing [that]."[27] On the crucial matter of the fiscal plan and its central recommendation for a transfer of direct taxes and corporate taxes to the dominion in return for large and needs-based unconditional grants to the provinces, St-Laurent "saw no objection." He favoured the federal takeover of taxation jurisdictions and did not share Sirois's concerns over Quebec losing access to estate taxes. St-Laurent agreed that debt refunding for provinces and municipalities should be highlighted while any appearance of federal control over future provincial borrowing should be avoided.[28]

St-Laurent argued that the plan did not represent an attack on provincial autonomy. When asked about the plan's acceptability to Quebec, he replied that he did not know. If the plan were represented as an attack on Quebec's "autonomy and ideals, it would be rejected." Regardless of how Duplessis reacted, in St-Laurent's view, the plan in itself "was not open to that criticism." A political realist, St-Laurent did note that Quebec would not appreciate having to "plead fiscal need before an outside body," such as a grants commission. This observation was an implicit criticism of one of the main institutional changes the commission had been considering and one that would fade over time. St-Laurent also warned against a declaration of "fundamental rights" that was being touted by Dafoe and Angus. Again, the consideration of such a declaration diminished over the following months.[29]

Stewart was more terse. He foresaw no problems with the major changes being proposed but urged clarification on the issue that there would be full "compensation" to the provinces for the tax areas surrendered to Ottawa. He thought that debt refunding for provinces and municipalities should be highlighted while any appearance of federal control over future provincial borrowing should be avoided.[30] The two advisors thus concluded that the fiscal plan was constitutionally and politically acceptable. Neither believed that it represented an attack on provincial autonomy, even though it recommended a dominion takeover of personal income and corporate taxes. There was at least the appearance of a general agreement on the fiscal plan. "We are now an undivided family again," Dafoe crowed. The sessions served as a critical litmus test for the Rowell-Sirois Commission. It was almost certainly the most important contribution Stewart and St-Laurent made to the commission.[31]

Once the commissioners agreed on the central plan, writing recommenced and drafts of several chapters for Books One and Two were finished during the summer of 1939.[32] They now estimated that the report would be a two-volume study of at least 300,000 words, with two series of supplemental publications, one a volume of the public accounts of Canada and the provinces since Confederation and the other the (seven) printed reports and (eleven) mimeographed special studies. Dafoe anticipated that about five more weeks of work would see them through: "The report proper – apart from the financial section, which I trust is well in hand – could be put into final shape with a week's revision; and I think we should hold fast to our June decision that the meeting at the end of the month should be, as intended, for the purpose of giving the report its final touches."[33] To a veteran newspaperman, writing to deadlines was second nature. But Dafoe failed to reckon with the stubbornness of the academics and bureaucrats.

The federal government, meanwhile, altered its position on the timing of the report's completion. In mid-June, Sirois encountered Ernest Lapointe on a train to Montreal. Lapointe "manifeste son etonnement en me demandant si cela voulait dire que le rapport ne serait pas presente avant le mois d'aout ou la fin d'aout." Sirois replied blandly: "nous n'envisagions pas la possibilitie de terminer le rapport plus tot." A few days later Lapointe, who was not particularly keen on the project from the start, telephoned Sirois to indicate that the prime minister was anxious to have the report as soon as possible. Sirois realized that the new timeline posed a serious challenge to the commission's credibility and possibly even its future.[34]

The prime minister proved to be less impatient than Lapointe but nonetheless reminded O.D. Skelton on 3 July that Sirois had promised a finished report by 1 July. Mackenzie King asked Skelton to get some indication of the completion date in order to inform cabinet. Lapointe gave Sirois the impression that the government would also appreciate some indication of the eventual recommendations. Sirois was not impressed by the political pressure. He fumed to MacKay and Angus: "[I don't] give a damn about the Government. What I want to do is to protect the reputation of the Commission." Sirois sent a scrupulous reply to the prime minister in French and English explaining in considerable detail the course taken by the commission since 1937, the many logistical and practical issues raised during the hearings and research phases, and the current status of the report. The work might still encounter difficulties but the commissioners aimed to finish by the early fall of 1939. MacKay and Angus were surprised but impressed by how galvanized the chief commissioner became when pushed. From that point forward, they did not question the leadership of Joseph Sirois.[35]

As they worked through the summer, the commissioners wrestled with the many ramifications of their recommendations. At the heart of these discussions was the broad question of the original meaning of Confederation and its impact on individual and provincial rights. While they continued to worry over their plan for fiscal rebalance between the dominion and provinces, they were most animated by matters of constitutional history. On the issue of rights, their disagreements were less over a list of rights than over whether there could be any entrenched encroachments on the power of government. None of them, not even Dafoe, believed that rights could be entrenched in the sense that later generations would understand it. They were an "innovation line to the underlying theory of government." Dafoe accepted that Angus was correct in arguing that no province could be prevented from "going wrong" without suborning the entire constitutional order and, indeed, that this limitation pertained also to the dominion. Angus argued in favour of a descriptive "citizenship rights" position, but his willingness to strengthen the courts gained little support. Based on the experience in the United States, MacKay expressed scepticism about judicial review. As Dafoe realized, "pedantically legal-minded" judges could not be trusted. The commissioners and their advisors accepted that the residual power in regard to citizenship rights, as with so many other areas, rested with the federal government through disallowance. According to Dafoe, the commission decided to be "detached" on most matters of constitutional interpretation. But Dafoe could not resist asserting that disallowance was the "key to the riddle of federation" in Canada. As he ruefully noted, "what old Sir John had to give with one hand to the provinces he took back with the other. He undoubtedly conceived the Federation (the greatest mystery of the whole thing is the use of the word Confederation – this must have been one of Macdonald's practical jokes) as a sort of Empire within the greater Empire." The provinces after 1867 were treated "as colonies with self-governing rights," but if they did not use these rights "in the way he thought right," Macdonald would "crack down on them with disallowance." Dafoe admitted that the commission did not dare state this opinion and indeed the report was content merely to admit there were divergent views of the meaning of Confederation and that disallowance was a key federal power. Discretion meant that "we will go pretty light on all these subjects," he commented to Grant Dexter.[36]

Joseph Sirois was not comfortable with discussions about reinterpreting the confederation agreement. Sirois had been merely nervous over the analysis of the other commissioners. His Quebec perspective brought him into real conflict with the views of Donald Creighton, the historian who, years later, would become a stout defender of the wisdom of John A. Macdonald and a ferocious advocate of a highly centralized federation.[37] When Sirois read Creighton's work, he insisted on a more balanced account regarding phrases in sections 91 and 92 of the British North America Act relating to specific and general powers. Creighton refused. He agreed to acknowledge one level of meaning (a very broad and entrenched interpretation of "property and civil rights" in Quebec law going back to the French regime and adopted with the Royal Proclamation of 1763), but he would not endorse this position. Creighton also dug his heels in on Privy Council decisions. This intervention displeased Sirois, who went so far as to consult with St-Laurent on the matter. St-Laurent agreed with Sirois. Skelton, MacKay, and Angus interceded to allow Creighton his rather limited revision, convincing Sirois and St-Laurent that it was a concession that might appease the "academic pundits in University circles in Toronto," such as Harold Innis and W.P.M. Kennedy.[38]

When the commissioners returned to Ottawa for what they thought would be a final session in late August, they again expressed concern about Skelton's slow pace in drafting Book One. They were making good headway with the writing of Book Two, but they remained at the mercy of "Skelton and his merry men" for the completion of Book One. Dafoe commented that Skelton was frustrating but indispensable. His considerable capacity for clear analysis and writing meant his contributions were essential, and, as an analyst, "he [could] even outpoint Angus." But there was growing concern that at any moment Skelton might be recalled to the Bank of Canada or lapse into distractions that might lead to further delays.[39]

Frustration with the pace of work paled in comparison with the developing situation in Europe. By the end of August, the realization loomed in Canadian governing circles that Germany was about to precipitate a war that would draw in not only Great Britain and France but also Canada. Dafoe was the most attentive to international events and the most eloquent in his observations. For years an advocate for the collective security project of the League of Nations, Dafoe had warned about the consequences of Britain's disregard of the League's fundamental goals and Canada's weak responses to Britain's moves. When the crisis in Europe deepened by late

August, Dafoe confessed to his wife that he was unable to rest in the evenings. He stayed up well into the nights listening to a radio that had been procured for him. The mood at lunches and dinners with his colleagues was increasingly fatalistic. On 31 August, while lunching at the Chateau Laurier, Dafoe observed the "grave faces" of a group of federal cabinet ministers among the diners. The commissioners were preparing to break for several weeks. The next day Dafoe reported being awakened at 6:00 a.m. by a telephone call: "It was Grant [Dexter] to tell me that the war was on and that Hitler was screaming over the radio." It was 1 September and Germany had invaded Poland. When Dafoe checked with George Ferguson at the *Winnipeg Free Press* and the head of the Sifton newspaper chain, Victor Sifton he found they both already knew. "The news gave me no sudden shock," Dafoe told Alice, "because, as you know, I have been sure for months if not for years that this wd. be the only result of Britain's policy of retreat and appeasement. But this town is full of people who two days ago were quite certain that there wd. be no war." Dafoe may have been resigned to the war but he realized the deep uncertainty it created. He reflected in closing his letter to Alice: "[we must] try to control our sensibilities under the strain of the frightful things that are going to take place or we shall be wrecked." The Dafoes had had two sons serve and survive the Great War; now their youngest was preparing to sign up for the coming war.[40]

The commissioners struggled to discern what the dark turn of events meant for their work. Dafoe met the staff members in their offices that morning and they spent some time discussing how the impending war would affect the commission. As veterans of the Great War, Angus and MacKay had no illusions about what was in store for the country. MacKay delayed his return to Halifax. Angus had already departed for Vancouver via a short trip to the annual Institute of Politics conference at Williams College in Massachusetts. While driving through New York State, he was intercepted by the State Police who informed him that the Canadian government needed his immediate presence. He turned around and headed for Ottawa. Skelton was advised that the government would likely want the report even sooner than promised. The commissioners agreed to cut out some of the work they had proposed and move more quickly towards completion. Dafoe also changed his plans and agreed to stay in Ottawa for two more weeks.[41]

The commissioners worked for the next several weeks. They moved to temporary quarters because the government requisitioned offices in the Roxborough Building. Staff members spent Labour Day moving into these smaller quarters. Over the next few days, Dafoe and Skelton debated whether the war would mean more or less pressure to finish. Dafoe heard that there would be a request for an interim report, but Skelton insisted that the government would await the completion of the full document. One thing was certain: there would be no election in the fall and therefore the report would not be needed by the sitting government.[42]

Dafoe attended the parliamentary debate of 8 and 9 September on the decision to declare war against Germany. He was surprised at the prime minister's eloquence: "It is the only speech I ever heard King make that I wd. rate higher than ordinary. King spoke well and at times magnificently ... Grant [Dexter] & I, with recollections of at least a dozen speeches of very different tenor ... looked at one another in some astonishment." Dafoe was also impressed by Ernest Lapointe's response to the leading French-Canadian isolationist, Maxime Raymond, who proposed neutrality: "Lapointe leaped to his feet the moment Raymond finished and made what I think I can say was the most effective political speech I ever heard." Dafoe was delighted that "after hammering the French extremists he gave the Toronto screamers at the other end of the scale a dose of the same medicine."[43]

As the reality of the war set in, the commission was forced to accept the fact that everything had changed. Robert Fowler admitted to Dafoe that the war "greatly altered the atmosphere into which the Commission's report [would] come." But perhaps, Fowler hoped, the recommendations would be "strengthened rather than weakened by the advent of war," thereby refuting "the easy and perhaps natural assumption that the report ha[d] become a dead letter." Dafoe shared in Fowler's wishful thinking. He hoped that the "too confident assumption in which so many people indulge[d], that the war washed up the work," would change to a "recognition that the war may add to the timeliness and value of the report."[44] The commissioners used this wishful thinking to force themselves to get back to work, revising Book Two and getting it ready for printing, while awaiting Skelton and the staff as they worked on Book One.

When the commission reconvened in mid-October, it admitted that the atmosphere of war was already obstructing their progress. MacKay remarked: "if we were a Royal Commission of one, and had no secretaries who wanted to write the report in their respective ways, time and trouble would be cut by at least 75%." But he realized that the delays could no longer be blamed solely on Skelton. Everyone's productivity had diminished. The "suppressed excitement" and "activity and enthusiasm" for the war in Ottawa was absorbing most of the energy. MacKay mused that it was too bad such determination and energy had not been devoted to the problems of unemployment, public health, and housing conditions over the previous decade.[45]

The work proceeded throughout the fall with more revisions and reconsiderations, particularly from Sirois, who still queried certain portions of the fiscal plan that seemed to suggest greater executive or central government authority. In particular, Sirois was concerned over a proposal for yet another version of a loan council that sounded like a dominion agency of control over provincial borrowing. He also had strong reservations over a related proposal for a permanent dominion-provincial secretariat. The commissioners sought to reassure Sirois that their visions of fiscal federalism were aligned. MacKay argued that an agency to review the federal transfers, dubbed a "Finance Commission," would be a technical agency of the two levels of government and not one before which the provinces would have to ask for fiscal adjustments. MacKay assured Sirois that their proposals would ensure that the unconditional grants system would be flexible enough to grow with governmental needs and not become subsumed under political pressures. The provinces would not have to "beg" the federal government for revisions. Sirois was finally convinced but reminded MacKay that any proposal for a loan council was dead and buried.[46]

The commissioners also grappled with the complicated questions of social services and issues of "insurance," such as health, pensions, and unemployment. They tried to reaffirm the legislative responsibility of the provinces with measures to ensure their fiscal capacity. While there was agreement on principle, it was a matter of careful attention to policy details. An election in Quebec, meanwhile, served as a satisfying distraction. With the support and even direct intervention of federal Quebec Liberals, the provincial Liberals under Adelard Godbout defeated Maurice Duplessis' Union Nationale. At least one of the three provincial obstacles to the commission's work was suddenly removed.[47]

By December, Book Two was readied for printing.[48] Book One, however, was not. The commission would have to continue working into the new year, probably until the end of January. Dafoe was hopeful that the texts might be approved in early January, although the editorial work would continue beyond that date. But the commission staff members were being poached for war-related activities. The capable secretary, Mary White, announced her resignation to take a position with the British High Commission. John Deutsch had made arrangements with Queen's University to teach for part of each week while Bill Mackintosh was drawn into full-time government work in the Department of Finance. Only Mary Rowland, still on secondment from the Bank of Canada, continued as a full-time commission employee, and she took on all of the increasingly difficult administrative duties until the commission wound up. Rowland sustained the commission's operations, but White was called back from her new job to work weekends and evenings as needed.[49]

In early January, the commissioners grew worried over the continuing delays. Sirois almost pleaded with Sandy Skelton to try and get at least the peripheral works – the research studies and Book Three – printed. He urged Skelton to ask if Mary Rowland could "use all pressure possible" to get the "Stationery Office" to finish printing and binding of the works they had. Skelton happily blamed the printers for the holdups but assured Sirois he had told the Prime Minister's advisors that they could not promise an immediate completion to the main volumes.[50]

Meanwhile, Dafoe was waylaid in Winnipeg for the second consecutive year with bronchitis and he would not be available until near the end of the month. He confessed that the commission was having "difficulty in bringing the ship into harbour." Skelton's slow pace "has got himself (& us) in a pretty pickle," Dafoe complained to Grant Dexter. Book Two was now at the printers, but the completion date for Book One was pushed back to mid-February.[51] The commissioners realized that the King government could ask for the report at any time, depending on the date set for the federal election. On 25 January, the government called an election for 26

March. This announcement provided the commission with a welcome extension of two months or longer.[52] Sirois had dutifully reported to King on 24 January that the second and third books were "in press" but the first was still being written. The prime minister informed Sirois that the election call meant the commission was not obligated to submit the report according to the original offer but, rather, to hold onto it until after the election was over and Parliament reconvened.[53]

The commissioners and staff were relieved. For a dinner on 1 February at Skelton's favourite haunt, Madame Burger's celebrated Hull restaurant, the Café Henry Burger, a souvenir menu was printed. They dined on such items as "Angus Appetizers," "Medaillons de the Monarch of the Plains," "Canada's Goose Cooked a la Sirois," and "Crepes nationales." It was served with a list of alcohol-free "Dafoe's Drinks," traditionally laced "Duplessis Cocktails," and ended with "Cognac Confederation," the latter Dr. Sirois's favoured brandy.[54] The evening was a well-deserved respite, but the celebration was premature.

The delays in Book One were not caused solely by Skelton's work habits. Fundamental disagreements again emerged over the interpretation of Confederation, not among the commissioners but once again with Donald Creighton. The historian had been called in to help edit Book One, but he pushed his own centralist interpretation, which increasingly went against the general tenor of the report. In mid-February, Sirois read Creighton's revised page proofs and recommended certain changes. Creighton refused. "I do not like the tone of these remarks," Sirois informed the other commissioners. He pointed out that the report was going to be signed by the four commissioners and that "Creighton ha[d] no responsibility whatever in connection with same." If the historian disagreed with the report's interpretation of Confederation, he was entirely free to criticize it later. As Dafoe explained to Sirois, Creighton was a "Federalist keenly interested in defending – and as opportunity offers extending – Federal power."[55] That advocacy was not going to be permitted in the final text.

To make matters worse, John Deutsch was tardy in finishing drafting the two remaining chapters on contemporary Canada and public finance. He was working on the chapters while also filling in for Bill Mackintosh at Queen's. Deutsch made his way from Kingston to Ottawa on most Fridays between January and March 1940. Although he plugged away, by his own testimony he usually spent one of his weekend days and most Saturday evenings enjoying Ottawa's winter social scene in the company of his new fiancée, Stephanie Heagerty, daughter of the dominion's chief public health officer and advocate of national health insurance, Dr. John Heagerty. MacKay and Angus fumed, and even the usually patient Sirois expressed irritation at the pace of his work.

Like Creighton, Deutsch did not take advice well, and Angus commented that he was not only slow to submit his work but also just as "obstinate" as Creighton in dealing with criticism.[56] Several commissioners objected to Deutsch's phrasing if not his arguments. He had argued that economic policy had "made Canada a nation," a position strongly criticized by Skelton, Dafoe, and Angus. The wording was revised to read, "the policies we adopted made Canada the kind of nation it is." Quite a difference and far more in keeping with the commissioners' views.[57]

Friction between the four commissioners and the staff boiled over yet again just after the February dinner. The commission met formally and agreed upon procedures for reviewing final drafts and editorial changes. They agreed that all material would be circulated among the commissioners with final approval given by Sirois, who would then hand it off to Skelton and Savard to supervise the actual printing. MacKay complained to Sirois that, after the meeting, the minutes as circulated were "inadequate" because they did not reflect these decisions. The commissioners' instructions were not being followed, and at times material was being sent on for printing that was still to be edited. MacKay then had a heated telephone conversation with Skelton over the procedures being followed, which he reported to his colleagues.[58]

MacKay later regretted suggesting there had been deliberate disregard of the commissioners' instructions. But even in backing down somewhat he pointed out several examples of flagrant mix-ups.[59] Skelton, who seems to have been shaken by the exchange with MacKay, responded in an apologetic manner that he was "at a loss" to know what instructions from MacKay or other commissioners had been ignored. Editorial changes stipulated by the commissioners had not been made, but he claimed that this failure had been inadvertent or based on mistaken understanding. He promised that "final page proofs" would be seen and approved by all commissioners.[60]

Thereafter, the work proceeded carefully, steadily but very slowly. As the drafts were submitted, they went through Mary Rowland's clearing-house to the commissioners. They were circulated across the country, usually from Angus to Dafoe to MacKay then Sirois. But between the mails and the editing, the final reviews and revisions took more than two months, extending in March and April. It was not until mid-April that the commissioners received the last section of the overdue chapters of Book One with Deutsch's work on contemporary Canada that had attracted their review.

The other upshot of MacKay's confrontation with Skelton was that, without warning and in the company of his father, Sandy Skelton departed at the end of February on a two-week vacation to Havana and Mexico City. The commissioners and staff were flabbergasted when they heard that Skelton had bolted town. As Sirois confessed to MacKay, "would I expose myself to an action in damages if I expressed to you my opinion that they are all gone crazy in Ottawa, save and except Miss Rowland?" Even the phlegmatic Dafoe admitted to "a degree of exasperation" with Skelton. MacKay managed to contain himself and even accepted that Skelton was entitled to a holiday. But Skelton's holiday meant that they would not meet the 20 March deadline.[61]

Commissioners and senior staff continued to edit, revise, and then review page proofs of these chapters until the end of the month of April. By then they had had to endure a potentially-harmful rumour that spread across Canada in the press in early March that the report was suppressed by the government for its own convenience.[62] By the last days, at Sirois's explicit directive, the final proofing was done by Savard and Skelton.[63] At last, in early May, the three volumes of the report and the eleven other booklets of special studies were all approved and the remaining sections sent for printing. Despite rumours at the time and suggestions long after, the report had not been completed earlier in the year and then held back for weeks at the government's convenience. Nor had it been composed by staff members and then signed off by the commissioners. Robert Fowler later asserted that, like the King James Bible, the Rowell-Sirois report was, as that august tome had explained in its preface, "a joint effort."[64]

9

Reinterpreting Canadian Federalism
May 1940

Economically Canada can be compared to a string of beads,
and they are not all pearls.

– Report, *1940, Book One, 186*[1]

The Commission does not consider that its proposals are either
centralizing or decentralizing in their combined effect, but
believe that they will conduce to the sane balance between
these two tendencies which is the essence of a genuine federal
system.

– Report, *1940, Book Two, 276*[2]

Nothing about the Rowell-Sirois Report proceeded without difficulties, not even its release. While the war obviously overshadowed the report, its contents were important enough to keep it in the political arena even in the critical times of 1940. Its arguments and recommendations have often been summarized or glossed over, but they are far more impressive than a synopsis can capture. The Rowell-Sirois Report was a product of the first flowering of Canadian social science, and its impact was grounded in that generation's reinterpretations of Canadian economic and political history as well as their innovative and creative recommendations.

When completion of the report was in sight early in 1940, plans for its launch began. The prime minister instructed his aide, J.W. Pickersgill, that the report had to be ready when Parliament reassembled on 25 January. Mackenzie King noted that he was not particularly concerned about the simultaneous release of the French-language translation, which was done in the same piecemeal fashion as the original report.[3] King wanted Pickersgill to ensure that "a proper précis of the report should appear in the press when it [was] tabled." This document, he instructed, should be prepared by the commission and not by the Prime Minister's Office.[4] Joseph Sirois intervened and strongly emphasized that both French and English versions must be ready at the same time. He also insisted upon delivering copies of the volumes to each provincial government prior to its tabling in the House of Commons, again avoiding any hint that the federal government had somehow received advance knowledge of its contents.[5]

All of this planning came to naught when the commission failed to meet its deadlines, just as Joseph Sirois had warned the government in mid-January. Fortunately for the commissioners, their failure coincided with the changing political strategies of the federal government. King made the decision to prorogue Parliament immediately after it was recalled and then call an election for 26 March.[6] The Liberals again won a majority. After many delays, the three volumes and the research studies were printed in oversize format and bound in red paper covers. All works were printed in both English and French versions.

O.D. Skelton and Arnold Heeney, clerk of the Privy Council, presented the prime minister with a new plan for releasing the report. This plan involved coordinating the delivery of copies to each provincial government, providing material for the media (major newspapers, the Canadian Broadcasting Corporation, and the Parliamentary Press Gallery), and preparing media releases. It was all to be done just prior to the official release to Parliament, scheduled for 10 May. Joseph Sirois again insisted on getting the entire report to the provinces in both official languages at the same time that it was delivered to the federal government. The commission, he argued, must show a consultative and even-handed approach.[7] The prime minister agreed to delay the official tabling of the report until after it was confirmed that the premiers had received their copies. Adjutor Savard, the French-language secretary, and Leonard Brockington, a Winnipeg lawyer and King's favourite speechwriter, were briefed so they could prepare "objective" national radio broadcasts for the CBC French and

English networks. These were given on 16 May.[8] Meanwhile, the commission staff learned at the last minute that John Dafoe, "without consulting anyone," had prepared his own summary for Grant Dexter, his *Winnipeg Free Press* parliamentary reporter, to distribute to the Press Gallery. The commission tried to prevent the leak but to no avail and no apparent damage.[9] When at last the entire set of volumes was lined up for presentation, Sirois telegraphed his colleagues to express his hope that "nearly three years of strenuous work ... may be of some help in solving our problems."[10]

The official release date was set for 10 May but, as was so often the case, fate intervened. In this instance, international events stole the commission's thunder. The Rowell-Sirois Report was scooped by the war. Amidst the alarming military news about the Nazi blitzkrieg suddenly unleashed against the Netherlands, Belgium, and France, the political news in the United Kingdom was just as unsettling. The prime minister, Neville Chamberlain, was unseated and Winston Churchill became the head of a new coalition government. Canadians, and above all Mackenzie King, were totally preoccupied by the political turmoil in Britain and the even more alarming military reports from Belgium and France. The German attack on Western Europe quickly led to the fateful turning of the tide against the French and British armies; the surrender of the Netherlands, Belgium, and even France; and the shocking, miraculous evacuation of the British Army trapped at Dunkirk. Domestically, King was dealing with three by-elections, preparation for the Throne Speech, and what he described as a "nervous breakdown" on the part of his closest cabinet associate, Ernest Lapointe. Delivered on 11 May, the report was tabled in the House of Commons on 16 May, the first day of the new parliamentary session. The manner in which the report's release was overshadowed by the war was yet another portent of problems to come. Regardless, the product of an inquiry that had taken thirty-two months of work and cost $533,600 was now in the public domain. The three-volume report was also available for public purchase for one dollar, the report plus research studies for ten dollars.[11]

The Rowell-Sirois Report provided not only a broad synthesis of economic and political history but also a serious reinterpretation of Canada as a federation. It supported rather than lamented the federal nature of the country and effectively sidestepped the questions of constitutional reform. Instead, it examined how the federal system could best fulfill the essential functions that governments faced under contemporary conditions. The report argued that the regions and the provinces were to be taken as seriously as the federal government in undertaking these functions. Through the "breathtaking" fiscal proposals, dubbed "Plan One," the recommendations claimed that a renewed federal system for Canada could escape what Norman Rogers had described as the "dead hand" that stymied reform of the existing federal system.[12]

In its introduction, the report claimed to stick closely to the terms of reference. These included a study of the constitutional allocation of revenue sources and governmental burdens, the character and amounts of taxes collected, public expenditure and public debt, and dominion subsidies and grants to provincial governments.[13] While the commission provided an examination of the constitutional and jurisdictional aspects of federalism, including the distribution of legislative powers, the report actually focused attention away from constitutional and towards the economic and fiscal aspects of government.[14]

The main question for the report was not whether it favoured centralization and a weakening of provincial autonomy or vice versa, as many contemporary and later observers asserted.[15] To the commissioners, such discussions would be fatal to their internal harmony, their capacity to retain credibility with both the federal government and the provinces, and finally, to their own understanding of the enterprise. Ottawa was not keen on constitutional combat, while the provinces were inevitably suspicious of federal intentions. The contentious hearings and the responses of the provinces, along with the challenges of writing the report, made clear the futility of proclaiming major constitutional change as one of the commission's goals. The published document went out of its way to explain Canadian federalism in a way that avoided inevitable and unnecessary confrontations based on old quarrels over jurisdiction, legislative powers, or even fiscal transfers. But it did not avoid offering controversial solutions.

The report reflected an intellectual as well as the political environment in which it was conceived and written. It was a study grounded in economic history and political economy, two modes of analysis that had been reconceived by leading academics and policy advisors in Canada during the 1920s and 1930s.[16] Almost all of the senior staff, and three of the commissioners, Angus, Dafoe, and MacKay, as well as their bureaucratic liaisons, O.D. Skelton and Clifford Clark, were leading members of the new professional association of economists and political scientists that attacked Canadian problems through the new methods and skills learned at the leading graduate schools, chiefly in the United States and Great Britain. This intellectual ferment, which saw the birth of modern social science in Canada, was based on a political economy approach that examined the interrelations among geography, policy, and markets. Canada's peculiar staples/natural resources economy, according to William Mackintosh, Harold Innis, and other economic historians, had expanded across the continent from the era of the old fur and timber trades to the age of wheat, mines, hydroelectric power, and pulp and paper.[17]

In the disciplines of political science and history, an outpouring of works on Canada was appearing just as the commission got under way. They affirmed the importance of the state and the North American and North Atlantic ties that shaped its political institutions. The first generation of constitutional scholars, including the likes of W.P.M. Kennedy, R. MacGregor Dawson, and Frank Scott, was developing syntheses of constitutional development to reflect the transformation of Canada's status both inside and outside the British Empire as well as the barriers to effective and active government within the country. Viewed in a broader context than federal-provincial conflict, the significance of this reconsideration in the era of "legal realism" was to avoid the fixation on judicial decisions and concentrate on ways to ensure effective government, including intergovernmental relations. The issues were less about which level of government had which rights and more about whether governments could intervene to positive effect. Norman Rogers made the point that "the principles which should guide these institutions [are devised] in order that they may achieve the purposes they are created to serve." The issues were rooted in expediency not theory. His specific criticisms of the controversial decisions of the Judicial Committee of the Privy Council were aimed at the "dead hand" of precedent because it prevented adequate governmental action and not because centralization was necessarily preferred. Even when some writers thought otherwise, they did so from a functional perspective. J.A. Corry believed that there was a certain inevitability to centralization in the modern world because more regulation and intervention had become essential to modern government.[18]

Canadian-born historians James T. Shotwell and J. Bartlett Brebner (both of whom ended up teaching at Columbia University) organized a series of volumes that examined the relationship between Canada and the United States. The resulting series, sponsored by the Carnegie Endowment for International Peace, supported more than forty volumes. The series included works by Henry Angus (on Canadian-American relations) and Donald Creighton (on the post-Conquest continental "commercial economy" of the St. Lawrence).[19] Dafoe contributed to a 1935 book entitled *Canada: An American Nation* that emphasized the two countries' shared political, economic, and cultural experience and practices.[20]

An important aspect of this intellectual background was the commission's grounding in the new concepts of economics and the role of the state that had emerged in the 1930s. Important theoretical critiques and stimulating practical advice emerged from the ferment that came to be identified as Keynesian economics. The term at the time was used less to identify strict adherence to Maynard Keynes's theories and more to identify debate over an active role for the state in managing fiscal and monetary policy.[21] These new approaches emphasized that the economic problems of the era were the result of the under-consumption of goods and capital, and that the state could engage in an appropriate and effective direction of economic output, or as the report put it, could function "to stimulate ... the national income." These measures were quite a departure from the traditional fiscal and monetary orthodoxy. They consisted of new goals based on interventionist monetary policy that disdained the discredited gold standard and called for efficient taxation and fiscal transfers unbound by budgetary orthodoxy.[22]

Book One was an economic and political history of Canada. It was a social scientists' history that was drawn from the new modes of economics and economic history. The influential historian Frank Underhill described it as "brilliant" and "convincing," but too "abstract." It amounted to "a ghostly ballet of bloodless categories."[23] Yet the work became a foundational reinterpretation of the country's national history, amounting to a reinterpretation of Canada's economic history.

The volume began with the claim that Confederation was "a great political achievement," based on a "conjuncture" of crises in each of the old British North American colonies at mid-century.[24] The first thirty years –

the era of the three basic national economic policies (transcontinental railway, western expansion, and tariff-based industrialization) – were "years of disappointment."[25] Canada became for the only time in its history an economic unit due to the national expansion of the wheat boom. Prairie settlement and "the magic of wheat" led to the transformation of the country.[26] But the political and economic unity was short-lived. The wartime period from 1914 to 1921 had the dual impact of creating a strong federal government while also producing bitter divisions among regions, classes, and ethnic groups.[27] The 1920s, although a time of "post-war prosperity," was one in which there was "an eclipse of Federal leadership" and "an ascendency of Provincial Governments."[28]

Finally, the decade of the 1930s was the time of Depression, where the "strangulation" of world trade and ill-advised Canadian policy had "extremely drastic" effects. The external cause was the crisis in world trade, a crisis that intensified due to the failures of international efforts and Canada's (and other countries') embrace of "economic nationalism." Canada's economy was dependent on world trade (one-third of national income) and highly dependent on "raw materials" (two-thirds of exports). The period after 1930 was disastrous. The policies of "expediency" (which meant maintaining a high dollar and embracing unprecedented levels of tariff protection) "widened the disparities in the losses" of individuals and governments alike.[29]

Book One argued that the 1930s ended Canada's phase of "national policy" development. By the 1920s, these old policies were no longer producing "their former expansionary and cohesive effects."[30] To address the highly regionalized economy and divergent regional conditions, new and more sophisticated approaches to monetary, trade, and fiscal policy had to be adopted to "redress the balance."[31] The commission's interpretation of Confederation and the ensuing decades of national expansion was a major corrective to a triumphalist interpretation of economic nation building.[32]

Book One highlighted the particular characteristics of Canadian economic development and the often-debilitating effects of public policy in the 1930s. The Rowell-Sirois Report did not affirm or refute the grievances and perspectives of the provinces; it did not directly address the sustained critique of national policies found in the presentations and written briefs of the four western provinces. But it did indirectly acknowledge and address them. The treatment of the 1930s contained a blunt critique of federal policies. It admitted that, since the onset of the Depression and due to its unprecedented effects, traditional monetary and tariff policies were no longer effective. They harmed resource and export sectors in particular, not only in the western provinces but also throughout the nation.[33]

Canada faced "almost entirely new" problems after 1930 and the country had two alternatives in dealing with the "international economic anarchy." The first option was "to counteract the factors which were responsible for the slump by attempting to maintain export volumes, to keep up activity in construction, and to prevent prices and costs from getting out of line." This choice was unorthodox and perhaps even radical, but it would have maintained national and regional incomes at the highest possible levels. It would have meant the full use of monetary policy to lower Canada's international exchange rate and thus maintain access to world markets in leading commodities such as wheat, lumber, and pulp. It would also have entailed generous grants to the provinces aiming to stimulate the job-rich construction sector.[34]

The alternative, and the one explicitly chosen by the dominion and most provinces, was "to avoid risky and unorthodox monetary measures and to endeavor to maintain income in the sheltered and protected sectors of the economy by drastic restrictions against imports." It meant following sound financial policies and facilitating the "operation of the natural forces of recovery."[35] This policy line entailed the combination of increased tariff protection, high dollar exchange rates, and the slashing of public spending and frozen grants to the provinces, which together worsened the divergent regional effects of the Depression. This was the policy anathema to the West.

Despite its originality as a synthesis of Canadian economic history, Book One stood firm on the legitimacy of the division of powers to sustain economic and fiscal functionality in an effective federation. It did not bemoan the divided authority of dominion and provinces over the economy. It did, however, point out how the provinces and the dominion alternated in the 1920s and 1930s in making aggressive interpretations of their governmental responsibilities with little regard for the consequences. Both the dominion and the provinces were impelled by "expediency."[36] Book One made absolutely no concession to the argument that they were trapped by the Constitution.

The analysis of Confederation, a source of considerable disagreement in the drafting stage, had become in the final version a subtler argument. The wording of the Constitution was not an insuperable obstacle to change and its provisions should not be read as restrictive. Interpretation and politics mattered. Confederation was a political achievement set against economic problems in each colony that "had many alarming and depressing features." The settlement of 1867 was designed to "lessen exposure to the effects of the economic policies pursued by the United States and Great Britain." Diverse motives and specific problems went into the Confederation agreement, with the result of "mutual concession" that "reconciled" national and local goals.[37] This historical factor led to a lesson on the nature of federalism and the interpretation of the BNA Act. According to the commissioners, "the vital core of a federal constitution is the division of legislative powers," the key factor that "represents the compromise between the forces which make union possible and those which inhibit the formation of a close union." The division of powers and the need to compromise delineate "the limits of what can be done by common agreement and the extent to which the separate states must be permitted to differ and work out their own destinies."[38]

The interpretation was a check on centralists and decentralists alike: a federal system meant the delineation of the "limits" for the central government and its constituent parts. A "mechanical application of the division of powers" was impossible due to the increasing complexity of the regional economies and the fact that "the neat logical divisions found in the constitution" no longer corresponded to the reality of "human affairs."[39]

The first volume tackled the vital question of whether the evolving interpretation of the BNA Act, through the Privy Council decisions, had somehow distorted the federal system. Did these decisions reflect the intentions of the Fathers of Confederation or did they reshape the federation? The Rowell-Sirois Report cautioned that the courts were not free to survey historical evidence as found in parliamentary debates and theoretical writings, but only the legal evidence. While the commission was prepared to examine this historical evidence, the result could not lead to the dismissal of Privy Council interpretations as somehow wrong or distorting.[40]

By its relentless emphasis on changing circumstances, the report warned of the dangers in remaining in the grip of the Confederation settlement and traditional economic, political, and constitutional orthodoxies. The solution to Canada's crisis in federalism lay in the future, not the past. While the role of government had changed due to the "revolutionary economic and social changes that ha[d] since taken place," the "intentions of the founders [could not], except by chance, provide solutions for problems of which they [had] never dreamed."[41]

Whether the analysis focused on the past, present, or future, the report hung its recommendations on the working of the federal division of powers. Book One ended in a carefully circumscribed depiction of the "constitution to-day."[42] This existing Constitution led to the main dilemma of the 1930s. The dominion government had unlimited access to revenues through its powers of direct taxation but limited power in the social policy areas that were crucial to the modern state. Meanwhile, the provincial governments had limited access to revenues but vast responsibilities in the social policy realm. In addition, the evolving federal system was becoming "more favourable to provincial power."[43]

There were difficulties, often considerable, over the "divided jurisdiction" of the modern federal system. But these difficulties were being overcome through forms of "voluntary agreement" and there was capacity for governments to find ways to engage in "co-operative ventures." The direction of public policy was towards forms of coordination and cooperation, including either joint administration or else delegation of functions. These issues of modern government, the report argued, rather than the allure of fundamental constitutional reform, must now be accepted.[44] Key aspects of the current federal system did not work, but they related less to the division of powers or "divided jurisdiction" than to the means to deal with them. The system of fiscal relations held the solution. This system, including negotiated grants to the provinces in the 1860s and conditional grants in the 1930s, did not work and had to be replaced by a totally different fiscal regime.[45]

The interpretation of Canada's economic history in Book One led directly to the forceful recommendations set out in Book Two. The strong linkage was hardly surprising. The two volumes were planned in tandem, even though the commissioners' volume was completed first, and the staffers' book completed second.

Book Two opened with the ringing declarations that the "maximum welfare" of all citizens was the goal of government and that "the goal of human welfare ... should determine the character of both the political and economic systems." This goal had three components: increasing national income, distributing income more efficiently, and providing greater social and economic security. The "stresses and strains" of the current era and the "unpredictable change" of the past seventy years meant that the report would not bow to the "sanctity" of the original 1867 Confederation agreement. "Bold departures" were needed to avoid "disastrous consequences" in the very near future.[46] Book Two proceeded to develop its arguments in support of these goals with an artful weaving of deduction and evidence, drawing on the eleven research studies and Thomson's statistical volume as well as the artful use of the hearings in support of its arguments. While not overly didactic, Book Two, like Book One, was an interpretation not a summary.

Two premises, stated in the introductory chapter, shaped a renewed federal system. The first was that there was no alternative to a major role for the state: "The growing complexity of our society, and the growing demands for governmental action to promote social welfare and control economic life, are compelling both the provinces and the Dominion to assume functions of government." The problem, however, was that governments were assuming roles for which they either had inadequate jurisdiction or inadequate revenues. Responsibility for social services, either directly through their own agencies or indirectly through funding quasi-public institutions, had become essential.[47]

The second premise was the role of the provinces in implementing policy. This took the form of the commission's oft-repeated support for "the general rule of provincial responsibility."[48] Existing constitutional arrangements should not be disturbed unless absolutely necessary. Governments had to recognize "pronounced differences in social philosophy between different regions." Governmental interventions had to be based on "economy and efficiency in administration." Finally, the "suitability of different jurisdictions" had to be gauged to carry out the financial burdens of government.[49]

Implicit in these arguments was a rejection of the need to turn the constitutional division of powers on its head. Instead, more effective governmental activities were required in certain areas (social services and stabilization of the economy) that were unheard of when the BNA Act was created. The "functional" roles of government had to be recognized. While there was a limited array of functions that should be allocated to or shared with the dominion, this was due to the need for uniformity of services and the "unequal financial ability of the provinces." Each province required the "ability to decide issues of peculiar importance to itself."[50]

Book Two turned to examine the purposes of modern government through discussions of social services, labour regulation, education, regulation of business, and interprovincial trade. Without advocating any particular mix to the positive state, it nonetheless made clear that interventions in areas of social policy and economic regulation were at the heart of modern government.[51] Each of these subjects included a review of the "allocation of functions" between the levels of government. The premise was that the provinces held the basic responsibility for social welfare services, with the exception of unemployment insurance.[52] The report emphasized the need to clarify the delegation of powers to deal with the many overlapping activities of the modern state.[53] These included economic jurisdictions such as trade and natural products marketing, company regulation and insurance, as well as social policy areas ranging from labour regulation and education to health and social insurance.

The issue of interprovincial trade drew two important points about dominion-provincial conflict. The first was that "local protectionism" was a challenge and would become a growing problem in Canada.[54] The problem of "safeguarding the freedom of interstate or interprovincial trade," however, was essential to a federal system. In the United States, the courts were used to enforce the constitutional rule of "free commerce." By contrast, in Canada, the power of disallowance was wielded to squelch provincial and municipal actions. Neither approach was considered ideal, but the commissioners concluded that federal disallowance was a "discretionary" power that quite simply should not be used. It was a political tactic that interfered with provincial legislative competency. In order to obtain agreements not to "obstruct" trade, the report proposed a tribunal with declaratory, not mandatory, powers in addition to discussions at intergovernmental conferences. The commissioners admitted that their recommendations on this issue were "vague." While the report strongly defended the principles of interprovincial freedom of trade, investment, and mobility, they had to be agreed upon by political leaders rather than imposed.[55]

The report recommended the institutionalizing of dominion-provincial conferences.[56] These conferences, like interprovincial conferences, had been held at irregular intervals between 1906 and 1935 but with ever greater frequency. The proposal for embedding the conferences, the commissioners noted, had widespread provincial support, and the value of them was by now "obvious." Like the delegation of powers, regular conferences would resolve problems of divided and conflicting governmental functions. Cooperation was essential because the powers of governments "tended to straddle" the two levels. The commission recommended a separate federal agency or department to entrench the innovation.[57]

Matters of jurisdiction were important, but the core of Canada's modern problems lay in public finance. Drawing freely on Book One's interpretation of Canadian economic history and current condition, Book Two set out its financial recommendations. Plan One was the commission's solution to the myriad problems besetting Canadian federalism. Originally conceived by Sandy Skelton, it was developed by Henry Angus, Robert Fowler, and Robert MacKay, and agreed upon by all the commissioners. It was the centrepiece of Book Two and, indeed, the report.[58] It was intended to deal with the fiscal crisis in which "no logical relationship exist[ed] between the local income of any province and the constitutional powers and responsibilities of the government of that province."[59] A more equitable distribution of governmental burdens and social service benefits was required, as was a "revenue system and a general fiscal policy designed to stimulate rather than depress the national income."[60]

In order to bring order and effective policy to the system, a four-part integrated programme was set out. First, it recommended a constitutional transfer of power over unemployment assistance. This proposal meant dominion assumption of the full cost of unemployment relief through a national unemployment insurance program. It included support for "unemployed employables" in the form of public works programs.[61]

Second, and most remarkably, Plan One called for a system of national adjustment grants. These were unconditional annual grants to each province, based on their individual tax bases and fiscal needs, and they would provide each province with the resources to meet "at least average Canadian standards for all other social services in all provinces."[62] The grants were to be administered by a joint federal-provincial national finance commission that would calculate and advise at five-year intervals. The basic grant could not be reduced, and it was based on provincial, not national, calculations of the provinces' capacity to tax.[63]

Third, the plan called on the federal government to take over net provincial debt service costs with the provinces repaying their debt based on a "fixed annual sum equal to the interest received by each province on its investments," with a special formula for Quebec, where provincial debt was low but municipal debt very high.[64]

Fourth and finally, Plan One recommended the transfer to the dominion of exclusive taxation in three areas: personal income, corporate income, and succession duties. This transfer in areas of direct taxation (a shared jurisdiction) was to be completed for not on the basis of constitutional change but through the practice of "delegation," which the report had shown to be a normal practice of the practice of federalism. This particular delegation was based upon the proviso that it would ensure the transfer of tax revenue through Ottawa to each of the provinces on a sufficiently large scale to sustain provincial social spending priorities. While this transfer was important, it was based on the precept that the revenues of the provinces would be untouched and, indeed, left inviolable since they were constitutionally guaranteed. These revenues included licences and fees, resource revenues, sales taxes such as gasoline taxes and the like, all of which were significant sources of provincial revenue in their own right.[65]

Plan One was supported by calculations showing how the tax transfers would affect each province. While most would gain, the surrender of corporate, individual, and succession revenues meant that Ontario and British Columbia would not presently qualify for the proposed National Adjustment Grants. Ontario alone would suffer a net loss on tax transfers. The report admitted that there was no direct benefit for Ontario and that, indeed, the transfer of taxes might well cost the province "in prosperous years." The benefits to Ontario would accrue, however, because the other parts of the country would be in a stronger fiscal situation. The report argued that all provinces, including Ontario, would end up in a stronger fiscal position. Their improved fiscal position would be due to the transfer of costs for the employable unemployed, to the easing of debt service charges, and to the fiscal gains for local governments.[66]

Plan One also called for a thorough overhaul of the tax system. It cautioned that only the establishment of "uniform" national taxes would enable Canada to finance a new fiscal regime. The income tax was "the most highly developed modern instrument of taxation." It had the potential to be "the most effective method yet devised, within the framework of the capitalist economy, for achieving the social and humanitarian objectives" of the modern state. Yet in Canada it was "crippled and seriously distorted by the present division of jurisdiction." Corporate taxes were identified as a crucial source of revenues that should be tapped nationally but without creating the current disincentives to business operations and new investments. The various provincial systems were described as "a chaos" that reveal "complexity beyond belief." The existing system was described as a hodgepodge of provincial tax grabs that did little more than take revenue inefficiently and without obvious benefits. Inheritance taxes represented a burgeoning revenue source, reflecting the Canadian economy's expansion and success. In other modern states, inheritance taxes were recognized as having the potential to serve as "an important instrument of social policy ... effecting some transfer of wealth from rich to poor." The commission hearings and submissions, however, indicated that in Canada inheritance taxes were widely criticized as "vexatious" and subject to "abuses" and "inequities."[67]

The plan called for a two-stage process that would reallocate responsibility for the collection of taxes to the federal authority and then distribute them to the provinces through a system of National Adjustment Grants. They were a means to establish "equity as between taxpayers, and as between provinces."[68] The maintenance of the national income of Canada required that "every government in Canada should provide adequate developmental, educational, and social services for its people. This is not reasonably possible today. Plan I would make it possible."[69]

As an alternative to the recommendations of Plan One, the report offered a second option. Drafted initially by Robert MacKay, the terse Plan Two was laid out in five unenthusiastic pages. It offered to transfer "full responsibility for unemployed employables" and a form of relief to provincial governments, on current levels of expenditure. But this shift, although perhaps tempting, would be "palliative" and fiscally "illusory." The report argued that, while Plan Two promised "somewhat greater advantages to the *governments* of some provinces ... it [did] not benefit the *residents* of these provinces equally with Plan I."[70] To emphasize the point, the distinction between governments and residents was italicized in the text. The basic aim of Plan One to "stimulate the national income" would not occur under Plan Two. Indeed, the report warned that the actual effects of the alternate plan would be "little short of disastrous" in terms of economic growth and equity. The current "scramble for revenue" would continue, the "confusion and conflict" between governments would continue, and worse, the sense of "injustice and bitterness" between governments and among the populace would continue and even intensify.[71]

Plan One was the creative centre of the Rowell-Sirois report.[72] It was based on respect for the sovereignty of two levels of government, each with its own responsibilities, but with a national economy that did *not* function as a single unit. When the commissioners were completing their work, Dafoe was adamant that Macdonald's National Policy, and its elaboration by Liberal prime minister Wilfrid Laurier, remained the source of Canada's problems because it aimed to create an economic unit under federal predominance. Reviewing the final draft, Dafoe parried what he saw as a tendency of commission staff to revert to the view that Canada was "an economic unit." He railed about this point to Sandy Skelton, urging rhetorical changes to Book One on national economic policies. Where the Deutsch-Skelton draft suggested a certain coherence to the national policies of land settlement, railways and tariffs, Dafoe disagreed. "Canada, of course, is not an economic unit; was not one at the height of the effectiveness of the integrating policies; is now less than it then was an economic unit, and will go broke tomorrow if it is obliged to become an economic unit." Dafoe understood that the economic ties that bound Canadians were not and could not be tight enough to offset the geographical, economic, and political ties that defined the provincial and regional parts of the country.[73]

Dafoe's arguments were successful. The later chapters of Book One on "Contemporary Canada" and "Public Finance" each made clear that there was neither a unified economy nor a coordinated public finance system.

The efforts at creating a single national economy had been based upon, and indeed led to, irreconcilable "divergent interests" between the export staple industries and a "protected domestic economy." These divergent sectors were regional, and any "unifying effect" had declined in the 1920s and 1930s.[74] Rather than attempting national integration, Plan One addressed the uneven distribution of government revenues and the federal division of constitutional responsibility. The fiscal problem was easily understood. The regions "may be economically complementary, and the existence of each vital to the welfare of the others," but "a very large proportion of the surplus – and taxable – income of the country is concentrated in a few specially favoured areas."[75]

While there was little doubt that the commission would recommend Ottawa take responsibility for unemployment, there was disagreement over the recommendation's ultimate goal. As historian Nancy Christie points out, the issue of unemployment became "one of the most intensely debated issues during the Rowell-Sirois Commission." In his submission, the director of social research at McGill University and an expert on unemployment, Leonard Marsh, argued that unemployment insurance must preserve the independent character of the "working man." He opposed including graded children's allowances because they might raise the family's total income to such a level as to invalidate the principle of lesser eligibility. Marsh took the position that, "if unemployment insurance provided too generously for dependents, it might interfere with the 'modern' concept of the singular family wage." Unemployment insurance "was meant to help break down older concepts of the family – wherein the wife and children contributed to the household economy – by forcing all dependents to survive, with no extra allowances, on the unemployment benefits 'earned' by the male contributor alone."[76]

The leading civil servants, such as Graham Towers and Clifford Clark, viewed unemployment insurance and relief as a way to regulate the workplace and an offshoot of public works programs. In their minds, these policies had to be in the control of the federal government. The foremost advocates of unemployment insurance, however, such as Arthur Purvis, Harry Cassidy, Leonard Marsh, and Charlotte Whitton, advocated making the provinces the exclusive preserve of all old age assistance, mothers' allowances, and child welfare programs. From their point of view, if all public assistance was to be integrated at the provincial and local levels, it was imperative to demote unemployment assistance to a needs-based category beyond federal jurisdiction. The federal government was intended to deal with all rights-based programs. As Cassidy explained to Purvis, "when it comes to the administrative organization of the public assistance services, I am inclined to adopt the same position as the Welfare Council – that unemployment assistance can best be administered by the provinces and local authorities." From his point of view, unemployment assistance was closely related to other types of assistance, such as general poor relief, old age assistance, and mothers' pensions.[77]

The Purvis Commission had proposed a broad-based federal response to the unemployment crisis. The King government shelved it while remaining committed in principle to federal control over an insurance scheme. And while the recommendation in the Rowell-Sirois Commission was not surprising, it was a more restrained and carefully shaped program that proved to be acceptable to all the provinces.[78] In almost every case except unemployment insurance, provincial responsibility "should be deemed basic and general." Dominion involvement "should be deemed an exception to the general rule, and as such should be strictly defined."[79]

The treatment of social services pointed towards the Rowell-Sirois Report's innovative call for an emphasis on fiscal need rather than on equality. "Provincial need," the commissioners claimed, "has not hitherto been expressly recognized as a principle of federal assistance, but we think it should be." This "new principle," it was hoped, would "underlie Canadian federalism in the future." The commission sought to ensure a minimum level of social standards across all provinces. National unity would be jeopardized "if the citizens of distressed provinces come to feel that their interests are completely disregarded by those of their more prosperous neighbours, and that those who have been their full partners in better times now tell them they must get along as best they can and accept inferior education and social services."[80] By embracing a fiscal needs approach, the commission "rejected any further leveling out of past inequalities of Confederation" as well as the concept that "all provinces were merely being afforded equal treatment." The commissioners came to the conclusion that this notion of equality of treatment would only result in perpetuating in-equalities for Canadians, depending on where they happened to reside. Differential payments were necessary.[81]

The commission feared that an attempt to create uniformity of benefits would actually produce the opposite result. In Esdras Minville's background study on social welfare and labour legislation in Quebec, he warned that uniform national unemployment benefits would mean that people living in regions with higher living standards would "complain about insuffi-ciency" while those in other regions with lower standards would be "in-clined to settle down to relief." A.E. Grauer sustained the position in his study. He questioned whether, "if the Dominion had sole authority over old age pensions, it might find it impossible for political reasons to maintain the differences in regional costs of living." For example, British Columbia in the late 1930s "had no serious rival to its claim for pre-eminence among the provinces in social welfare." BC feared that uniform federal programs would have a levelling effect, which explained why the province insisted on retaining control over all social welfare areas except unemployment relief. Grauer's research was rooted in sustained comparisons between the countries of Western Europe, the Commonwealth countries, and Canada, which revealed Canada's comparatively weak policy record.[82]

According to the report, "the principle reason" that the federal gov-ernment had to expand its jurisdiction into unemployment lay in "the readiness of industry in one province to complain it is taxed for social services which are provided out of general taxation in other provinces or are not provided at all in other provinces." Employers would be "in a pos-ition of competitive disadvantage in comparison with employers in prov-inces where there are not contributory social services," not to mention the "hindrance" on the mobility of a labour force tied to benefits in one province.

This recommendation was not intended to strip the provinces of con-trol over social services. The prime example was the commission's argument that any programs of health insurance must remain in provincial hands. Federal involvement in health policy would be strictly defined and limited to research, statistics, and leadership in the cooperative establishment of national standards in technical areas. Despite the realization that it may result in inequalities of taxes on industry between provinces, "experience with provincial social welfare legislation in the past has been that once an important reform is instituted in one province, it has been widely adopted relatively quickly by others."[83]

The commissioners recognized that the constitutional division of powers and thus jurisdictional autonomy underlay justifications for provincial dominance in the health care field. The division of powers was not an insuperable barrier to the changing role of government. While the BNA Act did not expressly allocate jurisdiction in public health, preponderant provincial authority in the field was inferred. The report asserted that "provincial responsibilities in health matters should be considered basic and residual." In keeping with this vision, provincial authority would centre on the core of health services, including authority over direct patient and institutional care, health education, preventative medicine, public health research, and professional qualifications. The commission adopted a limited view of the federal bases of power in health care. It cited only two direct sources of federal authority through marine hospitals and quarantine.

When it came to health issues, dominion activities would be limited and considered "exceptions to the general rule of provincial responsibility." Most notably, the commission proposed that the federal government voluntarily forego the use of fiscal transfers if it meant constraining the provinces in meeting their specific circumstances. The commission thus signalled its preference for near absolute provincial authority over all significant aspects of the health care field: "Every province might be put in a fiscal position to determine its own policies and to finance its own services in accordance with its own particular needs." The sole qualification was that the provinces should have the fiscal capacity to meet the average level of Canadian services.[84]

The report did not recommend any change to the current scheme of old age pensions, in which the dominion contributed 75 percent of the outlay and the provinces provided 25 percent, as well as the costs of administration. While J.A. Corry later pointed out that the cooperative efforts between Ottawa and the provinces "left something to be desired," a dominion takeover of the scheme would be too cumbersome, and the emphasis on local conditions would be lost. If sole responsibility were given to the provinces, the tax burden would simply be too heavy.[85]

The Rowell-Sirois Report recommended that the provinces should retain all residuary responsibility for social welfare expenditures. "Mere importance of a service," the report noted, "does not justify its assumption by the dominion." While the commission approved limited federal government grants for universities (without strings), and possibly a national research granting agency, it insisted that educational jurisdiction and, in effect, funding must remain under the provinces despite dire need in recent years.[86] The goal was for every province to be able to provide social services on the standards set by the provinces in the "peak" years of 1923 to 1931. As with other social services, if provinces wished to provide a different level or kind of service, Ottawa would promise to respect those tax fields left to the provinces and to allow them to set their own priorities.

About one-third of the report dealt with less momentous matters that nonetheless had often been raised in the hearings. These included issues of "administrative economies," problems of governmental "overlap," as well as transportation and the "special claims" of provinces such as British Columbia and New Brunswick. The matters of administrative economies included the familiar and interminable "modern" complaint that government expenditures in general were wasteful. Ontario had made this charge against other governments, particularly the western provinces, but business presentations reiterated the complaint with tedious regularity. Members of the research team conducted a special survey of federal and provincial services and identified three areas of overlap: transportation, tax collection, and police service duplication between the Royal Canadian Mounted Police and three provincial police forces. In the end, however, the commission found that the problem of overlap was misconstrued. The report noted that even Ontario did not provide evidence for its charge about profligate or wasteful overlaps among the provinces.[87]

The area of transportation provided examples of how alleged overlaps were exaggerated. In Canada there had emerged an effective division between the dominion, with its focus on railways (which had led to disastrous waste in the past) and air transport, and the provinces, with their focus on roads and highways. The increase in highway transportation demonstrated how readily the two levels of government coordinated their policies in areas ranging from research to planning to projects. An "intimate and cordial co-operation between the governments" was essential and generally realized. While fiscal means for provinces could be improved through Plan One, no transfer of power in one direction or the other was needed.[88] Even the thorny issue of railway freight rates and the request of smaller provinces for enhanced federal regulatory authority did not convince the commissioners that greater federal power even in the management of railways would be beneficial to the regions or the country.[89] Effective planning and not constitutional change (the tenets of coordination not subordination) were the means to more efficient transportation policy.

A final matter was the "special claims" for fiscal compensation for past underfunding. This examination took up an entire section and forty pages of text in order to review provincial charges of broken "contractual agreements" or "prejudiced" effects. The commission examined the claims of British Columbia, Saskatchewan, and the Maritime provinces. The commissioners had not been impressed by these claims, particularly BC's interminable demands, and sought to avoid becoming a "court of review" for provincial fiscal claims.[90] Regardless, the report dutifully examined the record, acknowledging BC's thirteen previous presentations to Ottawa, including requests that a specific commission of inquiry examine the issue. The commission found that "provincial subsidies in general no longer rest[ed] on consistent principles."[91] There was no way for the commission to adjudicate the history of compensation claims, but, regardless, the report attempted to find ways out of the mess. BC's special claims were rejected, albeit with a revised grant for the period prior to 1930 due to a recalculation of the historical population base.[92] Similar claims from Saskatchewan, New Brunswick, and Prince Edward Island were also considered. They were rejected in light of the report's contention that not only was the commission not a court of revision but that there had been no proof that federal policy had "prejudiced the financial position" of a province. Moreover, all of these issues would become irrelevant if a system based on fiscal need was implemented.[93]

Book Two briefly discussed several issues raised in the hearings that the commissioners believed were not part of their terms of reference. Each bore on social policy realms. One area was women's civil rights in Quebec. While the solution to the issue was Quebec's prerogative, the commissioners felt the issue had to be highlighted. Issues dealing with French-language rights, pertaining to New Brunswick and other provinces with a "substantial"

French-speaking minority, also needed airing. A broad and sympathetic treatment of language rights was worth supporting, but there was no question that education remained a provincial matter. Other issues dealing with "fundamental political rights and liberties" were identified as important but left unexplored.[94]

No such concerns were even hinted at regarding Indigenous peoples. The nearly complete lack of attention to their issues within the realm of dominion-provincial relations provided glaring proof of Canada's governmental approach to this neglected population. It was one the commissioners shared. They had reviewed it in their own deliberations and decide that the subject could be dispensed with.[95] During the hearings, federal and provincial officials raised the matter only tangentially in regard to Indigenous health care. The commission reviewed the issue briefly, concentrating on dire chronic diseases, particularly tuberculosis, and the peculiar policy gap between Ottawa and the provinces into which Indigenous health care fell. But the report ignored the legal, governmental, and socio-economic status of the Indigenous population in Canada.[96]

The Rowell-Sirois Report gave a new interpretation to the history of Canadian federalism. Plan One attacked the economic problems of a country whose economy was not working at full output and a federal system that was not in tune with the constitutional or functional realities of modern government. The federal system had to change. The objectives of the commission included a new kind of relationship in the form of cooperative federalism, a new basis for public finance with the adoption of the income tax and collection at the federal level, and a renewed fiscal partnership in the form of unconditional grants and the adoption of the new positive state.[97]

The report's concluding remarks offered defences against two obvious lines of criticism. The first addressed the unfortunate timing of its release. The commissioners asserted that the release of the report during wartime made no difference to its arguments or conclusions and should not affect the urgency with which they must be addressed. Indeed, the broad goals of providing Canadians with effective services and opportunities were "far more urgent" than ever. The "gravity of the hour" only underlined this urgency.[98]

The second statement addressed the inevitable provincial concerns that the recommendations would threaten their autonomy. The report emphasized that the recommendations were aimed at strengthening the federal system. The measures would enhance the capacity of *both* levels of government to deliver the services contemporary governments must provide in the most effective manner. In this regard, "the Commission does not consider that its proposals are either centralizing or decentralizing in their combined effect, but believe that they will conduce to the sane balance between these two tendencies which is the essence of a genuine federal system." This "sane balance" was the "most secure" basis for "Canadian national unity."[99] With that comment, the problem was handed to the governments of Canada for resolution. Whether the report would have any impact, or even gain consideration, was now up to the provinces and the dominion.

10

Dark Days
1940–41

*The experts of the Rowell-Sirois Commission gave a detailed
blueprint of the kind of federal governmental structure which
was needed to bring Confederation up to date. A Roosevelt
would have taken up such ideas and presented them in a
dramatic, dynamic appeal to the people. All that Mr. King did
was to get into an interminable controversy with provincial
demagogues.*

– Frank Underhill, September 1944[1]

When the Sirois Report, as it was being called, was unveiled, the initial
press response was positive. A month after the release a digest of press
reports was prepared by the Bank of Canada. The survey found that the
report was reviewed by 160 news stories and editorials from 88 newspapers
across Canada. The vast majority were favourable.[2]

Most of the coverage copied the Canadian Press summary, which
emphasized two main recommendations: federal responsibility for unemployment relief and federal assumption of provincial debt. Taxation
issues were not delved into in any detail. But there was a distinctly regional
bent to the reports. The Maritime newspapers gave prominence to transportation questions and the proposed merger of appeal courts. The western
press, influenced by the *Winnipeg Free Press* chain, emphasized the expected
benefits to municipalities and focused mainly on the unemployment situation that had crippled the region. French-language papers in Quebec

First ministers at the Dominion-Provincial Conference of 1941.
Library and Archives Canada, 3362880

focused on the question of provincial autonomy versus centralization, including such issues as labour legislation and education. The "big" papers from Ontario, including the *Globe and Mail*, the *Toronto Star*, and the *Financial Post*, were positive and provided detailed examinations of the various fiscal recommendations. They applauded the commission for providing greater stability for provincial finances through central Canadian lenders. Both the *Globe* and the *Post* presented the report as a call for an increase in federal powers and highlighted the recommendations that moved in this direction while downplaying the fiscal balance called for by the commissioners.[3]

Editorials across the country were mostly positive. On the subject of national finances, there was more concern that the report would not do enough to check the restless spending of provincial governments and that these governments would lose revenues by shifting direct taxation powers to Ottawa. The fear was that the provinces would spend on a greater per capita scale and then seek to qualify for higher adjustment grants rather than balance their budgets. There was also significant concern over the report's awkward timing. Editorialists were skeptical about dealing with significant issues for Canadian federalism, possibly even resulting in constitutional reform, during wartime. As the *Ottawa Citizen* observed in an extended metaphor, "the captain of the ship of state has called the passengers and crew together to discuss proposed changes in the rules of the game of shuffleboard, while enemy forces are moving into action to torpedo the ship."[4]

The press was justified in raising the unfortunate timing. The war certainly shaped the impact and evaluation of the Rowell-Sirois Report. The spring and summer of 1940 were among the darkest days of the Second World War. Germany was rampaging through Europe. The battle for France raged through May and June, fracturing the French Republic and eviscerating its armed forces. Great Britain faced a German onslaught throughout the spring and summer – the evacuation at Dunkirk and the aerial Battle of Britain – that threatened to lead to an invasion of the British Isles. The *Financial Post* commented: "coinciding with the smash of Nazi legions into Holland and Belgium, the Rowell-Sirois report on Dominion-provincial relations has found few Canadians so unabsorbed by war as to attempt a comprehensive digest of its findings."[5] Not surprisingly, Ottawa was not quick to engage the provinces in discussions.

The reaction of the press was one thing, the response of the provincial governments was quite another. It was a difficult time for the King government, already facing severe criticism for its lacklustre "limited liability" war effort from the newspapers and the Opposition. "With German panzers at the Channel," the *Globe and Mail* reported, "Mitch broke his long post-election silence when King released the report of the Rowell-Sirois Commission." Speaking in Premier Hepburn's absence, on 16 May, Provincial Secretary Harry Nixon stated that the commission's findings should not be considered until after the war. A week later, Hepburn charged that the prime minister "deliberately withheld publication of the Sirois Report with no other purpose in mind but to draw people's attention away from the lack of war effort." King released the report, Hepburn claimed, "with the design of shielding the heads of a Government leading a defenseless people." The Ontario premier refused to attend any meeting to discuss Rowell-Sirois. He was, however, prepared to attend a meeting to discuss a united war effort to "save ourselves from what appears to be obvious destruction."[6] It was a moot point since Hepburn was seriously ill with bronchial pneumonia for most of the spring. "I don't often wish that a man should pass away," King noted in his diary, "but I believe that it would be the most fortunate thing that could happen at this time."[7]

Other premiers were more positive. Thane Campbell of Prince Edward Island described the report as "comprehensive" and indicated that it required detailed study by the provinces. Angus Macdonald of Nova Scotia noted that he was "pleased" with the report. The premiers of New Brunswick, Alberta, and Quebec declined to comment until further study was possible. William Patterson of Saskatchewan considered the report "the most outstanding event in the constitutional development of the Dominion since Confederation." Duff Pattullo of British Columbia was notably less enthusiastic and argued that, if the main recommendations were accepted, his province would be forced to forego expanding certain sources of revenue in return for temporary savings. Fiscal cooperation between the provinces and the federal government was critical, Pattullo warned, but "if the views expressed in the Rowell-Sirois Report are carried out, Ottawa and not Victoria will indicate the extent and nature of that co-operation."[8]

The main supporter of Rowell-Sirois, Manitoba's John Bracken, urged the prime minister to call a conference immediately to discuss the report. He had waited impatiently for its release and had postponed the start of the 1940 legislative session in Manitoba in the hope of using it as a springboard to action. Bracken was convinced that Rowell-Sirois validated Manitoba's position. But when he called for an early conference, Mackenzie King responded to one of Bracken's strong letters of support and requests for its implementation by remarking that the federal government could not "touch" the report until the war was less perilous: "Until we had discussed the peace, we could not touch this local situation."[9] With the war in progress, "it would certainly be felt by many that the government should await developments before seeking to bring the provinces as a whole into conference with the Dominion on matters so all-important as those dealt with in the Commission's report."[10]

The Manitoba government had dug in with its support. In a speech in Winnipeg shortly after the report was published, provincial treasurer Stuart Garson echoed Dafoe's line that the commission was in fact "restoring, under the conditions of today, the intended substance of the financial plan created by the Fathers of Confederation in 1867." Like the founders, the commissioners, whom Garson dubbed "The Fathers of Reconfederation," recommended that the dominion take over the debts of the provinces. They recommended that Ottawa take over the chief taxing power. Whereas in 1867 this power consisted of the customs and excise duties, nowadays it was the personal income tax, corporation tax, and succession duties. The commissioners dealt with the issue of subsidies from the dominion to the provinces not on the basis of population, which would now be inadequate and inefficient, but on the basis of fiscal need. The recommendations, Garson noted, seemed almost too good to be true. But opposition would come from the affluent provinces, which would not presently receive adjustment grants. Garson feared that the nuances of the recommendations would be lost amidst a short-sighted, knee-jerk reaction against federal intrusions into provincial jurisdiction: "We must face frankly the possibility of opposition to this report upon the ground that it proposes to take away from provincial autonomy. So far as the Manitoba Government is concerned, it is prepared to affirm in the most positive terms that the carrying out of this report would increase rather than diminish provincial autonomy." The report, Garson trumpeted, "is Canada's financial Magna Carta." It would be a "profound tragedy" if its recommendations were not implemented.[11]

The economic dimensions of the war only added to the immediacy of the issues and the relevance of the Rowell-Sirois recommendations. Both the Department of Finance and the Bank of Canada pushed for engagement with the growing problems of taxation and expenditure. The budget of June 1940, delivered after J.L. Ralston replaced Charles Dunning as finance minister, called for major tax increases. Even though the majority of the budget was written prior to the fall of France, the dire situation was used to highlight the need for extra expenditures.[12] The objective was to use the "wisest financial methods of paying for the maximum effort which is physically possible." This would not simply mean extracting additional money from the economy but, rather, "producing soundly the maximum possible increase in our national income in the shortest possible time" and ensuring that the increase went directly to war purposes. "I come to you," Ralston announced in the budget speech, "to collect part of the price to which I have referred."[13] On a positive note, the economy had grown more than expected. More than 100,000 idle wage earners were drawn into employment in the twelve months prior to April 1940 and national income grew from $3.8 billion in 1939 to $4.5 billion for the fiscal year 1940–41.[14] But the government still needed more revenue, so a new excess profits tax was introduced. Average Canadians, however, would not escape. The budget opted for increases in income taxes rather than sales taxes because the former "approximates ability to pay."[15]

On 10 June, the crash of an Ottawa to Toronto airplane flight claimed the life of Norman Rogers, the defence minister. His death led to a cabinet shuffle. Ralston was moved from finance to defence, and the minister of revenue, James L. Ilsley, was promoted (reluctantly on Mackenzie King's part) to finance. Premier Angus Macdonald was persuaded to leave Nova Scotia, accept a federal cabinet post, and run in Rogers's seat of Kingston, Ontario. The changes also coincided with increased governmental legislative action. Rogers's fight for unemployment insurance while minister of labour found posthumous success. The bill to create unemployment insurance was introduced in mid-July, just four days after the amendment to the BNA Act was approved to transfer jurisdiction to the federal government.[16]

Clifford Clark and Bill Mackintosh, working together in finance, wanted the bill passed as quickly as possible because it would have a significant and immediate wartime benefit. Premiums would be paid to the federal government at a time when low unemployment meant few benefits would be paid out. The funds could then be redirected towards war production. The act was given royal assent on 7 August.[17] The King government also created the Unemployment Insurance Commission to administer the fund. The chief commissioner, appointed on 23 September, was Joseph Sirois.[18]

The establishment of a federal system of unemployment insurance dealt with a key recommendation of the Rowell-Sirois Commission. With this piece of the puzzle in place, the fiscal situation of the provinces began to appear more manageable, and with the war dominating public discourse, the specific pressure to implement the report's wholesale reforms diminished. Henry Angus thought so. "It is almost certain," he wrote, "that if the Commission's report is shelved until after the war, its recommendations may never receive proper consideration."[19] But Towers's influence at the Bank of Canada and Ilsley's ministerial lead in finance gave renewed impetus for fiscal change and possibly consideration of the report. Ilsley was a much more insightful finance minister than most of his predecessors. He understood the difficult fiscal situation, had a clear understanding of the issues of equity and efficiency in taxation, and grasped the economic arguments put to him by the senior officials in finance.[20]

In the summer of 1940, the finance department and the Bank of Canada made a serious push to build support for Rowell-Sirois. Towers held numerous meetings with provincial representatives, bankers, and investment dealers concerned with the continuing issue of debt refinancing.[21] Ilsley met with representatives of Canadian banks, and insurance and investment companies, who had put up substantial sums of money to avert provincial defaults while the commission was under way.[22]

The dual problems of provincial financial vulnerability and national war finance led the Bank of Canada to take the lead in support of the report. Sandy Skelton argued that only some form of major fiscal reform would resolve the problems of wartime finance. He focused particularly on the proposals for federal control of personal and corporate income taxes, and succession duties (which in 1939 had produced only $30 million in revenue for the provinces).[23] "In addition to being a necessary step to make the maximum war effort," Skelton noted, "it has constructive and lasting value for post-war difficulties. It need not be presented as war legislation, but it should have a very wide appeal to the many Canadians who are eager to see Canada brush aside petty sectional differences and selfish local interests which weaken her in the present emergency." Skelton concluded that the "need for implementing the Report [was] immeasurably greater than it was when the Report was written."[24]

Well supplied with evidence, Towers reiterated Skelton's arguments in a memo to Ilsley: "The need for developing an efficient taxation system which will yield the maximum of revenue with the least possible burden on the national income was never more urgent."[25] Like Sandy Skelton, Towers worried about "provinces and municipalities defaulting on their securities." In a meeting with the prime minister, Towers urged that the fiscal conundrum be dealt with "along the Sirois Report lines." Mackenzie King continued to express hope that the report could be left until after the war, but he was beginning to give ground to his advisors.[26]

In mid-August, Towers again pressed for not just consideration but adoption of Rowell-Sirois to resolve the problems of provincial government revenues. In a lengthy letter to the prime minister, he explained that a cascade of provincial defaults was possible. Alberta had again defaulted on its debts and that the other three western provinces and two of the Maritime provinces faced difficulty meeting interest payments. It was similar to the conditions that had led to the creation of the royal commission back in 1937, only worse. The provinces could not be allowed to default during wartime. Unless the fiscal recommendations as outlined in Plan One were adopted, Saskatchewan and New Brunswick would now face default. If New Brunswick defaulted, Nova Scotia would likely be unable to refund its debts and would also default. "It is hard to say how far the trouble would spread," Towers warned, "but I think it is safe to say that the repercussions would be very serious, and likely to have a bad effect on Dominion credit and the Dominion's war financing."[27]

Towers restated the "urgent" need for a reallocation of tax fields. The serious pre-war problem was only made worse by the war. Federal taxes had risen sharply during the war, but five provinces also increased their income or corporation taxes. The situation of tax inefficiency and ineffectiveness about which the Sirois Report warned was getting worse. An efficient tax system would be essential as taxes increased even more acutely during wartime than during peacetime. Towers agreed with finance officials that the federal unemployment insurance scheme was insufficient to repair Ottawa's revenue problems. Only one-quarter of the unemployed would be covered by unemployment insurance in the expected unemployment surge of the postwar period, and if Ottawa tried to insist that responsibility lay with the provinces or municipalities as it had in the past, workers would demonstrate even deeper resentment than they displayed during the Depression: "In the interests of peace, order and good government the Dominion may well have to assume full responsibility. But if it does so without having made other arrangements along the lines contemplated in the Sirois Report, the financial situation will be chaotic."[28]

Finally, Towers posed a rhetorical question: "If this were understood by the public, might not an effort to deal with the Report receive popular support; and, so far as the provinces are concerned, might action not be represented as the first constructive piece of work which the provinces could do on the home front?" He concluded that implementation of the report could not wait for peacetime: "In fact ... the necessity for solving the problems under discussion is rendered more acute by reasons of the war and inevitable post-war readjustments."[29]

By early September, it was clear to the senior bureaucrats in the King government that there were three possible moves: postpone action until after the war; call an immediate dominion-provincial conference; or implement the report's essential recommendations as war measures subject to a promise to hold a conference after the war.[30] The first option was viewed as unrealistic, so there were really two choices. The prime minister agreed to the creation of a special cabinet committee on dominion-provincial relations, headed by Ilsley, to chart a course for considering and possibly adopting the leading recommendations. King wanted Joseph Sirois on the committee. The veteran member of Parliament T.A. Crerar was also a member, providing Dafoe and Bracken with an ally.[31]

On 20 September, the Special Cabinet Committee on Dominion-Provincial Relations held an all-day meeting with officials in finance and the Bank of Canada. The morning session was spent discussing whether an attempt should be made to implement the recommendations and, if so, by what means. Federal officials realized that immediate action would help finance the war through the suggested transfer of taxes. It would help solve the problem of provinces facing default. At the same time, implementation could be pitched to the public as a wartime appeal for national unity as well as an opportunity to eliminate waste and inefficiency in the tax system at a time when the tax burden was becoming increasingly heavy and unpopular. Issues of foreign exchange would likely increase financial pressure on the dominion while, at the same time, gasoline rationing would further limit the fiscal capacity of the provinces.[32]

The committee realized that the federal government would be in a weaker position to bargain in the postwar period, once the appeal of wartime emergency had lifted. It also realized, however, that the same arguments would be used against implementation. Opponents would argue that the immediate and paramount problem was to fight the war and that any distractions and possible disturbances to the existing financial machinery were irresponsible and dangerous. The committee decided that the finance minister should approach each of the provinces to see how willing they were to implement the Rowell-Sirois Report. Ilsley was authorized to be firm with the reluctant provinces, warning them that if no action were taken, succession duties and corporation taxes would increase, as would liquor and gasoline rationing, thereby reducing provincial revenues regardless.[33]

Provincial reactions were fluid and varied from open support to grudging acceptance and outright rejection. According to *Winnipeg Free Press* parliamentary report, Grant Dexter, the proposal was offered to the three Maritime provinces "and all of them agreed to it – New Brunswick being very enthusiastic." The Liberal government in Quebec was "undecided but not aggressively antagonistic ... the inference [was] that if the rest of the provinces agree[d], Quebec [would] accept and make no trouble." The three Prairie provinces, even Alberta, would "fall in line" based on the lure of larger subsidies. The "uncertain provinces" were Ontario and British Columbia: "If Mitch should agree, the policy would be adopted regardless of B.C.'s attitude." Ilsley was "swinging quite a club in these conversations," Dexter noted. "He is pointing out that the pressure of the war must drive the Dominion into acts which cannot but affect the finances of the provinces." Ottawa might have to reduce unessential imports from the United States and ration the use of gasoline. This move would "go to the length of driving traffic off the roads and onto the rails. Such a policy would wreck the finances of Ontario." Any plans for Ontario's acceptance, however, depended upon a measured reaction from the Hepburn government.[34]

John Bracken was disappointed by the delay in considering the Rowell-Sirois recommendations. On 18 October, the Manitoba premier wrote a long letter to the prime minister in which he outlined the urgent need for a dominion-provincial conference. Bracken began by urging the federal government not to implement the proposals piecemeal, as he believed the Speech from the Throne hinted. He quoted the report in his justification: "We plead most earnestly that our proposals should not be considered one by one in isolation ... we have attempted to integrate them in a comprehensive plan of a constructive character, dependent for its harmony on the observance of the general principles which we have set out." Bracken argued that early implementation was a significant step towards "sound" wartime finance. Without it, "post-war complications may be almost as disastrous to the nation as the conflict itself." The present federal system had been "obsolete for at least the past twenty-two years." To expect it to stand the strain of the war as well as the postwar era was naïve at best: "Certainly if as a nation we cannot summon up sufficient energy and unity to implement this Report in order to face the awful emergencies of the war and its aftermath, how much less reason shall we have for such energy and unity for the same purpose in peacetime?" The recommendations were "framed to meet the exigencies not only of peace but of war."[35] But the premier was losing hope. Ottawa's delay contributed to Bracken's move to form a non-partisan coalition government in Manitoba and, in the words of Bracken's biographer John Kendle, to "give up" on the King Liberals "as a vehicle for change and action."[36]

Ontario's response was the most rebarbative. Premier Hepburn had gone through a brief period of self-reflection after his springtime illness, resulting in a seemingly less hostile attitude towards the King government, but this apparent shift in attitude worried federal officials. "'Mitch is friendly,' one hears on all sides," Norman Lambert informed the prime minister: "'He wants to heal the breach,' they say, but it should not lull the federal Government into a sense of security."[37] When the Rowell-Sirois Report was first released, acting premier Harry Nixon told a reporter: "My advice at this time is to concentrate all our energies on winning the war. We will debate these matters afterwards." An "unidentified treasury official" indicated that "there isn't a chance in the world of the Ontario government accepting the recommendations." Ottawa had little choice but to await Hepburn's official response. Grant Dexter predicted that it would be negative but hoped that the King government had "Mitch in the hole on this issue and [that] the logic of circumstances [would] be enough to force him to yield." As the financial burdens of the war increased, and Ottawa imposed heavier taxes through the War Measures Act, the public would likely punish any province that attempted to increase this burden further.[38]

On 21 October, Ilsley and his aides met with an Ontario delegation consisting of Premier Hepburn, Provincial Secretary Harry Nixon, Minister of Highways T.B. McQuesten, and Deputy Treasurer Chester Walters. Dexter gleaned from his Ottawa sources that the federal officials were disappointed with the results: "Mitch had been friendly but was absolutely and immovably opposed to Dominion action on the report. Sandy [Skelton] gathered that this would be the finish of it. He was down in the mouth," as was T.A. Crerar. While the Ontario premier admitted to not being "familiar with the findings," he was convinced "the commission had been biased, unfair, out to get Ontario." He was annoyed that the formula for the federal assumption of provincial debts favoured Quebec. Hepburn kept harping on one particular point, Crerar noted. The issue was a

> provision to lump municipal and provincial debt together in the take-over. This was grossly unfair to Ontario, whose municipalities had been thrifty and careful. Quebec municipalities had been spendthrift and reckless, and now this commission proposed to pull these Quebec municipalities out of the hole at the expense of the Dominion taxpayers, the bulk of whom were in Ontario ... He wanted peace and goodwill with Ottawa but on this issue he would fight – to the limit.[39]

This was fair comment and, while the Ontario response was rooted in the Hepburn-King feud, some of it was based on genuine policy differences. A study from the Ontario Department of Health explained one such point. The Sirois Report had found that most provincial health services were "inadequate" and advised formula funding for services. This approach would tend to curtail the present public health services in Ontario or at best to fix them at their present standard." Further improvements in provincial health services would be "inhibited by the necessity for conforming to the pace maintained by the less progressive provinces, or such improvements [would] be implemented by paying for them out of additional provincial taxation." There was some truth to the criticism that the commission was leaving health as a provincial responsibility while stripping the provinces of their ability to raise revenue through taxation or independent capital borrowing.[40]

Ilsley reported on the meeting to cabinet. Ernest Lapointe was critical of Ontario's stance as well as of the government "hotheads" who, he argued, were "carrying the issue to Hepburn." Lapointe argued that the proper course was to "maintain pressure on Hepburn and hope that he would not put himself on the record as opposed to the adoption of the report."[41] King read the letter from Bracken urging a conference, but the prime minister argued that Hepburn's opposition killed that idea. King claimed that the report would never be accepted "till Hepburn and in all probability his government along with him would be removed." If there was any possibility of agreement at a conference, the prime minister asserted, he would arrange one forthwith. Hepburn's response, however, made this highly unlikely.[42]

British Columbia, meanwhile, was opposed for other reasons. Premier Pattullo had previously proclaimed that, next to the war, the Sirois Commission was the most important matter facing the country. Now he argued that the report was based on a temporary situation and failed to understand the province's fiscal condition. British Columbia's fiscal well-being was tied to natural resources and they were not inexhaustible. Pattullo echoed his expert advisors in concluding that the Rowell-Sirois Report was not analytically sound, that it had provided a limited estimation of provincial fiscal need, and that it was fundamentally centralist.[43]

Pattullo issued a statement indicating that his government would have to study the report further. Ilsley phoned the premier requesting that he or a representative come to Ottawa immediately. Pattullo refused, claiming that he would not be rushed on such a crucial matter. "Some eastern interests," he replied, "such as the *Financial Post* of Toronto, seem desirous of pushing this matter to an immediate conclusion. Any time that the *Financial Post* of Toronto makes a recommendation, suspicion is at once created." The premier's obstructive attitude was harshly criticized in the provincial press.[44]

Studies done by the BC government argued that the calculation of taxation capacity was not compatible with the fiscal burdens on the province in such areas as social welfare and education. The report had not paid sufficient heed to BC's longstanding complaints of inadequate federal grants and the federal tariff burden. In addition, there were serious questions about the treatment of the "unemployable" (which would remain a provincial responsibility), about the negotiations of the "adjustment grant" (which was a low standard for calculating the national minimum), and about the authority of the province to negotiate loans (which, if they were not approved by Ottawa, would still count as part of the financial need when applying for an adjustment grant).[45]

The federal Department of Finance, meanwhile, had its gaze fixed on provincial tax realms. As far as Clifford Clark was concerned, the cabinet was painfully slow in recognizing the need for Ottawa to take over these areas. After a conversation with Sandy Skelton on 25 October, Dexter reported that the

> Cabinet, as a whole, are very complacent about war finance and general prospects economically – for reasons which nobody who is aware of the situation can understand. But the odd minister is becoming a little alarmed and Ilsley, under the constant prodding of Clark, Towers and the other experts, is beginning to see that if sound financial measures are to be taken, the Dominion must greatly enlarge its field of taxation and impose new taxation upon a scale which might well embarrass the provincial governments. That, of course, is putting it mildly.[46]

In effect, the finance department had worked out a "temporary" way of adopting the report. It was a scheme to manipulate its recommendations to the benefits of the federal government. The dominion could "shoulder the full burden of provincial debt during the war" and offer "larger grants than those outlined in the report of the commission" in return for being allowed to "invade" provincial taxation fields. In other words, a piecemeal approach to the report could be taken to entice the provinces with more money while the most advantageous recommendations for the federal government were adopted.[47]

The Bank of Canada joined the Department of Finance in an all-out push for the report. Ilsley assured "Sandy and the boys" that he was "fighting like hell for the report."[48] And the pressure was clearly working. Mackenzie King was worried about the wartime financial situation and, in particular, the tax burden placed upon the populace. He looked for other means to increase federal revenues. The prime minister argued in the Cabinet War Committee: "we must be careful to view the war as one likely to last three or four years and not get the country in a position where there will be a financial panic or collapse before the war is over." Clark was invited to a meeting of the War Committee to discuss financing on 24 October. The deputy minister reassured those present that national income was expanding and that Canada had the financial capacity to handle the increasing burden. King was relieved by Clark's assurances.[49] The conclusion was that the Sirois Report should be implemented: "The Dominion's share of the amount which may safely be diverted from ordinary consumption must be much greater, and the provinces and municipalities will have to yield still further. The only rational way of solving this problem is via the report."[50]

The issue of a dominion-provincial conference was debated throughout the autumn. King and most of the cabinet resisted. But the special committee formed to recommend strategy on Rowell-Sirois persevered. Led by Ilsley, the committee was unanimously in favour of arranging a conference to implement the major provisions.[51] The Ontario government might oppose adoption, but a conference would provide the opportunity for the federal government to take the lead and present "the national point of view." Buoyed by a survey of newspaper editorials, the committee was confident that public opinion would be on Ottawa's side.[52] Ilsley and Clark, as well as Towers and Skelton, were convinced that such a gathering was essential before any further action could be taken: "They believed that properly presented, the proposed fiscal changes would be well received as war measures, even in Ontario. They preferred to risk a confrontation with Mitchell Hepburn, and in view of the dire warnings of the financial experts about the need for speedy action, their views eventually carried the day."[53]

On 25 October, the committee officially recommended a dominion-provincial conference and, within a week, the cabinet fell in line. In November 1940, the cabinet established a new committee to organize the conference, consisting of O.D. Skelton, Graham Towers, W.A. Mackintosh, F.P. Varcoe (deputy minister of justice), and Joseph Sirois (now chief unemployment insurance commissioner).[54] Sirois soon withdrew due to failing health.

Grant Dexter's evaluation from Parliament Hill was guardedly optimistic. He informed his "chief," John Dafoe, that "the battle will now centre on the nature of the conference and the generalship which King shows." Towers and Skelton believed that, "unless King handle[d] the conference right, the report [might] become bogged in a morass of petty demands for revision." The prime minister seemed

inclined to let the conference proceed to a general discussion to be followed by a decision on the report. If this is done, the boys feel that many
of the premiers will want this or the other recommendation modified
and Mitch will pick up allies all along the line. But if King asks for a
decision on the principle at the outset and says that differences of detail
can be ironed out afterwards, they think Mitch will shrink from revolt.
He would almost certainly be isolated.[55]

The official letter inviting the premiers to a conference was careful in
both message and tone.[56] It proposed "consideration" of the report and
argued that its major recommendations were more relevant than ever
due to the wartime situation, but it did not threaten unilateral action. In
a draft letter King pencilled out the declaration that his government was
"wholly in favour of the Report" and substituted the more ambiguous
phrase: "The Report commends itself strongly to our judgment." But the
prime minister did call for "no time to be lost ... in order to secure, if
possible, the adoption of the Commission's recommendations." While
King pointed to the Depression as creating a financial situation in which
the traditional structure of federalism could no longer function, he claimed
that "the war has intensified the problem and emphasized the urgency of
its solution. While the cost of unemployment relief has been reduced, the
war has cast additional burdens on government and tax payers alike."
Competition between governments for tax revenues had increased. "If this
situation continues," King observed, "the war effort itself will inevitably
be hampered." The prime minister linked the patriotic call of wartime
necessity with the need to ensure postwar well-being. "We must think first
of winning the war, but we cannot afford to neglect the future."[57]

The cabinet discussed the upcoming conference on 13 December.
Despite the decision to move ahead, all members except Crerar expressed
the view that it would "amount to nothing." Even Ilsley was defeatist and
hoped at best that the gathering would last three days thereby allowing the
provinces to state their positions before it broke up "without too great
friction." According to the prime minister,

we would have to construct a mattress that would make it easy for the
trapeze performers as they dropped to the ground one by one. I have

never believed that the conference could succeed at this time of war. Were the government not to make the attempt, it would be blamed for whatever financial disasters will follow, as it certainly will, in the course of the next year or two.[58]

Even the bureaucrats expected the conference to fail. Sandy Skelton was "almost without hope of real achievement." According to Grant Dexter, Skelton no longer believed that "the pen is mightier than the sword and would [have] like[d] nothing better than an assignment to strangle Mitch with his bare hands." Crerar was trying to "get King to screw his courage up to the fighting point." Crerar "would [have gone] so far as to have a general election on the issue. But King [would] not do anything of this nature. He [would] speak bravely for the report on the opening day but if the provinces [wouldn't] have it, the conference [would] be adjourned and he [would] use the taxation method of skinning the cat."[59]

Despite the spirit of resignation, preparations for the conference continued. The planning committee recommended that the conference open with a public session that would include general reactions to the report. It would then divide into working committees, including finance, unemployment, special problems, and the Constitution. Following the completion of these deliberations, the conference would reassemble to consider methods of implementation.[60]

In early January 1941, Mackenzie King turned his full attention to the conference. He read articles summarizing the commission's work by Dafoe and Fowler, which he described as "excellent."[61] As usual, the prime minister was critical of the preparations by those around him. Only a couple of his ministers, King groused, "seem to have concerned himself in the least either reading up for the conference or its arrangements. The latter fell back again on my office."[62] When King began to draft his opening speech, he wanted to strike a diplomatic tone, "conciliatory, not dogmatic nor dictatorial or threatening but placing as largely as possible responsibility on the provinces themselves for method of proceeding." He reminded cabinet that Hepburn and the other dissenters would be seeking "an opening to make a stage play." The tactic, King argued, would be "to draw all to make a very sympathetic approach to the provinces; get them in conference in [the]

"Strike of the Three Wreckers" – editorial cartoon, 17 January 1941.
Winnipeg Free Press

right mood, and then allow developments to shape themselves as might be inevitable, but certainly to do nothing that would prejudice the larger task for future years." Nova Scotia's Angus Macdonald was now in the federal cabinet as minister of naval services. As a supporter of Rowell-Sirois, he was, King noted, "a great help in presenting the position." But that was only within cabinet. Macdonald, who might have been a valuable emissary to the premiers, was held in the background.

Material prepared by Clifford Clark, O.D. Skelton, and Sandy Skelton was submitted to the prime minister for inclusion in his opening speech. King was annoyed by the lack of flexibility: "It went the length of insisting upon the whole financial scheme being accepted in the form in which it is, and protesting against any kind of modification or any attitude of approach which suggested changes." Federal officials in finance outlined the arguments for using taxation rather than inflation or borrowing to pay for the war. The strategy was to use the war as the pretext for having the provinces acquiesce, but if they refused, the dominion would take the required taxes regardless. "There might have been grounds," historian J.L. Granatstein adjudged, "for thinking that the bureaucracy was using the war as a spur towards fiscal centralization."[63] King criticized the bureaucrats' approach as "entirely the wrong way to go about affecting that end" and again called for a "conciliatory approach." If the federal government adopted a "take it or leave it attitude, that attitude would be blamed for the failure of the conference." The pressure from federal financial interests "to have their own way [was] the greatest danger the conference face[d]." The Department of Finance and the Bank of Canada were right in holding to "sound money methods in time of war," but the "velvet glove" was necessary at present. "There is nothing that Hepburn and Aberhart would like better," King noted,

> than for the Federal Government and myself in particular to take an arbitrary and dictatorial position. Hepburn would run his provincial campaign on the effort of Ottawa to take from Ontario all its powers, privileges, rights, to sacrifice them to Quebec or the Prairies. There never was a conference which required more in the way of tact, and the avoidance of certain attitudes than the forthcoming one.[64]

As the conference approached, the prime minister began to think that something substantial could be achieved. "I am a little more hopeful tonight than I have been thus far of getting somewhere with the conference," mused King. He hoped that a "true foundation" had been laid that could be built upon in the future:

> In my thoughts, as I dictate, I think of how strange it is that I should be taking the part I am in this particular conference which aims at the strengthening of Confederation by maintaining our national unity on the recognition of Responsible Government in all its applications. Surely a prayer of early life has been answered that I might help to carry on the work which my grandfather and those associated with him began. Somewhere, surely, he and Sir Wilfrid will be conscious of this fruit of his effort.

King's political calculations were less ethereal: "It will serve the advantage of enabling our government to state clearly the financial problem as it presents itself to the government at this time of war. It will lay the ground for such action as may shortly become imperative, and it should help to advance the necessary reforms by at least a step." If the provinces resisted, the prime minister realized the conference could still achieve the desired result of justifying an expansion of federal taxation.[65]

Back to his editorial duties in Winnipeg, J.W. Dafoe was uneasy about the fate of the report. Even amidst war, governments were playing politics. Dafoe was delighted that the King administration had called a conference to discuss the report, but he doubted whether it had the courage to make fiscal reform an election issue. Writing in the *Winnipeg Free Press* on 9 November, Dafoe had expressed hope that the broad principles of the report would at least be accepted. He warned that "the Report of the Commission and the attendant studies have made it clear to all that our existing Federal system is no longer adequate to the requirements of Canada; and that to persist in retaining it intact will be to invite disaster and perhaps to make disaster inevitable."[66] Robert Fowler, ensconced at the Wartime Prices and Trade Board, warned Dafoe that cabinet ministers and senior bureaucrats were at times defeatist about the Rowell-Sirois Report. Henry Angus had returned to the University of British Columbia. On the eve of the conference, he noted that their report was no longer criticized for "recommending greater centralization."[67]

Premier Hepburn agreed to attend the conference, but his formal confirmation repeated the argument that the issues should be postponed so as not to impair national unity and the effective prosecution of the war. While awaiting the conference, "he maintained an uncharacteristic silence on the subject of dominion-provincial relations, although this did not indicate any change of heart." From Ontario's perspective, the federal government was using "extensive propaganda" to push the report: "Members of Parliament and Senators were being button-holed in the streets urging that the report be adopted."[68] Hepburn told C.G. Power that he was coming to Ottawa "with blood in [his] eye and dandruff in [his] mustache," adding, "but of course that's the way you expect me."[69] Ominously, he met with Pattullo and Aberhart upon their arrival in Ottawa to discuss strategy.[70]

Pattullo had been irked when he received the final agenda a few days prior to meeting with the prime minister in Ottawa. In his reply to King accepting the invitation to the Conference, he raised a number of concerns. He was annoyed that the conference would focus only on the Rowell-Sirois Commission.[71] Pattullo reiterated the core of BC's objections: "So far as our Province is concerned, we will be in such a position of incapability to move forward or even to maintain existing standards, as will assuredly lead to grave dissatisfaction and friction. Herein I think the Commission erred in its approach to the problem." The BC premier dismissed the notion that the regions of Canada could be made more equal: "Each of these units is distinctive and there is nothing to be gained and much to be lost in attempting to bring them to a common level ... The tendency of the course recommended by the Commission would be to lower the general standard of development rather than to raise it. It would be a backward instead of a forward step." Pattullo rejected the idea of a federal commission overseeing the estimation and distribution of the National Adjustment Grants. It was based on "the assumption that the Provinces must be curbed, and checked after curbing, and that the central authority is the medium through which this is to be accomplished." He concluded that the real intent of Plan One was to "exercise a measure of control over provincial operations."[72]

Whether right or wrong, this argument had to be met. As usual Pattullo craved attention from the prime minister and got it in this instance. King hosted Pattullo for dinner at the Chateau Laurier a few days before the conference. King did not change the premier's mind. "He is opposing the Commission's recommendations," King noted, "but will try to be helpful in as many directions as possible."[73]

A week before the conference opened, a throne speech was delivered in Quebec. The speech not only referred to the upcoming gathering and promised the full cooperation of Quebec towards a more harmonious federalism but also emphasized the "integral conservation of provincial autonomy." Opposition leader Maurice Duplessis was having none of it. He demanded the correspondence between Liberal premier Godbout and the federal government dealing with the report. The royal commission received a rough ride in the Quebec National Assembly. Speakers almost unanimously argued against any surrender of provincial prerogatives.

Duplessis described the report as "an attempt to drain away the source of the life of the province."[74] Against this fulmination, the most powerful Quebec federal cabinet minister, Ernest Lapointe, argued that the report was entirely in Quebec's interest. When Quebec Liberal senator L.M. Gouin wrote to point out the widespread hostility in the province to its main recommendations, Lapointe countered that 99 percent of the opponents were not conversant with the details and likely had not even read it. Moreover, "loin d'avoir ete fait pour nuire aux provinces et detruire leur autonomie, a eu pour objet d'assurer leur survivance en leur permettant de trouver les moyens de rencontror leur obligations. D'ailleurs, la Commission a eu un soin jaloux de voir a ce que tous les droits des provinces soient respectes."[75] Lapointe had moved some distance over the years of waiting.

Amidst this uncertain atmosphere, the Dominion-Provincial Conference of 1941 opened at 10:30 a.m. on 14 January in the House of Commons chamber. The federal government went to considerable lengths to provide a grandiose atmosphere. Crerar described the opening scene to Dafoe:

> It was decided ... to surround the Conference with all the dignity possible, especially in its opening session ... with all the members of the Federal Government who were in Ottawa and with the Provincial delegates and their advisors on the floor of the chamber. In addition, many Members of Parliament were present. The result was that practically every seat in the House of Commons was occupied. The general public had the galleries. In this setting, the Prime Minister sat at the head of the Clerk's Table and the nine premiers were seated around it in order of their precedence.[76]

Prime Minister Mackenzie King began by defending the decision to call the conference in wartime due to the urgent need to readjust the federal fiscal relationship. The Rowell-Sirois Commission provided a study not just of the problems of the federal government but of "the federal system." The report, he argued, was more important now than ever. These problems would continue to loom over the country regardless of the war and its outcome. King warned that "the sooner the pressing financial problems were settled the better for fighting the war and coping with post-war problems." He pointed out that "we do not approach the conference with our minds closed. We do not say 'all or nothing' or 'everything at once.'" The changes proposed by the royal commission, he concluded, did not require major constitutional changes, nor did they amount to increased centralization or endanger provincial autonomy. Instead, the report aimed at "rescuing autonomy from the perils of confused and overlapping jurisdictions, and making clear definitions between the functions of the federal and provincial governments." Certain regions would make more immediate gains, but all the provinces would enjoy fiscal benefits in the long term.[77]

Mitch Hepburn spoke immediately after King. Several observers noted that "Mitch seemed not to listen as King spoke, and did not join in the polite applause."[78] Instead, the Ontario premier delivered a speech full of the hyperbolic verbiage that so often distracted audiences from the substantive policy arguments: "Ontario was as unalterably opposed to the commission's recommendations as ever." The premier claimed that he had never publicly criticized the report. He was, however, critical of the timing of its consideration. Federal finance minister Ilsley had come to Toronto to discuss the advisability of implementing the recommendations and, at that time, Hepburn had "almost begged him to use his influence to prevent this becoming a national issue during wartime." But Mackenzie King, as usual, ignored his pleadings. Hepburn again complained about the lack of Ontario representation on the commission after Rowell's withdrawal and noted that the report should be omitted altogether from discussions. He mocked it as the "five hundred-thousand dollar report – the product of the minds of three professors and a Winnipeg newspaper man." He sneered that "the propaganda machine made it appear that to implement this document would make the provinces richer and, at the same time, make the Dominion richer by the simple process of transferring debts and revenues to the central government." To Hepburn this was bad economics: "Inasmuch as there are only two parties to the deal, surely one need only to have an elementary knowledge of economics to appreciate the fact that both cannot win."[79]

The war, Hepburn asserted yet again, rendered the commission irrelevant. The unemployment issue sat at the heart of the recommendations, but the war eliminated the problem. It was "unadulterated humbug" to claim that the federal government was now doing the provinces a favour by taking full responsibility for the unemployed. On the contrary, the move would help federal coffers by allowing Ottawa to avoid its present duty to provide 40 percent of the cost of food, clothing, and shelter for those on relief. The only taxes left to the provinces would be from liquor, vehicle licences, and gasoline, but these were being rationed during wartime. Where, Hepburn asked, would provincial revenue come from? Ontario would be forced to go begging to the federal government with "tin cup in hand." The premier also pointed out that there was no issue of overlapping with the collection of income taxes by the province and dominion. Ontario had already gone out of its way to cooperate with Ottawa during wartime. Federal income taxes were allowed as a deduction from the provincial levy so that every increase by Ottawa reduced the provincial tax base. In addition, capital spending was postponed and foreign exchange had been added through American tourism. The War Measures Act was already in effect and Ottawa possessed "extreme, even dictatorial power." It was shameful that the King government was "fiddling while London [was] burning." The pressure to implement the report, Hepburn claimed, emerged from "a well-cooked, nefarious deal to make good the losses in depreciation of certain bonds held largely by financial houses, to collect unpaid interest on Alberta bonds and to cause a sharp appreciation in the bonds of certain provinces."[80] He concluded with a ringing defence of provincial rights in all its manifestations, from Quebec's autonomy to the basic rights of the provinces.[81] Hepburn concluded that "this is a peace-time document, and we believe honestly and sincerely that the time to discuss it is not now, but only when the menace to our democracy, Christianity and freedom is removed by the complete defeat and even annihilation of the ruthless axis powers."[82]

Premier Adelard Godbout of Quebec followed, but he spoke very briefly. Although he commended the report, he argued that it was unwise to make fundamental changes to the federal system during wartime. Godbout accepted that the war imposed an urgency that could not be avoided and averred that Quebec did not "fear" negotiations or take a "selfish" view of proposals for change. Provincial autonomy, he asserted, was built on financial independence and that, by invading the provincial tax fields, such autonomy would inevitably be curtailed: "Should an overbearing Federal

Government decide to reduce our autonomy to nothing, all they would have to do would be to tighten the screw gradually and they would soon find us on our knees." The system for administering the adjustment grants, the premier argued, would be "humiliating for us because it [would] force us, after having released the best of our revenues to Ottawa, to go begging for grants from the Federal Officers." Acknowledging claims that the report was not promoting centralization, he feared that "each readjustment would drift towards centralization." Quebec's autonomy could be diminished. This warning delivered, Godbout nonetheless ended with a pledge to work with the dominion to further the war effort and to find ways to reform the fiscal system.[83] The Quebec premier was carefully non-committal. He was burdened by easily aroused suspicions in Quebec that the provincial Liberal government was the creation of its federal counterpart.

The positions put forward by Nova Scotia and New Brunswick deviated in tone from their prior assurances of support. Nova Scotia's new premier, A.S. MacMillan, who had replaced Angus Macdonald the previous summer, initially indicated his willingness to support the report. But at the opening session, MacMillan seemed to back away. He argued that the National Adjustment Grant as calculated was "woefully" insufficient. Nova Scotia would require $3 million rather than $800,000 to bring it up to the standards of the rest of the country. If it came to providing a "categorical answer" on the spot, MacMillan asserted, it would be "no." Nova Scotia was not overtly dismissive of the conference or the report, and privately quite sympathetic, yet its public stance was insipid compared to Angus Macdonald's advocacy of "fiscal need" in 1938.[84]

New Brunswick's premier, J.B. McNair, also gave tepid support. McNair had been the province's attorney general during the hearings. He made it clear that New Brunswick was less averse to changes to the federal system than it had been in 1938, but he was annoyed by the report's rejection of the province's historical claim for compensation. McNair's remarks suggested that New Brunswick could live with the main outlines of Plan One and welcomed further negotiation on areas of contention. Like MacMillan, McNair did not convey convey any enthusiasm, even though the provincial government he led did favour it.[85]

The last to speak in the morning was Premier John Bracken of Manitoba. As expected, his comments about the report were favourable. His theme was that the conference was a chance to reset the federal state founded in 1867 with the benefit of seventy years of experience and an impressive report. His excessively detailed exposition took up more than twice the time taken by any other premier, and was so extensive it spilled over from the morning into the afternoon session.

Bracken opened with the statement that the war made the present conference even more important than the one that created Confederation: "It is fortunate that the wisdom of the Fathers of Confederation makes our task a much easier one than theirs. They had to envisage the needs of a Federal State that did not then exist; and they had to conceive and implement the legislation under which those needs could be met. We, now, on the basis of seventy years' experience, have only to adjust their plans to the conditions of today." The task as Bracken well knew was anything but easy. The Manitoba premier engaged in a very lengthy point-by-point analysis of Plan One and its implications. He described Rowell-Sirois as "one of the most intensive and complete public enquiries ever undertaken in the British Empire on the workings of a Federal State." National unity, he argued, "must be based on provincial autonomy, and provincial autonomy cannot be assured unless a strong feeling of national unity exists throughout Canada."[86]

Bracken concluded that if notorious foes like John A. Macdonald and George Brown could compromise in the interest of political union and national growth, then surely Mackenzie King and Mitchell Hepburn could do the same. Bracken's defence of the report was tied firmly to the preservation of provincial fiscal autonomy. The expansion not only of responsibilities but also of limitations had burdened the provinces with debt and then gutted them during the Depression. These were not just cyclical problems, they were structural. Plan One was the solution.

Duff Pattullo followed Bracken, and he was almost brusque. The premier went straight at the report's "centralizing" agenda. Under Plan One, he claimed, provincial powers would be "taken away" and what remained would be "largely influenced by and subject to central control." BC would be incapable of moving forward or even maintaining its own existing standards. There were five regions in Canada. British Columbia was distinct from the Prairie region and there was "nothing to be gained and much to be lost in attempting to bring them to a common level." The result of adopting the report would be to "turn the treadmill of mediocrity in perpetuity." Under Rowell-Sirois, "we would be so circumscribed that instead of the new hegemony engendering harmony, it would only aggravate disharmony." Pattullo joined Hepburn in rejecting the claim that the report's implementation was necessary to prosecute the war.[87]

Thane Campbell of Prince Edward Island, on the other hand, criticized those who cast the report as centralist. This assertion, the premier argued, was an exaggeration and amounted to fearmongering. He did criticize the commission for not being sympathetic enough to PEI's problem of communication with the mainland and for not fully understanding the plight of agricultural producers and their struggles under dominion policy. While agreeing that it was not intrinsically centralist, Campbell was concerned that the federal finance commission would "give rise to an increase rather than a decrease of bureaucracy." PEI was also concerned that the federal takeover of unemployed employables still left seasonal workers as the responsibility of the provinces. But the premier supported the transfer of tax fields and the specific recommendations of Plan One as "entirely satisfactory."[88]

Premier William Patterson of Saskatchewan spoke next. He was clear about his province's support for the main recommendations, but he also reiterated hopes for major constitutional change to guarantee fiscal reform. He tackled the argument that wartime was no time to deal with such domestic concerns. While it was essential that Canada carry out an effective war effort, the effective functioning of the federal system was essential to this effort. If the adoption of the report "will make for greater effectiveness," Patterson claimed, "then I say the change cannot be made too quickly or too soon, and the Province of Saskatchewan favors early action." He ended by backing away from his remarks about constitutional change admitting that the report's adoption did not of course require any such changes.[89]

The last speaker of the day was Alberta premier William Aberhart. Prior to the conference, the provincial government gave the impression that it was open to negotiations. Provincial Treasurer Solon Low had acknowledged in late 1940 that the report deserved careful assessment and that it proposed fiscal changes that might well benefit Alberta.[90] Upon arriving in Ottawa for the conference, Aberhart met with Hepburn and Pattullo.

The Alberta premier came away convinced that the report should be set aside until the war was over. His remarks reflected this stance.

Aberhart's theme was based on the Social Credit catechism. The real problems confronting the country, he pontificated, were not created by constitutional or fiscal arrangements but by the international financial system. These matters could not be dealt with adequately until the war was won, and even then, they were not susceptible to mere tinkering. Only transformation of the global financial system would accomplish this feat. National unity, Aberhart announced, was at risk. The unemployment situation could be dealt with immediately by the dominion, but the debts of the provinces could be put off: "Under our present stupid debt-creating system of finance we shall have accumulated so many debts after this war that we shall then be able to deal with them in a wholesale fashion instead of piecemeal." A federal propaganda campaign had been pushing the Rowell-Sirois recommendations for weeks, Aberhart charged, yet Canadians had no real sense of what the report actually contained. If adopted, the recommendations would neither alleviate the burden of debt on western Canada nor reduce taxes. The only ones likely to benefit were the "large corporations and financial institutions." It was "dangerously criminal," he went on, "to sit calmly and indifferently while we are being hoodwinked and inveigled into a financial dictatorship or a Fascist state at a time when we are giving the best of our manhood to the Empire."[91] Aberhart simultaneously endorsed more centralization for the sake of the war but withheld approval for major changes to federal-provincial fiscal relations and policies.[92]

Aberhart finished speaking at 6:15 p.m., and the prime minister adjourned the conference for the day. The next morning the governments were scheduled to go into committee work. Later that night, Mackenzie King congratulated himself on "the contrast between Hepburn's attitude and [his] own, particularly in the manner of speaking." He accused Pattullo of going "much too far in his position," and Aberhart, while "amusing and plausible," of being "all humbug."[93] The prime minister was disappointed that Godbout, McNair, and MacMillan had not been "more positive and better prepared." He found that Bracken spoke "much too long and by being argumentative as he was, helped rather to create the impression that the conference was being forced more or less at his instance."[94] King reiterated his impatience with Hepburn's "demagoguery." He had not disguised this reaction during the session. A *Globe and Mail* reporter observed that, "when he is upset, Mr. King has a mannerism of tapping his fingers; sometimes he twiddles his glasses or his thumbs. He did all three today while the Ontario Premier spoke."[95]

King mused in his diary about why the conference and the commission were facing serious opposition. His reflections consisted of a very broad criticism of both private- and public-sector interests, whose disparate goals were distorting the political debate: "My own feeling is that there are two influences that are militating strongly against acceptance of the Report. Above all, financial interests having played it up so much through the press, Bank of Canada, etc. and the other: Manitoba has been so insistent on it all." The financial interests to which King was referring included banking and finance institutions and the Bank of Canada, all of them obsessed with the stability of the financial sector. On the other side was the "Manitoba influence," including not only John Bracken and J.W. Dafoe but also Grant Dexter, T.A. Crerar, and even advisors attached to the Prime Minister's Office such as Leonard Brockington and Jack Pickersgill. It was, King deduced, "largely a Dafoe report." King added to this mix of overly influential outsiders by throwing in the Queen's University economists and their representatives and progeny now in the federal Department of Finance and Bank of Canada. Altogether the baleful interest groups severely distorted the deliberations at the conference, leaving little room for apt compromise. It was a shame, King summed up, that Rowell "was not spared to complete the work," because it was "eventually too highly coloured by the needs of the Prairies."[96]

The next day, the conference itinerary proposed dividing into four committees – finance, labour and unemployment, constitutional, and "special Problems" – each chaired by a senior cabinet minister and an official secretary.[97] The discussions would certainly have been informed and animated. But they never occurred. Hepburn refused to take any action that even suggested he supported adoption of the report. After an hour of hallway wrangling, Lapointe and Crerar informed King that the Ontario premier, supported by Pattullo and Aberhart, refused to go into committees to discuss the recommendations.

After a lengthy adjournment in which many private discussions occurred, Lapointe announced in mid-afternoon that there was "a difference of opinion" and that three premiers were refusing to discuss the report in detail. The minister of finance would address the "whole financial situation." Pattullo and Aberhart agreed to let Ilsley speak, while Aberhart requested that the conference discuss the report but not consider its recommendations. King overruled Aberhart, arguing that the conference was held to examine whether and how to adopt the report and not to have a general discussion about its contents. Hepburn, however, responded that he would only give the floor to the federal minister of finance if Ontario was allowed an opportunity to respond. King granted the request.[98]

Ilsley began "rather timidly" and was recorded as asking King in an aside whether he should "avoid any controversial topics." The prime minister abruptly replied: "Oh no, go ahead."[99] Ilsley may have started out softly but he ended with a bang. Ilsley first made it clear that he was not prepared to make any statement about the current financial situation of the government and pointed to the pressures to carry out a maximum war effort that demanded extraordinary spending. He responded to the critics' charges. Support for Rowell-Sirois did not come from bond speculators, as Hepburn had charged. "The commissioners, he noted, had been careful to call for a capital gains tax on the sale of depreciated bonds to eliminate speculative profits." More generally, the recommendations aimed to "safeguard" governments from such exploitation. Ilsley then rejected the claim that Plan One would destroy provincial fiscal autonomy or, as Pattullo had argued before and during the Conference, "curb" their discretionary powers. Both of these objections were based on a misunderstanding of Plan One.[100]

The finance minister offered arguments in favour of adopting the report. The existing federal tax system remained an unfair "jumble" of regressive and overlapping taxes. It was both inefficient and ineffective. Moreover, it was incapable of addressing the major problems of financing the war effort or stabilizing the financial system of the country. Beyond that, the existing allocation of revenues did not enable governments, provincial or federal, to deliver the necessary and appropriate minimum level of services expected by Canadians. Finally, there was nothing in the existing allocations of revenues and responsibilities to prepare for a postwar world.

Ilsley threatened that reform of the taxation, and indeed the fiscal, system was essential and would be implemented regardless of the conference outcome. He concluded by stating that there was no question as to the urgency of action, of the unlimited right of the dominion to tax in any area, or whether the federal government had the power to act unilaterally.[101]

Ilsley concluded with a strong message:

> We preferred to call this conference and to try to reach by agreement a satisfactory solution of the problems that Canada faces. We tried to do it in the democratic way. It is wholly unfair to accuse us of lukewarmness in our support of this Report because we went about the matter decently instead of with the big stick. We are not lukewarm in support of the Report nor of its recommendations. We believe it is the best solution yet devised for the solution of our problems, which are problems of staggering magnitude.

He advised the premiers that, if they had another solution: "they should, I respectfully submit, certainly be made and made now."[102] In the words of historian J.L. Granatstein, "the velvet glove that Mackenzie King and the Cabinet had carefully drawn on had been removed by the Minister of Finance."[103]

Not surprisingly, the Ontario delegation met the strong tone and veiled threats head on. Highways Minister T.B. McQuesten read a lengthy statement that was to be used in the finance committee. Ontario, he claimed, had steadily improved its level of social services since 1934 and had balanced its budget since 1936. Yet under Plan One the province would give up $40 million in revenues and its municipalities $5 million, for which it would receive only $23 million in return. This loss would only be the beginning because the cost of social services was certain to rise. McQuesten bristled at a suggestion that Hepburn should try to live up to the example of George Brown in the struggle for Confederation: "Hepburn has been living up to the tradition of Brown, and has defended and upheld all that Brown stood for, and is safeguarding the rights and responsibilities vested in the separate provinces of confederation ... provincial autonomy without adequate revenues for discharging the functions of government for which provinces are responsible is but little more than a farce." McQuesten reiterated that Ontario was withdrawing from the conference, leaving "the rest of the members to continue their efforts to do what we are bound to say would result in wrecking confederation, as we understand it, and in destroying provincial autonomy and rights."[104]

Hepburn then "leapt to his feet to amplify these criticisms." He called Ilsley's arguments "ridiculous." On one hand the finance minister claimed that provincial revenues would not be affected and then, on the other, he threatened to impose gasoline rationing. The premier again maligned the Rowell-Sirois Commission as the product of "a few college professors and a Winnipeg newspaperman, who has had his knife into Ontario ever since he was able to write editorial articles." Its recommendations were tantamount to disaster: "I myself will not sell my province down the river for all time to come and allow our social services to remain a victim of dictatorial methods of a bureaucracy to be set up in Ottawa." Pounding the table, he challenged the prime minister: "We are not behind you; we are ahead of you, and if you want to do something as a war measure, go ahead and do it. But don't smash this confederation and stir up possible racial feuds in your effort." Hepburn concluded that implementation was "nefarious work" conducted by "wreckers of confederation, under the guise of patriotism."[105]

The prime minister asked for further comments. The premiers responded, but their remarks merely followed the scripts they had delivered the previous day. Pattullo was obdurate, although he insisted that he was not being obstructive and was prepared still to have a general discussion about the report. Godbout seemed more intent on shoring up his provincial rights defences against future changes. He restated his willingness to study the recommendations, but he could not sacrifice provincial autonomy or submit to changes that would, it seemed, actually involve "serious financial sacrifice" on the part of Quebec. Unless a civil tone could be maintained, further discussion would be unwise.[106] Aberhart claimed that he did not want to be labelled a dissenter but held to his position.[107] Bracken made no attempt to hide his disdain for his fellow premiers. The situation, he argued, had now reached the point of absurdity. The federal government had been handed the means and justification to invade the provincial taxation fields in order to finance the war effort and the provinces would get nothing in return. How did this position make sense? The Manitoba premier questioned why the three dissenting provinces would not agree to measures that would raise the standard of services and stabilize the fiscal situation for the other provinces. Bracken was also frustrated with the prime minister, who gave him every indication of sitting idly by rather than working to save the conference and the Rowell-Sirois Report.[108]

Bracken was right about one thing: Mackenzie King was prepared to allow the conference to fail. The prime minister was not, however, going to allow the dissenting premiers to have the last word. The federal cabinet ministers were instructed to respond to Ontario's statements, or at least to counter Hepburn's "stage play" mockery. A phalanx arose and in varying degrees defended the commissioners and the report.[109]

Angus L. Macdonald did not have to be prodded. While he abstained from the discussion at the conference, "lest he be seen as a second representative of Nova Scotia," he "quietly tried to salvage something" and "worked to mend fences and get negotiations moving."[110] Macdonald argued for several years that Rowell-Sirois was the "culmination of a 'new liberalism' which embraced a 'positive' role for the state in building infrastructure and establishing social insurance programs – that had developed between the wars." It was "the last best chance for the economically weaker provinces to direct their own affairs while providing modern services to their citizens."[111] At the conference, Macdonald sent King a scrawled note urging the prime minister to show flexibility: "Mr. Aberhart is willing to consider the Sirois Report, along with other matters. Hepburn is willing to talk about the war. If we accepted the idea of discussing *something*, could we by degrees get to a consideration of the Report?"[112]

Ilsley was the last cabinet minister to respond. He claimed that the Ontarians had just declared themselves "observers" and that he had to set the record straight by strongly objecting to the accuracy of McQuesten's statistics about the impact on Ontario of the federal fiscal proposals. The comments rankled Hepburn:

> I just want to summarize the whole situation in a few words by saying that the Sirois report was conceived as a peace-time measure. What has happened in the interval? You have dressed it up with the garments of patriotism and cloaked it with the exigencies of war as well, and have said to those of us who represent the provinces, "We want you to accept

the findings of this report as a war measure in perpetuity." Now this is where we disagree. We say that we will help you in every conceivable manner so far as prosecuting this war is concerned, but we are not going to sell out our respective provinces, and generations to come, under the exigencies of war.[113]

The prime minister had no intention of gambling on further negotiations. He adjudged the outbursts to be a political gain for the federal government and he "was not prepared to snatch defeat from the jaws of victory."[114] During a ten-minute adjournment, King met privately with his ministers. The result was a statement read to the conference indicating that it was over. In his closing remarks, King admitted that, while there were differences of opinion in cabinet over proceeding with fundamental constitutional changes during wartime, the conference had been necessary, particularly if changes to the financial system of the federation were required. Privately, the prime minister was more frank: "Far from being a failure, the conference has resulted in achieving beyond expectation the principal aim for which it was called, namely the avoidance of any excuse for protest on the part of provincial governments once the Dominion government begins, as it will be obliged very soon to do, to invade fields of taxation which up to the present have been monopolized in whole or in part by some of the provinces."[115] Justice Minister Ernest Lapointe demonstrated greater optimism, at least in public. Rowell-Sirois might be "discarded to-day," but "it will not be killed." The report was a "monument" and its "ideas" would eventually be reconsidered and adopted in part if not in full.[116]

The conference of 1941 broke up on its second day at 6:35 p.m. "Thus ended," historian Christopher Armstrong notes, "at the hands of the representative of the province of Ontario the most serious effort to that date to restructure the Canadian confederation."[117] But even in calling the conference closed, King left open the possibility for reconvening it if the provinces agreed. The "first ministers" and their colleagues rose and sang "O Canada" to end the proceedings. "Later on," Liberal MP Paul Martin recalled, "I found out that King never liked federal-provincial conferences; they unsettled him and, he felt, disturbed the political structure and the nation as well."[118]

A dinner had been planned for the second evening at the Ottawa Country Club. The banquet had been carefully arranged with a seating plan to ensure that the premiers and their ministers, as well as selected federal and provincial officials, were appropriately spaced amidst federal ministers and the prime minister. King would be seated at the apex of a long L-shaped table beside the premiers of Quebec and Ontario, with the other premiers either close beside or opposite them. Hepburn did not show up. The premier was called away by "urgent business" at Queen's Park

Despite the failure of the conference, King was very pleased with the dinner arrangements and his own performance. "I do not recall any gathering where I ever received a finer ovation, more spontaneous and enthusiastic. Everyone seemed to have been delighted with the way in which I got through the conference at the close, and at the avoiding of any rancor throughout. The dinner, by general consent," King claimed, "was as happy and congenial as any we have ever had at the Country Club. It brought together men from all parts of the Dominion and I feel did an awful lot to strengthen our government with the different governments." Upon arriving home at the end of the evening, King could not have been happier. He commented on the beautiful night sky and how the heavens themselves seemed to be parting:

> Felt distinctly relieved and happy about the whole conference ... I took care throughout to make clear while the conference had been called because of the report, the report was simply to be a basis of discussion of matters referred to therein. Had I gone the length of those financial men and intelligentsia around me would have wished, saying that the whole thing was to be taken or nothing, I would have played completely into the hands of Hepburn, Pattullo and Aberhart. As it was, I had enough in what I said, to save the situation, and to put us in our true position. Felt immensely relieved that the conference was out of the way.[119]

Two days after the conference ended, King learned that Joseph Sirois had died. Increasingly ill with heart problems in late 1940, Sirois had returned to Quebec after his work in Ottawa and taken no part in the conference. "I have no doubt that the attacks on his report in his condition of health hastened the end," King recorded. "I should not be surprised if

Rowell passed away fairly soon. It would be a blessing to his wife and himself if he did."[120] Despite King's premonition, Newton Rowell lingered in ill-health. He died on 22 November 1941. Eerily enough, two weeks after Sirois's death, another champion of the commission unexpectedly died. Oscar Skelton, overworked as usual and harried by the endless problems of domestic as well as foreign policy and politics, suffered a fatal heart attack on 28 January 1941. The death of the under-secretary of state for external affairs was a serious blow to the government of Canada. Skelton was as much a domestic as a foreign policy advisor.[121]

The deaths of Sirois and Skelton foreshadowed the eclipse of Rowell-Sirois as an immediate policy document. The events of January 1941 ended the most active phase but not the impact of the "commission on reconfederation." From that point on, it served as a set of principles and a source of policy ideas about federalism that would define an era and guide a generation.

11

The Aftermath
1941–46

Whether or not governments use the information provided or follow the proposals that are made is unimportant from the perspective of the royal commission as an instrument of executive choice. For the government of the day, the royal commission is a valuable tool of public policy; it not only defines issues, it authenticates those that are chosen for investigation over those that are ignored.

– David E. Smith, 1995[1]

An article in the Canadian edition of *Liberty* magazine on the eve of the 1941 Dominion-Provincial Conference assessed the low expectations and the uninspiring state of federalism in Canada. "Will Canadian Re-Confederation be achieved in 1941?" it asked with rhetorical flourish. "Will our numerous governments – Dominion, provincial, and municipal – end the disgraceful era of bungling and buck-passing and get down to business and good administration?" Aside from the war, the article claimed, the Sirois Report was "the most important and the most urgent matter before the Canadian public today." The central problems included the unemployment and drought situations caused by the Depression, an "outworn Constitution," and a "pitiful period in our national history; a period of fumbling, of friction and futility." The royal commission offered solutions, and the Canadian public was onside, but a few provinces were obstructing progress. To *Liberty*, the reason for the opposition was easy to discern:

"Doesn't He Look Natural!"– editorial cartoon. *Acadia University Archives*

selfishness and short-sightedness. The three dissenting provinces of Ontario, Alberta, and British Columbia would not presently receive National Adjustment Grants yet they would have to surrender certain tax sources. As the business and financial centre of Canada, Ontario enjoyed a large share of income taxes, while Alberta's developing oil wealth was a new taxable boon and BC's timber market was an important tax resource. The greatest opposition came from Ontario, but it was not "sectional"; rather, it came from the personal antagonism between Mitch Hepburn and Mackenzie King: "Unless these men can forget their quarrel, the conference will be a waste of time."[2] The article was correct, and the conference was a botched opportunity. Yet the report remained at the centre of federal reconstruction for the rest of the wartime period.

At the Bank of Canada, Sandy Skelton monitored the press response. In the days that followed the end of the 1941 conference, most newspapers emphasized national unity. They denounced the "three wreckers" without fully embracing the cause of Rowell-Sirois. Despite the reaction, however, press support had diminished since the time the report was first released.[3]

The Prairie papers (three of which were owned by the Siftons) stood apart from the rest. They were, Skelton reported, "practically unanimous in their approval of the Report and disappointment in the failure of the conference." Most editorials "followed the leadership of the *Winnipeg Free Press* in its whole-hearted support." Elsewhere the reaction was different. The Maritime papers, despite the positions of the region's premiers, were generally opposed to the adoption of the report, particularly during wartime. The *Halifax Chronicle* and *Halifax Herald* considered it a "dead pigeon." They argued that the failure to find agreement was orchestrated by Ottawa.

The reaction in the French-language press in Quebec was one of relief at the adjournment. *Le Devoir* led the opposition in arguing that the report was a threat to the rights of French Canadians: "Most arguments in its favour will go unheeded as long as that fear remains." In a series of ten articles in *Le Devoir* from 21 January to 3 February, writer Leopold Richer, a moderate *nationaliste*, laid out Quebec's opposition. It was based on the traditional need to protect provincial autonomy so Quebec could continue to defend its culture. Premier Godbout received particular criticism for being weak and waffling, and for supporting Ottawa by not resisting. Godbout "could not oppose the Report because Mr. Lapointe approved of it." *Le Devoir* complained of the "presumption of Manitoba and Saskatchewan politicians in thinking that the other provinces should pay with their autonomy for the costs of the stupid policies of these two provinces." The people of Quebec were warned "to remain watchful to safeguard their rights as the threat to their autonomy embodied in the Sirois Report was by no means a thing of the past."

Most Ontario newspapers took the position that the failure was regrettable but that Hepburn's behaviour was a fiasco. The *Globe and Mail* argued that politics wrecked the conference and that the Hepburn-King feud stole the show. The *Toronto Telegram* claimed that Rowell-Sirois had to be rejected because it was out to make Ontario pay for the "past extravagance" of the Prairie provinces and Quebec. Even the *Toronto Star* was ambivalent about the report and argued: "the trouble with the Sirois Report was that it made rescue of western finances part of an elaborate and unnecessary new financial set-up which disturbed the balance now existing between provinces which are financially sound." In British Columbia, the press was unclear about the substantive issues while ganging up on Pattullo for his obstructionist stance. In general, the press coverage across Canada was more focused on allocating blame for the failure than on analyzing the issues involved.[4]

In a post-conference article for *Liberty,* journalist Grattan O'Leary offered a perspective on the failed meeting that criticized both the dominion and provincial camps. "Shocked by the sectional discord, veiled threats, and recriminations," the piece opened, "where do we go from here?" The conference "was pathetically mismanaged." The prime minister "fluttered a white flag" from the outset while the premier of Ontario was present "only to scoff." The various premiers demonstrated their "crass ignorance" of the report while the federal finance minister's guidance came after the conference was already "dead." It was doubtful, O'Leary charged, "whether half the delegates who came to Ottawa had read the Report through, let alone studied it." The bureaucrats understood its importance, but they failed to bother explaining this importance to the nation at large. Hepburn, meanwhile, was more focused on continuing his "guerrilla war" against the King government. As a result, "the whole business was muffed pitiably."[5]

The politicians' reactions to the failure of the conference demonstrated the recalcitrant positions of the participants. Publicly, the premier of Ontario was "remarkably restrained." Hepburn went home pleased he had blocked Rowell-Sirois "indefinitely." Despite press criticism, he was confident that he expressed the majority view of Ontarians.[6] Privately, however, Hepburn was "incensed" by his treatment at the conference and then after by the press. The Ontario government placed large ads in newspapers in an attempt to set the record straight. Hepburn refuted reports that the Ontario delegation had withdrawn. The province, he claimed, was willing to discuss all avenues of cooperation to maximize the war effort. Ontario could not accept the Rowell-Sirois recommendations because they would cut into provincial revenues and add hundreds of millions to the federal debt. As far as Hepburn was concerned, "not only would adoption of the report threaten the high level of education and social services, but [it] would also lead to the centralization of power and the growth of a bureaucracy which would undermine federalism and threaten democracy."[7] In the Ontario legislature, Hepburn attacked Bracken, accusing the Manitoba premier of "wanting his bonds endorsed so that these extravagant provinces could go on with the same kind of extravagance." In a speech to the Ontario Property Owners' Association on 11 February, the Ontario premier claimed that adoption of the report would cost the province $20 million a year.[8]

Duff Pattullo had to deal with harsh criticism by the regional and national press. The BC premier was thrown in with Hepburn and Aberhart as one of "The Three Saboteurs." Pattullo brushed off the charge as attacks by centralizers who viewed any strong provincial stand as obstructionist, but the criticisms struck harder than he acknowledged. Instead of returning home to explain why the conference failed, Pattullo remained in Ottawa for several days and then travelled to New York to be outfitted for new suits.[9] Upon his return, he was again admonished, most notably in the *Vancouver Province* and the *Vancouver Sun*. There were also grumblings of discontent within the BC Liberal Party and in the provincial cabinet, including calls for an election.[10]

On 13 and 20 February, the provincial secretary, George Weir, gave two radio broadcasts that defended the premier and alluded to more serious policy differences beyond political wrangles. Rowell-Sirois, he argued, would end up reducing BC's revenues to a national average and force the province to depend on unreliable consumption taxes, such as liquor and gasoline. Ultimately, the report would benefit Quebec, Saskatchewan, and Manitoba, while hampering British Columbia. Conditional grants-in-aid were preferable to unconditional National Adjustment Grants because the former were aimed towards a specific goal while the latter were mere subsidies. Weir took direct aim at the adjustment grants, which the province would not receive until it had "dropped to a so-called national average." This amount was lower than anything experienced by BC during even the worst years of the Great Depression. "The way to national unity does not lie in penalizing certain provinces in order to aid others."[11] Pattullo responded to the press attacks by claiming that British Columbia would "suffer" more than any other province under Rowell-Sirois.[12]

On 13 March, Pattullo gave a radio address aimed at his "armchair critics" and the "smug and pharisaical propagandists" of the press. He assured the populace that the BC government was cooperating fully with the federal war effort. But it would not cooperate with the "proposed radical changes to our constitution" that would bring "disagreement and discord." The calling of the conference in wartime "was a mistake, a fact recognized by the Dominion Government." Pattullo complained about the short notice and the failure to provide a copy of the agenda until two days before he was to depart for Ottawa.

Pattullo's most serious criticism was aimed at the taxation proposals, which would strip the provinces of major revenue sources, and the overall "centralization of authority and control of provincial activities," resulting from the creation of the finance commission: "It would jeopardize all of our social welfare measures, would render impossible government developmental policies in respect of our natural resources and industrial activities," he claimed, "and we would be left without money on Capital Account for roads and bridges, except such as might be approved by central authority." Income taxes and succession duties, the premier argued, made up more than a third of total provincial income: "Our whole provincial economy has been built up on our authority to levy the Provincial Income Tax and we are now asked to surrender this flexible tax on which we have become so dependent." The premier dismissed the criticism that he had left the conference without discussing the report. It was discussed "for two days in open conference and had already been given weeks of study by some of us before the conference met." The "propagandists" were now trying "to ink the waters," but "all the ink they can splash across Canada cannot change the report of the Commission, and that is the real and important factor." Within a year, Pattullo, who was flailing around on many more issues than just the Rowell-Sirois Report, lost the premiership.[13]

William Aberhart, the last in the trio of so-called wreckers, expressed disappointment that the conference had ended so abruptly. Like Pattullo, he portrayed the report as a means to undermine the fiscal autonomy of the provinces. He claimed that, regardless of whether they would accept the report, the premiers had expected to have been invited to discuss the general state of dominion-provincial affairs. In a radio address on 4 February, the Alberta premier noted that, "had we allowed the international financiers to have slipped the recommendations of the Sirois report into our hands, each of the provinces would have had a real live wildcat by the tail." He refused to hand the people of Alberta "bound and gagged into the clutches of the financial tyrants ... that would divest the people of every vestige of autonomy and democratic freedom that they at present enjoy."[14] In a letter to Hepburn, Aberhart defended their stance at the conference as in the best interests of the country.[15]

Before leaving Ottawa, John Bracken and Stuart Garson met with federal officials to determine "where to go from here." The normally phlegmatic Bracken had been quite "hopeful" that the report would be implemented substantially if not fully. The failure to proceed took Manitoba back to its gloomy starting point regarding provincial debt. Bracken and his colleagues were "sadly disappointed."[16] When Bracken and Garson met with Graham Towers and Donald Gordon of the Bank of Canada on 17 January, Garson explained that he was anxious because he felt the collapse of the conference and the warnings issued by Ilsley would make it essential for Manitoba to reconstitute the provincial debt at lower interest rates. Garson asked if the bank would assist Manitoba and its debenture holders in working out a plan to borrow through the market. "If this cannot be done," he noted, "Manitoba can hardly hope to persuade its people that what Alberta did in 1936 was wrong." Towers warned of the "real effects of default." But something had to be done. "If we do nothing now but just drift into suspension," Garson argued, "we may hurt many other interests than our own and certainly would hurt other Provinces." The following morning Garson met with the deputy minister of finance. Clifford Clark hoped that "something [might] be accomplished, either in the nature of the Report or an alternative." Garson's response reflected Manitoba's mood: "I do not share your optimism with respect to the Report, that it will be reconsidered in any short period of time."[17]

Upon his return to Winnipeg, Bracken told the press that Canadians could not afford to let a problem of such importance remain unsolved, particularly in wartime. "Nor," the premier argued, "can the nation afford to sit by and see a major policy scuttled because three governments out of ten refuse to sit down with the others to consider it." On 27 January, Bracken gave a radio address in which he called for Ottawa to override provincial obstruction and implement Rowell-Sirois. He called the actions of Hepburn, Pattullo, and Aberhart "a new low in democratic behavior." The dissenting premiers were not unpatriotic, but their study of the report was "insufficient" and their knowledge of its contents "inadequate." They were "wrong" and the results were highly "disruptive." The premier's harshest criticism was aimed at Hepburn, and he issued a direct threat to Ontario. The province, he claimed, was the "chief beneficiary of Confederation." If the report was not allowed to redistribute the wealth of the nation, then: "the only logical course for us to take is to reduce to a minimum the amount of business we do with these concerns ... by doing business with them, we enable them to transfer large amounts of wealth from the taxing authority of Manitoba to the taxing authority of Ontario. And if this process is to be only a one way traffic, we shall have to do our best to stop it before it pauperizes us."[18]

On 20 February, Stuart Garson defended the Rowell-Sirois recommendations. Speaking to the Manitoba Associated Boards of Trade, he piled on the three dissenting premiers. He claimed that no opposing arguments were even put forward other than a fallacious claim that the commission was designed for peacetime and could not meet the exigencies of war. Garson reminded those gathered that implementation of the findings would result in an annual gain to municipalities in Manitoba of $2.5 million and to the province an annual National Adjustment Grant of $2.1 million. Failure to implement these terms would result in the province losing revenue through the elimination of federal relief payments as well as the federal invasion of provincial tax fields. The end would be either default or greater indebtedness. Garson spent considerable time explaining that, while the report recommended giving the dominion exclusive control over income, corporation, and inheritance taxes, the detractors focused attention on how this would diminish provincial autonomy rather than focusing on how it would alleviate the burden on taxpayers:

> If the Sirois Report is not implemented, the provinces and the municipalities will continue to have these mounting social services and relief costs to provide for out of their limited tax base. If the responsibilities of the province are not reduced, they will need every cent of revenue that they can get. They cannot afford to have the Dominion Government invading their sources of revenue. Several of the provinces already

have their credit seriously strained by relief burdens, and one is in default as is.

In order to avoid the kind of fiscal calamity created during the Great War, Ottawa should use direct taxation, such as income taxes, on a large and increasing scale. If the report was not implemented, these heavy increases would be piled on top of the present provincial taxes, which were already imposed unevenly across the nation. The result would be "a crazy-quilt set of income and corporation tax rates which vary in the various provinces." Garson claimed that the federal government was coming for direct taxation sources regardless. The only question for the provinces to consider was what they were going to get in return: "The Sirois Report contains by far the best suggestion."[19]

The responses of the other provinces emphasized the argument that a crucial opportunity to repair the federal system was being squandered. The Saskatchewan premier, Billy Patterson, responded to the conference failure by trying to assure the public that, in time, the logic and merits of Rowell-Sirois would win out. He gave three radio broadcasts in support of the report in February.[20]

The other leaders changed their stances after the January conference. In Prince Edward Island, Premier Thane Campbell stated in a radio address on 18 February that nearly all the recommendations of the report could be carried out through voluntary agreement by the provinces and the dominion without revising the BNA Act. Income tax, succession duties, and corporation taxes were not lucrative enough sources of provincial revenue. The adoption of the report would be of very substantial benefit to PEI, and Campbell hoped that fair and thorough consideration would be given at a later date. Premier MacMillan of Nova Scotia attributed the conference failure to the "dog in the manger" attitude of the three provinces that "ganged up" in an "unholy triple alliance." He blasted Hepburn for a position based on personal animosities and political ambitions. Premier McNair of New Brunswick mourned the failure because he believed it could have been the starting point for the solution of many of Canada's federal problems. He was most appalled that an attempt to bring the nation's statespersons to the table and discuss matters of joint concern had not only failed but broken down in animosity. McNair rejected the argument that the conference was ill timed, and he pointed to examples in Britain where partisan lines were being crossed to discuss serious matters of concern. New Brunswick "stood to lose tremendously" if Rowell-Sirois was not adopted. The provincial government hoped that wiser heads would prevail in time and that the conference would be reconvened.[21]

In Quebec, the political response was more complicated. Premier Adelard Godbout held a press conference on 1 February in which he rejected charges that the report was unsympathetic to Quebec. Union Nationale leader Maurice Duplessis had certainly viewed the report in this light. In a statement released on 15 January, the Opposition leader attacked Rowell-Sirois for favouring "the centralization in Ottawa of all financial powers." If it were adopted, "Quebec would have the right to live ... but they are taking the means to prevent her from breathing."[22] Godbout rejected that position, but, like that of the other premiers who supported the report, his endorsement was too little and too late to matter.

Not surprisingly, the commissioners were disappointed by the failure of the conference. After witnessing the provincial responses during the hearings, they were not surprised by the obstructionist attitudes displayed at the conference. "I am not particularly disturbed about the storm which is now blowing up" over the report, Dafoe had commented to Angus on the eve of the conference:

> The Report is now part of Canadian politics in place of being sidetracked and ignored. Its beneficial effects will be evident in the coming years, but it may take a considerable period of time before they manifest themselves. I often said to myself, and perhaps to others, when we were working on the Commission that an estimate of twenty years, during which time the Report in one form or another would be a factor in politics, would probably not be too long a period to envisage.[23]

When the conference ended, Dafoe at first despaired, remarking that "two years of demanding work was washed down the drain by a flood of petty provincialism and political partisanship." Crerar commiserated with Dafoe. "It seems a strange phenomenon," he replied, "that men like Hepburn and Pattullo and Aberhart can be placed in high positions of responsibility and maintained there by our democratic system. Are people losing their capacity to reflect and think and can any demagogue win and hold the ear of the people against any appeal to reason and common sense?"[24]

Dafoe rallied and argued that the "performance" by the "three mosquitoes" would actually "expedite things." Dafoe expressed his views in an editorial entitled "The True Wreckers," in which he warned that Ottawa would now invade provincial fields of revenue because, "confronted with the unreasoned and bitter prejudice of the three wreckers, it must."[25] Henry Angus commented that "we had prepared a delayed-action bomb and then run away to wait for the explosion, fearing sometimes the noise and sometimes that we have prepared a dud."[26] Like Dafoe, he concluded that the peculiar outcome of the conference would prove positive and that the "definite bust-up was much better than prolonged and fruitless debate."[27] The commissioners were convinced that their plan remained valid.

Regardless of the fallout surrounding the conference, the federal government had issued an ultimatum and intended to carry it through. The conference failure prevented the implementation of Rowell-Sirois, but that failure could now be blamed on provincial obstruction, narrow thinking, and sectional selfishness. Mackenzie King viewed the conference as a success because the antagonistic provinces would end up allowing for a greater federal invasion into provincial taxation than the report ever contemplated. "While, to appearances it has been a failure," the prime minister recorded, "in reality it has served the purpose we had had in view, of avoiding attack for not having called the conference, and particularly for what would certainly have followed, invasion of provincial sources of revenue." He noted that the dissenting premiers were caught in their own trap: "We have now got the pledge of the provinces to let us take their revenues if we need them – a tremendous achievement."[28]

While Mackenzie King was not generally in favour of increased federal powers, wartime conditions necessitated action, and the Sirois Report justified the method. In one of his last conversations with O.D. Skelton, King claimed that the dominion had been "forced" into holding the conference through the influence of the Bank of Canada, and the departments of finance and external affairs, while he and Lapointe were "absolutely opposed to anything of the kind at this time."[29] Finance Minister Ilsley was prepared to invade the provincial tax realms but his thinking about the commission was shaped by Clark and Towers. The essence of the report,

Ilsley thought, was not about tax fields but "on the principle that no part of the country can be allowed to lag far behind another part in standards of living, education, social services, and so on." And it was this attempt to create national minimum standards that caused "considerable resistance to this theory in the more favoured parts of Canada."[30]

The federal government unilaterally moved to invade the provincial tax fields. Walter Gordon, special assistant to the deputy minister of finance, later claimed to have raised the specific plan with Clifford Clark several days after the conference ended. "I thought there might be a solution to the problem," he reflected years later, "not one that would accomplish the social objectives of the Rowell-Sirois Commission, but it was at least a method of financing the wartime budgets." Ottawa would announce the taxes that it intended to take while at the same time offering to enter into an agreement with any province that would surrender its rights to levy the taxes for the duration of the war. These provinces would be paid a fixed amount each year based roughly on the amounts of their present tax revenues and augmented in the case of the poorer provinces. The federal government would make it clear that no province was being forced to enter an agreement but remained free to continue levying its own taxes. In this case, however, the provinces would not qualify for the fixed amounts to be paid by Ottawa: "Moreover, the taxpayers in any province that failed to enter an agreement would be required to pay a total level of taxation that would not be bearable; the full tax rates to be levied by the federal government, plus the taxes imposed by a province that was unwilling to enter an agreement, would exceed one hundred per cent of taxable income in many cases."[31] In other words, the provinces could choose to transfer temporarily their tax fields to Ottawa or maintain them and have both levels of government heavily tax the populace.

Contrary to Gordon's claim, Ilsley had been contemplating such a plan prior to the conference, and forethought was certainly evident in his ultimatum delivered to the provinces. Over the previous year and a half, Clark and Mackintosh had also discussed this heavy-handed move as a necessary if temporary wartime measure.[32] Alex Skelton circulated a paper on the subject on 11 February 1941 entitled "The Aftermath of the Sirois Conference," in which several options were suggested, including the federal takeover of direct taxation.[33] By the end of March, the cabinet agreed that the "tax rental" measure would be announced in the budget.[34] It would be temporary and Prime Minister King assuaged himself with the view that that the commission's most crucial recommendations would be implemented in the postwar period. "What is now being done," King recorded, "will last until the year after the war which may mean that, at that time, the provinces will have come to see that the Sirois Report is, after all, what is best for them as well as for us. It is a bold and far-reaching policy but will, I believe, succeed."[35]

The budget was brought down on 29 April 1941. Ottawa moved decisively to centralize control of Canada's taxation system. Ilsley announced that the federal government would raise income and corporate taxes significantly, in effect forcing the provinces from these fields. Wartime Tax Agreements would be negotiated with the provinces to "rent" their tax fields in exchange for a subsidy representing their value. As compensation, the provinces would be offered either the revenue they actually collected from this source in 1940 or the net cost of the debt service in 1940 (less their revenue from succession duties) and also a subsidy based on fiscal need, if need could be shown. Ilsley declared that the agreements would be a "temporary step" and not "an attempt to get the provinces out of those tax fields permanently."[36] According to historian J.L. Granatstein, "Plan 1 of the Rowell-Sirois Report was now dead, but the needs of the war had been met." Adherents of the commission within the federal government were not yet prepared to bury Rowell-Sirois, but they knew it was comatose. The budget presented the necessary heavy increase in federal taxation, but it was part of the broader policies of war finance, notably the recently completed Hyde Park Agreement with the United States, which gave Canada access to American orders for its wartime Lend-Lease Agreement with the United Kingdom. Wartime needs were met by extraordinary means, including the federal invasion of provincial taxation realms.[37]

Some observers in Ottawa tried to convince themselves that the recommendations were actually being implemented. Others, more discerning about what was being done, hoped that the budget proposal was a temporary measure that would be binding only until the actual recommendations of the commission could be implemented after the war. Crerar claimed that the "really important provisions of Plan One were provided for in the budget." Grant Dexter stated that the budget might be read as "the rear entrance of the Sirois report." Sandy Skelton thought that, at worst, the budget was not the end of Plan One, although it was a "very poor second best." According to Dexter, the premiers of Nova Scotia and New Brunswick now regretted their stance at the conference: "They had come to Ottawa absolutely certain that the report would be adopted and therefore they talked more to the folks back home and in the hope that they might better their position." They were now "very sorry." Regardless, Ilsley made it clear that "there was no chance of giving them the grants as outlined in the report."[38]

Dafoe's hopes diminished. He condemned the tax rental plan as a system of separate settlements drawn up "under political pressure, with resultant charges, often well based, of unfairness, discrimination and political corruption." He told Skelton that he was now "pretty philosophical about the probable future of Dominion-Provincial relations," adding: "[I] just cannot see how, in the post-war world, Canada can be other than a highly integrated country, with the provinces relegated to a relatively unimportant role."[39] Dexter reported that Sandy Skelton was in despair over what was happening. Over the years of work on the commission, Skelton had grown increasingly sympathetic to the position of the provinces even if they were not convinced by his advocacy of reform. Ottawa would now end up with the tax sources after "buying out the 'sons-of-bitches.'" Most important for Skelton, the inequalities between the provinces were "largely frozen." Any future grants would be paid "not upon the basis of maintaining a minimum standard of government but on absolute fiscal need – just enough to enable the provinces to get by. Instead of getting cake, they [would] get only crumbs."[40]

The negotiations for the Wartime Tax Agreements between Ottawa and the provinces were arduous and took over a year to conclude. The federal government made two further concessions: it guaranteed the provincial governments the amount of their gasoline tax revenues in 1940 and their liquor revenues in the amount collected in the twelve months ending 30 June 1942. The second guarantee did not subsequently involve the federal government in any payments, while the first required payments of $11.6 million in 1943. In each agreement the federal government promised in the year after termination "to reduce its rates of taxes by such an amount as will enable the Province again to use the income tax and corporation tax fields, and in particular the Dominion undertakes to reduce its rate of tax on corporation incomes by at least ten percent of such incomes." The preamble to each agreement stated that the province should not "be deemed to have surrendered, abandoned, or given over to the Dominion any of the powers, rights, privileges or authority" vested in it.

The most contentious issue of the tax rental agreements involved determining the amount of the fiscal need subsidies for the provinces in return for temporarily vacating the fields of income and corporation taxes. Meetings were held between dominion and provincial finance ministers and officials in December 1941. The objective, as far as Ottawa was concerned, was to fix an amount that would "permit the provinces to stand on their own feet until the end of the war, without coming back to the Dominion for further assistance." Ilsley admitted that the relative level of services in the various provinces was unequal, but it was not the time to deal with the issue. "We are not applying the principle of bringing the levels of social services throughout the Dominion up to a national standard, which was the principle suggested in the Rowell-Sirois report," Ilsley noted. "That was rejected and we do not think that we can import that principle into these fiscal need subsidies." No subsidies would be paid to Quebec, Ontario, Alberta, or British Columbia. The situation in the Maritime provinces was complicated by existing federal grants as a result of the Duncan Commission and the White Commission. These provinces would lose if they gave up these previous grants. As a result, the federal government agreed to make up the losses. "The citations from the report of the Sirois Commission," Ilsley noted, "should not be taken as having any bearing on what we do here either in this or in any other respect."[41]

Ontario tried to hold out but Hepburn was trapped. With a large provincial surplus, the premier of Ontario was under pressure to make concessions in order to assist in prosecuting the war. The provincial government agreed to negotiate and discussions began on 30 September 1941. In return for vacating the personal and corporate income tax fields, Hepburn demanded that Ottawa guarantee provincial revenues from gasoline taxes, vehicle licences, and liquor board profits for the province. "My worry," Hepburn informed Ilsley, "is that we are going to be left with the super structure and all the revenues will be taken from us. If this is a move which has as its final objective the elimination of the provinces we might as well know it."[42] Not surprisingly, these negotiations proved particularly acrimonious and lasted over six months. Provincial officials accused their federal counterparts of attempting to reduce the amount to be paid to Ontario so that existing levels of social services could not be maintained. The negotiations dragged on into the early months of 1942, and Hepburn even adjourned the provincial legislature to show his displeasure with the failure to reach a settlement. In the end, the federal government agreed to allow the municipalities to collect their corporation taxes until the end of 1943. Ontario finally gave way and signed an agreement in March 1942.[43]

As the months passed, Manitoba continued to lament the sidelining of Rowell-Sirois. Premier Bracken could not help but contrast the new tax rental agreements with the commission's recommendations and regret what could have been. There would be no attempt to create conditions of social equality through minimum standards across the provinces. Previously negotiated special subsidies were being replaced by fiscal needs subsidies. These grants did not provide the provinces with an average level of social services but, rather, granted "pressing necessity for money to maintain its present public services," even if they were below an adequate level. Any positive gains from the tax rental agreements, Bracken emphasized, were temporary rather than permanent, and "even these would accrue on a more satisfactory basis and in larger measure, by the implementation of the Rowell-Sirois Report."[44] Manitoba, he claimed, was receiving one-seventh of the benefits under the tax rental agreement it would have received under Rowell-Sirois.[45] In December 1942, Bracken, frustrated by the never-ending fiscal issues and Mackenzie King's strategies, left the premiership he had held since 1922. He succumbed to the blandishments of federal Conservatives and became leader of the newly named Progressive Conservative Party, a sop to Bracken's Prairie perspectives. Manitoba's capable Provincial Treasurer Stuart Garson took over as premier.[46]

Facing a divided caucus and suffering from deteriorating health, Mitch Hepburn resigned as premier of Ontario in October 1942. Mackenzie King was relieved to say the least. "Ambition, combined with venom," the prime minister recorded, "has helped to bring about his destruction." King went on to gloat: "[I feel] this morning as if the atmosphere has been cleansed, as if the province and the Dominion had been freed of a corrupt and corroding influence, something really loathsome."[47] The divided Liberals in Ontario carried on for nearly a year, but they were falling apart. George Drew and the Conservatives won the provincial election with a minority government in the summer of 1943. In the words of historian P.E. Bryden, "Drew inherited a province that faced a much more muscular federal government than had any of his predecessors."[48] Yet Ontario still had political and economic "muscle" of its own.

The Canadian government had been preparing for postwar reconstruction almost since the war began, but by late 1942, when confidence of an eventual Allied victory increased, there was greater emphasis on decontrol, demobilization, and reconstruction. The cabinet and several departments, notably pensions and health, worked on the postwar plan for social security. Healthcare insurance, family allowances, and comprehensive veterans' benefits became central to the Liberal government's social policy agenda between 1942 and 1945.[49] This new agenda was encapsulated by the goals of "reconstruction" planning. These goals were coordinated if not initiated by the powerful interdepartmental Economic Advisory Committee chaired by Clifford Clark. After late 1944, the efforts were led by a new department, the Ministry of Reconstruction, headed by wartime cabinet minister C.D. Howe, with W.A. Mackintosh as his deputy.

The war years led to increased support for comprehensive social services in the postwar world. Policy proposals were put forward both within government and with the general public. In early 1943, two large policy studies prepared for federal advisory committees advocated major expansions of social services. *Report of the Advisory Committee on Health Insurance*, compiled under the lead of Dr. J.J. Heagerty, long-time federal director of public health services, argued in favour of a federally led comprehensive public health insurance system. An even broader plan was found in the *Report on Social Security in Canada*, written by Leonard Marsh, a prominent McGill University social work professor. Both works emerged from the enthusiastic support of Minister of Pensions and National Health Ian Mackenzie, whose personal and departmental energies focused on building national programs with little concern for provincial relations or fiscal needs.[50]

Marsh proposed a comprehensive plan of social security measures, again under federal authority. Each study was the culmination of state-led social policy reform proposals that had been percolating for a number of years in academic, social service, and government circles. While aware of the complexity of the fiscal and jurisdictional issues involved, each plan was predicated on federal access to major revenue sources as well as on provincial enthusiasm for federal leadership and coordination. By embracing conditional grants, neither study seemed concerned about the delicacies of federalism, and they ignored the principles and discussions of the Rowell-Sirois Report. Neither study adjudged as insurmountable the jurisdictional or fiscal barriers to a strong federal lead with provincial administration. The two reports created a flurry of interest but aroused more irritation than support in the upper reaches of the federal government. As Grant Dexter opined, "there wasn't anything practical in the Marsh report."[51]

In the larger policy community, the Rowell-Sirois perspective was upheld against these blueprints for the welfare state. Charlotte Whitton was critical of the Heagerty and Marsh proposals as well as of their United Kingdom counterpart, the Beveridge Report. In a short book commissioned by the new Progressive Conservative leader, John Bracken, she emphasized the primacy of the provinces in areas of social services as well as the need for their expansion. She used Rowell-Sirois to support her rejection of wholesale fiscal or administrative centralization.[52] In 1943, another prominent academic and former League for Social Reconstruction stalwart, Harry Cassidy, strongly advocated for the universalization of social services. His work drew extensively on Rowell-Sirois in highlighting the jurisdictional and fiscal limits on any comprehensive schemes, but he gave ground in proposing the limited use of some conditional funding along with unconditional federal tax transfers. In the years that followed, Cassidy argued that social services under provincial administration could be financed through Ottawa's lead and the judicious use of conditional grants. Like many observers since, he ignored the emphasis on unconditional grants and the diverse provincial "fiscal need" that comprised the bedrock of the Rowell-Sirois plan.[53]

Although the provincial advocates of Rowell-Sirois remained true to the commission, its supporters in Ottawa had begun to change their positions. From a federal perspective, gains were now being made without having to "transfer constitutional power" or share tax revenue along carefully assessed lines of fiscal need. While some proposals, such as health care, were based on seeking cooperation with the provinces, others, such as family allowances (despite the obvious intrusion into provincial jurisdiction), bypassed them altogether. Guided by the lodestar of full employment rather than social security, a comprehensive reform of the federal system seemed less important. In the words of finance official Robert Bryce, it seemed possible to solve the problem of the tax fields "without constitutional change by applying the principles of the wartime agreements."[54] The objective was to maintain the tax rental agreements into the postwar era. "Wartime experience," reflected prime ministerial advisor (and later a Liberal cabinet minister) Jack Pickersgill, "suggested there were certain inadequacies in the Rowell-Sirois recommendations."[55] Another dominion-provincial conference was being planned to deal with the postwar era. Clifford Clark intended to use the opportunity to knock the provinces into line. "To hell with the provinces," was Clark's position. "With him," reported Dexter in mocking Mackenzie King's electoral slogan of 1935, "it is tax agreements or chaos."[56]

Several influential federal bureaucrats who had worked from the sidelines on Rowell-Sirois, such as Clifford Clark, Bill Mackintosh, and Sandy Skelton, remained active in the resolution of issues raised by the royal commission. But their goals also shifted. As he worked on reconstruction planning after 1943, Skelton continued to accommodate provincial fears about their fiscal security in a world of high social security payments. He often returned to the solution provided by the Rowell-Sirois Report. Mackintosh, on the other hand, who became deputy minister of reconstruction by war's end, embraced the Keynesian agenda of full employment and gave less importance to the role of the provinces. Clark, the most influential of the three bureaucrats, focused on sustaining Ottawa's fiscal situation and gave little thought to provincial fear and suspicion over federal assurances of adequate compensation in return for their loss of direct tax sources.[57]

The commissioners themselves were no longer involved. Sirois had died in January 1941, not long after the failure of the Dominion-Provincial Conference. Dafoe continued to observe and receive information from afar, but his health was failing. His writing concentrated on international relations, although he still spoke in public as late as 1943 on the continuing relevance of Rowell-Sirois. He died in January 1944. The younger commissioners, Henry Angus and Robert MacKay, remained active throughout the decade and for years after, but neither was engaged in public advocacy over federalism or domestic policy making. Angus and MacKay spent part of the war in Ottawa working in the external affairs department, far from federal-provincial issues.

Ottawa's proposals for postwar federalism were presented at the Dominion-Provincial Conference on Reconstruction, convened on 5 August 1945. Known as the "Green Book" (or, more formally, as the *Proposals of the Government of Canada*), the federal plan was published in a fifty-two-page report bound in mint-green covers. The volume contained three main proposals: a plan for the transition from the managed wartime economy to a peacetime "private enterprise" economy; an outline for systematic "public enterprise" activities; and a program of social security based on protections for the individual against "risks," "hazards," and "disabilities." The package was based on a new set of "financial arrangements" as well as on the broad proviso that an open market economy would emerge internationally.[58]

The reconstruction plan included a specific list of federal actions, ranging from "decontrols" to "industrial conversion," and a package of veterans' benefits, housing programs, agricultural supports, and major labour market reforms including collective bargaining rights. An emphasis on job creation underlay the proposals.[59] The most innovative portions of the Green Book, however, were contained in the plans for "public investment" and "social security." These two aspects were particularly important because they sought to avoid the crises that had decimated the economy after the Great War. The public investment agenda concentrated on natural resource development, transportation expansion, and technical education projects. It had to involve "cooperation" and "coordination" with the provinces. All of this would sustain high employment and incomes.[60] The extensive social security measures were justified on both "humanitarian" and "economic" grounds. They encompassed design of a public health care system that included health insurance, extended unemployment insurance, and national old age pensions.[61]

To support the three areas, the Green Book set out a controversial outline for an agreement on a permanent federal fiscal regime. Only a new set of financial arrangements would ensure full employment and social security in Canada's postwar world. Citing Rowell-Sirois, the Green Book asserted that Canadians and their governments should remember that, prior to the war, Canada had been "harassed" by economic problems, including inadequate systems of taxation and fiscal relations. These systems were inefficient, they were "inadequate" for the provinces, and they "undermined" federalism. The proposed fiscal regime included a tax agreement in which Ottawa took over income, corporation, and succession taxes but provided the provinces in return with an unconditional grant. The federal government proposed to pay each province twelve dollars per capita annually, with the amount an "irreducible minimum" and adjusted to grow in accordance with the national output and provincial population. Ottawa also offered to share costs in specific social service areas based on specific ratios, holding out the suggestion that there would be variations in the ratios depending on provincial need.[62]

Although there had been prior discussions between governments, and the issues were certainly well known, the specific Green Book proposals were only brought to the provinces at the conference. The premiers and their advisors were taken aback by the far-reaching nature of the federal proposals that lacked prior provincial consultation. Premier George Drew of Ontario intervened early in the conference to denounce the proposals as centralist: "Centralization is an evil principle of government," he declared. "Hitler is the prototype of the centralizer. Centralization always leads to Hitlerism." Rhetoric aside, Drew wanted to negotiate. Along with Quebec premier Maurice Duplessis (who had been returned to office in mid-1944), Ontario was prepared to accept federal collection of personal and corporate taxes under certain conditions. Such a scheme, however, would involve complex negotiations, and they could not be accomplished at a meeting over a few days.[63] Drew led the move to secure a delay in the proceedings and then departed to Toronto to study the proposals. Duplessis soon followed. The conference adjourned.

While many in the federal government tried to associate the Green Book proposals with the Rowell-Sirois recommendations, the commission's supporters saw through the guise. Although Dafoe had died, his *Winnipeg Free Press* colleagues followed the issues with rapt attention. Grant Dexter commented on how the chances to remake Canadian federalism continued to diminish. Ottawa's path forward bore faint resemblance to that laid out by Rowell-Sirois. In a long and thoughtful letter to fellow *Winnipeg Free Press* journalists George Ferguson and Bruce Hutchison, Dexter vented his frustration. He advised the two editorialists on how to write about the failed 1945 conference. News stories should focus on the fact that the Rowell-Sirois solution to the crisis in federalism was slipping into the background. "You will have to excuse me," Dexter noted sarcastically, but after "putting in considerable time" studying the commission and the report, it was disheartening to observe how neither the tax rental agreements nor the Green Book proposals bore a strong resemblance to the Rowell-Sirois recommendations. The only aspect of the Green Book "which [could] honestly claim warrant in the Sirois report" was the transfer of direct taxes to the dominion. The federal government was doing exactly what the commissioners warned it not to: Ottawa was taking a piecemeal approach. The present proposals, Dexter claimed, afforded "only a temporary solution to the problem of Dominion-provincial financial relations." The recent conference led Dexter to go back to his "Sirois library," and the exercise proved enlightening. The King government had "abandoned the very pith and basis of the commission's findings." By rejecting the National Adjustment Grants, Dexter noted, "[the] one thing that seemed of supreme importance to the commission in seeking to solve the Dominion-provincial problem, has been thrown overboard."[64]

Grant Dexter emphasized that, in its historical analysis, Rowell-Sirois had made clear that the "curse" of dominion-provincial relations was "the equal per capita grant system inaugurated at Confederation." The provinces were not equal in 1867, and this imbalance was recognized through "special dispensations" to New Brunswick and Nova Scotia. Equality of treatment was never possible. Yet it had been attempted repeatedly "until the last shreds of logic were stripped from the per capita system." The "subsidy problem," Dexter argued, led to claims for special terms, resulted in political protest, and generated a hatred of central Canada. It was disruptive to national unity. The basic recommendation of Rowell-Sirois was to eliminate the per capita system on a basis of equality: "That was the first essential step in solving the problem." The provinces disliked the federal financial commission that was to determine the grants. The criticism, Dexter claimed, was "weak" because an independent tribunal was possible without its being political. The federal government now turned to the Green Book proposals, but they "fell far short of what [was] required." The provision for an equal upward revision of the new grants in keeping with increases in the national income "mitigate[d] the thing somewhat," he admitted, "but [didn't] touch the basic point that the provinces [were] unequal." Dexter proposed that Ferguson and Hutchison emphasize editorially that Rowell-Sirois offered permanent remedies while the Green Book offered only temporary measures. The "evils of the past" would emerge again and the "basic problem so far as the weaker provinces [were] concerned ha[d] not been touched." The "old rancours" would continue because there was "no alternative to the Sirois recommendations."[65]

When the conference adjourned in August 1945, discussions over the Green Book moved into study groups and intergovernmental consultations that went on for nine months. This gestation period was marked by serious if intermittent policy discussions within and between governments. Sandy Skelton worked heroically to coordinate these consultations. No longer hampered by the Hepburn-King feud, Ontario took a leading role among the provinces in seeking to offer solutions to peacetime fiscal revenue sharing. Even Mackenzie King was impressed.[66] British Columbia, now led by the capable John Hart, also demonstrated a willingness to find grounds for agreement.[67] Manitoba, Nova Scotia, and Saskatchewan, each led by premiers who supported the Rowell-Sirois Report, were committed to finding a comprehensive agreement. While Rowell-Sirois was seldom referred to directly, the commission's report was always hovering in the background.[68]

The "Reconstruction Conference" was reconvened between 25 April and 3 May 1946. Despite the sense of optimism, and the best efforts of bureaucrats such as Sandy Skelton who continued to carry much of the burden of coordinating federal-provincial negotiations, once again the dominion-provincial gathering bogged down in disagreement. Even an increase in the unconditional per capita grant from twelve to fifteen dollars failed to overcome provincial concerns that they would not receive revenue increases to meet expanded social services programs, not to mention the rising costs of transportation and education. The "weaker provinces" remained convinced that their commitments would outstrip their fiscal resources, just as they had in the 1920s and 1930s. Premier Duplessis of

Quebec abruptly left the conference at noon on 3 May and, after further discussions, the proceedings ended "with vitriol but without agreement." Mackenzie King blamed his inflexible colleagues in the Department of Finance and the Bank of Canada for the breakdown.[69]

Following the second adjournment of the Reconstruction Conference, the federal government announced its plans. If a province agreed to withdraw from the personal and corporate income tax and succession duty fields for five years, it would receive an annual per capita subsidy based on population and gross national production. The unilateral announcement led Ontario to call for a return to Rowell-Sirois. Speaking in Winnipeg, Premier George Drew claimed he supported a

> National Adjustment Grant such as was recommended by the Rowell-Sirois Report. I made it clear that we are ready to agree to any system of administration which will be acceptable to the provinces receiving National Adjustment Grants, and that we are ready to agree to any financial basis for these grants approved by the Conference. I might remind you that the Dominion proposals exclude this very essential recommendation in the Rowell-Sirois Report. We attach considerable importance to this proposal and we want a provision for an adequate National Adjustment Grant included in the agreement.[70]

Some members of the audience might have shaken their heads to make sure they had heard the Ontario premier correctly. But Ontario treasurer Leslie Frost expressed similar sentiments. The provinces were in "a frame of mind" to participate in "a big deal" over taxation. The federal government, however, would not give any ground.[71]

The federal government proceeded on its own, retaining the lion's share of direct taxes that it had swept up since 1941, while the provinces continued to mull over what social welfare state measures each or all could enact.[72] For months, the federal and provincial governments made at least a pretense of negotiating a permanent solution to the division of taxation. The premiers, including Quebec's Maurice Duplessis and Alberta's Ernest Manning, informed the prime minister that the provinces were keen to come to an agreement.

Other provinces continued to call for a return to Rowell-Sirois. Not surprisingly, Manitoba, led by Premier Stuart Garson (until he too succumbed to the lure of federal politics in 1948), and Saskatchewan, under CCF premier Tommy Douglas, continued to make strong pleas for the report. Garson had approached the 1945–46 conferences as well as the subsequent negotiations as occasions for the "less well-to-do" provinces to make provisions for continuing effective fiscal transfers even if the wealthy provinces did not accept them. Douglas noted at one point that he was "taking it for granted that the purpose of any federal-provincial conference [would] be to discuss the main recommendations of the Sirois Report." Throughout the rest of the decade and into the 1950s, the Saskatchewan government viewed the Rowell-Sirois recommendations as the starting point for all dominion-provincial agreements.[73] Angus Macdonald, meanwhile, had returned to provincial politics as Nova Scotia premier in late 1945, and he remained a vocal supporter of Rowell-Sirois. He enthusiastically reminded his federal counterparts that the basis for a resolution of an improved national tax system was to be found in the report. By the end of 1946 he admitted defeat. "The work of the Sirois Commission has been pretty thoroughly scrapped [and] cast aside." The postwar proposals returned to the old per capita subsidy as if Nova Scotia could "get along on the same basis as Ontario."[74]

As Grant Dexter predicted, the years immediately following the end of the Second World War witnessed further moves towards centralization. Mackenzie King was not comfortable with this direction, but a new generation of politicians and civil servants increasingly directed policy. King was never "keen" about the tax rental agreements. He had difficulty embracing the notion of one government taxing and another spending.[75] "The Finance Department, behind which is the Bank of Canada," King observed in January 1946, "have completely changed the generally accepted procedure which has been to keep as largely as possible the spending authority responsible for the tax-raising. I think their effort is in the direction of centralization of financial control. That may be desirable from the point of view of more effective administration, etc., from Ottawa's end, but politically it will not be possible."[76] Regardless, because it was politically effective, he presided over the new direction until his resignation in late 1948.

In January 1947, the new finance minister, Douglas Abbott, who had replaced the exhausted J.L. Ilsley, announced that Ottawa would continue the separate tax rental arrangements with each province.[77] According to historian P.E. Bryden, "Canada thus entered the post-war period without a blueprint for action. Instead of coordinated activity, ad hoc arrangements governed the sharing of tax fields and the responsibility for expensive social policies, and the uncoordinated statutory subsidies remained the only way in which provincial inequalities were balanced."[78] All the efforts to create a coordinated federal fiscal system had failed, and by 1947 new agreements were negotiated with each province.

Conclusion
Appraising Rowell-Sirois

*The doubting ones who have used the lack of immediate
positive results to illustrate their views on the impotency of
royal commissions generally, and this one in particular, seem
to have stopped at this preliminary judgment and never
explored below the surface.*

— *Ronald M. Burns, 1961*[1]

Rowell-Sirois haunted federal-provincial relations in the years that followed
the Second World War. In 1950, a dominion-provincial conference on finances and social security was held. The conference agreed upon a revised
national old age pension plan, but the overall result was a continuation of
the ad hoc and federally dominated postwar system. The tax rental arrangements were maintained despite considerable provincial discontent
from Quebec and the weaker provinces and would continue until a different
system, known as "equalization," was worked out in 1962.[2]

In preparation for the 1950 conference, senior federal officials reconsidered Rowell-Sirois. Clifford Clark and Robert Bryce in the Department
of Finance credited the royal commission for highlighting "the uncoordinated and aimless development of the tax structure at both the federal
and provincial levels," for recognizing the need for "a broader approach to
intergovernmental finance," and for "insisting on the necessity of a franker
recognition of regional differences of wealth and income and a more vigorous effort on the part of the Dominion to reduce these disparities." They

praised it for showing that the prewar subsidy system was "chaotic and illogical" and that conditional grants were "inherently unsatisfactory." This was not faint praise, but federal officials downplayed Rowell-Sirois due to limitations in the National Adjustment Grant proposal. The proposal provided no specific methods for calculating provincial needs or variations in needs. It did not provide for an expansion of social services. It was unfair to the prosperous provinces since there was no compensation to them for the loss of tax revenue they would suffer. It was a document, federal officials claimed, rooted in the slump of the 1930s and not the boom of the present.[3]

Despite these limitations, the federal view asserted that the tax rental agreements were "undoubtedly the offspring of the Rowell-Sirois recommendations" by providing the federal government with control over the tax fields. The other aspect of the recommendation about unconditional grants, however, was ignored. Compensation for this invasion of provincial jurisdiction was "considerably different in character from the National Adjustment Grants proposed by the Commission." The purpose of Rowell-Sirois was to "relieve the social and economic disparities between regions of Canada and it was inherent in the plan that proportionately the largest payments would go to the least wealthy provinces." By contrast, the tax rental payments were "essentially the price that had to be paid to rent from the provinces their rights to impose certain direct taxes for the period of the war, and it was inevitable, therefore, that the largest payments would be received by the provinces where the tax fields had most value."[4]

The federal officials admitted that the atmosphere for dominion-provincial relations improved after the war, but opposition from the affluent provinces to a system of National Adjustment Grants remained an obstacle. The "three prosperous provinces" would be asked to vacate their richest tax fields and receive no grants by way of compensation "except the implied prospect of assistance in times of extreme adversity." They had been offered escape from their expenditures for relief and for servicing their public debt, "but those compensations, which may have been sufficient in 1937 now seem to be outweighed by their loss of revenue and the potential reduction in their independence." The objective of the Rowell-Sirois Commission was to relieve the provinces of their most burdensome expenditures while helping them meet their expenditures through federal

unconditional grants: "The Commission was not concerned with providing for possible increases in the functions of provincial governments, which
it considered to be already over-extended." Finance officials believed that
increases had indeed occurred with such provisions as health insurance.
As provincial costs for social programs increased, "eventually, the largest
portion of provincial revenues would be derived from fiscal need grants
whose size would be never certain from one year to the next."[5]

Despite their shifting views, federal officials in 1950 claimed that
Canadian federalism was following the general course charted by Rowell-
Sirois. The report was "in itself a form of tax rental agreement" and had
"already been partially implemented by the 1941 and 1947 tax agreements."
Most of the recommendations "ha[d] been carried out in whole or in part."
The main difference between the commission proposals and the tax rental
agreements, they asserted, was simply a matter of "emphasis." The former
was concerned with recovery from the Depression, the latter with counter-
cyclical fiscal policy; the former was based on the "adjusted deficit" concept,
the latter on "per capita expenditure."[6]

Despite their best attempts to weave a narrative of consistency, federal
officials could not avoid one glaring weakness in their argument. However
much the postwar economy had grown, the vulnerabilities in Canada's
federal structure had not been solved and, instead, temporary measures
became the norm. "Conditions have been particularly propitious for the
attainment of federal aims," officials admitted, "it cannot be assumed that
they will remain so in the future."[7] Yet few of the underlying needs of the
citizens of Canada had been fully addressed. The weaker provinces and
their residents did not have sufficient access to social security, ranging
from education to health care to pensions. The most powerful provinces
scuttled Rowell-Sirois in 1941, but after the war it was federal officials like
Clark and Bryce who refused to reconsider or elaborate upon the recommendations: "Whatever may have been the merits of the recommendations
of the Rowell-Sirois Commission in the context of 1939," they concluded
in 1950, "they are, in many respects, no longer relevant."[8]

Perhaps the one area the officials did find satisfactory was that Rowell-
Sirois undoubtedly was successful in recommending regular federal-
provincial conferences. The era of these "first ministers" meetings was
initiated after the 1941 and 1945–46 conferences. Put in mere numbers,

in the twenty-five years between the first conference in 1906 and the 1941 summit on the Rowell-Sirois Commission, there were nine formal conferences. In the twenty-five years after 1945, there were twenty-six, a rate that continued into the early twenty-first century, when Canadian leaders either tired of or learned to avoid the big formal meetings.[9]

Outside government, the interpretation of Rowell-Sirois by academic observers was more varied. Starting in the 1940s, the report was often viewed as a centralizing document, just as interventionist government was viewed as centralizing. This view started with the scathing critique by the influential University of Toronto economist Harold Innis in 1940 and was sustained by the more positive account by Queen's University political scientist (and former inquiry staff member) J.A. Corry. Innis was fearful of the growth of state power by the 1940s, claiming the report invited Ottawa to "abuse" its powers over the provinces. Corry did not take that position, but he worried that contemporary economic and political forces threatened the "compromise" of federalism and the "parcelled out" sovereignty between two levels. Corry argued chiefly from the case of the United States, but he offered no specific panaceas for Canada.[10]

Similar assessments were taken up by other scholars over the next two decades. The story went that Rowell-Sirois laid the foundation for postwar Canadian federalism as part of the general move towards a more centralized and powerful federal government. For the next twenty years, the nuances of the recommendations led most analysts and commentators to simplify them into a struggle between centralization and provincial rights. Few academics recognized these nuances. Based on the centralist direction that Ottawa pursued after the war, it was assumed that this was the path recommended by Rowell-Sirois.[11] While the arguments about the evolution of the Canadian economy and governmental system remained influential, the recommendations for remaking federalism in Canada slipped away.

There were a few observers who dissented from the dominant interpretation. Not surprisingly, these were often some of the experts involved with the commission. Henry Angus and Bill Mackintosh reflected on the commission a decade after its completion as well as on the broader shifts in federal-provincial relations. They approved the moves towards unconditional grants and transparency in the federal fiscal system. But, as Angus argued, they were not pleased with the anemic resolution of "chronic disparities" between regions and the unequal distribution of national income.[12] Their dissent was later taken up by others. In a 1961 festschrift for Henry Angus, the deputy treasurer of Manitoba and formerly a BC treasury official, Ronald M. Burns, made another important point:

> The doubting ones who have used the lack of immediate positive results to illustrate their views on the impotency of royal commissions generally, and this one in particular, seem to have stopped at this preliminary judgment and never explored below the surface. Perhaps on a box-score basis the Commissioners do not fare well, but investigations of this nature and scope cannot be dismissed so superficially.

According to Burns, the legacy of Rowell-Sirois lay in the "knowledge and direction" it offered: "We should take into account not just what was immediately achieved but rather the atmosphere for change and development created through both the recommendations themselves and the vast background of information assembled in the course of the enquiry." The commissioners "put forward certain fundamental ideas and principles which if read and assimilated might well have gone far to discredit some of the more irresponsible and parochial views that unfortunately for our national interests are still held widely and used to practical political effect."[13]

The political scientist Donald Smiley worked diligently for years, starting in the early 1960s, to reinterpret the importance of Rowell-Sirois. On the surface, he admitted, the commission failed and "its analysis of federal-provincial relations has had surprisingly little influence on the direction that the theory and practice of Canadian federalism have taken since 1945." The concept of provincial autonomy was "central" to the commission's argument but it was "denied explicitly or implicitly" by the Green Book proposals submitted at the 1945 conference, by the Massey Commission of 1951, as well as by the "actual developments in federal-provincial relations since the Second World War." Smiley realized that, below the surface, Rowell-Sirois offered something distinct. The "master-solution" of the report aimed at ensuring that each province was able to provide a level of provincial services at average national standards without subjecting its citizens to provincial taxation above the national average. The commission opted for "inter-provincial equalization based on fiscal need rather than compensation for these alleged disabilities." The preoccupations of the war combined with provincial obstructionism prevented the implementation of Rowell-Sirois, but according to Smiley, these obstacles did not fully explain the report's failure. The federal government was already moving in a different direction. By 1945, Ottawa had committed itself to a "new Grand Design." This design was based on "the Keynesian imperative" that the main economic role of national governments was to ensure appropriate levels of aggregate demand through generalized fiscal and monetary policies and through lowering barriers to international trade and investment. Of particular note, it avoided the "explicit widening of the constitutional powers of the national government." Since "peacetime capitalist economics faced chronic deficiencies of aggregate demand, the 1945 proposals included an important role for the federal authorities in public investment and, in cooperation with the provinces, in establishing and sustaining a Canadian welfare state."[14]

In contrast, by the 1970s and 1980s, the interpretation of Rowell-Sirois among many Canadian historians became further entrenched in a centralist metanarrative. Rather than examining the innovations of the commission, historians tended to reiterate arguments about its centralizing intent. Concentrating, as many did, on the building of national political institutions, they did not deviate from their explanations about the powerful central state that was created in the postwar period, though they were well aware of the counterforce of provincialism. They did not share Innis's suspicion of centralized government, and they wrote as if centralization was the way of the wartime and postwar world.[15]

While the vast majority of historians embraced the centralist metanarrative, a few examined Canadian political developments from a provincial position and, as result, proposed a different view of the Rowell-Sirois Commission.[16] This perspective, which was devised by a number of historians examining the regions and the provinces, was synthesized by Stephen Henderson, who argued that an "unfortunate conflation" occurred in the literature of federalism in which the interests of the federal government were bound by the "aspirations" of the country. The provincial side was "neglected or, worse, feared and mistrusted." In the "absence of rigorous historical scrutiny of the development of post-war federalism, statements about the sweetness and light of Ottawa's side of the federal balance [were] accepted at face value. Similarly, articulations of provincial concerns about the federal system [were] often dismissed as petty, self-interested, and short-sighted."[17]

How then should we evaluate the historical significance of the Rowell-Sirois Commission? There is no disputing the fact that the commission failed to direct policy. The Dominion-Provincial Conference on the report in 1941 was a fiasco. The recommendations were not implemented. Canadian federalism went in a different direction. Yet the Rowell-Sirois Commission fully exposed the troubled and even dysfunctional condition of Canadian federalism, and it served as a touchstone for the remaking and rethinking of federalism for many years.

Seventy years after Canada became a nation in 1867, Confederation had faltered. Federalism was fraught with difficulties emerging from the Great War and from the challenges of the "modern era" of government. But the Great Depression threatened to break Confederation. Coinciding with the most serious economic crisis ever to grip the nation was the arrival of a group of aggressive, bombastic, colourful, and populist premiers. Canada has never again encountered such a group, and their personalities shaped the life of the royal commission. The Rowell-Sirois Commission was established to repair the broken system and perhaps to "Re-Confederate" Canada.

Rowell-Sirois had limited chances for success against the likes of such extravagant public figures as Mitch Hepburn, Maurice Duplessis, Duff Pattullo, and "Bible Bill" Aberhart in office. Likewise, however, the commission would never have been established without the influence and support of John Bracken and Angus L. Macdonald, but they were far less imposing national figures than the leaders of the largest provinces. On the federal side, the story is much the same. There is little doubt that the interparty feud between Liberal prime minister Mackenzie King and Liberal premier Mitch Hepburn hampered the commission's work and contributed to its ultimate fate. King did not lead the federal response to Rowell-Sirois. The roles of highly influential federal civil servants in the Department of Finance (Clifford Clark) and the Bank of Canada (Graham Towers and Sandy Skelton) loom over this story. But, with the exception of Skelton, they did not shape the report.

The commissioners and their staff collaborated fully in shaping and writing Rowell-Sirois. As a group, they were convinced of the seriousness of their endeavour and they were determined to produce an inquiry that would help break the log jam of policy. They were committed to their role in the governmental structure as a temporary extension of the executive branch. Despite the crises faced by the inquiry in its two and a half years of operation – from the loss of key personnel, to tensions with the staff, to the obstructive antics of the premiers, to the backdrop of a world war – the commissioners remained steadfast and produced a remarkable document. While none of them were radicals, all had the capacity to argue against the grain of received mainstream public policy. The commission's research plan drew upon the leading social scientists of the time just as a generation of work was coming to fruition. The innovative nature of Plan One was testament to the creative thinking of the disparate core groups of Skelton and his political economist associates on one side, and Angus and MacKay abetted by Robert Fowler on the other. The stabilizing forces of Sirois and Dafoe ensured that the work was completed successfully despite creative and temperamental differences.

Over the years, the younger commission staff fared better than their report. Skelton remained a senior civil servant and a voice for cooperative federalism, until his untimely death in 1950. He drowned sailing the treacherous Lagos Lagoon while working on a British commission of inquiry investigating federal finance in Nigeria. Skelton's senior research colleagues, Mackintosh, Corry, Deutsch, and Eggleston, went on to illustrious academic careers. The first three became successive Principals of Queen's University, while Eggleston established the School of Journalism at Carleton University. Rowell's aide, Robert Fowler, moved ever more prominently in the world of law and business, and headed a 1957 federal inquiry into broadcasting that reshaped the regulatory model for television and radio. Angus, unimpressed by his work at external affairs during the war, returned to UBC, which he helped build into a major research institution. MacKay flitted between Dalhousie and the federal government until the mid-1940s, when he entered the diplomatic corps, engaging in such projects as bringing Newfoundland into the Confederation.

The Rowell-Sirois Report set down specific policy observations and recommendations that ultimately reset a federalist agenda that reverberated for decades. A crucial argument in Book One was that the era of the national policy and an integrated east-west economy had come to an end by the 1920s. Canadian economic policy was moving from one national policy era to another. The era of national growth based on western settlement, tariff protection, and east-west transportation links was succeeded by full employment, social welfare, and trade liberalization. This new era of "compensatory liberalism" based on Keynesian fiscal policy and the so-called welfare state contrasted with the state-shielded market economy of the nineteenth century. By the end of the twentieth century, this second era came to a close with the shift towards free trade, the decline of the welfare state, and the emergence in the 1980s of a third national policy, described as "market liberalism," or "corporate neo-liberalism."[18] This is the truncated liberal democracy of the early twenty-first century.

The most important aspect of Rowell-Sirois was Plan One, the scheme for the reallocation of taxation and its national redistribution. Plan One was to be accomplished through agreement and delegation in the areas of income and succession taxes accompanied by the unconditional reallocation of revenues through the National Adjustment Grant. This proposal aimed to provide funding to the provinces based not on specific programs but solely on varying provincial needs. Long-standing debates over centralization and decentralization, between the federal and the provincial powers, were not important to the commission's recommendations. Traditional, outdated, and legalistic ways of thinking had to be abandoned.[19]

The report made it clear that conceiving of the federal system within a legal-constitutional framework did not reflect the ways of modern politics and government. Rowell-Sirois sidestepped the area of formal constitutional change almost entirely (the unemployment insurance power being the exception), but this was not simply a means of avoiding conflict. In the world of complex overlapping jurisdictions and intergovernmental responsibilities, policy decisions were political and had to be placed within the purview of politicians. By restating the agenda of the federal system and the big issues of public policy within what Edwin R. Black once called the "strange vocabulary" of fiscal federalism, the commission was successful.[20]

The Rowell-Sirois Commission reinforced the fundamental reconsideration of the purposes of government occurring in the middle decades of the twentieth century. It asserted that government policy must concentrate on the general welfare of all and that redistribution was central to that objective. It also asserted that formalistic, rigid structures of federalism were unworkable. A workable federal system required a flexible and changeable set of inter-governmental relations, oriented by temporal matters and a high degree of autonomy for the levels of government. Despite its achievements, there were omissions and failings. A critical example was the commission's refusal to examine the social and economic conditions of Indigenous population in Canada. Another was the complete absence of considering the role of women in the public sphere. A third was its obtuseness about Quebec's particular policy relationships with the rest of Canada. Each of these failings was to catch up to Canadian governments within a generation.

The report constituted a fundamental shift in public discourse. It prescribed a new view of the relations between governments as well as the role of government.[21] The commissioners articulated a vision of federalism far removed from the nineteenth-century model they were called upon to renovate and they rose above the conventional views of their time. Their original instructions were to tinker with the federation, the machinery of government, but their recommendations were nothing less than to remake Canadian federalism into a system designed to provide the "maximum welfare" of all its citizens.

Notes

Introduction

1 Edwin R. Black, *Divided Loyalties: Canadian Concepts of Federalism* (Montreal and Kingston: McGill-Queen's University Press, 1975), 3.

2 Among many works on the subject of inquiries, the following have been particularly useful: Neil Bradford, *Commissioning Ideas: Canadian National Policy Innovation in Comparative Perspective* (Don Mills: Oxford University Press, 1998); *Commissions of Inquiry and Policy Change: A Comparative Analysis*, ed. Greg Inwood and Carolyn Johns (Toronto: University of Toronto Press, 2014); Innis Christie and Paul A. Pross, "Commissions of Inquiry: Introduction," *Dalhousie Law Journal* 12, 3 (1989–90): 1–18; Barbara Lauriat, "'The Examination of Everything': Royal Commissions in British Legal History," *Statute Law Review* 31, 1 (2010): 24–46.

3 The arguments about the radical change in Canadian federalism shaped by Rowell-Sirois are found in many works, most pertinently the following: Alan C. Cairns, *Reconfigurations: Canadian Citizenship and Constitutional Change* (Toronto: McClelland and Stewart, 1995), 19; Donald V. Smiley, "The Rowell-Sirois Report, Provincial Autonomy, and Post-war Canadian Federalism," *Canadian Journal of Economics and Political Science* 28, 1 (1962): 54–69; R.B. Bryce, *Maturing in Hard Times: Canada's Department of Finance through the Great Depression* (Montreal and Kingston: McGill-Queen's University Press, 1986), 218; Ronald M. Burns, "The Royal Commission on Dominion-Provincial Relations: The Report in Retrospect," in *Canadian Issues: Essays in Honour of Henry F. Angus*, ed. Robert M. Clark (Toronto: University of Toronto Press, 1961), 143, 148; Stephen T. Henderson, *Angus L. Macdonald: A Provincial Liberal* (Toronto: University of Toronto Press, 2007), 8–9; Christopher Armstrong, *The Politics of Federalism: Ontario's Relations with the Federal Government, 1867–1942* (Toronto: University of Toronto Press, 1981), 3; Doug

Owram, *The Government Generation: Canadian Intellectuals and the State, 1900–1945* (Toronto: University of Toronto Press, 1986), 39; and Bradford, *Commissioning Ideas*, 37–40.

4 Of American origins in the late twentieth century, the "new political history" responded to the marginalization of traditional political history and argued that its interpretative plausibility or relevance needed more explicit grounding in institutional/governmental foundations, in intellectual and social circumstances, and (crucially) in drawing explicitly from works in political science and political thought as well as history. A forum in the *Canadian Historical Review*, although perhaps overstating the novelty of the perspectives, exemplifies the refreshed views they bring to political questions. Matthew Hayday, Mary-Ellen Kelm, and Tina Loo, "From Politics to the Political: Historical Perspectives on the New Canadian Political History," 564–71; Stephane Savard, "Rethinking the Quiet Revolution: The Renewal of Political History through the Expansion of the 'Political Field,'" 572–87; and P.E Bryden, "Foxes, Hedgehogs, and the Changing Shape of English-Canadian Political History," 588–601. All in *Canadian Historical Review* 100, 4 (2019).

5 James H. Gray, *The Winter Years: The Depression on the Prairies* (Toronto: Macmillan, 1966); Barry Broadfoot, *Ten Lost Years: Memories of Canadians Who Survived the Great Depression* (Toronto: Doubleday, 1973). These works are in print to this day.

6 Library and Archives Canada (LAC), Mackenzie King Papers, O.D. Skelton to Mackenzie King, 20 April 1937; H.F. Angus, "An Echo of the Past: The Rowell-Sirois Commission," *Canadian Tax Journal* 1, 5 (1953): 439 and "Autobiography," 274.

7 This "break with the past" is examined in the Canadian political world by David Tough, *The Terrific Engine: Income Taxation and the Modernization of the Canadian Political Imaginary* (Vancouver: UBC Press, 2018), esp. chap. 1. The ways the "modern," "modernity," and their meanings pervade mid-twentieth-century social and political thought in Canada has had lots of attention in recent years, most helpfully to us in Clarence Karr's *Authors and Audiences: Popular Canadian Fiction in the Early Twentieth Century* (Montreal and Kingston: McGill-Queen's University Press, 2000) and Leonard Kuffert's two works, *A Great Duty: Canadian Responses to Modern Life and Mass Culture 1939–1967* (Montreal and Kingston: McGill-Queen's University Press, 2003) and *Canada before Television: Radio, Taste, and the Struggle for Cultural Democracy* (Montreal and Kingston: McGill-Queen's University Press, 2016).

8 Neil Bradford, "Writing Public Philosophy: Canada's Royal Commissions on Everything," *Journal of Canadian Studies* 34, 4 (1999–2000): 137; and Neil Bradford, *Commissioning Ideas*, 37–40 et seq.

9 The rise and influence of the elite cadre are examined in J.L. Granatstein, *The Ottawa Men: The Civil Service Mandarins, 1935–1957* (Ottawa: Deneau, 1984); and Owram, *Government Generation*.

10 Thomas Lockwood, "A History of Royal Commissions," *Osgoode Hall Law Journal* 5, 2 (1967). Lockwood cites the *Revised Statutes of Canada, 1952*, "Inquiries Act," but it is virtually the same as the text of the *Revised Statutes, 1926*, "Inquiries Act," that governed the Rowell-Sirois Commission. Alan C. Cairns, "Reflections on Commission Research," *Dalhousie Law Journal* 12, 3 (1989–90): 87–108, quotation 91; The basic distinction is used in Canada, Privy Council Office, "Commissions of Inquiry," www.pco-bcp.gc.ca.

11 Arthur H. Cole, compiler, *A Finding-List of Royal Commission Reports in the British Dominions* (Cambridge, MA: Harvard University Press, 1939); H.M. Clokie and J. William Robinson, *Royal Commissions of Inquiry* (Stanford: Stanford University Press, 1937); J.E Hodgetts, "Royal Commissions of Inquiry in Canada," *Public Administration Review* 9, 1 (1949): 22; Thomas Lockwood, "A History of Royal Commissions," *Osgoode Hall Law Journal* 5, 2 (1967): 172–209. A complete list of 370 (and counting) is found in Canada, Privy Council Office, "Commissions of Inquiry," www.pco-bcp.gc.ca.

12 See Lauriat, "Examination of Everything"; Clokie and Robinson, *Royal Commissions of Inquiry*; Christie and Pross, "Commissions of Inquiry"; G. Bruce Doern, "The Role of Royal Commissions in the General Policy Process and in Federal-Provincial Relations," *Canadian Public Administration* 10, 4 (1967): 417–33; and in general J.E. Hodgetts, W. McCloskey, Reg Whitaker, and V. Seymour Wilson, *The Biography of an Institution: The Civil Service Commission of Canada, 1908–1967* (Montreal and Kingston: McGill-Queen's University Press, 1971). Data are in *Historical Statistics of Canada*, 2nd ed., ed. F.H. Leacy (Ottawa: Canadian Government Publications Centre, 1983), series Y293-5.

13 Bradford, *Commissioning Ideas*; Bradford, "Writing Public Philosophy"; and, most recently, Gregory J. Inwood and Carolyn M. Johns, eds., *Commissions of Inquiry and Policy Change: A Comparative Analysis* (Toronto: University of Toronto Press, 2014). All of these works stand in contrast to the more critical perspective of the literature from the 1930s to the 1980s, as cited below.

14 *Royal Commission on Maritime Claims*, A.R. Duncan, chair (Ottawa: King's Printer, 1927); *Royal Commission on the Natural Resources of Manitoba*, W.F.A. Turgeon, chair (Ottawa: King's Printer, 1929); *Royal Commission on the Natural Resources of Saskatchewan*, A.K. Dysart, chair (Ottawa: King's Printer, 1935); *Royal Commission on the Natural Resources of Alberta*, A.K. Dysart, chair (Ottawa: King's Printer, 1935); *Royal Commission on Financial Arrangements between the Dominion and the Maritime Provinces*, Thomas White, chair (Ottawa: King's Printer, 1935); *Royal Commission on Banking and Currency in Canada*, Hugh Pattison Macmillan, chair (Ottawa: King's Printer, 1933); *National Employment Commission, Final Report*, Arthur Purvis, chair (Ottawa: King's Printer, 1938).

15 These inquiries include *Royal Commission on Canadian Arts, Letters and Sciences* [1949–51] (Ottawa: King's Printer, 1950); *Royal Commission on Canada's Economic Prospects* [1955–57] (Ottawa: Queen's Printer, 1958); *Royal Commission on Bilingualism and Biculturalism* [1963–70] (Ottawa: Queen's Printer, 1970); *Royal Commission on the Economic Union and Development Prospects for Canada* [1983–85] (Ottawa: Supply and Services, 1985); *Royal Commission on Canada's Aboriginal People* [1991–96] (Ottawa: Assembly of First Nations, 1996); and the *Commission on the Future of Health Care* [2001–02] (Saskatoon: The Commission, 2002).

The importance of such inquiries has been assessed in several fine works of history and political science written over the past three decades: Paul Litt's *The Muses, the Masses and the Massey Commission* (Toronto: University of Toronto Press, 1992); Gregory Inwood's *Continentalizing Canada: The Politics and Legacy of the Macdonald Royal Commission* (Toronto: University of Toronto Press, 2005); Valerie Lapointe-Gagnon's, *Panser le Canada: Une histoire intellectuelle de la commission Laurendeau-Dunton* (Montreal: Boreal, 2018); and Bradford's *Commissioning Ideas*.

Chapter 1: A Federation Turned Upside Down

1 J.W. Pickersgill, *The Liberal Party* (Toronto: McClelland and Stewart, 1962), 117.

2 Edwin R. Black, *Divided Loyalties: Canadian Concepts of Federalism* (Montreal and Kingston: McGill-Queen's University Press, 1975), 1.

3 Among many works, a clear summary and a useful corrective to the position long dominant in English Canada is Wade Wright and Peter Hogg, "Canadian Federalism, the Privy Council and the Supreme Court: Reflections on the Debate about Canadian Federalism," *UBC Law Review* 38, 2 (2005): 329–52. A full investigation is in the collected essays of R.C.B. Risk, compiled by G.B. Baker and Jim Phillips, *A History of Canadian Legal Thought: Collected Essays* (Toronto: University of Toronto Press, 2006).

4 In the English Canadian literature, this shift starts with Black, *Divided Loyalties*, and includes key works such as Robert Vipond, *Liberty and Community: Canadian Federalism and the Failure of the Constitution* (Albany: SUNY Press, 1991); John Kendle, *Federal Britain: A History* (London: Routledge, 1997); Paul Romney, *Getting It Wrong: How Canadians Forgot Their Past and Imperilled Confederation* (Toronto: University of Toronto Press, 1999); Peter C. Oliver, *The Constitution of Independence: The Development of Constitutional Theory in Australia, Canada, and New Zealand* (New York: Oxford University Press, 2005); and David E. Smith, *Federalism and the Canadian Constitution* (Toronto: University of Toronto Press), 2010. There is a vast contrary position as well.

5 Oliver, *Constitution of Independence,* 112–13, 118–23.

6 These excerpts are taken from the British North America Act, 1867, cited in *Report of the Royal Commission on Dominion-Provincial Relations*, Book Three, *Documentation* (Ottawa: King's Printer, 1940), Part B, British North America Act, 1867, 30 Victoria, chap. 3, ss. 91 and 92.

7 See British North America Act, 1867, VIII Revenues, Debts, Assets, Taxation, especially s. 118. The fiscal settlement is summarized in *Report,* Book One, *Canada 1867–1939,* 41–46. An accessible recent summary of Canada's fiscal history with excellent graphics is Livio Di Mateo, *A Federal Fiscal History, Canada 1867–2017* (Vancouver: Fraser Institute, 2017), 6–11 et seq.

8 See the measured historical account of political and legal ideas by Kendle, *Federal Britain,* 18–36, and the classic Canadian work on modes of federalism by Black, *Divided Loyalties,* 1–20.

9 Many works have examined these changes. A brief account is Wade Wright and Peter Hogg, "Canadian Federalism, the Privy Council and the Supreme Court: Reflections on the Debate about Canadian Federalism," *UBC Law Review* 38, 2 (2005): 329–52. Extensive arguments are found throughout Risk, *History of Canadian Legal Thought.*

10 The phrase is in P.E. Bryden, *"A Justifiable Obsession": Conservative Ontario's Relations with Ottawa, 1943–1985* (Toronto: University of Toronto Press, 2013), 3. While constitutional cases have been examined by scores of work, the Ontario story is carefully examined in Christopher Armstrong, *The Politics of Federalism: Ontario's Relations with the Federal Government, 1867–1942* (Toronto: University of Toronto Press, 1981).

11 Lord Watson, in *Maritime Bank v. Receiver-General of the Province of New Brunswick,* 1892, cited in many sources, e.g., Smith, *Federalism and the Canadian Constitution,* 70, and Peter A. Russell, Rainer Knopff, Ted Morton, *Federalism and the Charter: Leading Constitutional Decisions* (Montreal and Kingston: McGill-Queen's University Press, 1981), 52.

12 David Tough has explored the political ideas and themes of the "modern" in several works, including *The Terrific Engine: Income Taxation and the Modernization of the Canadian Political Imaginary* (Vancouver: UBC Press, 2018). See in general Robert Craig Brown and Ramsay Cook, *Canada 1896–1920: A Nation Transformed* (Toronto: McClelland and Stewart, 1974), 228–48. The primary work is Vernon C. Fowke, *The National Policy and the Wheat Economy* (Toronto: University of Toronto Press, 1957, 1983), esp. chap. 9. See also J.R. Mallory, "Disallowance and the National Interest: The Alberta Social Credit Legislation of 1937," *Canadian Journal of Economics and Political Science* 14, 3 (August): 343.

13 Brown and Cook, *A Nation Transformed,* chap. 12, show the importance of the federal move. E.A. Heaman argues that this change was the last and perhaps most important

of the "tax revolts" and a move that reconstructed federalism. See E.A. Heaman, *Tax, Order and Good Government: A New Political History of Canada, 1867–1917* (Montreal and Kingston: McGill-Queen's University Press, 2017), 376–458. While many had debated the benefits of direct taxation, O.D. Skelton was one of the most articulate exponents arguing in favour of the many benefits of this transformation, as first explained in Barry Ferguson, *Remaking Liberalism: The Intellectual Legacy of Adam Shortt, O.D. Skelton, W.C. Clark, and W.A. Mackintosh* (Montreal and Kingston: McGill-Queen's University Press, 1993), 168–85.

14 Canada, Canadian Intergovernmental Conference Secretariat, *First Ministers' Conferences, 1906–2004* (Ottawa: n.p., n.d.), 3. On the failed efforts in those crucial years of the 1910s to breech federal-provincial conflict particularly related to the Prairie provinces, the literature is extensive, epitomized by Fowke, *National Policy and the Wheat Economy*; and W.L. Morton, *The Progressive Party in Canada* (Toronto: University of Toronto Press, 1950). A recent work focusing on intergovernmental relations is Mary Janigan, *Let the Eastern Bastards Freeze in the Dark: The West versus the Rest since Confederation* (Toronto: Vintage Canada, 2012), 1–24 and 225–43.

15 As quoted in R. MacGregor Dawson, *William Lyon Mackenzie King: A Political Biography*, vol. 1, *1874–1923* (Toronto: University of Toronto Press, 1958), 300.

16 For overviews see Thompson and Seager, *Decades of Discord*, 104–37; and Robert Bothwell, Ian Drummond, John English, *Canada 1900–1945* (Toronto: University of Toronto Press, 1990), 199–209.

17 The standard work remains Dennis H. Guest, *The Emergence of Social Security in Canada*, 3rd ed. (Vancouver: UBC Press, 2003), chap. 1.

18 The term is in Chester Martin's 1938 book, *Dominion Lands Policy*, reprint edited by L.H Thomas (Toronto: McClelland and Stewart, 1973).

19 Thompson and Seager, *Decades of Discord*, 132; J.A. Maxwell, "Expenditures of Canadian Provincial Governments," *Contributions to Canadian Economics* 3 (1931): 41.

20 Thompson and Seager, *Decades of Discord*, 132–33.

21 Livio Di Matteo's synthesis shows the trend: *A Federal Fiscal History: Canada 1867–2017* (Vancouver: Fraser Institute, 2017), 32–39.

22 Thompson and Seager, *Decades of Discord*, 133–35.

23 The terminology is the current usage of the Privy Council Office and its Intergovernmental Conference Secretariat. Canada, "First Ministers Conferences, 1906–2004," Canadian Intergovernmental Conference Secretariat, http://www.scics.ca/en/.

24 Christopher Armstrong, "Ceremonial Politics: Federal-Provincial Meetings before the Second World War," in *National Politics and Community in Canada*, ed. Kenneth R. Carty and Peter W. Ward (Vancouver: UBC Press, 1986), 119.

25 As cited in Armstrong, "Ceremonial Politics," 112–14, 120.

26 Mary Janigan, *Let the Eastern Bastards Freeze in the Dark,* 312–28; and H. Blair Neatby, *William Lyon Mackenzie King,* vol. 2, *1924–1932: The Lonely Heights* (Toronto: University of Toronto Press, 1963), 232–43.

27 Canada, *Dominion-Provincial Conferences/Conferennces Federales-Provinciales* [November 1927, December 1935, January 1941] (Ottawa: King's Printer, 1951), 6–7.

28 On Maritime Rights see E.R. Forbes's indispensable *The Maritime Rights Movement, 1919–1927* (Montreal and Kingston: McGill-Queen's University Press, 1979). The rise and fall of Prairie protest has been written about by many historians for many years, but a recent examination of Prairie claims over natural resources is in Janigan, *Let the Eastern Bastards Freeze in the Dark,* 306–29.

29 Canada, *Dominion-Provincial Conferences/Conferennces Federales-Provinciales,* précis of 1927 conference, 19, 23–25, 33–36; Thompson and Seager, *Decades of Discord,* 136 and 135–37.

30 Canada, *Dominion-Provincial Conferences/Conferences Federale-Provinciale,* précis of 1927 conference, 11–12. The alliance of Ontario and Quebec is described in Thompson and Seager, *Decades of Discord,* 134–35, 137. Ontario's espousal of the position is examined in Armstrong, *Politics of Federalism,* chap. 7.

31 Thompson and Seager, *Decades of Discord,* 131–33. The sea-change in constitutional practice is explained in Alan Cairns's foundational piece, "The Judicial Committee and Its Critics," *Canadian Journal of Political Science* 4, 3 (1971): 301, 302ff, 311; and in the recent overview of Smith, *Federalism and the Canadian Constitution,* 42, 99–101, 114ff.

32 Library and Archives Canada (LAC), Mackenzie King Diaries, 3–10 November 1927, quotation 10 November 1927.

33 W.P.M. Kennedy, "Crisis in the Canadian Constitution," *Round Table* 96 (September 1934): 803–19.

34 Vincent C. MacDonald, "Judicial Interpretation of the Canadian Constitution," *University of Toronto Law Journal* 1, 2 (1936): 260; F.R. Scott, "The Development of Canadian Federalism," *Papers and Proceedings of the Canadian Political Science Association* 3 (1931): 231–47; J.A. Corry, "The Federal Dilemma," *Canadian Journal of Economics and Political Science* 7, 2 (1941): 216; H.F. Angus, "The Working of Confederation: A Western View," *Canadian Journal of Economics and Political Science* 3, 3 (1937): 345–54. R.C.B. Risk described Scott, MacDonald, and Kennedy as the three leading proponents of a new synthesis propounding centralization in "The Scholars and the Constitution," *Manitoba Law Review* 23 (1996): 496–523. The "League" views are carefully assessed in Michiel Horn, *The League for Social Reconstruction: Intellectual Origins of the Democratic Left in Canada, 1930–1942* (Toronto: University of Toronto Press, 1980).

35 Norman McLeod Rogers, "The Political Principles of Federalism," *Canadian Journal of Economics and Political Science* 1, 3 (1935): 337–47, esp. 344–45; and "The Dead Hand," *Canadian Forum*, August 1934. See also V.W. Bladen, "The Economics of Federalism," *Canadian Journal of Economics and Political Science* 1, 3 (1935): 348–51; D.C. MacGregor, "The Provincial Incidence of the Canadian Tariff," *Canadian Journal of Economics and Political Science* 1, 3 (1935): 384–95; and W.J. Waines, "Problems of Public Finance in the Prairie Provinces," *Canadian Journal of Economics and Political Science* 3, 3 (1937): 355–69, quotations 357.

36 See the detailed arguments about the ideas behind constitutionalism by David Schneiderman, "Haldane Unrevealed," *McGill Law Journal* 57, 3 (2012): 608–11; and "Harold Laski, Viscount Haldane, and the Law of the Canadian Constitution in the Early 20th Century," *University of Toronto Law Journal* 48, 4 (1998): 521ff.

37 The literature on the Depression is voluminous and contentious. Although a global phenomenon, it was most acute in many ways in the United States. The international impact was severe due to the US's massive international trade and investment. See Charles P. Kindleberger, *The World in Depression, 1929–39*, rev. ed. (Berkeley: University of California Press, 1986); and Dietmar Rothermund, *The Global Impact of the Great Depression, 1929–1939* (London: Routledge, 1996).

38 The broad impact of the Depression is examined in Bothwell et al., *Canada 1900–1945*, 245–58; Thompson and Seager, *Decades of Discord*, 193–221; and K. Norrie, D. Owram, and H. Emery, *A History of the Canadian Economy*, rev. ed. (Toronto: Nelson, 2007), 317–42. Still the basic outline of the Depression is the Royal Commission on Dominion-Provincial Relations, *Report*, Book One, *Canada 1867–1939* (Ottawa: King's Printer, 1940), 138–50 and 160–71.

39 In addition to the two key surveys cited in the previous note, see A.E. Safarian, *The Canadian Economy in the Great Depression* (Montreal and Kingston: McGill-Queen's University Press, 2009); and H. Blair Neatby, *The Politics of Chaos: Canada in the Thirties* (Toronto: Macmillan, 1972); plus the Royal Commission on Dominion-Provincial Relations, *Report*, Book One, *Canada 1867–1939*, chap. 6. A concise overview is Michiel Horn's booklet, "The Great Depression of the 1930s in Canada," *Canadian Historical Association Historical Booklet 39* (1984).

40 See Canada, Canadian Intergovernmental Conference Secretariat, *First Ministers' Conferences 1906–2004* (Ottawa: n.p., n.d.), passim.

41 A recent concise overview of the Bennett government is P.B. Waite, *In Search of R.B. Bennett* (Montreal and Kingston: McGill-Queen's University Press, 2012), chaps. 3–6.

42 As quoted in R.B. Bryce, *Maturing in Hard Times: Canada's Department of Finance through the Great Depression* (Montreal and Kingston: McGill-Queen's University Press, 1986), 173.

43 Bryce, *Maturing in Hard Times*, 173; Waite, *In Search of R.B. Bennett*, chap. 3.

44 John Kendle, *John Bracken: A Political Biography* (Toronto: University of Toronto Press, 1979), 127ff.

45 Among many works, see R.A. Young, "'And the People Will Sink into Despair': Reconstruction in New Brunswick, 1942–52," *Canadian Historical Review* 59, 2 (1988): 130.

46 See Canada, *Dominion-Provincial Conferences/Conferences Federales-Provinciales*, précis of 1927 conference, 11–12; and Armstrong, "Ceremonial Politics," 125–26.

47 Archives of Manitoba (AM), Bracken Papers, box 71, Bennett to Bracken, 9 March 1933.

48 Bryce, *Maturing in Hard Times*, 174, 109–15.

49 In addition to the general works cited already, see the flip side on Britain's position in Ian Drummond, *Imperial Economic Policy, 1917–1939: Studies in Expansion and Protection* (Toronto: University of Toronto Press, 1974); and R.F. Holland, "The End of an Imperial Economy: Anglo-Canadian Disengagement in the 1930s," *Journal of Imperial and Commonwealth History* 11, 2 (1983): 159–74.

50 George Watts, *The Bank of Canada: Origins and Early History* (Ottawa: Carleton University Press, 1993); E.P. Neufeld, *Bank of Canada Operations 1935–54* (Toronto: University of Toronto Press, 1955). A succinct history is found in Michael and Angela Redish, eds., "70 Years of Central Banking," *Bank of Canada Review*, special issue (Winter 2005–06). See *Report on Banking and Currency in Canada*, chair Baron Macmillan [Hugh Pattison Macmillan] (Ottawa: King's Printer, 1933).

51 Robin Fisher, *Duff Pattullo of British Columbia* (Toronto: University of Toronto, 1991), 253–64; Bryce, *Maturing in Hard Times*, 174–75; Robert Wardhaugh, *Behind the Scenes: The Life and Work of W.C. Clark* (Toronto: University of Toronto Press, 2010), 77–78.

52 Bryce, *Maturing in Hard Times*, 175–76; Wardhaugh, *Behind the Scenes*, 77–81.

53 Doug Owram, *The Government Generation: Canadian Intellectuals and the State, 1900–1945* (Toronto: University of Toronto Press, 1986), 142–43.

54 Wardhaugh, *Behind the Scenes*, 157, 218. The work of creating a national accounting system – the basis for macro-economic policy – in the 1930s is described in Duncan McDowall, *The Sum of the Satisfactions: Canada in the Age of National Accounting* (Montreal and Kingston: McGill-Queen's University Press, 2008), chaps. 2 and 3.

55 Kendle, *John Bracken*, 112–33.

56 Bryce, *Maturing in Hard Times*, 175–76.

57 Ibid., 176–77; Kendle, *John Bracken*, 112ff.

58 AM, Bracken Papers, "Dominion-Provincial Conference–January 1934."

59 AM, Bracken Papers, "Sub-Conference on Financial Questions," 13–14 January 1936; and "Dominion-Provincial Conference 1935," Finance [Treasurer's] Dept. FOO83 – location code B-6-1-20, temporary box 5.15–28; Nova Scotia, Royal Commission,

Provincial Economic Inquiry (Halifax: King's Printer, 1934), summarized as *The Jones Report on Nova Scotia's Economic Welfare Within Confederation* (Halifax: n.p., 1934).

60 AM, Bracken Papers, "Dominion-Provincial Conference – January 1934"; Bryce, *Maturing in Hard Times*, 176–77.

61 Fisher, *Duff Pattullo*, 266–70; Bryce, *Maturing in Hard Times*, 177–78; British Columbia Archives (BCA), Pattullo Papers, vol. 68/1, mfm. A-1809, R.B. Bennett to T.D. Pattullo, 19 December 1934, and Mackenzie King to Pattullo, 23 January 1934.

62 Bryce, *Maturing in Hard Times*, 178–79.

63 *Winnipeg Free Press*, 4 September 1934.

64 Thompson and Seager, *Decades of Discord*, 253.

65 Keith G. Banting, *The Welfare State and Canadian Federalism* (Montreal and Kingston: McGill-Queen's University Press, 1987), 62–63. Graphic presentation of this takeover by Ottawa and its surprisingly robust fiscal base is shown in Di Mateo, *Federal Fiscal History*, 34–44.

66 Thompson and Seager, *Decades of Discord*, 261–66; Larry Glassford, *Reaction and Reform: The Politics of the Conservative Party under R.B. Bennett, 1927–1938* (Toronto: University of Toronto Press, 1992), 153–57; and Waite, *In Search of R.B. Bennett*, 196–204.

67 Cited in J.R.H. Wilbur, *The Bennett New Deal: Fraud or Portent?* (Toronto: Copp Clark, 1968), 80–81.

68 H. Blair Neatby, *William Lyon Mackenzie King III, 1932–1939: The Prism of Unity* (Toronto: University of Toronto Press, 1976), 86; Thompson and Seager, *Decades of Discord*, 261–66.

69 Waite, *In Search of R.B. Bennett*, chap. 6. On the constitutional questions, see the summary in John T. Saywell, *The Lawmakers: Judicial Power and the Shaping of Canadian Federalism* (Toronto: University of Toronto Press, 2002), chap. 9.

70 Thompson and Seager, *Decades of Discord*, 133; and Bryden, *"Justifiable Obsession,"* 4.

Chapter 2: Towards a Royal Commission: 1935–37

1 Library and Archives Canada (LAC), Diaries of Mackenzie King, 26 August 1936. All citations in this book are to the online version: bac-lac.gc.ca, Diaries of William Lyon Mackenzie King.

2 As emphasized by King's principal biographer, H. Blair Neatby, and never subsequently challenged. See H. Blair Neatby, *William Lyon Mackenzie King 1932–1939: The Prism of Unity* (Toronto: University of Toronto Press, 1976), chap. 9.

3 Debates in the Department of Finance are examined in Robert Wardhaugh, *Behind the Scenes: The Life and Work of William Clifford Clark* (Toronto: University of Toronto Press, 2010); and in the Employment Commission in James Struthers, *No Fault of Their Own: Unemployment and the Canadian Welfare State, 1914–41* (Toronto:

University of Toronto Press, 1983). See also R.M. Dawson, "The Federal Constitution," in *Canada,* ed. George W. Brown (Berkeley: University of California Press, 1950), 294–95.

4 W.R.C Jay, "The Australian Loan Council," *Publius: The Journal of Federalism* 7, 3 (1977): 101–17; R.S. Gilbert, *The Australian Loan Council, 1890–1965* (Canberra: Australian National University Press, 1991). A highly critical contemporary study of the plan is J.A. Maxwell, "The Recent History of the Australian Loan Council," *Canadian Journal of Economics and Political Science* 6, 1 (1940): 22–38.

5 A recent work on Dunning's "mature" reorientation is Don Nerbas, *Dominion of Capital: The Politics of Big Business and the Crisis of the Canadian Bourgeoisie* (Toronto: University of Toronto Press, 2013), 69–113.

6 Wardhaugh, *Behind the Scenes,* 107–13; Neatby, *The Prism of Unity,* 150–57. See also LAC, Graham Towers Papers, Graham Towers, "Memorandum on Dominion Provincial Discussions re Loan Council," 18 April 1936, file 15.

7 Previous conferences had been called in 1906, 1918, and 1927.

8 Archives of Manitoba (AM), Bracken Papers, GR 754, "Dominion Provincial Conference, 1935 – Ottawa, December 9th to 13th, 1935 – Sub-Conference on Financial Questions and the Continuing Committee on Financial Questions – Ottawa, January 13th and 14th 1936"; Bank of Canada Archives, Research Dept. 2B-400 (1), A. Sk., "Canadian Loan Council," 10 September 1935; ibid., G.H. Herbert, Background Memo ... A Loan Council for Canada, 8 January 1936; ibid., Provincial Treasurers' Conference Ottawa, "Loan Council," 13 and 14 January 1936. Finance Minister Dunning revealed the outlines of the proposal in his 1936 Budget Speech of 1 May 1936. See *Hansard* 1936 2365ff.

9 See Robin Fisher, *Duff Pattullo of British Columbia* (Toronto: University of Toronto Press, 1991*),* 285–86; and John T. Saywell, *"Just Call Me Mitch": The Life of Mitchell F. Hepburn* (Toronto: University of Toronto Press, 1991), 248–49. The specific expressions of support for a comprehensive review of the distribution of taxation and fiscal powers are found in detailed reports of the 1935 conference and its aftermath kept by the Manitoba treasury department. See AM, GR 754, "Sub-Conference on Financial Questions," 13–14 January 1936; and "Dominion-Provincial Conference 1935," Finance [Treasurer's] Dept. FOO83, location code B-6-1-20, temporary box 5, 52–77. The official record is Canada, *Dominion-Provincial Conference* [December] 1935 (Ottawa: King's Printer, 1936).

10 AM, Bracken Papers, GR 754, "Dominion Provincial Conference, 1935 – Ottawa, December 9th to 13th, 1935 – Sub-Conference on Financial Questions and the Continuing Committee on Financial Questions – Ottawa, January 13th and 14th 1936."

11 Ibid.

12 Canada, *Royal Commission on Maritime Claims*, A.R. Duncan, chair (Ottawa: King's Printer, 1927); Nova Scotia, *Report of the Royal Commission, Provincial Economic Inquiry*, J.H. Jones, chair (Halifax: King's Printer, 1934). Macdonald's academic and governmental interests are deftly portrayed in Stephen Henderson, *Angus L. Macdonald: A Provincial Liberal* (Toronto: University of Toronto Press, 2007). The "provincial" in the title is intentionally ironic.

13 Christopher Armstrong, *The Politics of Federalism: Ontario's Relations with the Federal Government, 1867–1942* (Toronto: University of Toronto Press, 1981), 199; Saywell, *"Just Call Me Mitch,"* 248.

14 LAC, Department of Finance Papers, vol. 3985, W.C. Clark to Charles Cockcroft, 14 March 1936. On Alberta's about-face, see the fiscal analysis by Eric Hanson, *Financial History of Alberta, 1905–50*, reprint ed. (Calgary: University of Calgary Press, 2003), 172–76; Wardhaugh, *Behind the Scenes*, 107–13.

15 Bank of Canada Archives, research files, 2B-400, A. Sk., "Canadian Loan Council" 10 September 1935; ibid., file 2B-400; A. Skelton, "Federal Provincial Finance," 10 March 1936; ibid., Graham Tower Fonds, file 15, Towers "Memos," nos. 14–16, April 1936; ibid., "Memorandum on Dominion Provincial Discussions re Loan Council," 18 April 1936.

16 Robert Bothwell, Ian Drummond, John English, *Canada 1900–1945* (Toronto: University of Toronto Press, 1987), 269–71; Neatby, *Prism of Unity*, 147–51; Fisher, *Duff Pattullo*, 285–86; Saywell, *"Just Call Me Mitch,"* 247–49; Wardhaugh, *Behind the Scenes*, 110–13. King's thinking can be followed in LAC, Mackenzie King Diaries, 18 January 1936, 25, 28 and 30 March 1936, 25 April 1936.

17 There is information about Canadian interest in the Australian model in Mary Janigan, "The Art of Sharing: The Richer Provinces versus the Poorer Provinces since Confederation" (PhD diss., York University, 2017), passim.

18 Canada, *Dominion-Provincial Conference* [December] 1935 (Ottawa: King's Printer, 1936), Mackenzie King's statements, 62, 8–9.

19 Struthers, *No Fault of Their Own*, chaps. 5 and 6; Hugh Grant, *W.A. Mackintosh: The Life of a Canadian Economist* (Montreal and Kingston: McGill-Queen's University Press, 2015), chap. 7; Georges Campeau, *From UI to EI: Waging War on the Welfare State* (Vancouver: UBC Press, 2005), chap. 4.

20 National Employment Commission, *Final Report*, 26 January 1938 (Ottawa: King's Printer, 1938), esp. 29. See Appendix A, Interim Report, July 1937, 52ff and Appendix D, Information Service Bulletins, 75ff.

21 Struthers, *No Fault of Their Own*, chap. 6; Grant, *W.A. Mackintosh*; and Campeau, *From UI to EI*. The quotation is from National Employment Commission, *Final Report*, 29; Mackenzie King's ire is expressed in the King Diaries, 26 July 1937, 20–24 December 1937, 12 and 23–25 January 1938.

22 Bank of Canada Archives, Research Department File 2b-400, A. Skelton, "Provincial Debt Conversion and Loan Proposals," 4 January 1936; ibid., file 2b-400, G.H. Herbert, "The Control of Provincial and Federal Borrowing: A Loan Council for Canada," 8 January 1936.

23 Bank of Canada Archives, Research Department File 2B-400, vol. 1, 1935–36, ASK [Skelton], "Memo: Federal Provincial Finance," 20 March 1936.

24 Nova Scotia, *Report of the Royal Commission Provincial Economic Inquiry*, J.H. Jones, chair (Halifax: King's Printer, 1934); and ibid., *The Jones Report: A Digest* (Halifax: Government of Nova Scotia, 1934), quotation 9; W.A. Carrothers, "Problems of the Canadian Federation," *Canadian Journal of Economics and Political Science* 1, 1 (1935): 26–40, quotation 27.

25 Bank of Canada Archives, Research Department File 2B-170, 1935–39, A.E. Grauer, "The Distribution of Taxing Powers in Canada," August 1936, 65 pp., esp. 1–3 and 48–65.

26 R.B. Bryce, *Maturing in Hard Times: Canada's Department of Finance through the Great Depression* (Montreal and Kingston: McGill-Queen's University Press, 1986), 190–91; Douglas Fullerton, *Graham Towers and His Times* (Toronto: McClelland and Stewart, 1986), 79–81.

27 LAC, Department of Finance Papers, vol. 22, D.A. Skelton, confidential memorandum, "The Case for a Royal Commission Enquiry on Provincial Finances."

28 Ibid., W.C. Clark, confidential memorandum, "Royal Commission on Economic Basis of Confederation," 7 December 1936.

29 All quotations from LAC, Department of Finance Papers, vol. 22, W.C. Clark, "Royal Commission on Economic Basis of Confederation," 7 December 1936.

30 Ibid.

31 Ibid.

32 LAC, Department of Finance Papers, RG 19, vol. 3985, Dunning to Aberhart, 25 June 1936.

33 Ibid., Aberhart to King, 26 August 1937.

34 LAC, Mackenzie King Papers, series J-1, W.C. Clark to W.L.M. King, 30 November 1936, 185139-43; AM, Bracken Papers, GR 754, "Proceedings of the Permanent Committee on Financial Questions," 9 December 1936.

35 AM, Bracken Papers, GR 754, "Proceedings of the Permanent Committee on Financial Questions," 9 December 1936.

36 Ibid.

37 Ibid.

38 See Supreme Court of Canada, *Reports*, 64, 1922, United Kingdom Privy Council, 66, 1924. Quebec's lead attorney was Louis St-Laurent. A full treatment of the issue

is Shirley Tillotson, *Give and Take: The Citizen-Taxpayer and the Rise of Canadian Democracy* (Vancouver: UBC Press, 2017), 69–74.

39 AM, Bracken Papers, GR 754, "Proceedings of the Permanent Committee on Financial Questions," 9 December 1936.

40 Glenbow-Alberta Archives, Fred Kennedy Fonds, series 1, file 4, "Black Book" [Diary], 18 December 1936.

41 AM, Bracken Papers, GR 754, "Proceedings of the Permanent Committee on Financial Questions," 9 December 1936.

42 Bryce, *Maturing in Hard Times,* 191–92, 209–10.

43 Doug Owram, *The Government Generation: Canadian Intellectuals and the State, 1900–1945* (Toronto: University of Toronto Press, 1986), 236.

44 AM, Bracken Papers, GR 754, "Proceedings of the Permanent Committee on Financial Questions," 9 December 1936; John Kendle, *John Bracken: A Political Biography* (Toronto: University of Toronto Press, 1979), 148–49.

45 LAC, Mackenzie King Diaries, 12 December 1937, 15 December 1936.

46 Bank of Canada Archives, Graham Towers Fonds, "Memorandum of Conversation with Mr. Dunning," 5 January 1937.

47 LAC, Mackenzie King Diaries, 9–21 December 1936, 4 January 1937.

48 Ibid., 6 January 1937.

49 Ibid., 8 January 1937.

50 Ibid., 6 and 8 January 1937.

51 Ibid., 8 January 1937; University of Manitoba Archives (UMA), Dafoe Papers, box 7, file 5, T.A. Crerar to J.W. Dafoe, 11 January 1937.

52 Bryce, *Maturing in Hard Times,* 194; Kendle, *John Bracken,* 151–52.

53 LAC, Mackenzie King Diaries, 20 January 1937.

54 Ibid., 21 January 1937.

55 Ibid.

56 Bryce, *Maturing in Hard Times,* 194.

57 LAC, Mackenzie King Diaries, 23 January 1937.

58 Ibid., 27 January 1937.

59 Bryce, *Maturing in Hard Times,* 195. The details of Towers's visit and his report is found in LAC, Department of Finance Papers, GR 754 F0083, loc. code B-6-1-20, temporary box 5, "Very Confidential Province of Manitoba," February 1937, 132. Towers's thinking was conveyed in several conversations with business and government officials in early February. See ibid., "Memorandum re: Possible Debt Conversion," 2 February 1937, "Confidential Treasury Memo" [Garson], 8 February 1937.

60 AM, Bracken Papers, Bracken to Dunning, 8 February 1937, box 101; and ibid., temporary box 5, Bank of Canada Report, 11 February 1937, 124, Towers to Bracken,

12 February 1937, Report, 129. See also AM, Bracken Papers, temporary box 5, "Confidential" memo [Garson], 8 February 1937.

61   Bank of Canada, "Reports on the Financial Position of the Provinces of Manitoba, Saskatchewan and Alberta 1937," *Canada Sessional Papers* 1937, nos. 169, 169a, 169b (Ottawa: Government of Canada 1937); ibid., no. 169, Manitoba (tabled 11 February 1937), 25–26: letter of conveyance, Towers to Bracken, 11 February 1937. The consolidated report is reviewed and cited in Bryce, *Maturing in Hard Times*, 195ff.

62   LAC, Mackenzie King Diaries, 16 February 1937.

63   Donald Creighton, *Canada's First Century* (Toronto: Macmillan, 1970), 227. Creighton's positive judgment should be noted; he was a participant in the resulting commission of inquiry.

64   LAC, Mackenzie King Papers, (J4), memoranda and notes, vol. 206, 16 February 1937, 242308-11.

65   Bank of Canada, "Reports on the Financial Position of the Provinces of Manitoba, Saskatchewan and Alberta 1937," sessional paper 169a, Saskatchewan, 6 March 1937, 27–28.

66   Ibid., sessional paper 169b, Alberta, 7 April 1937, 34–42.

67   Bryce, *Maturing in Hard Times*, 195–96; R.B. Bennett, House of Commons *Debates*, 16 February 1937, 922–23.

68   Bryce, *Maturing in Hard Times*, 196–98; Hanson, *Financial History of Alberta*, 322.

69   P.B. Waite, *In Search of R.B. Bennett* (Montreal and Kingston: McGill-Queen's University Press, 2012), 251–52; R.B. Bennett, House of Commons *Debates*, 31 January 1938, 29ff.

70   Glenbow-Alberta Archives, Fred Kennedy Fonds, series 1, "Black Book," 17 February 1937, and indeed the diary for the period from 1935 through 1938. There have been many overviews of Alberta's policy perambulations; the most modern treatment is Robert L. Ascah, *Politics and Public Debt: The Dominion, the Banks, and Alberta's Social Credit* (Edmonton: University of Alberta Press, 1999).

71   Neil Bradford, "Writing Public Philosophy: Canada's Royal Commission on Everything," *Journal of Canadian Studies* 34 (2000): 143; Neatby, *Prism of Unity*, 200.

72   LAC, Mackenzie King Papers, correspondence (J1), O.D. Skelton to Mackenzie King, 20 April 1937.

73   LAC, Mackenzie King Diaries, 20 April 1937.

Chapter 3: Organizing the Commission: Summer 1937

1   Harold Innis, "The Rowell-Sirois Report," *Canadian Journal of Economics and Political Science* 6, 4 (1940): 254–55.

2 Geoffrey Parsons, *Punch,* 24 August 1955, cited in Barbara Lauriat, "'The Examination of Everything': Royal Commissions in British Legal History," *Statute Law Review* 31, 1 (2010): 36.

3 British Columbia Archives (BCA), GR 1222, Premiers Papers, box 95, file 7, T.D. Pattullo to Mackenzie King, 1 March 1937, C.A. Dunning to T.D. Pattullo, 5 March 1937, and Pattullo to Dunning, 8 March 1937.

4 BCA, GR 1222, Premiers Papers, box 95, file 7, Pattullo to Dunning, 29 June 1937, Dunning to Pattullo, 13 July 1937.

5 Library and Archives Canada (LAC), O.D Skelton Papers, vol. 5, file 3, misc. memos.

6 LAC, O.D. Skelton Papers, vol. 5, file 3, memos I, III and IV, undated 1937. The memos comprise a file of eleven numbered in roman numerals, most but not all signed by Skelton.

7 LAC, O.D. Skelton Papers, vol. 5, file 3, memo VII, 24 July 1937.

8 See LAC, Ernest Lapointe Papers, MG 27 III, B 10, vol. 16, file 39, "nominations aux postes de la commission." On Robinson, see Don Nerbas, *Dominion of Capital: The Politics of Big Business and the Crisis of the Canadian Bourgeoisie, 1914–1947* (Toronto: University of Toronto Press, 2013), 27ff.

9 As seen by his many earnest consultations with Dafoe and others in Winnipeg. See the definitive work by J.E. Rea, *T.A. Crerar: A Political Life* (Montreal and Kingston: McGill-Queen's University Press, 1997), passim.

10 University of Manitoba Archives (UMA), Dafoe Papers, box 7, file 5, T.A. Crerar to J.W. Dafoe, 11 January 1937; Queen's University Archives (QUA), Crerar Papers, box 104, T.A. Crerar to J.W. Dafoe, 17 April 1937.

11 John W. Dafoe, "Revising the Constitution," *Queen's Quarterly* 37, 1 (1930): 1–17.

12 This series is put into context by Jeffrey Brison in his *Rockefeller, Carnegie and Canada: American Philanthropy and the Arts and Letters in Canada* (Montreal and Kingston: McGill-Queen's University Press, 2005), 151ff.

13 QUA, Crerar Papers, box 104, Crerar to Dafoe, 20 April 1937, Dafoe to Crerar, 21 April 1937. This letter is also in UMA, Dafoe Papers, box 14, file 1.

14 LAC, Mackenzie King Diaries, 22 and 23 July 1937; UMA, Dafoe Papers, box 14, file 2, King to Dafoe, 23 July 1937, Dafoe to King, 24 July 1937; LAC, Lapointe Papers, vol. 16, file 39, Lapointe to Rinfret, telegram 24 July 1937, Rinfret to Lapointe, 1 August 1937, Lapointe to Rinfret, 13 August 1937.

15 Margaret Prang, *N.W. Rowell: Ontario Nationalist* (Toronto: University of Toronto Press, 1975), 489–90; LAC, Mackenzie King Diaries, 22 July 1937; LAC, O.D. Skelton Papers, vol. 5, file 3, memo VI, July 1937, VII, 24 July 1937. See also Terry Crowley, *Marriage of Minds: Isabel and Oscar Skelton Reinventing Canada* (Toronto: University of Toronto Press, 2003), 222–23.

16 LAC, Mackenzie King Papers, Primary series correspondence (J1), Rowell to King, 4 August 1937, 207240ff; ibid., Mackenzie King Diaries, 4 August 1937.

17 LAC, Mackenzie King Diaries, 13 August 1937; ibid., Mackenzie King Papers, Primary series correspondence (J1), King to Rowell, 12 August 1937, 207243, Rowell to King, 13 August 1937, 207244.

18 BCA, GR 1222, Premiers Papers, vol. 95, file 7, Pattullo to King, 10 August 1937, King to Pattullo, 12 August 1937.

19 On Robinson, see Don Nerbas, *Dominion of Capital: The Politics of Big Business and the Crisis of the Canadian Bourgeoisie, 1914–1947* (Toronto: University of Toronto Press, 2013), chap. 1, esp. 51. On Stewart, see Barry Cahill, *The Thousandth Man: A Biography of James McGregor Stewart* (Toronto: University of Toronto Press, 2000), chap. 8, esp. 117–19; LAC, O.D. Skelton Papers, vol. 5, file 3, memo III.

20 LAC, Mackenzie King Diaries, 21 July 1937, 23 July 1937, 11 and 13 August 1937.

21 As quoted in Prang, *N.W. Rowell*, 489.

22 Prang, *N.W. Rowell*, 489; LAC, Rowell Papers, vol. 89, Rowell to King, 28 October 1937; UMA, Dafoe Papers, box 14, file 2, Dafoe to King, 24 July 1937.

23 Prang, *N.W. Rowell*, 489–90.

24 J.W. Dafoe, *Canada: An American Nation* (New York: Columbia University Press, 1935), 79–80.

25 Ibid., 80–84.

26 UMA, Dafoe Papers, box 14, file 2, Dafoe to Crerar, 21 April 1937.

27 Ibid.

28 Ibid.

29 Ibid., 24 July 1937; Ramsay Cook, *The Politics of John W. Dafoe and the Free Press* (Toronto: University of Toronto Press, 1963), 216.

30 G.V. Ferguson, *John W. Dafoe* (Toronto: Ryerson Press, 1948), 88–90.

31 QUA, Dexter Papers, Dafoe to Dexter, 28 August 1937.

32 UMA, Dafoe Papers, box 3, file 3, Dafoe to V. Sifton, 27 July 1937.

33 Ferguson, *John W. Dafoe*, 88–89.

34 See Robert Wardhaugh, "Balancing Both Sides of the Ledger: J.W. Dafoe and Mackenzie King," in *Mackenzie King, Citizenship, and Community*, ed. John English, Ken McLaughlin, and P. Whitney Lackenbauer (Toronto: Robin Brass Studio, 2003), 80–98.

35 R.A. MacKay, *The Unreformed Senate of Canada* (Toronto: Oxford University Press, 1926); R.A. MacKay, "After Beauharnois What?," *Maclean's*, 15 October 1931; Archives of Nova Scotia, A.L. Macdonald Papers, vol. 532, file 1330, "Minutes of First Meeting of Group," 13 January 1931.

36 H.F. Angus, *Citizenship in British Columbia* (Victoria: King's Printer, 1926); and H.F. Angus et al., *The Legal Status of Aliens Resident in Canada* (Toronto: University of

Toronto Press, 1931). On the threatened terminations of MacKay and Angus, see Michiel Horn, *Academic Freedom in Canada: A History* (Toronto: University of Toronto Press, 1999), 101–2, 108–10; and Michiel Horn, "Academic Freedom" *History of Intellectual Culture* 4, 1 (2004): 1–15.

37 R.B. Bryce, *Maturing in Hard Times: Canada's Department of Finance through the Great Depression* (Montreal and Kingston: McGill-Queen's University Press, 1986), 212.

38 P.B. Waite, *In Search of R.B. Bennett*, 251–52; Bennett in House of Commons *Debates*, 31 January 1938, 29–30.

39 *Edmonton Journal*, 8 November 1937; House of Commons *Debates*, 16 February 1937, 927.

40 LAC, Mackenzie King Papers, Primary series correspondence (J1), Aberhart to King, 26 August 1937, 198182-5; King to Aberhart, 2 September 1937, 198187-9.

41 Christopher Armstrong, *The Politics of Federalism: Ontario's Relations with the Federal Government, 1867–1942* (Toronto: University of Toronto Press, 1981), 208; LAC, Mackenzie King Papers, J-1, C-4279, T.B. McQuesten to Mackenzie King, 27 March 1937, 142372.

42 John T. Saywell, *"Just Call Me Mitch": The Life of Mitchell F. Hepburn* (Toronto: University of Toronto Press, 1991), 376.

43 Conrad Black, *Duplessis* (Toronto: McClelland and Stewart, 1977), 148; Saywell, *"Just Call Me Mitch,"* 338–42; BCA, Pattullo Papers, vol. 73/2 (mfm. A-1810), Hepburn to Pattullo, 27 July 1937, Pattullo to Hepburn, 9 August 1937.

44 Robin Fisher, *Duff Pattullo of British Columbia* (Toronto: University of Toronto Press, 1991, 316–19.

45 Kendle, *John Bracken*, 154–58.

46 Government of Canada, Order-in-Council P.C. #1908, 14 August 1937; see LAC, Mackenzie King Papers, Primary series correspondence (J1), King to Rowell, 14 August 1937 (two letters), 207245, 207248. The order-in-council was published in many Canadian newspapers on 16 August and it is reprinted in full in Royal Commission on Dominion-Provincial Relations, *Report*, Book One, *Canada 1867–1939* (Ottawa: King's Printer, 1940), "Terms of Reference," 9–11.

47 A carefully researched look into Alexander Skelton is found in Norman Hillmer, *O.D. Skelton: A Portrait of Canadian Ambition* (Toronto: University of Toronto Press, 2015), 174, 178, 194–95. This account corrects the myth-making of Skelton's friends in the economics and banking trades. See Bryce, *Maturing in Hard Times*, 212–13; cf. LAC, Mackenzie King Diaries, 25 August 1937; UMA, Dafoe Papers, Dafoe to Skelton, 27 August 1937.

48 LAC, Mackenzie King Papers, Primary series correspondence (J1), W.L.M. King to Governor-in-Council, n.d. August 1937 and attachment W.C. Clark to O.D. Skelton, 21 August 1937, "Remuneration."

49 Prang, *N.W. Rowell*, 490. LAC, Mackenzie King Papers, memoranda and notes, C-4279, memo, King to Henry, 11 September 1937, 142406.

50 LAC, MacKay Papers, vol. 7, bound volume, "Secretary's Minutes," 8–10 September, 15 September 1937; Royal Commission, *Report*, 13–18. The fees for the counsel are noted in Cahill, *Thousandth Man*, 129. By the reckoning of the Bank of Canada Inflation Calculator, $150 in 1937 is well over $2,500 in today's terms. See www.bank ofcanada.ca. LAC, Department of Finance Papers, vol. 22, file 101–85, Royal Commission General File 1937–40, Alex Skelton to C.A. Dunning, 14 September 1937.

51 It was published as *Volume III, Documentation*, when the report was completed in 1940.

52 UMA, Dafoe Papers, box 5, file 1, Dafoe to A. Skelton, 27 August 1937, box 14, file 2, Dafoe to Rowell, 9 November 1937, Dafoe to Skelton, 17 November 1937.

53 LAC, MacKay Papers, vol. 7, bound volume, "Secretary's Minutes," 8–10 September 1937 and 27 November 1937; UMA, Dafoe Papers, vol. 14, file 5, extract of "Privy Council Minute," 11 September 1937, and the *Report*, Book One, *History of the Commission*, 13–18. The emphasis on the equal importance of the special academic studies with the hearings and provincial government reports is found in the commission's "Program of Activities," 3 November 1937. See UMA, Dafoe Papers.

54 Robert M. Fowler, "The Role of Royal Commissions," in David C. Smith, *Economic Policy Advising in Canada: Essays in Honour of John Deutsch* (Montreal: C.D. Howe Institute, 1981), 96, 100–1. An overview of the influx of academics into government work in this period is Barry Ferguson and Doug Owram, "Social Scientists and Public Policy," *Journal of Canadian Studies* 15, 4 (1981): 3–17. A thorough and stimulating examination of intellectuals in public life during the 1930s and 1940s is Doug Owram, *The Government Generation: Canadian Intellectuals and the State, 1900–1945* (Toronto: University of Toronto Press, 1987).

55 LAC, Mackenzie King Diaries, 16 August 1937.

Chapter 4: Setbacks and Recovery: Autumn 1937

1 J.A. Corry, "The Report of the Royal Commission on Dominion-Provincial Relations," *Canadian Banker* 47, 4 (1940): 387.

2 "Program of Activities Outlined by Chairman," Canadian Press news wire, Ottawa, 3 November 1937; Library and Archives Canada (LAC), Rowell Papers, vol. 89, Newton to Mary, 1 August 1937.

3 LAC, Mackenzie King Papers, Primary series correspondence (J1), Rowell to King, 3 September 1937, 207260, King to Rowell, 4 September 1937, 207262.

4 LAC, MacKay Papers, vol. 7, secretary's minutes, 8–10 September 1937. At this meeting, only the commissioners and Skelton were in attendance: LAC, RG 19, Department of Finance, vol. 22, file 101-85-15, Skelton to Dunning, 14 September 1937.

5 LAC, Mackenzie King Papers, Primary series correspondence (J1), Rowell to King, 7 September 1937, 207263ff; ibid., Rowell to King, 13 September 1937, 207268.

6 LAC, MacKay Papers, vol. 7, "Secretary's Minutes," 8–10 September 1937.

7 Ibid., vol. 8, "Sirois," MacKay and Angus, "Suggested Readings," 10 September 1937.

8 Neil Bradford, *Commissioning Ideas: Canadian National Policy Innovation in Comparative Perspective* (Don Mills: Oxford University Press, 1998), 39

9 LAC, MacKay Papers, vol. 7, "Secretary's Minutes," 15 September 1937; vol. 8, "Skelton" file, 24 August and 1 September 1937. This liberal (non-Marxian) "political economy tradition" has been examined in several works, including C.D.W. Goodwin, *Canadian Economic Thought* (Durham, NC: Duke University Press, 1961); Robin Neill, *A History of Canadian Economic Thought* (London: Routledge, 1991); Barry Ferguson, *Remaking Liberalism: The Intellectual Legacy of Adam Shortt, O.D. Skelton, W.C. Clark, and W.A. Mackintosh* (Montreal and Kingston: McGill-Queen's University Press, 1993). On the wartime and postwar origins of the entire apparatus of modern quantitative economic analysis as the basis of policy-making, see Neill's *History of Canadian Economic Thought* and Duncan MacDowall's work describing the creation of the new methods of analysis and systems of measurement for "national accounts," *The Sum of the Satisfactions: Canada in the Age of National Accounting* (Montreal and Kingston: McGill-Queen's University Press, 2008).

10 University of Manitoba Archives (UMA), Dafoe Papers; LAC, MacKay Papers, vol. 7, secretary's minutes, 27 November 1937; Wilfrid Eggleston, *While I Still Remember* (Toronto: Ryerson, 1968), 217–51.

11 LAC, MacKay Papers, vol. 7, "Secretary's Minutes," 7 October 1937; LAC, Rowell Papers, vol. 89, Newton [Rowell] to Nell [Rowell], 22 September 1937.

12 Ibid.

13 In 1934, the United Farmers of Alberta (UFA) premier John Brownlee was sued for seduction by his family's former babysitter, Vivian MacMillan. The ensuing scandal forced Brownlee's resignation as premier.

14 LAC, MacKay Papers, vol. 7, secretary's minutes, 7 October 1937; ibid., O.D. Skelton Papers, vol. 5, file 3, memo VII, July 1937; ibid., Rowell Papers, vol. 89 (mfm.939), Newton to Nell, 24 and 25 September 1937. Biographical material on Waite and Schmidt, as well as Hansen and Upgren, is found in various Minnesota sources, e.g., Willard W. Cochrane, "Agricultural Economics at the University of Minnesota 1886–1979," Department of Agriculture and Applied Economics, *University of Minnesota Miscellaneous Publications*, 21, 1983: www.http:/hdl.handle.net/11299/112651.

15 British Columbia Archives (BCA), Premiers Papers, vol. 95, file 6, 10 September 1937; LAC, Rowell Papers, Newton to Nell, 25 September 1937, telegrams Rowell to

Pattullo, Pattullo to Rowell; ibid., MacKay Papers, vol. 7, "Secretary's Minutes," 7 October 1937; BCA, Premiers Papers, vol. 95, file 6, 10 September 1937, Rowell to Pattullo, 3 November 1937, Pattullo to Rowell, 9 November 1937.

16 LAC, R.A. MacKay, vol. 8, correspondence A-W, MacKay to Campbell, Dysart, and Macdonald, 2 September 1937, 23 September 1937.

17 MacKay pointed out that Maritimers were on the staff, including New Brunswick-born-and-raised Stanley A. Saunders. The constitutional advisor, Vincent MacDonald of Dalhousie, hired a Saint John lawyer, John Fisher, to assist him. LAC, MacKay Papers, vol. 8, correspondence A-W, MacKay to Campbell, Dysart, and Macdonald, 2 September 1937, 23 September 1937; ibid., A.A. Dysart to R.A. MacKay, 4 November 1937, MacKay to Dysart, 5 and 6 November 1937, MacKay to Skelton, 6 November 1937; LAC, Rowell Papers, vol. 89, Rowell to MacKay, 8 and 9 November 1937.

18 LAC, Rowell Papers, vol. 89, Newton to Nell, 15 and 17 October 1937.

19 "Program of Activities Outlined by Chairman," Canadian Press news story, 3 November 1937.

20 See *Report of the Royal Commission on Dominion-Provincial Relations,* Book One (Ottawa: King's Printer, 1940), 15.

21 R.B. Bryce, *Maturing in Hard Times: Canada's Department of Finance through the Great Depression* (Montreal and Kingston: McGill-Queen's University Press, 1986), 212; Margaret Prang, *N.W. Rowell: Ontario Nationalist* (Toronto: University of Toronto Press, 1975), 490–91; cf. LAC, Rowell Papers, vol. 89 (mfm. 939), Newton Rowell to Mary Rowell, 1 August 1937.

22 As quoted in Murray Donnelly, *Dafoe of the Free Press* (Toronto: Macmillan, 1968), 165–66; UMA, Dafoe Papers, box 5, file 1, Dafoe to A. Skelton, 27 August 1937.

23 G.V. Ferguson, *John W. Dafoe* (Toronto: Ryerson Press, 1948), 90–91. The assumption that Dafoe was a commanding presence was denied in later years by Angus, Fowler, and MacKay. They said he was collegial and committed to the process. LAC, MacKay Papers, vol. 10, additional items, MacKay to Robert Fowler, 2 August 1963, Fowler to MacKay, 6 August 1963; ibid., Angus Papers, "Autobiography," 264–66.

24 Bryce, *Maturing in Hard Times,* 213; UMA, Dafoe Papers, box 5, file 1, Dafoe to A. Skelton, 27 August 1937.

25 Rowell's remarks are cited in Prang, *N.W. Rowell,* 490–91. Original in LAC, Mackenzie King Papers, Primary series correspondence (J1), Rowell to King, 28 October 1938, 207273-5. Dafoe's views are noted in LAC, Ernest Lapointe Papers, vol. 16, file 39, Rowell to Lapointe, 29 October 1937.

26 He recovered his health and served another seventeen years on the Supreme Court, including ten as chief justice, and lived to age eighty-two.

27 LAC, Mackenzie King Papers, Primary series correspondence (J1), Morin to King, 3 November 1937, 205610, King to Morin, 4 November 1937, 205611.

28 Ibid., Rowell Papers, vol. 89, Rowell to Dafoe 12 November 1937.

29 Ibid., Mackenzie King Papers, Primary series correspondence (J1), Rowell to King, 28 October 1937, 207273-5; ibid., Ernest Lapointe Papers, vol. 16, file 39, Rowell to Lapointe, 29 October 1937; ibid., Mackenzie King Diaries, 2 November 1937, 4 November 1937; ibid., MacKay Papers, vol. 7, "Secretary's Minutes," 6–7 October 1937; ibid., MacKay Papers, vol. 8, "Rowell" file, Rowell to MacKay, 5 November 1937.

30 Dale Thomson, *Louis St-Laurent: Canadian* (Toronto: Macmillan, 1967), 94–97; and Sylvio Normand, "Joseph Sirois," *Dictionary of Canadian Biography*, vol. 16. The official appointment was by Order-in-Council P.C. 2880, 18 November 1937. See LAC, Rowell Papers, vol. 89 C938, Rowell to Dafoe, 19 and 23 November 1937.

31 As quoted in Prang, *N.W. Rowell*, 491. See LAC, Rowell Papers (mfm. 939), vol. 89, Newton to Nell, 24 and 25 November 1937.

32 LAC, Mackenzie King Diaries, 24–25 November 1937.

33 On the preparation of transcripts, see BCA, GR 1222, Premiers Papers, vol. 95, file 6, Wilfrid Eggleston to Duff Pattullo, 29 November 1937.

34 Thomson, *Louis St-Laurent*, 94–97; LAC, MacKay Papers, vol. 8, MacKay to Rowell; and ibid., MacKay Papers, Rowell to MacKay, 12 November 1937, vol. 7, secretary's minutes, 27 November 1937.

35 LAC, MacKay Papers, vol. 8, MacKay to Rowell; and ibid., MacKay Papers, Rowell to MacKay, 12 November 1937, vol. 7, "Secretary's Minutes," 27 November 1937. On the work of the two counsels, see Thomson, *Louis St-Laurent*, 94–97; and Barry Cahill, *The Thousandth Man: A Biography of James McGregor Stewart* (Toronto: University of Toronto Press, 2000), 121–23.

36 The most authoritative survey of Prairie economic, social, and political conditions is G.A. Friesen, *The Canadian Prairies: A History* (Toronto: University of Toronto Press, 1984), chap. 15.

37 UMA, Dafoe Papers, box 2, Dafoe to G.V. Ferguson, n.d. March 1938.

38 Archives of Manitoba (AM), Bracken Papers, Bracken to Solon Low, 6 May 1937, Bracken to Low, 25 May 1937, Low to Bracken, 18 May 1937, T.C. Davis to Bracken, 8 October 1937, Bracken to Davis, 12 October 1937, Bracken to Viner, 6 May 1937.

39 John Kendle, *John Bracken: A Political Biography* (Toronto: University of Toronto Press, 1979), 158; LAC, Rowell Papers, vol. 89, Newton to Nell Rowell, 27 November 1937; ibid., MacKay Papers, vol. 10, Robert to Kathleen, 28 November 1937.

40 See Ramsay Cook, *The Politics of John W. Dafoe and the Free Press* (Toronto: University of Toronto Press, 1963), 271–72; Kendle, *John Bracken*, 57, 95, 120–22.

41 AM, Bracken Papers, G643, Bracken to Viner, 6 May 1937, Bracken to Viner, 1 June 1937, Viner to Bracken, 21 May 1937, Viner to Bracken, 5 June 1937.

42 LAC, MacKay Papers, vol. 10, Robert to Kathleen, 28 November 1937. According to W.L. Morton, the report "became almost an obsession" with Bracken. See W.L.

Morton, *Manitoba: A History* (Toronto: University of Toronto Press, 1967), 450. The correspondence from the Garson Papers shows a very high level of oversight from the provincial treasurer.

43 Government of Manitoba, *Manitoba's Case* (Winnipeg: King's Printer 1937); AM, GR 1661, Executive Council, box G 639, file 1200, "Knight Report." The eighteen volumes of the economic survey were in some instances explicitly drawn from the work done preparing *Manitoba's Case*. See R.M. Pearson, *Provincial Finance in Manitoba* (Winnipeg: Manitoba Economic Survey Board, 1938), 1–3.

44 John Bracken testimony, in Royal Commission on Dominion-Provincial Relations, "Transcripts of Public Hearings 1937–38" (hereafter cited as "Public Hearings"), 29 November 1937, 11ff. The official records are in two series, "Submissions 1937–38" [written statements] and "Transcripts of Public Hearings 1937–38." The originals are in LAC, RG 33/23 Royal Commission on Dominion-Provincial Relations, vols. 1–30. The 20,000+ pages have been digitized in the invaluable Heritage project: www.heritage.canadiana.ca reels C-6980-89 for "Submissions" and C-8989-96 for "Public Hearings."

45 *Manitoba's Case*, part 2, *The Constitutional Relations of the Dominion and the Provinces*, passim, 12, 43, 40–41, 42–43. Like all the provincial government submissions, *Manitoba's Case* is a stand-alone volume but may be found in Royal Commission on Dominion-Provincial Relations, "Submissions," vol. 1.

46 See *Manitoba's Case*, part 3, *The Effects of Federal Monetary Policy on Western Canadian Economy* and Nova Scotia, *Royal Commission Provincial Economic Inquiry* (Halifax: King's Printer, 1934), "The Provincial Incidence of the Canadian Tariff," 88–99.

47 This refers to the detailed estimates of the cost of monetary policy to the West presented in *Manitoba's Case*, part 3, *The Effects of Federal Monetary Policy*, 6–7. Bracken's waffling was noted as summarized in York University Archives (YUA), Robert Fowler Papers, box 2, file 1, "Summary of the Hearings," 2 December 1937. See also Bracken testimony, "Public Hearings," 29 November 1937, 11–12. For details see *Manitoba's Case*, part 3, *The Effects of Federal Monetary Policy*, and part 4, *Tariff Policy*, 15–17, 19–22 plus tables.

48 *Manitoba's Case*, part 3, *The Effects of Federal Monetary Policy* and part 7, *Analysis of Manitoba's Treasury Problem*, 85; *Winnipeg Free Press*, "Commission Hears Dominion Monetary Policy Criticized," 30 November 1937, 1; *Winnipeg Free Press*, "Farm Slump Blamed," 1 December 1937, 2. In general, see James A. Jackson, *The Centennial History of Manitoba* (Toronto: McClelland and Stewart, 1970), 231.

49 *Manitoba's Case*, part 6, *The Financial Problems of Municipalities and School Districts*, and part 7, *Manitoba's Treasury Problem*; YUA, Robert Fowler Papers, box 2, file 1, "Summary of the Hearings," 2 December 1937. See also the overview in Richard

Simeon and Ian Robinson, *Society, and the Development of Canadian Federalism* (vol. 71 of the Macdonald Royal Commission Research Studies) (Toronto: University of Toronto Press, 1990), 84–85.

50   As summarized in Donnelly, *Dafoe of the Free Press*, 167–68; YUA, Robert Fowler Papers, box 2, file 1, "Summary of the Hearings," 1 December 1937.

51   Kendle, *John Bracken*, 158–59. For details, see *Manitoba's Case*, part 7, *Manitoba's Treasury Problem*, passim; YUA, Robert Fowler Papers, box 2, file 1, "Summary of the Hearings," 1 December 1937.

52   "Public Hearings," 75ff; YUA, Robert Fowler Papers, box 2, file 1, "Summary of the Hearings," 1 and 2 December 1937; Prang, *N.W. Rowell*, 491–92.

53   YUA, Robert Fowler Papers, box 2, file 1, "Summary of the Hearings," 30 November 1937, 3, and 30 November 1937, 133–34.

54   "Confederation Clinic," 1 December 1937; Louis St-Laurent, "Public Hearings," 30 November 1937, 162ff, 196E-F.

55   Stuart Garson, "Public Hearings," 75ff; YUA, Robert Fowler Papers, box 2, file 1, "Summary of the Hearings," 1 and 2 December 1937; Prang, *N.W. Rowell*, 491–92; "Confederation Clinic," 30 November, 1–4 December, 7 December 1937.

56   See *Manitoba's Case*, parts 6 and 7; and YUA, Robert Fowler Papers, box 2, file 1, "Summary of the Hearings," 1 December 1937 (Garson) and 3 December 1937 (Bracken). The phrase used by Garson is in *Manitoba's Case*, part 7, 37.

57   LAC, Rowell Papers, vol. 89, Newton to Nell, 27 November 1937, 28 November and 5 December 1937.

58   LAC, MacKay Papers, vol. 10, Robert to Kathleen, 30 November, 4 and 5 December 1937.

59   LAC, Eggleston Papers, vol. 12, file 11, Wilfrid to Lena, two undated letters and 7 December 1937. His memoir, *While I Still Remember*, chap. 3, tells several tales about Skelton.

60   Donnelly, *Dafoe of the Free Press*, 167–68; "Confederation Clinic," 8 December 1937.

61   Donnelly, *Dafoe of the Free Press*, 166–67; "Confederation Clinic," 8 and 9 December 1937.

62   YUA, Robert Fowler Papers, box 2, file 1, "Summary of the Hearings," 4, 7, 8 December 1937.

63   As quoted in John T. Saywell, *"Just Call Me Mitch": The Life of Mitchell F. Hepburn* (Toronto: University of Toronto Press, 1991), 376.

64   UMA, Dafoe Papers, Dafoe to Ferguson, 12 March 1938.

65   QUA, Crerar Papers, box 104, T.A. Crerar to Dafoe, 18 December 1937.

66   LAC, MacKay Papers, vol. 10, Robert to Kathleen, 5 December 1937.

67   "Confederation Clinic," 11 December 1937.

68   UMA, Dafoe Papers, box 21, file 6, Jack to Alice, 9 December 1937; LAC, MacKay Papers, vol. 10, Robert to Kathleen, 9 December 1937; "Confederation Clinic," 11 December 1937.

69   What may be just as interesting about the university's contributors is that they became the mainstays of the Saskatchewan government's many submissions on federal-provincial relations over the course of many years under both Liberal and CCF governments. See Shirley Spafford, *No Ordinary Academics: Economists and Political Scientists at the University of Saskatchewan, 1910–1960* (Toronto: University of Toronto Press, 2000), passim.

70   Province of Saskatchewan, *A Submission by the Government of Saskatchewan to the Royal Commission on Dominion Provincial Relations* (Regina: King's Printer, 1937), iii–iv; University of Saskatchewan Archives Board, T.C. Davis Radio Broadcasts, 3 February 1938; Beth Bilson, "William J. Patterson," in *Saskatchewan Premiers of the Twentieth Century*, ed. Gordon Barnhart (Regina: Canadian Plains Research Center, 2004), 139–61.

71   LAC, MacKay Papers, vol. 10, Robert to Kathleen, 9 December 1937.

72   Premier Patterson, "Public Hearings," Regina, 9 December 1937, 1184. Newspaper reports made much of the table used in the House itself: "Historic Table Scene of Talk of Confederation," *Regina Leader-Post*, 9 December 1937, 1; "Province Asks Debt Refunding at Lower Interest," *Regina Leader-Post*, 9 December 1937, 1.

73   *Submission by the Government of Saskatchewan*, 1.

74   Ibid., pt. 2, 6–8, quotation 6, and pt. 12, 330.

75   In addition to Friesen's overview in *Canadian Prairies*, see the recent examination of the wretched situation of 1930s Saskatchewan in W.A. Waiser, *Saskatchewan: A New History* (Calgary: Fifth House, 2005), chap. 14; and Garrett Wilson's study of the dry belt economic collapse of the 1930s, *In the Temple of the Rain God* (Regina: Canadian Plains Research Center, 2012).

76   *Submission by the Government of Saskatchewan*, 1–3, quotation 1.

77   Ibid., 4–11, quotation 7; University of Saskatchewan Archives Board, T.C. Davis Radio Broadcasts, 3 February 1938.

78   Saskatchewan Archives Board, T.C. Davis Radio Broadcasts, 3 February 1938. *A Submission by the Government of Saskatchewan*, on tariffs, 223ff, quotation 228, on monetary policy, 233ff, quotation 233.

79   *Submission by the Government of Saskatchewan*, "Federalism and Fiscal Relations," 16; Saskatchewan Archives Board, T.C. Davis Radio Broadcasts, 3 February, 10 February 1938, also found in "Public Hearings" 10 December 1937, 1339–40.

80   Thomson, *Louis St-Laurent*, 94–97; *Submission by the Government of Saskatchewan*, 331–35. The phrase "fiscal need" is cited in YUA, Robert Fowler Papers, box 2, file 1, "Summary of the Hearings," 9 and 17 December 1937.

81 "Confederation Clinic," 11 December 1937; LAC, Rowell Papers, vol. 89, Newton to Nell Rowell, 10 December 1937; Thomson, *Louis St-Laurent,* 94–97.

82 LAC, Rowell Papers, vol. 89, Newton to Nell, 10 and 14 December 1937; ibid., MacKay Papers, vol. 10, Robert to Kathleen, 11 December 1937.

83 LAC, Eggleston Papers, vol. 12, file 11, Eggleston to Lena, n.d. 1937 and 15 December 1937, Eggleston to E. Weber, 12 December 1937 and 16 December 1937.

84 LAC, Rowell Papers, vol. 89, Newton to Nell, 27 November 1937, vol. 59, Rowell to King, 21 December 1937, King to Rowell, 23 December 1937.

85 Prang, *N.W. Rowell,* 492–93; Eggleston, *While I Still Remember,* and Ferguson, *John W. Dafoe,* note Dafoe's disapproval of partying and boisterousness. J.B. McGreachy's "Confederation Clinic" is replete with comments about Rowell's quiet ways and humorous tone.

86 QUA, Crerar Papers, Crerar to Dafoe, 18 December 1937; LAC, Rowell Papers, vol. 89, Newton to Nell, 10 December 1937.

Chapter 5: Winter of Discontent: January–March 1938

1 Library and Archives Canada (LAC), Mackenzie King Diaries, 21 December 1937.

2 Ibid., Mackenzie King Papers, Primary series correspondence (J1), Mackenzie King to Premiers, 5 November 1937, and their replies. Even Maurice Duplessis favoured the project. See King to Duplessis, 5 November 1937, 200746-7, Duplessis to King, 22 November 1937, 200748-9.

3 National Employment Commission, *Final Report,* January 1938 (Ottawa: King's Printer, 1938), passim. A recent overview is Hugh Grant, *W.A Mackintosh* (Montreal and Kingston: McGill-Queen's University Press, 2016), 151–71. See the broader treatments of unemployment by Jim Struthers, *No Fault of Their Own: Unemployment and the Canadian Welfare State* (Toronto: University of Toronto Press, 1983); and Georges Campeau, *From UI to EI: Waging War on the Welfare State* (Vancouver: UBC Press, 2005). See also W.A. Mackintosh, "Canadian Economic Policy from 1945 to 1957 – Origins and Influences," in *The American Economic Impact on Canada,* ed. Hugh Aiken (Durham, NC: Duke University Press, 1959), 53.

4 In his diaries Mackenzie King vents his rage at the commission, the political economists, and adventurist policy-making in general. LAC, Mackenzie King Diaries, 20–23 December 1937, 22, 23, and 25 January 1938, the last entry expressing his warning to cabinet.

5 LAC, Mackenzie King Diaries, 18 March 1938; R.B. Bryce, *Maturing in Hard Times: Canada's Department of Finance through the Great Depression* (Montreal and Kingston: McGill-Queen's University Press, 1986), 185–87; Grant, *W.A. Mackintosh,* 152ff.

6   LAC, Rowell Papers, Newton to Nell, 20 January 1938, Rowell to Frederick Rowell, 23 and 27 January 1938; LAC, MacKay Papers, vol. 10, Robert to Kathleen, 14 and 19 January 1938, 27 January 1938.

7   J.B. McGeachy, "Confederation Clinic," 18 January 1938.

8   E.H. Coleman, Under-Secretary of State, in Royal Commission on Dominion-Provincial Relations, "Public Hearings 1937–38," 26 January 1938, 3459ff; McGeachy, "Confederation Clinic," 27 January 1938.

9   The key source is Department of Mines and Resources, memo, Royal Commission on Dominion-Provincial Relations, "Submissions 1937–38," Exhibit #396, 32–33; ibid. Charles Camsell, Deputy Minister of Mines and Resources, and W.H. McGill, Director of Indian Affairs, "Public Hearings," 30 May 1938, 9617-9, 9640-2.

10   Royal Commission on Dominion-Provincial Relations, "Submissions," BC Director of Welfare memo, Exhibit #191, 8, "Public Hearings": Manitoba, 731–33, New Brunswick, 8672, Nova Scotia, 4134, Saskatchewan, Department of Health memo, Exhibit #77. The commission summary is in Royal Commission on Dominion-Provincial Relations, *Report,* Book Two (Ottawa: King's Printer, 1940), 15, 35.

11   See *Report,* Book Three, "Exhibits and Hearings," 209ff: Ottawa, 17–31 January 1938, and exhibits 87–139, 15–16 February 1938, and exhibits 163–71, 25 May–2 June 1938, and exhibits #380–412.

12   Jessica Squires, "Creating Hegemony: Consensus by Exclusion in the Rowell-Sirois Commission," *Studies in Political Economy* 81 (2008): 159–90.

13   See *Report,* Book Three, *Documentation,* "Exhibits and Hearings," 209–14, and "List of Witnesses," 215–19.

14   McGeachy, "Confederation Clinic," 18–22 January 1938 and 25–27 January 1938, quotations 18 January, and 21 January 1938.

15   York University Archives (YUA), Fowler Papers, box 2, file 1, "Summary of the Hearings," Ottawa, 17–18 January 1938; McGeachy, "Confederation Clinic," 18–19 January 1938.

16   YUA, Fowler Papers, "Summary of the Hearings," Ottawa, 18 January 1938. See also Arthur Pedoe, "Federal versus State Supervision of Insurance: A Canadian View," *Law and Contemporary Problems* 15 (Autumn, 1950): 584–85.

17   J.A. Corry, "Constitutional Trends and Federalism," *Canadian Issues: Essays in Honour of Henry F. Angus,* ed. Robert M. Clark (Toronto: University of Toronto Press, 1961), 15. The inconsistent position was noted at the time in McGeachy's "Confederation Clinic."

18   YUA, Robert Fowler Papers, box 2, file 1, "Summary of the Hearings," Ottawa, 20 January 1938. McGeachy caught Rowell's enthusiasm for Mackenzie's subject. See McGeachy, "Confederation Clinic," 21 January 1938; LAC, MacKay Papers, vol. 10, Bert to Kay, 14, 27, and 28 January 1938.

19 Margaret Prang, *N.W. Rowell: Ontario Nationalist* (Toronto: University of Toronto Press, 1975), 492–93; LAC, MacKay Papers, vol. 10, Robert to Kathleen, 21 January 1938; and ibid., Rowell Papers, Newton to Nell, 20 January 1938.

20 YUA, Robert Fowler Papers, box 2, file 1, "Summary of the Hearings," Ottawa, 19 January 1938; *Canada – One or Nine* is found in "Submissions," Exhibit #99.

21 Scott's remarks are as quoted in Sandra Djwa, *The Politics of Imagination: The Life of F.R. Scott* (Vancouver: Douglas and McIntyre, 1989), 153–54. Scott's views were developed in essays like the key 1931 paper "The Development of Canadian Federalism," reprinted in his *Essays on the Constitution* (Toronto: University of Toronto Press, 1976), 35–48. See also LAC, F.R. Scott Papers, vol. H1283, correspondence, 1938–40.

22 YUA, Robert Fowler Papers, box 2, file 1, "Summary of the Hearings," Ottawa, 20 January 1938; McGeachy, "Confederation Clinic," 29 January 1938. See the book, League for Social Reconstruction, *Social Planning for Canada* (Toronto: Nelson, 1935).

23 YUA, Robert Fowler Papers, box 2, file 1, "Summary of the Hearings," Ottawa, 21 January 1938; McGeachy, "Confederation Clinic," 22 January 1938.

24 LAC, Rowell Papers, Newton to Nell, 30 January 1938; McGeachy, "Confederation Clinic," 31 January 1938; Dr. Bruning, "Public Hearings" Ottawa, 26 January 1938, 3656–775.

25 Stephen T. Henderson, *Angus L. Macdonald: A Provincial Liberal* (Toronto: University of Toronto Press, 2007), 61.

26 As quoted in T. Stephen Henderson, "'A New Federal Vision': Nova Scotia and the Rowell-Sirois Report, 1938–1948," in *Framing Canadian Federalism*, ed. Dimitri Anastakis and P.E. Bryden (Toronto: University of Toronto Press, 2009), 54. The social scientists who prepared briefs were Norman Rogers, R.M. Dawson, S.A. Saunders, and R.A. MacKay.

27 Henderson, *Angus L. Macdonald*, 91.

28 *Royal Commission into the Finance Arrangements between the Dominion and the Maritime Provinces* (Ottawa: King's Printer, 1935), 20–21, 22–24.

29 Henderson, *Angus L. Macdonald*, 62–67.

30 LAC, MacKay Papers, vol. 8, MacKay, memo on the commission hearings, 20 January 1938. The Duncan Commission was officially entitled *Report of the Royal Commission on Maritime Claims* (Ottawa: King's Printer, 1926), 45; the Jones Report was published as *Royal Commission, Provincial Economic Inquiry* (Halifax: King's Printer, 1934), 27.

31 LAC, MacKay Papers; ibid., Rowell Papers, Newton to Nell, 3 February 1938.

32 Macdonald's remarkable academic background and skills are examined in Henderson's *Angus L. Macdonald*. The atmosphere in Halifax is described in McGeachy, "Confederation Clinic," *Winnipeg Free Press*, 3 and 4 February 1938

33 *Submission by the Government of the Province of Nova Scotia to the Royal Commission on Dominion-Provincial Relations* (Halifax: King's Printer, 1938). McGeachy commented on this manner of argument (see ibid.).

34 McGeachy, "Confederation Clinic," 3 February 1938. Nova Scotia's position and its hopes for the commission are set out in Stephen Henderson's excellent "New Federal Vision," 53, 55–56, and his larger study of Macdonald's premierships, *Angus L. Macdonald*, 4004ff.

35 Henderson, "New Federal Vision," 55.

36 *Manitoba's Case*, part 2; and Saskatchewan, *Submission*, 5–11.

37 Nova Scotia, *Submission*, part 2, 8–17 et seq., quotation 9. The "propositions" are argued in Nova Scotia, *Submission*, 18–52.

38 This argument was made in the Jones Report of 1934 in an appendix written by R.A. MacKay. See *Royal Commission, Provincial Economic Inquiry*, app., 18–40.

39 This argument is crucial to the report, written by Norman Macleod Rogers, by 1938 a federal cabinet minister. See *Royal Commission, Provincial Economic Inquiry*, chaps. 8–19, 88–116.

40 In general, see Nova Scotia, *Submission*, 2 and 25ff., 8–52, 61–67, and 72–78. The fundamental importance of "sufficient revenue" based on "fiscal need" is stated time and again in Nova Scotia's *Submission*, 9 and 16, and "Public Hearings," e.g., 3 February 1938, 3858 (Macdonald), 3864–66 (MacQuarrie), and 4 February 1938, 3979–81 (Macdonald). Macdonald's "new liberal" frame of mind is examined in Henderson, *Angus L. Macdonald*, passim.

41 "Public Hearings" 4 February 1938, 4004ff, 4042–43, quotation 4045, 4062–70, 4165ff; Nova Scotia, *Submission*, 67–69 and 72–78. See also YUA, Robert Fowler Papers, box 2, file 1, "Summary of the Hearings," 3 February 1938.

42 LAC, Rowell Papers, vol. 89, Newton to Nell, 1, 3, 4 February 1937, Rowell to Frederick Rowell (son), 3 February 1937.

43 McGeachy, "Confederation Clinic," 8 February 1938; LAC, Eggleston Papers, vol. 12, file 11, Eggleston to Weber, 6 February 1938.

44 LAC, Rowell Papers, vol. 89, Rowell to Frederick [Rowell], 3 February 1938, Newton to Nell, 4 February 1938; ibid., Eggleston Papers, box 12, file 5, Wilfrid to Lena, 2 and 4 February 1938, cf. Wilfrid to Lena, n.d. December 1937.

45 Murray Donnelly, *Dafoe of the Free Press* (Toronto: Macmillan of Canada, 1968), 170; Wilfrid Eggleston, *While I Still Remember* (Toronto: Ryerson, 1968), 228. See also LAC, Eggleston Papers, vol. 12, file 5, Wilfrid to Lena, [10] February 1938.

46 LAC, Rowell Papers, vol. 89, Newton to Nell, 10 and 13 February 1938; ibid., Eggleston Papers, vol. 12, file 11, Eggleston to Weber, 13 February 1938.

47 LAC, Eggleston Papers, vol. 12, file 11, Wilfrid to Magdalena, 2, 4, 6 February 1938, Eggleston to Weber, 6 February 1938.

48 *The Case of Prince Edward Island* (Charlottetown: Irwin, 1938), 1.

49 McGeachy, "Confederation Clinic," 10 and 11 February 1938; YUA, Robert Fowler Papers, box 2, file 1, "Summary of the Hearings," 11 February 1938.

50 *The Case of Prince Edward Island*, 3ff, 7ff, 36ff; YUA, Robert Fowler Papers, "Summary of the Hearings," 10 February 1938.

51 *The Case of Prince Edward Island*, passim, quotations 1, 7. Recommendations are on 44–54, quotation 54; McGeachy, "Confederation Clinic," 11 and 14 February 1938.

52 LAC, Rowell Papers, vol. 89, Newton to Nell, 10 and 13 February 1937; McGeachy, "Confederation Clinic," 10 February 1937. McGeachy described the tone of the PEI case as simply an appeal for more money rather than an entrenched grievance. See McGeachy, "Confederation Clinic," 11 February 1938

53 The rural population was 68.7 percent in 1931 and 69.1 percent in 1941. See R.A. Young, "'And the People Will Sink into Despair': Reconstruction in New Brunswick, 1942–52," *Canadian Historical Review* 69, 2 (1988): 130.

54 Prang, *N.W. Rowell*, 493; LAC, Rowell Papers, vol. 89, Newton to Nell, 13 February 1938, Rowell to Frederick Rowell, 3 March 1938.

55 Prang, *N.W. Rowell*, 493; LAC Rowell Papers, vol. 89, Newton to Nell, 13 February 1938, Rowell to Frederick Rowell, 3 March 1938.

56 LAC, Mackay Papers, vol. 8, Robert to Kathleen, 8 and 11 March 1938; ibid., Rowell Papers, Newton Rowell to Frederick Rowell, 3 March 1938.

57 Robin Fisher, *Duff Pattullo of British Columbia* (Toronto: University of Toronto Press, 1991), 319; Donnelly, *Dafoe of the Free Press*, 170; Eggleston, *While I Still Remember*, 230–33.

58 British Columbia Archives (BCA), GR 1222, Premiers Papers, vol. 95, file 7, J.W. deB. Farris to John Hart, 13 August 1937, file 6, Dr. W.A. Carrothers, "Suggested Outline of Brief for British Columbia for Royal Commission ... & Bibliography of Research Material ...," 9 December 1937; 23 November 1937, Weir (Provincial Secretary) to Pattullo, 24 November 1937, Hart (Finance) to Pattullo, 24 November 1937, 24 November 1937, Wismer (AG) to Pattullo, 26 November 1937, Cathcart (Lands) to Pattullo, 26 November Munro to Macdonald (Agriculture).

59 Fisher, *Duff Pattullo*, 319; Eggleston, *While I Still Remember*, 233.

60 *British Columbia in the Canadian Confederation* (Victoria: C.F. Banfield, 1938), passim; McGeachy, "Confederation Clinic," 17 March 1938; YUA, Robert Fowler Papers, box 2, file 1, "Summary of the Hearings," 16 March 1938.

61 *British Columbia in the Canadian Confederation*, part 2, "Confederation Settlement and Better Terms," quotation 22.

62 BCA, GR 1222, Premiers Papers, vol. 95, file 6, Pattullo to Rowell, 29 November 1937.

63 Ibid., "Received from Senator Farris," n.d. 1937/38, file 7, Farris to Hart, 13 August 1937.

64   Ibid., file 7, J.W. deB. Farris to John Hart, 13 August 1937.

65   YUA, Robert Fowler Papers, box 2, file 1, "Summary of the Hearings," 16 March 1938; McGeachy, "Confederation Clinic," 17 and 18 March 1938; Prang, *N.W. Rowell*, 494; LAC Rowell Papers, Newton to Nell, 17 and 25 March 1938.

66   McGeachy, "Confederation Clinic," 19 March 1938; "Public Hearings" 17, 18, and 21 March 1938, 4978ff, 5108ff, 5254ff; BCA, Pattullo Papers, vol. 68/8, Farris Invoice, 20 December 1938, 17 May 1939, 18 May 1939, 22 May 1939.

67   Fisher, *Duff Pattullo*, 319–22.

68   LAC, Rowell Papers, vol. 89, Newton to Nell, 22 March 1938; ibid., MacKay Papers, vol. 8, Robert to Kathleen, 16 and 18 March 1938; ibid., Eggleston Papers, vol. 12, file 11, Eggleston to Weber, 24 March 1938. See also *British Columbia in the Canadian Confederation*, 351–54.

69   LAC, MacKay Papers, vol. 8, Robert to Kathleen, 18, 22, 24 March 1938; ibid., Rowell Papers, vol. 89, Newton to Nell, 17, 25, 26 March 1938.

70   LAC, Mackenzie King Papers, Primary series correspondence (J1), King to Aberhart, 19 February 1937, 198154; ibid., Mackenzie King Diaries, 23 February 1937.

71   John Herd Thompson and Allen Seager, *Canada, 1922–1930: Decades of Discord* (Toronto: McClelland and Stewart, 1986), 295; J.R. Mallory, "Disallowance and the National Interest: The Alberta Social Credit Legislation of 1937," *Canadian Journal of Economics and Political Science* 14, 3 (1948): 349. A full treatment of the matter is found in his *Social Credit and the Federal Power in Canada* (Toronto: University of Toronto Press, 1958), chaps. 6 and 7. The "revival" was discerned by Eugene Forsey, "Disallowance of Provincial Acts, Reservation of Provincial Bills, and Refusal of Assent by Lieutenant-Governors since 1867," *Canadian Journal of Economics and Political Science* 4, 1 (1938): 58.

72   As quoted in Robert A. Wardhaugh, *Mackenzie King and the Prairie West* (Toronto: University of Toronto Press, 2000), 217.

73   The phrase is Alvin Finkle's in his critical study, *The Social Credit Phenomenon* (Toronto: University of Toronto Press, 1987). See Edward Bell, *Social Classes and Social Credit in Alberta* (Montreal and Kingston: McGill-Queen's University Press, 1993), 80–85; LAC, Department of Finance, RG 19, vol. 3985, King to Aberhart, 9 June 1938.

74   Prang, *N.W. Rowell*, 494–95; LAC, Rowell Papers, Newton to Nell, 28 and 29 March 1938; LAC, MacKay Papers, vol. 7, "Secretary's Minutes," Edmonton, 28 and 30 March 1938; ibid., MacKay Papers, vol. 8, A. Skelton to R.A. MacKay, 13 December 1938.

75   LAC, MacKay Papers, vol. 8, 30 March 1938; ibid., Angus Papers, "Autobiography," 275–78; ibid., Mackenzie King Papers, Correspondence, mfm C3723, Aberhart to King, 27 August 1937. An astute point, the meaning of which is explored at length in Clark Banack's recent *God's Province: Evangelical Christianity, Political Thought,*

and Conservatism in Alberta (Montreal and Kingston: McGill-Queen's University Press, 2016), chap. 4.

76 McGeachy, "Confederation Clinic," 30 March 1938; LAC, MacKay Papers, vol. 10, Robert to Kathleen, 30 March 1938.

77 Prang, *N.W. Rowell*, 495.

78 Eric John Hanson, *Financial History of Alberta, 1905–1950* (Calgary: University of Calgary Press, 2003), 178–79.

79 At a cost of $11,000, reported by both R.A. MacKay and J.B. McGeachy. See LAC, MacKay Papers, vol. 7, "Secretary's Minutes," 7 October 1937, ibid., vol. 10, Robert to Kathleen, 30 March 1938; McGeachy, "Confederation Clinic," 28 and 29 March 1938.

80 *The Case for Alberta* (Edmonton: King's Printer, 1938), part 1, "Alberta's Problems and Dominion-Provincial Relations," passim.

81 *Case for Alberta*, part 1, chaps. 3–15, passim.

82 Ibid., part 2, "The Urgent Need for Social and Economic Reform," passim. See Edward Bell, *Social Classes and Social Credit in Alberta* (Montreal and Kingston: McGill-Queen's University Press, 1993), 124–26.

83 *Case for Alberta*, part 1, "Recommendations," 374–77, part 2, 17, 31, 45–46; University of Manitoba Archives (UMA), Dafoe Papers, box 14, file 1, Dafoe to A. Skelton, 5 September 1938; LAC, MacKay Papers, vol. 8, C.A. Dunning to Sirois, 10 December 1938, A. Skelton to MacKay, 13 December 1938.

84 *Submission by Edmonton Chamber of Commerce* (Edmonton: n.p., 1938), 64. See in particular the sections on "Fundamental Rights," 13–15, the "Disabilities of Alberta," 19–43, "Taxation," 44–49, and "Public and Private Debt," 54–56.

85 McGeachy, "Confederation Clinic," 29–31 March, 2 and 4 April 1938; LAC, Rowell Papers, vol. 89, Newton to Nell, 30 and 31 March 1938; ibid., MacKay Papers, vol. 8, Robert to Kathleen, 30 March 1938, 1 April 1938.

Chapter 6: Stormy Spring: April–June 1938

1 As quoted in John T. Saywell, *"Just Call Me Mitch": The Life of Mitchell F. Hepburn* (Toronto: University of Toronto Press, 1991), 377–78.

2 An edited version is "Text of Ontario Submission," *Globe and Mail*, 4 May 1938, 8. Also quoted in Christopher Armstrong, *The Politics of Federalism: Ontario's Relations with the Federal Government, 1867–1942* (Toronto: University of Toronto Press, 1981), 212. The three-part *Statement by the Government of Ontario* is found in "Submissions," Exhibit #296 "Prime Minister's Statement," #297 "General Statement," #298 "Appendix and Tables." See also the citation in note 42 of this chapter.

3 As quoted in Armstrong, *Politics of Federalism*, 209.

4 Margaret Prang, *N.W. Rowell: Ontario Nationalist* (Toronto: University of Toronto Press, 1975), 487.

5 Murray Donnelly, *Dafoe of the Free Press* (Toronto: Macmillan, 1968), 171–72. The book had exclusive access to Dafoe family correspondence that decades later became part of the Dafoe Papers in the University of Manitoba Archives.

6 Neil McKenty, *Mitch Hepburn* (Toronto: McClelland and Stewart, 1967), 159–60.

7 As quoted in Armstrong, *Politics of Federalism*, 211.

8 Ibid.

9 Richard Alway, "Hepburn, King, and the Rowell-Sirois Commission," *Canadian Historical Review* 48 (1967): 118.

10 Armstrong, *Politics of Federalism*, 4.

11 Alway, "Hepburn, King, and the Rowell-Sirois Commission," 117.

12 McKenty, *Mitch Hepburn*, 159–60. This event lay behind Thomas Crerar's warning to John Dafoe about the forces aligning against the federal government and the commission. See Queen's University Archives (QUA), Crerar Papers, Crerar to Dafoe, 18 December 1937.

13 Library and Archives Canada (LAC), Mackenzie King Diaries, 10 December 1937.

14 Archives of Ontario, RG 1–13, Hepburn Papers, 14 February 1938; Saywell, *"Just Call Me Mitch,"* 377–78.

15 Archives of Ontario, RG 1–13, Hepburn Papers, Hepburn to Duplessis, 24 January 1938.

16 Saywell, *"Just Call Me Mitch,"* 378.

17 As quoted in Armstrong, *Politics of Federalism*, 209–10.

18 Archives of Ontario, RG 1–13, Hepburn Papers, Duplessis to Hepburn, 31 January 1938.

19 Ibid., Hepburn to Duplessis, 14 February 1938; Saywell, *"Just Call Me Mitch,"* 378.

20 Paul-Andre Linteau, Rene Durocher, Jean-Claude Robert, Francois Ricard, *Quebec Since 1930* (Toronto: Lorimer, 1991), 115–16.

21 Alway, "Hepburn, King, and the Rowell-Sirois Commission," 120.

22 As quoted in Saywell, *"Just Call Me Mitch,"* 379; and Armstrong, *Politics of Federalism*; LAC, MacKay Papers, vol. 10, Bert to Kay, 21–22 April 1938.

23 University of Manitoba Archives (UMA), Dafoe Papers, box 22, file 1, Jack to Alice, 22, 23, 24 April 1938; LAC, MacKay Papers, vol. 10, Bert to Kay, 22, 25, 27 April 1938 and 8 May 1938.

24 J.B. McGeachy, "Confederation Clinic," *Winnipeg Free Press*, 25 April, 3 May 1938.

25 Archives of Ontario, Hepburn Papers, RG 1–13, Gordon Conant to Hepburn, 22 April 1938.

26 Ibid.

27 J.B. McGeachy, "Confederation Clinic," 29 April 1938.

28 Canadian Chambers of Commerce, "submission," 8, in Canada, Royal Commission on Dominion-Provincial Relations, "Public Hearings" (hereafter cited as "Public Hearings"), 30 May 1938, 9506ff, 9552.

29 LAC, MacKay Papers, vol. 10, Bert to Kay, 30 April 1938, 3 May 1938; UMA, Dafoe Papers, box 22, file 1, Jack to Alice, 25, 28 April, 1 May 1938.

30 LAC, MacKay Papers, vol. 10, Bert to Kay, 30 April 1938.

31 Hepburn, "Public Hearings" 2 May 1938, 7396–456B. See also "Text of Ontario Submission," *Globe and Mail*, 4 May 1938, 8. See *Statement by the Government of Ontario to the Royal Commission on Dominion-Provincial Relations* (Toronto: King's Printer, 1938), "Book 1, Prime Minister's Statement," 30ff.

32 Hepburn, "Public Hearings" 2 May 1938, 7396–456B. See also Armstrong, *Politics of Federalism*, 212.

33 "Text of Ontario Submission." See also Saywell, *"Just Call Me Mitch,"* 380–81; and Alway, "Hepburn, King, and the Rowell-Sirois Commission," 120, 130–31.

34 "Text of Ontario Submission." See also McKenty, *Mitch Hepburn*, 161.

35 "Text of Ontario Submission." Also quoted in Armstrong, *Politics of Federalism*, 212.

36 Saywell, *"Just Call Me Mitch,"* 379. Saywell follows Dafoe's account to Alice Dafoe. See UMA, Dafoe Papers, vol. 1, J.W. Dafoe to Alice Dafoe, 2 May 1938; J.B. McGeachy, "Confederation Clinic," *Winnipeg Free Press*, 2 May 1938; York University Archives (YUA), Robert Fowler Papers, box 2, file 1, "Summary of the Hearings," Toronto, 2 May 1938.

37 Prang, *N.W. Rowell*, 495–96; UMA, Dafoe Papers, vol. 1, Dafoe to Alice Dafoe, 2 May 1938; LAC, MacKay Papers, vol. 1, Bert to Kay, 3 May 1938.

38 Rowell, "Public Hearings" 7452B; and cited in Armstrong, *Politics of Federalism*, 212; UMA, Dafoe Papers, vol. 1, John to Alice Dafoe, 2 May 1938.

39 John Kendle, *John Bracken: A Political Biography* (Toronto: University of Toronto Press, 1979), 161.

40 "Confederation Clinic," *Winnipeg Free Press*, 3 May 1938.

41 McKenty, *Mitch Hepburn*, 161.

42 It is an elusive document. As noted above, book 1, Hepburn's statement, was printed in the *Globe and Mail* on 4 May 1938. The full report is to be found in some libraries as *Statement by the Government of Ontario to the Royal Commission on Dominion-Provincial Relations*, 3 vols. (Toronto: King's Printer, 1938). Hepburn's statement was filed as an "Exhibit," #296 and printed as book 1 of the *Statement by the Government of Ontario*.

43 Saywell, *"Just Call Me Mitch,"* 381; YUA, Robert Fowler Papers, box 2, file 1, "Summary of the Hearings," 2, 4, 5 May 1938.

44 "Public Hearings" 3 May 1938, K.W. Taylor, 7472–509; *Statement by the Government of Ontario*, book 2, 22ff, C. Walters 7509–602, 7527–29 and 7575. A summary of the

overall testimony is in McKenty, *Mitch Hepburn*, 160–61. The most thoughtful account of the Ontario government perspective remains Armstrong, *Politics of Federalism*, passim.

45 As quoted in Saywell, *"Just Call Me Mitch,"* 382; "Public Hearings" 3 May 1938, 7483.

46 "Public Hearings" 3 May 1938, 7497–98, 7504, 7508, reflecting points made in *Statement by the Government of Ontario*, book 2, 14ff.

47 Armstrong, *Politics of Federalism*, 213; Public Hearings" 4 May 1938, 7611–614, 7614.

48 "Public Hearings" 3 May 1938: Taylor, 7492–96 and 7505–9, Rowell, 7507.

49 Donnelly, *Dafoe of the Free Press*, 172.

50 LAC, MacKay Papers, vol. 10, Bert to Kay, 8 May, 15 May 1938. This letter is also cited at length in Saywell, *"Just Call Me Mitch,"* 383; Prang, *N.W. Rowell*, 495–96; Armstrong, *Politics of Federalism*, 216.

51 Ibid.

52 Lang, "Public Hearings" 6 May 1938; *Statement by the Government of Ontario*, book 2, 2–6.

53 Archives of Ontario, RG 1-13, Hepburn Papers, Gordon Conant to Hepburn, 9 May 1938.

54 "Public Hearings" 6 May 1938: Conant-Rowell, 7963–72, cf. Lang-Rowell, 7946–52; YUA, Robert Fowler Papers, box 2, file 1, "Summary of the Hearings," 6 May 1938.

55 As quoted in Armstrong, *Politics of Federalism*, 216; UMA, Dafoe Papers, vol. 1, Dafoe to Alice Dafoe, 6 May 1938.

56 The crucial argument is made in P.E. Bryden's study of the post-1943 decades of Ontario-Ottawa relations and then demonstrated through the rest of her book. It is more implicit but just as clear in Christopher Armstrong's work on the previous era of Ontario's fractious relationship with Canada, which was coming to an end by the late 1930s. See Armstrong, *Politics of Federalism*, passim; P.E. Bryden, *"A Justifiable Obsession: Conservative Ontario's Relations with Ottawa, 1943–1985* (Toronto: University of Toronto Press, 2013), 4 et seq.

57 LAC, Mackenzie King Diaries, 3 May 1938.

58 Ibid., Mackenzie King Papers, memoranda and notes, "Mr. Hepburn and the Federal Government," C-4263, 1938, 121372-121516; ibid., E.A. Pickering to W.L.M. King, 25 April 1938, C-4279, 142394; LAC, O.D. Skelton Papers, vol. 5, file 3, memo XI, 9 May 1938.

59 Bank of Canada Archives, Graham Towers Fonds, memorandum, 5 May 1938.

60 Donnelly, *Dafoe of the Free Press*, 73; UMA, Dafoe Papers, personal correspondence, box 1, Dafoe to Alice Dafoe, 18 April and 23 April 1938; box 3/3, Dafoe to Mackenzie King, 11 May 1938. On Rowell's deterioration in health, see Prang, *N.W. Rowell*, 496.

61 LAC, MacKay Papers, vol. 10, 8 May 1938.

62 UMA, Dafoe Papers, box 22, file 1, Jack to Alice, 8 May 1938; LAC, MacKay Papers, vol. 10, Bert to Kay, 8 May 1938.

63 Alexander Brady, "Quebec and Canadian Federalism," *Canadian Journal of Economics and Political Science* 25, 3 (1959): 265; UMA, Dafoe Papers, Jack to Alice, box 22, file 1, 12 May 1938.

64 Duplessis's comments to Hepburn are cited in McKenty, *Mitch Hepburn*, 157–58.

65 Dale Thomson, *Louis St-Laurent: Canadian* (Toronto: Macmillan, 1967), 97–98.

66 Conrad Black, *Duplessis* (Toronto: McClelland and Stewart, 1977), 180. See "Brief Submitted by the Quebec Government," 12 May 1938, Hearings and Exhibitions, vol. 13, file 341A, passim.

67 This position is explained by Alain-G. Gagnon in "Quebec-Canada's Constitutional Dossier," in *Quebec: State and Society*, ed. Alain-G Gagnon (Toronto: University of Toronto Press, 2004), 127–49.

68 Quoted in Black, *Duplessis*, 180. See "Brief Submitted by the Quebec Government," 12 May 1938, Hearings and Exhibitions, vol. 13, file 341A, passim; YUA, Robert Fowler Papers, box 2, file 1, "Summary of the Hearings," 12 May 1938.

69 UMA, Dafoe Papers, box 22, file 1, Jack to Alice, 13 May 1938. Also quoted in Donnelly, *Dafoe of the Free Press*, 173.

70 "L'Origine du pacte de la Confédération est contestée," *Le Soleil*, 13 May 1938, 1.

71 "Public Hearings" 13 and 14 May 1938.

72 Donnelly, *Dafoe of the Free Press*, 173–74, a depiction originating from MacKay. See LAC, MacKay Papers, vol. 10, Bert to Kay, 15 May 1938; UMA, Dafoe Papers, box 22, file 1, Jack to Alice, 13 May 1938 and 15 May 1938.

73 LAC, MacKay Papers, vol. 10, Bert to Kay, 15 May 1938.

74 Donald Creighton, *Canada's First Century* (Toronto: Macmillan, 1970), 232; UMA, Dafoe Papers, box 22, file 1, Jack to Alice, 13 May 1938.

75 UMA, Dafoe Papers, box 1, Dafoe to Alice Dafoe, 15 May 1938; LAC, MacKay Papers, vol. 10, Bert to Kay, 15 May 1938.

76 LAC, Mackenzie King Papers, Primary series correspondence (J1), Dysart to King, 29 December 1937, 200771-2; E.A.P[ickering], "memo," 4 January 1938, 200773; King to Dysart, 4 January 1938, 200774.

77 *Submission of the Government of New Brunswick to the Royal Commission on Dominion-Provincial Relations*, 1938 (New Brunswick: King's Printer, 1938). The *Submission* is reviewed in Cory Slumkoski, "'... A Fair Show and a Square Deal': New Brunswick and the Renegotiation of Canadian Federalism, 1938–1951," *Journal of New Brunswick Studies* 1 (2010): 124–42. See also T. Stephen Henderson, "'A New Federal Vision': Nova Scotia and the Rowell-Sirois Report, 1938–1948," in *Framing Canadian Federalism*, ed. Dimitry Anastakis and P.E. Bryden (Toronto: University of Toronto Press, 2009), 54.

78 J.B. McGeachy, "Confederation Clinic," *Winnipeg Free Press*, 18, 19, 20, 23 May 1938.

79 LAC, MacKay Papers, vol. 10, Robert to Kathleen, 22 May 1938; UMA, Dafoe Papers, box 22, file 1, Jack to Alice, 20 May 1938.

80 Premier A.A. Dysart, "Public Hearings" 18 May 1938, 8494–99.

81 Cited in Donnelly, *Dafoe of the Free Press*, 174.

82 "Public Hearings" 21 May 1938, 9506ff, quotation 8571. See the exchanges with commissioners, 8524–27, 8531, 8534.

83 As put in Edwin R. Black, *Divided Loyalties: Canadian Concepts of Federalism* (Montreal and Kingston: McGill-Queen's University Press, 1977); 164; Slumkoski, "A Fair Show and a Square Deal," 126; YUA, Robert Fowler Papers, box 2, file 1, "Summary of the Hearings," 18 May 1938.

84 UMA, Dafoe Papers, box 22, file 1, Jack Dafoe to Alice Dafoe, 20 May 1938; ibid., box 14, file 2, W.C. Kierstead to J.W. Dafoe, 4 June 1938; ibid., box 2, J.W. Dafoe to G.V. Ferguson, 26 May 1938; J.B. McGeachy, "Confederation Clinic," *Winnipeg Free Press*, 19 May 1938.

85 J.B. McGeachy, "Confederation Clinic," 26, 27, 30 May 1938 and 1 June 1938; "Public Hearings" 1 June 1938, 9775–903.

86 Tim Buck, "Public Hearings" vol. 79, 2 June 1938, 9775–877. The talk is reported in J.B. McGeachy, "Confederation Clinic," 3 June 1938; and the luncheon in Eggleston's *While I Remember*.

87 Gunnar Myrdal, "Public Hearings" 9108–54. On fiscal policy, see 9118–19, monetary policy etc., 9131–34.

88 J.B. McGeachy, "Confederation Clinic," 3 February 1938.

89 YUA, Robert Fowler Papers, box 2, file 1, "Summary of the Hearings," 2 June 1938; "Public Hearings" 2 June 1938, 9958–59, 9970–71, 9972–73, 9974–75, 9979–80.

90 LAC, MacKay Papers, vol. 10, Bert to Kay, 29 May and 3 June 1938.

Chapter 7: Hard Seasons: Summer and Fall 1938

1 Library and Archives Canada (LAC), Mackenzie King Papers, Memoranda and notes (J4), O.D. Skelton, "Memorandum on Dominion-Provincial Relations," 16 July 1938, 114360-3.

2 Rowell's breakdown and continuing illness after mid-1938 are described in Margaret Prang, *N. W. Rowell: Ontario Nationalist* (Toronto: University of Toronto Press, 1974), 496–97.

3 University of Manitoba Archives (UMA), Dafoe Papers, Crerar to Dafoe, 18 December 1937; LAC, Mackenzie King Diary, 6 January 1938; John T. Saywell, "*Just Call Me Mitch*": *The Life of Mitchell F. Hepburn* (Toronto: University of Toronto Press, 1991), 385–86; LAC, Mackenzie King Diaries, 26 and 29 April 1938, 2–6 May 1938.

4 Saywell, "*Just Call Me Mitch*," 385–86.

5 LAC, Mackenzie King Diaries, 2–4 May 1938.

6 Ibid., 18 May 1938; Saywell, *"Just Call Me Mitch,"* 387.

7 LAC, Mackenzie King Papers, Hepburn to Dunning, 15 June 1938, Dunning to Hepburn, 18 June 1938; Archives of Ontario, Hepburn Papers, F10, Hepburn to King, 29 June 1938; Christopher Armstrong, *The Politics of Federalism: Ontario's Relations with the Federal Government, 1867–1942* (Toronto: University of Toronto Press, 1981), 218.

8 LAC, MacKay Papers, vol. 7, Hepburn to Alex Skelton, 13 July 1938. Copy of Hepburn to King, 29 June 1938 as cited in the above note.

9 LAC, MacKay Papers, vol. 8, Skelton to MacKay, 22 July 1938, copy in UMA, Dafoe Papers, box 14, file 3, Skelton to Dafoe, 22 July 1938.

10 L.E. Beaulieu to J. Sirois, 14 May 1938, M. Duplessis to J. Sirois, 20 May 1938, Sirois to Duplessis, 25 May 1938, in Royal Commission on Dominion-Provincial Relations, "Submissions," vol. 13, #341a/b.

11 Archives of Ontario, RG 13, Hepburn Papers, Aberhart to Hepburn, 9 September 1938.

12 As quoted in Armstrong, *Politics of Federalism,* 218.

13 LAC, Mackenzie King Papers, Memoranda and notes (J4), O.D. Skelton, "Memorandum on Dominion-Provincial Relations," 16 July 1938, 114360-3.

14 Saywell, *"Just Call Me Mitch,"* 388–90.

15 UMA, Dafoe Papers, box 3, file 3, Dafoe to Mackenzie King, 11 May 1938; ibid., box 2, Dafoe to G.V. Ferguson, 26 May 1938; ibid., box 14, file 1, Dafoe to A. Skelton, 2 July 1938, Angus to Dafoe, 9 July 1938, Fowler to Dafoe, 23 July 1938; ibid., 14, file 4, Nell Rowell to Alex Skelton, 15 August 1938; LAC, MacKay Papers, Sirois to MacKay, 20 July 1938.

16 LAC, Mackenzie King Papers, Memoranda and notes (J4), O.D. Skelton, "Memorandum on Dominion-Provincial Relations," 16 July 1938, 114360-3; R.B. Bryce, *Maturing in Hard Times: Canada's Department of Finance through the Great Depression* (Montreal and Kingston: McGill-Queen's University Press, 1986), 213–15; LAC, Mackenzie King Diaries, 2 June 1938.

17 LAC, Mackenzie King Papers, Memoranda and notes (J4), O.D. Skelton, "Memorandum on Dominion-Provincial Relations," 16 July 1938, 114360-3.

18 See David Ricardo Williams, *Duff: A Life in the Law* (Vancouver: Osgoode Society and UBC Press, 1984).

19 LAC, Mackenzie King Papers, Memoranda and notes, (J4), O.D. Skelton, "Memorandum on Dominion-Provincial Relations," 16 July 1938, 114360-3.

20 Ibid., Mackenzie King Diaries, 16 July 1938.

21 LAC, Henry Angus Papers, "Autobiography," 273.

22 Bryce, *Maturing in Hard Times,* 215; LAC, Henry Angus Papers, file 1 "Autobiography" 272–73; J.A. Corry, *My Life and Work: A Happy Partnership* (Kingston: Queen's

University, 1981), 108–9. See also W.A. Mackintosh, "Douglas Alexander Skelton (1906–1950)," *Canadian Journal of Economics and Political Science* 17, 1 (1951): 89–91; on the standing of Café Henry Burger in Ottawa society, see June Callwood, "Dining Over at Madame Burger's." *Maclean's Magazine*, 1 November 1950, 14ff.

23 LAC, MacKay Papers, vol. 8, Skelton to Rowell, 8 April 1938, vol. 7, "Secretary's Minutes," 25 April 1938.

24 LAC, MacKay Papers, vol. 8, Skelton to Rowell, 8 April 1938, vol. 7, "Secretary's Minutes," 25 April 1938, 7 May 1938, 8 August 1938.

25 Ibid., MacKay Papers, vol. 7, "Secretary's Minutes," Ottawa, 11 May 1938; ibid., MacKay Papers, vol. 8, Skelton to MacKay, 23 June 1938.

26 Ibid., Eggleston Papers, vol. 30/1, Wilfrid to Lena, 28 July 1938, and several other undated letters of July 1938.

27 LAC, Mackenzie King Papers, Memoranda and notes (J4), E.A.P[ickering], memo, 26 July 1938, 142401; J.W. Pickersgill to W.L.M. King, 16 August 1938, 142412. See also British Columbia Archives (BCA), GR 1222, Premiers Papers, vol. 95, file 7, Skelton to Pattullo, 29 April 1938, Secretary to Pattullo to Skelton, 9 May 1938, 14 and 19 July 1938, Skelton to Pattullo, 12 and 18 August 1938, Skelton to Pattullo and reply, 8 and 14 October 1938, Skelton to Pattullo and reply, 14 November 1938, Pattullo to Skelton, 17 November 1938, Pattullo to J. deB. Farris, 17 November 1938, Skelton to Pattullo.

28 The letter was sent to the commissioners: LAC, RG 33, Royal Commission on Dominion-Provincial Relations Papers, vol. 56, Skelton to Sirois, 23 July 1938; LAC, MacKay Papers, vol. 8, Skelton to MacKay, 23 June 1938; UMA, Dafoe Papers, 14/1, Skelton to Dafoe, 23 June 1938.

29 UMA, Dafoe Papers, box 14, file 4, Fowler to Angus, 23 June 1938, "extract" to Dafoe.

30 Ibid.

31 UMA, Dafoe Papers, box 14, file 2, Angus to Dafoe, 28 June 1938, and 9 July 1938; ibid., file 1, Dafoe to Angus, 5 July 1938; ibid., file 2, Dafoe to A. Skelton, 2 July 1938.

32 LAC, MacKay Papers, vol. 8, MacKay to Sirois, 16 July 1938, Sirois to MacKay, 20 and 23 July 1938, quotation 21 July 1938.

33 Ibid., RG 33 23, Royal Commission on Dominion-Provincial Relations Papers, vol. 56, Skelton to Sirois, 23 August 1938, Sirois to Skelton, 26 August 1938.

34 Ibid., MacKay Papers, vol. 7, "Secretary's Minutes," 8 August 1938.

35 Ibid., Royal Commission on Dominion-Provincial Relations Papers, vol. 4, Clark to Rowell and Skelton, 17 February 1938, Rowell to Skelton, 19 February 1938, Sirois to Rowell, 6 April 1938, Rowell to Sirois, 7 April 1938.

36 UMA, Dafoe Papers, box 22, file 2, Dafoe to Elizabeth Dafoe, 9 August 1938, Dafoe to Alice Dafoe, 10 August 1938; LAC, MacKay Papers, vol. 10, Robert to Kathleen,

9 August 1938, vol. 7, MacKay to Sirois, Dafoe, and Angus, 12 and 15 August 1938, and Sirois to MacKay, 14 August 1938. Since Giblin's testimony was in camera, the record of "Public Hearings" merely noted he testified on 8 August 1938.

37 LAC, MacKay Papers, vol. 7, minutes, 4 and 8 August 1938, A. Skelton to Hepburn, 12 August 1938. A copy of the minutes found its way to the Department of Finance: LAC, Department of Finance Papers, RG 19, vol. 2201, "Minutes of August 4th 1938 Meeting of the Royal Commission on Dominion-Provincial Relations."

38 BCA, Pattullo Papers, vol. 75/6, Pattullo to King, 5 August 1938; LAC, Mackenzie King Papers, memoranda and notes, C-4279, "Memorandum of Discussions," 26 September 1938, 142413.

39 LAC, MacKay Papers, vol. 8, A. Skelton to H.E. Crowle, 9 June 1938, Crowle to Skelton, 10 June 1938, Crowle to MacKay, 26 October 1938; ibid., Royal Commission on Dominion-Provincial Relations Papers, vol. 56, Rowell to Skelton, 7 February and 11 April 1938, Skelton to Kennedy, 16 November 1937, Kennedy to Skelton, 23 November 1937, Kennedy to M. Rowland, 10 March 1939. It is notable that both MacDonald and Kennedy were among the most critical constitutional English Canadian authorities regarding Judicial Committee of the Privy Council decisions and advocates for centralization. See R.C.B. Risk, "The Scholars and the Constitution," *Manitoba Law Review* 23 (1996): 505–13.

40 A.E. Grauer, "Public Assistance and Social Insurance," "Public Health," "Housing." Research Studies for the Royal Commission on Dominion-Provincial Relations (Ottawa: King's Printer, 1940).

41 LAC, MacKay Papers, vol. 7, "Secretary's Minutes," 8 August 1938, vol. 10, Robert to Kathleen, 11 and 13 August 1938; UMA, Dafoe Papers, box 22, file 2, Jack Dafoe to Alice Dafoe, 12 August 1938. See also Dafoe Papers, box 22, file 2, Dafoe to Elizabeth Dafoe, 9 August 1938; LAC, MacKay Papers, vol. 10, Robert to Kathleen, 9 and 11 August 1938.

42 Ibid., Robert to Kathleen, 9 and 11 August 1938; LAC MacKay Papers, vol. 8, MacKay to Sirois, 16 July 1938, Sirois to MacKay, 17 August 1938.

43 LAC, Eggleston Papers, vol. 12, file 11 contains many letters to his wife and to his former high school teacher, Ephraim Weber, in Regina, Saskatchewan.

44 UMA, Dafoe Papers, box 14, file 3, A. Skelton to Dafoe, 22 July 1938; LAC, MacKay Papers, vol. 7, "Secretary's Minutes," 8 August 1938, vol. 8, Sirois to MacKay, 17 August 1938; UMA, Dafoe Papers, box 14, file 1, Dafoe to Skelton, 5 September 1938; LAC, MacKay Papers, vol. 8, Fowler to MacKay, 13 September 1938; UMA, Dafoe Papers, box 14, file 1, Fowler to Dafoe, 19 September 1938.

45 LAC, MacKay Papers, vol. 7, "Secretary's Minutes," 3–5 October 1938; UMA, Dafoe Papers, box 14, file 2, Stuart Garson to Dafoe, 26 October 1938 and 1 November 1938.

46 UMA, Dafoe Papers, box 14, file 2, MacKay to Dafoe, 2 September 1938; ibid., file 1, Dafoe to MacKay, 9 September 1938, Dafoe to A. Skelton, 9 September 1938; ibid., file 3, Skelton to Dafoe, 12 September 1938.

47 LAC, Mackenzie King Papers, Primary series correspondence (J1), N.W. Rowell to Hon. E. Lapointe, 19 October 1938, 219614; Nellie Rowell to Mackenzie King, 11 November 1938, 219622-3; Mackenzie King to Nell Rowell, 12 and 23 November 1938, 219624, 219626. The Prime Minister had of course been kept informed of Rowell's situation all through the summer and fall. See ibid., Nellie Rowell to Mackenzie King, 29 May 1938, enclosure Dr. C. Lusk to Mrs. Rowell, 28 May 1938, 219615-6 and 219617.

48 Order-in-Council P.C. 2946, 1938.

49 LAC, MacKay Papers, vol. 7, "Secretary's Minutes," 7 May 1938, 8 August 1938, 9 October 1938, 22 November 1938; LAC, MacKay Papers, vol. 8, MacKay to Savard, 10 September 1938, Savard to MacKay, 23 September 1938.

50 UMA, Dafoe Papers, box 14, file 2, Dafoe to MacKay, 9 September 1938, Dafoe to Skelton, 9 September 1938; ibid., private correspondence, box 1, Dafoe to Alice Dafoe, 6 October 1938.

51 UMA, Dafoe Papers, box 22, file 2, Jack to Alice, 6 October 1938; LAC, MacKay Papers, vol. 10, 6 and 8 October 1938. See also LAC, Henry Angus Papers, "Autobiography," 270–71.

52 LAC, MacKay Papers, vol. 10, 6, 8, and 10 October 1938; ibid., MacKay Papers, vol. 10, 20 and 27 October, 1938, 7 November 1938; UMA, Dafoe Papers, box 22, file 2, 12 October, 19 October, 22 October, n.d. October 1938, 2 November 1938, 28 November 1938.

53 This is gleaned from many comments over the period from July to September: UMA, Dafoe Papers, box 14, file 3, Skelton to Dafoe, 22 July 1938, Fowler to Dafoe, 19 September 1938; ibid., file 5, Skelton to Dafoe, Dafoe to Skelton, 5 September 1938, Dafoe to Skelton, 12 September 1938.

54 LAC, Royal Commission on Dominion-Provincial Relations Papers, vol. 53, commission correspondence, Deutsch to Creighton, 30 November 1937, Creighton to Skelton, 30 December 1937, 14 April 1938, 30 June 1938, Skelton to Creighton, 6 August 1938, Creighton to Skelton, 15 September 1938, Skelton to Creighton, 16 September 1938.

55 UMA, Dafoe Papers, box 14, file 1, Dafoe to Alex Skelton, 30 December 1938, enclosing MacGibbon's comments.

56 LAC, MacKay Papers, vol. 10, MacKay to Katherine MacKay, 21 October 1938, 27 October 1938.

57 Ibid., 27 October 1938, 7 November, 1938; UMA, Dafoe Papers, vol. 2, Dafoe to Ferguson, 11 October, 19 November, 29 November 1938.

58 LAC, Royal Commission on Dominion-Provincial Relations Papers, vol. 53, Skelton to Innis, 19 September 1937, Innis to Skelton, 1 October 1937, Miss Rowland to Mr. Macfarlane, 10 November 1938, Innis to Skelton, n.d. [November] 1938, Skelton to Innis, 17 and 21 December 1938.

59 Ibid., Innis to Skelton, 29 December 1938, 3 January 1939.

60 LAC, MacKay Papers, vol. 10, MacKay to Katherine MacKay, 27 October 1938, 7 November 1938; ibid., Royal Commission on Dominion-Provincial Relations Papers, vol. 53, Innis to Skelton, 3 January 1939, Skelton to Innis, 5 January 1939.

61 LAC, Royal Commission on Dominion-Provincial Relations Papers, vol. 53, Skelton to Innis, 5 January 1939, Innis to Skelton, n.d. January 1939.

62 LAC, Mackenzie King Papers, Primary correspondence series (J1), King to Sirois, 8 October 1938, 221790.

63 Ibid., Sirois to King, 14 October 1938, 221791-2, 26 November 1938, 2221794; cf. UMA, Dafoe Papers, Dafoe to Skelton, 9 September 1938.

64 Alvin H. Hansen, "Public Hearings" Ottawa, 29 November 1938, 10375-10428, esp. 10376, 10397-99, 10419ff.

65 Jacob Viner, "Public Hearings" Ottawa, 30 November 1938, 10579-10612, quotes 10579, 10584; Stuart Garson, "Public Hearings" Ottawa, 1 December 1938, 10614-33, quotes 10615, 10617.

66 LAC, Mackenzie King Diaries, 2 December 1938.

67 Annie Margaret Angus, "Cursory Rhymes for Commissioners," LAC, Henry Angus Papers, "Autobiography."

Chapter 8: Toil and Trouble: 1939 and 1940

1 University of Manitoba Archives (UMA), Dafoe Papers, box 14, file 2, Dafoe to Fowler, 30 September 1939.

2 Bennett would spend the rest of his days there as Viscount Bennett, a peer of the realm. Library and Archives Canada (LAC), MacKay Papers, vol. 7, royal commission minutes and instructions, 22 November 1938. See also LAC, MacKay Papers, vol. 8, Sirois to Bennett, 26 November and 3 December 1938, Bennett to Sirois, 29 November; ibid., vol. 7, minutes, 8 December 1938.

3 LAC, MacKay Papers, vol. 8, Robert MacKay to A. Skelton, 23 November 1938, A. Skelton to Graham Towers, 19 December 1938, Towers to Skelton, 11 January 1939.

4 UMA, Dafoe Papers, box 14, file 3, D.A. Skelton to W.C. Clark, 16 November 1938, W.C. Clark to D.A. Skelton, 22 November 1938, Charles A. Dunning to Dr. Sirois, 10 December 1938.

5 LAC, MacKay Papers, vol. 7, "Secretary's Minutes," 8 December 1938.

6 UMA, Dafoe Papers, box 14, file 1, Dafoe to Fowler, 21 September 1938.

7   These summaries and précis are found in various places, including UMA, Dafoe Papers, box 14, file 8; and LAC, MacKay Papers, vol. 8. They are also found in York University Archives (YUA), Robert Fowler Papers, box 2, file 1, "Summary of the Hearings." Skelton explains some of the process to Dafoe. See UMA, Dafoe Papers, box 14, file 3, Skelton to Dafoe, 12 October 1938; ibid., file 1, Dafoe to Fowler, 16 December 1938.

8   UMA, Dafoe Papers, box 14, file 1, Dafoe to Skelton, 15 December 1938; ibid., file 2, 10 January 1939. Dafoe was dwelling on Martin's arresting arguments starting with *The Natural Resources Question: The Historical Basis of Provincial Claims* (Winnipeg: King's Printer, 1920) and *Dominion Lands Policy* (Toronto: McClelland and Stewart, 1973 [1938]). Mackintosh edited and contributed to the large, comprehensive critical eight-volume study of the course of western settlement, "Frontiers of Settlement," which published Martin's 1938 book as well as his own on Prairie settlement and agriculture *Prairie Settlement: The Geographical Setting* (Toronto: Macmillan, 1934) and *Economic Problems of the Prairie Provinces* (Toronto: Macmillan, 1935).

9   UMA, Dafoe Papers, box 14, file 1, Skelton to Dafoe, 21 December 1938.

10 *Economic Reconstruction: Report of the Columbia University Commission,* Robert M. MacIver, chairman (New York: Columbia University Press, 1934). On the Chicago Economics study, see Ronnie J. Phillips, "The 'Chicago Plan' and New Deal Banking Reform," *Working Paper No. 76,* June 1992, Jerome Levy Economics Institute of Bard College. The quotation is in MacIver et al., *Economic Reconstruction,* vi.

11 *Report on Indian Constitutional Reforms* (Calcutta: Superintendent Government Printing, India, 1918).

12 UMA, Dafoe Papers, box 22, file 1, Dafoe to Alice Dafoe, 12 August 1938; ibid., box 14, file 1, Dafoe to Angus, 5 July 1938; ibid., box 14, file 2, Angus to Dafoe, 8 July 1938.

13 UMA, Dafoe Papers, box 14, file 2, Dafoe to Skelton, 10 January 1939.

14 Ibid., file 1, Angus to Dafoe, 3 January 1939, 21 February 1939.

15 LAC, MacKay Papers, vol. 10, Bert to Kay, 29 January 1939, 19 February 1939. This assessment was shared by Angus in retrospect. See LAC, Henry Angus Papers, "Autobiography," 267–68.

16 LAC, MacKay Papers, vol. 10, Bert to Kay, 2, 4, 8, 11, 15 February 1939.

17 Angus, "Public Hearings" Victoria, BC, 21 March 1938, 5260, Toronto, Ontario, 9 May 1938, 8117. A few public organizations did support it.

18 LAC, MacKay Papers, vol. 10, Bert to Kay, 19 February 1939; UMA, Dafoe Papers, box 14, file 1, Dafoe to MacKay, 6 July 1939, 24 July 1939, Mackay to Dafoe, 11 July 1939, 18 July 1939. The issue "Fundamental Rights" was discussed in a précis, 10 October 1938. See citations in note 8 above. The *Report* acknowledged the possibility of a bill of rights but dismissed its practicality in Book One, 224–25.

19 LAC, MacKay Papers, vol. 10, Bert to Kay, 9 March 1939.

20 Ibid., 12 and 14 March 1939, 22 March 1939, 26 March 1939; LAC, Mackenzie King Papers, Primary correspondence series (J1), King to Sirois, 14 March 1939, 236923; Sirois to King (two letters), 15 March 1939, 236926 and 236931-3; Sirois to O.D. Skelton, 15 March 1939, 236929; A.D.P. Heaney to W.P. Turnbull, 20 March 1939, 236928.

21 LAC, MacKay Papers, vol. 10, Bert to Kay, 19 April 1939, 9, 14, and 21 May 1939.

22 Ibid., 23 April, 9, 13, and 18 May 1939.

23 Ibid., 9 May (on Skelton) and 14 May (on the plan) 1939.

24 The fiscal plan, which was called "Plan One," was unveiled in the *Report*, Book One, 81–86. It is explained in greater detail in the next chapter.

25 LAC, MacKay Papers, vol. 10, Bert to Kay, 9 May 1939, 14 May 1939; ibid., Henry Angus Papers, "Autobiography," 267, 269; UMA, Dafoe Papers, box 2, Dafoe to G.V. Ferguson, 8 May 1939, 17 May 1939, 19 May 1939, MacKay to Fowler, 2 August 1963, Fowler to MacKay, 6 August 1963. This memo appears to have been lost, and it does not appear in records consulted for this study.

26 LAC, MacKay Papers, vol. 10, Bert to Kay, 8 June 1939, n.d. [likely 10] June 1939; UMA, Dafoe Papers, box 2, Dafoe to Ferguson, 14 June 1939; LAC, Henry Angus Papers, "Autobiography," 282–83.

27 LAC, MacKay Papers, vol. 7, RCDPR, "Secretary's Minutes," 12 and 13 June 1939.

28 Ibid.

29 Ibid.

30 Ibid.

31 Ibid.; UMA, Dafoe Papers, vol. 2, Dafoe to Ferguson, 14 June 1939; ibid., vol. 14, précis of discussions, 17 and 18 November 1938; LAC, Henry Angus Papers, "Autobiography," 282–83. Angus emphasizes that, for the most part, the two legal counsel had very little influence over the commissioners.

32 Wilfrid Eggleston, *While I Still Remember* (Toronto: Ryerson, 1968), 248–50; and LAC, Eggleston Papers, diary, May–June 1939; ibid., Angus Papers, "Autobiography," 282ff; J.A. Corry, *My Life and Work*, 106–7.

33 LAC, Mackenzie King Papers, Memoranda and notes (J4), King to Skelton, 3 July 1939, 142414; UMA, Dafoe Papers, box 22, file 3, Dafoe to Elizabeth Dafoe, 4 July 1939; LAC, MacKay Papers, vol. 8, Dafoe to MacKay, 7 July 1939.

34 LAC, Royal Commission on Dominion-Provincial Relations Correspondence, vol. 56, 4/4, Sirois to Savard, 28 June 1938, Sirois to Alex Skelton, 29 June 1939, Savard to Sirois 4 July 1939, Skelton to Savard, 4 July 1939.

35 LAC, MacKay Papers, vol. 10, Robert to Kathleen, 8 and 10 July 1939; UMA, Dafoe Papers, box 14, file 2, MacKay to Dafoe, 10 July 1939; LAC, Mackenzie King Papers, Primary correspondence series (J1), King to Sirois, 5 July 1939, 236933; Sirois to

King, 12 July 1939, 236934-9; A.D.P. Heaney to Sirois, 13 July 1939, 236934; Sirois to Heeney, 15 July 1939, 236935.

36 UMA, Dafoe Papers, box 3, Corry to Dafoe, 31 July 1939, Dafoe to MacKay, 15 August 1939; Queen's University Archives (QUA), Dexter Papers, additions, 11 August 1939.

37 See Donald Wright, *Donald Creighton: A Life in History* (Toronto: University of Toronto Press, 2015), 135, 137, 139. Wright does not delve into the details of Creighton's work for the commission. Creighton's extreme advocacy of a centralist and Anglo-Canadian Canada may be sampled in his *Towards the Discovery of Canada: Selected Essays* (Toronto: Macmillan, 1972).

38 LAC, MacKay Papers, vol. 8, Sirois to MacKay, 29 December 1939, MacKay to Sirois 4 January 1940, Sirois to MacKay, 4 January 1940, MacKay to Angus and Sirois, 5 January 1940; ibid., Royal Commission Papers, vol. 53, Creighton to Skelton, 20 September 1939, 6 January 1940; *Report*, Book One, 32–36; UMA, Dafoe Papers, box 14, file 2, MacKay to Dafoe, 10 July 1939, 18 July 1939; LAC, MacKay Papers, Dafoe to MacKay, 22 July 1939, 31 July 1939.

39 UMA, Dafoe Papers, box 2, Dafoe to Ferguson, 29 August 1939, 2 September 1939; ibid., box 22, file 3, Jack to Alice, 24, 26, and 28 August 1939.

40 UMA, Dafoe Papers, box 22, file 3, Jack to Alice, 26 and 31 August 1939, 1 September 1939.

41 Ibid., 1 September 1939.

42 Ibid., 4 and 7 September 1939.

43 Ibid., 9 September 1939, 14, 17, and 18 September 1939.

44 Ibid., box 14, file 1, Fowler to Dafoe, 24 September 1939; ibid., file 2, Dafoe to Fowler, 30 September 1939.

45 LAC, MacKay Papers, vol. 10, Bert to Kay, 14 October 1939.

46 Ibid., vol. 7, MacKay to Sirois, 12 August 1939, Sirois to MacKay, 14 August 1939, MacKay to Sirois, 15 August 1939, Sirois to Skelton, 25 September 1939, MacKay to Sirois, 6 October 1939, Angus to MacKay, 9 October 1939, Sirois to MacKay, 14 October 1939. Cf. *Report*, Book Two, 83–84.

47 LAC, MacKay Papers, vol. 10, Bert to Kay, 25 and 27 October 1939.

48 Ibid., vol. 7, "Social Services," MacKay to Skelton, 3 December 1939, "Insurance," Fowler to MacKay, 8 December 1939.

49 Ibid., MacKay Papers, vol. 10, Bert to Kay, 15 December 1939, 28 December 1939; UMA, Dafoe Papers, box 22, file 4 and box 22, file 6, Jack to Alice, 7 December 1939, 10 December 1939, 12, 13, 14 December 1939, 16 and 17 December 1939.

50 LAC, Royal Commission on Dominion-Provincial Relations Correspondence, vol. 56, Sirois to Kelton, 3 January 1940, Skelton to Sirois, 4 January 1940.

51 LAC, MacKay Papers, vol. 8, MacKay to Sirois, 28 December 1939; ibid., vol. 10, Bert to Kay, 28 December 1939, 1 January 1940, 23 January 1940. MacKay's letters to his

wife were not preserved after that date. UMA, Dafoe Papers, vol. 1, Dafoe to H.F. Armstrong, 4 January 1940; ibid., vol. 2, Dafoe to Ferguson, 23 January 1940; QUA, Dexter Papers, Dafoe to Dexter, 9 January 1940.

52 LAC, Mackenzie King Papers, Memoranda and notes (J4), King to Pickersgill, 5 January 1940, 227159; O.D. Skelton to Prime Minister, 10 January 1940, 227160-2; Skelton to Pickersgill, 11 January 1940, 227166; A.D.P. H[eeney] to Prime Minister, 25 January 1940, 227168. The considerations of the King government in this period are explained in J.L. Granatstein, *Canada's War: The War Policies of the Mackenzie King Government, 1939–1945* (Toronto: University of Toronto Press, 1974), chap. 3.

53 LAC, Mackenzie King Papers, Primary series correspondence (J1), Sirois to King, 24 January 1940, King to Sirois, 29 January 1940, 252040-1, 252042; Sirois circulated King's letter: see ibid., MacKay Papers, vol. 8, King to Sirois, 29 January 1940.

54 LAC, Eggleston Papers, vol. 12, file 12, "Memorabilia," printed menu of 1 February 1940.

55 Ibid., MacKay Papers, vol. 7, Sirois to MacKay and others, 15 February 1940, Dafoe to MacKay, 17 February 1940, MacKay to Sirois, 19 February 1940, Sirois to MacKay, 21 February 1940; UMA, Dafoe Papers, box 14, file 1, Angus to Dafoe, 21 February 1940. Creighton's interpretation of the intentions of the "founders" is summarized in Donald Wright, *Donald Creighton: A Life in History* (Toronto: University of Toronto Press, 2015), passim, esp. chaps. 8 and 11.

56 Deutsch's work is documented for the period 1939–40. A fascinating series of letters from Stephanie Heagerty, his fiancée, plots Deutsch's regular trips between Kingston and Ottawa during the winter. See QUA, Deutsch Papers, vol. 1, file 2, correspondence 1939–40, Stephanie to John, 9, 17, 24 January, 14, 21, 28 February, 6, 14, 19, 24 March 1940. On the commissioners' reaction to Deutsch's work, see LAC, MacKay Papers, vol. 8, Sirois to MacKay, 7 March 1940; UMA, Dafoe Papers, box 14, file 2, Angus to Dafoe, 21 February 1940; LAC, MacKay Papers, vol. 8, MacKay to Sirois, 1 March 1940.

57 See UMA, Dafoe Papers, box 14, file 3, Skelton to Dafoe, 8 April 1940, Angus to Dafoe, 20 April 1940.

58 LAC, MacKay Papers, vol. 7, "Secretary's Minutes," 1 February 1940; ibid., vol. 8, MacKay to Sirois, 12 February 1940.

59 LAC, MacKay Papers, vol. 8, MacKay to Skelton, 13 February 1940.

60 Ibid., Sirois to MacKay, 14 and 15 February 1940; ibid., vol. 7, Sirois to Skelton, 14 February 1940. It is likely but not clear that the latter letter was copied to Angus and Dafoe.

61 LAC, MacKay Papers, vol. 8, Sirois to MacKay, 5 March 1940, MacKay to Sirois, 1 March 1940; QUA, Dexter Papers, Dafoe to Dexter, 9 March 1940; UMA, Dafoe Papers, box 14, file 1, Dafoe to Angus, 29 March 1940; LAC, MacKay Papers, vol. 8,

MacKay to Dafoe, 7 March 1940, Dafoe to MacKay, 17 March 1940, MacKay to Angus, 25 March 1940, Angus to MacKay, 22 and 27 March 1940, MacKay to Angus, 4 April 1940.

62 E.g., LAC, Mackenzie King Papers, Memoranda and notes (J4), G.M. Weir to Mackenzie King, 12 March 1940, King to Weir, 12 March 1940, 277174, 277175ff. In *Commissioning Ideas: Canadian National Policy Innovation in Comparative Perspective* (Don Mills: Oxford University Press, 1998), 42n82, Neil Bradford is misled by his cited sources (Fransen's thesis who was misled by earlier sources) into asserting that the report was finished by mid-February and that delays were the doing of Mackenzie King. That was not the case. Newspapers of the time had delighted in charging the government with deliberate suppression. A near-contemporary printed source for all that, which probably influenced others, was the odd and erroneous claim by Wilfrid Eggleston in 1946 that the report was finished by mid-February and "held back." See *The Road to Nationhood* (Toronto: Oxford University Press, 1946), 117.

63 LAC, MacKay Papers, vol. 8, Angus to MacKay, 22 and 27 March 1940, MacKay to Angus, 4 April 1940; UMA, Dafoe Papers, box 14, file 3, Skelton to Dafoe, 8 April 1940, Angus to Dafoe, 20 April 1940; LAC, MacKay Papers, vol. 8, Sirois to MacKay, 25 April 1940.

64 This too is more than a moot point and worth emphasis. Writing credit for many of the significant inquiries of later periods seems to go to staff members working, no doubt, under direction. Sources for the explanation about writing credits for Rowell-Sirois are chiefly the recollections of Angus, MacKay, and Fowler as well as Eggleston. See LAC, Angus Papers, "Autobiography," 256ff; ibid., MacKay Papers, vol. 10, additions, MacKay to Fowler, 2 August 1963, a memo, "Personal Reminiscence ... 26/7/63," and Fowler to MacKay, 6 August 1963. MacKay and Fowler disagreed with Ramsay Cook's just published book on John W. Dafoe, *The Politics of John W. Dafoe and the Free Press* (Toronto: University of Toronto Press, 1963), which made a strong claim for Dafoe's predominant role. Eggleston's remarks are in his autobiography, *While I Still Remember* (Toronto: Ryerson, 1968), chap. 14, 217ff. and his earlier book, *The Road to Nationhood*, 97ff.

Chapter 9: Reinterpreting Canadian Federalism: May 1940

1 *Report of the Royal Commission on Dominion-Provincial Relations* (Ottawa: King's Printer, 1940), Book One, 186.

2 *Report of the Royal Commission on Dominion-Provincial Relations* (Ottawa, King's Printer, 1940), Book Two, 276.

3 The commission hired two translators, one a Laval graduate student, Marcel Trudel, in later years a professor of history at Laval and Ottawa and no friend of Quebec clerical nationalism.

4 Library and Archives Canada (LAC), Mackenzie King Papers, Memoranda and notes (J4), King to Pickersgill, 5 January 1940, 277159.

5 Ibid., Skelton to King, 10 January 1940 and Skelton to Pickersgill, 11 January 1940. See also LAC, MacKay Papers, vol. 8, Sirois to MacKay, 12 January 1940 and 6 February 1940.

6 LAC, MacKay Papers, vol. 8, MacKay to Dafoe, 7 March 1940.

7 Ibid., RG 33, Royal Commission Papers, vol. 55, Sirois to Skelton, 13 May 1940.

8 Ibid., Mackenzie King Papers, Memoranda and notes (J4), Skelton to King, 29 April 1940, 277179; A.D.P. H[eeney] to Prime Minister, 2 May 1940, 277180, Skelton memo (King "approved"), 3 May 1940, 277182-4; Mackenzie King to Heeney, 7 May 1940, 277188; A.D.P. H[eeney] to Prime Minister, 7 May 1940, 227189; ibid., Mackenzie King Diaries, 16 May 1940.

9 LAC, Mackenzie King Papers, Memoranda and notes (J4), Skelton to King, 10 May 1940, 277185-7. Dexter prepared a careful summary – worth reading still – for the *Winnipeg Free Press* but was inadvertently denied authorial credit, to Dafoe's embarrassment. See Queen's University Archives (QUA), Grant Dexter Papers, additions, Dafoe to Dexter, 16 May 1940.

10 University of Manitoba Archives (UMA), Dafoe Papers, box 13, file 4, Sirois to Dafoe (telegram), 11 May 1940.

11 LAC, Mackenzie King Diaries, 10, 11, 16, 18 May 1940; Canada, *Sessional Papers*, 95–1940; George F. Henderson, *Federal Royal Commissions in Canada 1867–1967: A Check-List* (Toronto: University of Toronto Press, 1967), 134. The total was not much less than the annual budget of the auditor general of Canada.

12 The useful distinction between "federation" and "federalism" is found in Preston King's 1979 work, which underlines the legitimacy of the division of sovereign authority as central to federal thinking. See his *Federalism and Federation* (London/Baltimore: Croom Helm/Johns Hopkins University Press, 1982). Rogers's essay was a short piece written in 1934 that dismissed worship of the original centralist vision of 1867. See Norman McLeod Rogers, "The Dead Hand," *Canadian Forum*, August 1934.

13 Terms of Reference, Order-in-Council P.C. 1008, 1937, cited in *Report*, Book One, 9–10, and summarized in *Report*, Book One, 13–14.

14 Ibid., 10 and 14.

15 A prime example was Frank Scott's prediction in his influential 1938 survey of Canada that the commission would force Canada to decide between a more centralized or a looser federation. See Frank Scott, *Canada Today: A Study of Her National Interests and National Policy* (London: Oxford University Press, 1938), 79. We have examined this issue as part of a review of the broader reception of the report in a previous essay, "Reconsidering Rowell-Sirois," in *Constructing Tomorrow's Federalism*,

ed. Ian Peach (Winnipeg: University of Manitoba Press, 2007), 34–49. A recent examination is the clear analysis of the economic and fiscal possibilities in the report by Hugh Grant, *W.A Mackintosh* (Montreal and Kingston: McGill-Queen's University Press, 2016), 173ff.

16 There are many studies examining the history of the academic social sciences in Canada. Among the most helpful general works for this account" have been the following: Carl Berger, *The Writing of Canadian History* (Toronto: University of Toronto Press, 1976, revised 1990); Edwin R. Black, *Divided Loyalties: Canadian Concepts of Federalism* (Montreal and Kingston: McGill-Queen's University Press, 1975); Neil Bradford, *Commissioning Ideas: Canadian National Policy Innovation in Comparative Perspective* (Don Mills: Oxford University Press, 1998); J.L. Granatstein, *The Ottawa Men: The Civil Service Mandarins 1935–1957* (Ottawa: Deneau, 1982); Robin F. Neill, *A History of Canadian Economic Thought* (London: Routledge, 1991); Peter C. Oliver, *The Constitution of Independence: The Development of Constitutional Theory in Australia, Canada, and New Zealand* (New York: Oxford University Press, 2005); Doug Owram, *The Government Generation: Canadian Intellectuals and the State, 1900–1945* (Toronto: University of Toronto Press, 1987); Donald Wright, *The Professionalization of History in English Canada* (Toronto: University of Toronto Press, 2005).

17 The Rowell-Sirois Report and its authors built upon the scholarship of the day and, in particular, the eight-volume Canadian Frontiers of Settlement series, edited and designed by W.A. Mackintosh. The series that Mackintosh put together (using Rockefeller Foundation funding) was replete with studies of the economic expansion of Canada to the west, the characteristics of Canadian settlement policy, and the rise and crisis of the wheat economy. The Canadian Frontiers of Settlement series constituted a remarkable explanation and critique of western settlement policy and practice. See Marlene Shore, *The Science of Social Redemption: McGill, the Chicago School, and the Origins of Social Research in Canada* (Toronto: University of Toronto Press, 1987), 162–94; and Jeffrey D. Brison, *Rockefeller, Carnegie and Canada: American Philanthropy and the Arts and Letters in Canada* (Montreal and Kingston: McGill-Queen's University Press, 2005), 156–59. Mackintosh's work is examined in Barry Ferguson, *Remaking Liberalism: The Intellectual Legacy of Adam Shortt, O.D. Skelton, W.C. Clark, and W.A. Mackintosh* (Montreal and Kingston: McGill-Queen's University Press, 1993); and Grant, *W.A. Mackintosh*. Innis, wary of government consultation, did not participate directly in the work of the commission, but he had some influence through his Toronto acolyte Donald G. Creighton. Innis did read the research studies. See LAC, Royal Commissions, RG 33, Royal Commission on Dominion-Provincial Relations Papers, vol. 53, "H.A. Innis" file. See Donald

Creighton, *Harold Adams Innis: Portrait of a Scholar* (Toronto: University of Toronto Press, 1957); and Grant, *William Mackintosh*. Creighton shows that Innis was chary of other economists' government service at the expense of autonomous university work, and he criticized the recommendations of Book Two but lauded the social science of Book One. See Harold Innis, "The Rowell-Sirois Report," in *Staples, Markets, and Cultural Change: Selected Essays [of Harold A. Innis]*, ed. Daniel Drache (Montreal and Kingston: McGill-Queen's University Press, 1995), 253. Grant shows that Mackintosh had the opposite view of the value of applied research for government.

18 A most instructive historically grounded reconsideration is R.C.B. Risk, "The Scholars and the Constitution," *Manitoba Law Journal* 23 (1996): 496–523. Specific works that show this underlying goal are Norman McLeod Rogers, "The Dead Hand," *Canadian Forum*, August 1934; Norman McLeod Rogers, "The Political Principles of Federalism," *Canadian Journal of Economics and Political Science* 1, 3 (1935): 337–47; F.R. Scott, "The Development of Canadian Federalism," *Papers and Proceedings of the Canadian Political Science Association* 3 (1931): 231–47; J.A. Corry, "The Federal Dilemma," *Canadian Journal of Economics and Political Science* 7, 2 (1941): 215–28; H.M. Clokie, "Judicial Review, Federalism and the Canadian Constitution," *Canadian Journal of Economics and Political Science* 8, 4 (1942): 537–56.

19 Henry Angus was a co-author of two volumes, *Canada and Her Great Neighbour* (New Haven/Toronto: Yale University Press/Ryerson Press, 1938) and *British Columbia and the United States* (New Haven/Toronto: Yale University Press/Ryerson Press, 1938), while Creighton wrote his career-making monograph, *The Commercial Empire of the St. Lawrence* (New Haven/Toronto: Yale University Press/Ryerson Press, 1937).

20 On "The Relations of Canada and the United States," see Berger, *Writing of Canadian History*; and Brison, *Rockefeller, Carnegie and Canada*, 161–65, works that emphasize the simultaneous "continentalist" and nation-centred treatment of Canadian history that emerged from the volumes. John Dafoe's *Canada: An American Nation* (New York: Columbia University Press, 1933) was from a series of lectures on Canadian international relations.

21 The adoption of Keynesianism is subject of long-standing debate, some seeing it emerging early, while others remain sceptical about that. Economists Robert Campbell, *Grand Illusions: The Politics of Keynesianism in Canada, 1945–1975* (Toronto: University of Toronto Press, 1977) and Owram, *Government Generation*, along with Grant, *W.A. Mackintosh*, are well-informed pillars of a discussion of great significance.

22 *Report*, Book Two, 79 and Book One, 151. Historical studies of twentieth-century economic thought sustain this point, as in the magisterial Eric Roll, *A History of*

Economic Thought, 5th ed. (London: Faber and Faber, 1992). Recent Canadian work has zeroed in on this point. See Bradford, *Commissioning Ideas;* Robert Wardhaugh, *Behind the Scenes: The Life and Work of W.C. Clark* (Toronto: University of Toronto Press, 2010); Grant, *W.A. Mackintosh;* Shirley Tillotson, *Give and Take: The Citizen-Taxpayer and the Rise of Canadian Democracy* (Vancouver: UBC Press, 2017).

23   Frank H. Underhill, *In Search of Canadian Liberalism* (Toronto: Macmillan, 1961), 20.

24   *Report*, Book One, 19 et seq.

25   Ibid., 52 et seq.

26   Ibid., 66ff.

27   Ibid., 93–94.

28   Ibid., 132, 133.

29   Ibid., 138–51 and 151–60, quotation 140, 143, 172, and 151.

30   Ibid., 182–85, quotation 185.

31   Ibid., 178ff, especially 182–86, quotation 182.

32   On this theme, the report echoed the findings of Mackintosh's study for the commission. *The Economic Background of Dominion-Provincial Relations*, Royal Commission on Dominion-Provincial Relations Research Study #3 (Ottawa: J.O. Patenaude, 1939) noted the perils and costs of national expansion and the absence of unifying effects.

33   *Report*, Book One, 151–60.

34   Ibid., 151.

35   Ibid.

36   *Report*, Book One, 172–73.

37   Ibid., 29.

38   Ibid., 30.

39   Ibid., 31.

40   Ibid., 31–32, 32.

41   All quotations *Report*, 1940, Book One, 36, Book One, 246; UMA, Dafoe Papers, box 3, file 6, Dafoe to MacKay, 15 August 1939. See also UMA, Dafoe Papers, box 7, file 3, Dafoe to Corry, 26 and 31 July 1939.

42   *Report*, Book One, 247.

43   Ibid., 247–49, quotation 248.

44   Ibid., 254–57, quotations 256, 254.

45   Ibid., 254–57, 257–59.

46   *Report*, Book Two, 9 and 10. The theoretical statement here at least alludes to if it does not rely on a version of liberalism – too seldom identified in Canada but commonly ascribed in the broader Anglo-American world – of reformist or developmental liberalism, which emerged from political science and economic reform

theorists from the 1880s to the 1920s in Great Britain and Europe, in the United States, and, to an extent, in Canada. See Peter Clarke, *Liberals and Social Democrats* (Cambridge: Cambridge University Press, 1978); James T. Kloppenberg, *Uncertain Victory: Social Democracy and Progressivism in European and American Thought, 1870–1920* (Oxford: Oxford University Press, 1988); Ferguson, *Remaking Liberalism*; and, above all in its sweeping conceptualization, C.B. Macpherson, *The Life and Times of Liberal Democracy* (New York: Oxford University Press, 1977).

47 *Report*, Book Two, 14 et seq. While this point may seem self-evident, it was hardly so in the 1930s when the role of non-governmental social service institutions was vastly greater than it would be later on in the century. Moreover, the commissioners had spent several months in 1937 and 1938 listening to a myriad of these agencies lobbying for governmental aid but not state takeover of their roles, testimony that did not lead to any direct defense of these agencies. Showing this breakthrough is the point of a number of works, starting with Owram's *Government Generation*.

48 *Report*, Book Two, 30.

49 Summarized in *Report*, Book Two, 13.

50 Ibid., 13 and 14.

51 *Report*, Book Two, chaps. 1–4, 15–67. Almost all of the eleven research studies revealed these many ways through examinations of Canadian and other governments' policies in the contemporary period.

52 *Report*, Book Two, 24.

53 Ibid., 72–73.

54 Ibid., 62–63. The discussion referred vaguely to some testimony and to L.M. Gouin and Brooke Claxton, *Legislative Expedients and Devises Adopted by the Dominion and the Provinces*, Royal Commission on Dominion-Provincial Relations, Research Report #8, (Ottawa: J.O. Patenaude, 1938).

55 *Report*, Book Two, 62, 65, 66–67. Gouin and Claxton, "Legislative Expedients."

56 *Report*, Book Two, 68–72.

57 Ibid., 14.

58 Ibid., 75–129.

59 Ibid., 78.

60 Ibid., 79.

61 Ibid., 81, 83. For the umpteenth time in the decade, the recommendation for extensive unemployment relief was heard.

62 *Report*, Book Two, 81, 83. In their discussions the commissioners acknowledged the origins of the principles in Nova Scotia's testimony and submission, but they may have found it impolitic to refer to this in the report. In any case, Manitoba and Saskatchewan independently called for this form of grant. See UMA, Dafoe Papers,

box 14, file 1, "Precis of Discussions," "fiscal need," 17 and 18 November 1938. See also Stephen Henderson, "A New Federal Vision: Nova Scotia and the Rowell-Sirois Report, 1938–48," in *Framing Canadian Federalism*, ed. Dimitry Anastakis and P.E. Bryden (Toronto: University of Toronto Press, 2009), 51–74.

63 *Report*, Book Two, 83–84. The proposed commission was totally unlike the Australian commission, which was a true joint state-commonwealth agency, although it too was merely advisory.

64 *Report*, Book Two, 82.

65 Ibid., 83, 86. In one of the few places where rewrites and summaries seem to stand out, the Rowell-Sirois Report inelegantly attempted to summarize Plan One after describing it in detail. It claimed the plan had seven features, starting with "relief to the Provinces," their "withdrawal" from "certain Tax Fields," a "surrender of federal subsidies" save for their inarguable areas of indirect taxation, the "new" revenue from the National Adjustment Grant, plus a framework for future borrowing either inside or outside the National Adjustment Grant plus, debt relief framework, plus "freedom of Provinces" from direct dominion control (Book Two, 86). This summary so little resembled the previous outline that it may have misled more readers than it enlightened, though it probably didn't fool too many politicians, bureaucrats, or academic readers with its use of the language of public relations, namely, "freedom of Provinces." See *Report*, 1940, Book Two, 86.

66 *Report*, Book Two, the details for each province took twenty pages, 87–107, on Ontario 96–97, and in general 85. See Angus, "Autobiography," 287.

67 *Report*, Book Two: on income taxes 111–13, quotation 111; on corporate taxes 113–16, quotation 113; on succession taxes 117–20, quotation 117. In Shirly Tillotson's recent study, the common perception of the era was that "the system wasn't fair." See Tillotson, *Give and Take*, 170.

68 *Report*, Book Two, 111, 113, 119. O.D. Skelton had written a number of essays during the Great War extolling the fairness and redistributive benefits of the income tax, and his acolytes, Clifford Clark and W.A. Mackintosh, trained as neo-classical economists, shared his perspective. See Ferguson, *Remaking Liberalism*, 161–86; Grant, *W.A. Mackintosh*, 169–72; Wardhaugh, *Behind the Scenes*, passim. The important book that pulls together the tax reform movement as a redefinition of the rights of citizens and the role of the state in this period is Tillotson's *Give and Take*.

69 *Report*, Book Two, 157. The broad discussion is on Book Two, 150–62. There is a very spirited treatment of the deficiencies of the existing tax system, regressive in its treatment of individuals and crippling in its effect on business, in Book One, 210–15.

70 *Report*, Book Two, 131–36, quotation 133; LAC, MacKay Papers, vol. 10, Robert to Kathleen, 9 May 1939.

71 Quotations in *Report*, Book Two, 134, 135.

72 J.W. Dafoe, "The Canadian Federal System under Review," *Foreign Affairs* 18, 4 (1940): 653; Luella Gettys, "Canadian Federalism: Report of the Royal Commission on Dominion-Provincial Relations," *American Political Science Review* 35, 1 (1941): 103-4.

73 *Report*, Book One, 178-82; UMA, Dafoe Papers, box 14, file 2, Dafoe to Skelton, 2 April 1940. This was also the point that Jacob Viner had argued during the proceedings in presenting Manitoba's critique of national tariff policies. See "Public Hearings," vol. 85, 10580-82; W.A. Mackintosh, *The Economic Background of Dominion-Provincial Relations*, Royal Commission on Dominion-Provincial Relations Research Study #2 (Ottawa: J.O. Patenaude, 1939), 83-85.

74 *Report*, Book One, 182-85, quotations 185, 186, 186-201; ibid., Book One, 214-15, 212-13, quotations 213. The entire chapter was the work of Deutsch but was revised after strong objections from commissioners.

75 *Report*, Book Two, 77, 78.

76 Nancy Christie, *Engendering the State: Family, Work, and Welfare in Canada* (Toronto: University of Toronto Press, 2000), 238-39.

77 Ibid., 240-42.

78 See Georges Campeau, *From UI to EI: Waging War on the Welfare State* (Vancouver: UBC Press, 2005), 56ff.

79 *Report*, Book Two, 24-42, on unemployment see 24-29 and 38-40, quotation 24.

80 Ibid., 233. As quoted in Christopher Armstrong, *The Politics of Federalism: Ontario's Relations with the Federal Government, 1867-1942* (Toronto: University of Toronto Press, 1981), 220-21.

81 See *Report*, Book Two, 38-40; Anthony G.S. Careless, *Initiative and Response: The Adaptation of Canadian Federalism to Regional Economic Development* (Montreal and Kingston: McGill-Queen's University Press, 1997), 22-23. As quoted in Bryce, *Maturing in Hard Times*, 173.

82 Esdras Minville, *Labour Legislation and Social Service in the Province of Quebec*, Royal Commission on Dominion-Provincial Relations Research Study #5 (Ottawa: J.O. Patenaude, 1939), 86; and A.E. Grauer, *Public Assistance and Social Insurance*, Royal Commission on Dominion-Provincial Relations Research Study #6 (Ottawa: J.O. Patenaude, 1939), 31. The issues are surveyed and the provincialist position explained in Keith G. Banting's crucial work, *The Welfare State and Canadian Federalism* (Montreal and Kingston: McGill-Queen's University Press, 1987), 91-93.

83 *Report*, Book Two, 36 and 43. These are cited and explored at greater length in Banting, *The Welfare State and Canadian Federalism*, 64-66.

84 Peter Graefe and Andrew Bourns, "The Gradual Defederalization of Canadian Health Policy," *Publius: The Journal of Federalism* 39, 1 (2009): 194–97; *Report*, Book Two, 42–43, quotations 44.
85 *Report*, Book Two, 31–32; J.A. Corry, "The Report of the Royal Commission on Dominion-Provincial Relations II," *Canadian Banker* 48, 1 (1940): 22.
86 *Report*, Book Two, 50–52. See also Edwin R. Black, *Divided Loyalties: Canadian Concepts of Federalism* (Montreal and Kingston: McGill-Queen's University Press, 1977), 117–18.
87 J.A. Corry, *Difficulties of Divided Jurisdiction*, Royal Commission on Dominion-Provincial Relations Research Study #7 (Ottawa: J.O. Patenaude, 1939), passim; *Report*, Book Two, 165–66, 183.
88 Ibid., 187–219.
89 Ibid., 199.
90 LAC, MacKay Papers, box 8, memo on the commission hearings, 20 January 1938; UMA, Dafoe Papers, box 14, file 4, W.C. Clark to D.A. Skelton, 22 November 1938, refers to Finance Minister Dunning's direct request.
91 *Report*, Book Two, 243.
92 Ibid., 243.
93 Ibid., 230, 259.
94 Ibid., 224–25 and footnote 14. The commission received several briefs supporting a bill of rights from a diverse range of advocacy groups but no provincial governments. See UMA, Dafoe Papers, box 14, file 8, "Precis of Discussions," "Fundamental Rights and Disallowance," 16 October 1938.
95 See UMA, Dafoe Papers, box 14, file 8, "Precis of Discussions": "Indians," 1 November 1938.
96 Ibid., report, 35, 178.
97 The approach of cooperative federalism and unconditional grants marks one of the key styles of federal government, as numerous Canadian analyses of federalism point towards. This list would include the work of many political scientists and a few historians, notably (but not exclusively) Donald Smiley, *Canada in Question;* Edwin Black, *Divided Loyalties;* Keith Banting, *The Welfare State and Canadian Federalism;* Anthony Careless, *Initiative and Response:The Adaptation of Canadian Federalism to Regional Development* (Montreal and Kingston: McGill-Queen's University Press, 1977); Armstrong, *Politics of Federalism;* Guy Laforest, *Trudeau and the End of a Canadian Dream* (Montreal and Kingston: McGill-Queen's University Press, 1993).
98 *Report*, Book Two, 275, 276.
99 Ibid., 276.

Chapter 10: Dark Days: 1940–41

1 Frank Underhill, *Canadian Forum*, September 1944, reprinted in Frank H. Underhill, *In Search of Canadian Liberalism* (Toronto: Macmillan, 1960), 116, 132.

2 Library and Archives Canada (LAC), Department of Finance, vol. 2701, file 300-1(2), "Newspaper Comment on the Royal Commission Report," 22 pp., prepared by Miss Costello, Bank of Canada, 15 June 1940. Also found in LAC, MacKay Papers, vol. 8, "Press Reports – Digest 1940–41."

3 LAC, Department of Finance, vol. 2701, file 300-1(2), "Newspaper Comment on the Royal Commission Report," 15 June 1940.

4 Ibid.

5 Ibid.

6 *Globe and Mail*, 22 May 1940; LAC, Mackenzie King Diaries, 22, 23 May 1940.

7 LAC, Mackenzie King Diaries, 15 June 1940.

8 Ibid., Department of Finance, vol. 2701, "Newspaper Comment on the Royal Commission Report," 15 June 1940.

9 Ibid., Mackenzie King Diaries, 27 May 1940; John Kendle, *John Bracken: A Political Biography* (Toronto: University of Toronto Press, 1979), 173.

10 LAC, Mackenzie King Papers, Primary series correspondence (J1), Bracken to King, 23 August 1940, 23950-1, King to Bracken, 23 September 1940, 239752, A.D.P. H[eeney] to Prime Minister, Re Sirois Report, 239753; Bracken to King, 18 October 1940, 239754ff.

11 Ibid., Memoranda and notes (J4), Stuart Garson, "A Manitoba Viewpoint on the Sirois Report: Remarks before the Financial Bureau of the Winnipeg Board of Trade," 7 June 1940, 227199-210.

12 J.L. Ralston, *House of Commons Debates* (24 June 1940), 1011; David Slater, *War Finance and Reconstruction: The Role of Canada's Department of Finance, 1939–46* (Ottawa: n.p., 1995), 35.

13 J.L. Ralston, *House of Commons Debates* (24 June 1940), 1011.

14 Ibid., 1013–18.

15 *House of Commons Debates* (24 June 1940), 1022, J.L. Ralston; Slater, *War Finance and Reconstruction*, 41–45.

16 Jim Struthers, *No Fault of Their Own: Unemployment and the Canadian Welfare State, 1914–1941* (Toronto: University of Toronto Press, 1983), chap. 6, esp. 194–204.

17 *House of Commons Debates* (30 July 1940), 2128, J.L. Ralston.

18 *Labour Gazette*, October 1940, 995–96. The two others were R.J. Tallon, secretary of the Trades and Labour Congress, and A.M. Mitchell, head of a Montreal manufacturing firm.

19 LAC, Department of Finance, RG 19, vol. 2701, "Newspaper Comment on the Royal Commission Report," 15 June 1940.

20 Detailed accounts are in many works, most recently, Robert Wardhaugh, *Behind the Scenes: The Life and Work of W.C. Clark* (Toronto: University of Toronto Press, 2010), chaps. 5–9; Hugh Grant, *W.A. Mackintosh: The Life of a Canadian Economist* (Montreal and Kingston: McGill-Queen's University Press, 2015), chap. 7. For details of the fiscal transformation, see Colin Campbell, "J.L. Ilsley and the Transformation of the Canadian Tax System: 1939–1943," *Canadian Tax Journal* 61, 3 (2013): 633–70.

21 Douglas Fullerton, *Graham Towers and His Times* (Toronto: McClelland and Stewart, 1986), 151–52.

22 LAC, Department of Finance, vol. 2701, "Memorandum re Sirois Report and the War," Graham Towers to J.L. Ilsley, 24 September 1940; Christopher Armstrong, *The Politics of Federalism: Ontario's Relations with the Federal Government, 1867–1942* (Toronto: University of Toronto Press, 1981), 223.

23 Referred to in Fullerton, *Graham Towers and His Times*, 152. Memo is found in three or four places, including Queen's University Archives (QUQ), W.A. Mackintosh Papers, box 6, A. Skelton, "Sirois Report and the War," 24 July 1941, "Copy 4 of 4."

24 As quoted in Christopher Armstrong, *The Politics of Federalism: Ontario's Relations with the Federal Government, 1867–1942* (Toronto: University of Toronto Press, 1981), 223.

25 J.L. Granatstein, *Canada's War: The War Policies of the Mackenzie King Government, 1939–1945* (Toronto: University of Toronto Press, 1974), 162–63.

26 LAC, Mackenzie King Diaries, 26 July 1940.

27 Ibid., Mackenzie King Papers, Primary series correspondence (J1), Graham Towers to King, 15 August 1940, 252692-7; Armstrong, *Politics of Federalism*, 223.

28 LAC, Mackenzie King Papers, Primary series correspondence (J1), Towers to King, 15 August 1940, 272692-7.

29 Ibid., also quoted in Granatstein, *Canada's War*, 163.

30 LAC, Department of Finance, vol. 2701, "Memo on the Report of the Sirois Commission," 11 September 1940. See also LAC, King Diaries, 19 September 1940. See also Granatstein, *Canada's War*, 164.

31 LAC, Department of Finance, vol. 2701, file 300-1(2), Heeney to Ilsley, 23 September 1940. See also LAC, Mackenzie King Diaries, 19 September 1940.

32 LAC, Department of Finance, vol. 2701, Special Cabinet Committee on Dominion-Provincial Relations Report and Emergency Measures, 20 September 1940, and memorandum on the report of the Sirois Commission, 11 September 1940.

33 Ibid.; see also Armstrong, *Politics of Federalism*, 224.

34 F.W. Gibson and Barbara Robertson, eds., *Ottawa at War: The Grant Dexter Memoranda* (Winnipeg: Manitoba Record Society, 1994), Dexter to Dafoe, 17 October 1940, 78–81.

35 Archives of Manitoba (AM), Bracken Papers, vol. 119, Bracken to King, 18 October 1940.

36 Kendle, *John Bracken*, 173–75.

37 As quoted in John T. Saywell, *"Just Call Me Mitch": The Life of Mitchell F. Hepburn* (Toronto: University of Toronto Press, 1991), 453–54.

38 Gibson and Robertson, *Ottawa at War*, Dexter to Dafoe, 17 October 1940, 79–80.

39 Ibid., 24 October 1940, 81–82.

40 Archives of Ontario, Hepburn Papers, RG 3-10, "Observations Regarding the Report and Recommendations of the Report on Dominion-Provincial Relations Public Health Province of Ontario," Harold J. Kirby to Hepburn, 6 December 1940; Armstrong, *Politics of Federalism*, 224.

41 Gibson and Robertson, *Ottawa at War*, Dexter to Dafoe, 25 October 1940, 82–84.

42 LAC, Mackenzie King Diaries, 22 October 1940.

43 Robin Fisher, *Duff Pattullo of British Columbia* (Toronto: University of Toronto Press, 1991), 324–29, quotes Pattullo's statement, and 330ff on BC's critical position.

44 Fisher, *Duff Pattullo*, 327–29; BCA, Premiers Papers, vol. 70, file 4, Pattullo to Mackenzie King, 31 October 1940, vol. 95, file 2, King to Pattullo, 2 November 1940.

45 British Columbia Archives (BCA), Premiers Papers, vol. 95, file 2, G.N. Perry to Pattullo, 16 October 1940, W.A. Carrothers to Pattullo, 16 December 1940.

46 Gibson and Robertson, *Ottawa at War*, Dexter to Dafoe, 25 October 1940, 81–85.

47 Wardhaugh, *Behind the Scenes*, 181, 185.

48 Gibson and Robertson, *Ottawa at War*, Dexter to Dafoe, 25 October 1940, 81–85.

49 LAC, Mackenzie King Diaries, 24 October 1940.

50 Gibson and Robertson, *Ottawa at War*, Dexter to Dafoe, 25 October 1940, 82.

51 LAC, Mackenzie King Papers, Memoranda and notes (J4), A.D.P. H[eeney], "Memo re Special Committee on Report of the Royal Commission on Dominion-Provincial Relations," 31 October 1940, 227235-6.

52 LAC, Mackenzie King Papers, Memoranda and notes (J4), Report of the Cabinet Sub-Committee appointed to consider the Report of the Royal Commission on Dominion-Provincial Relations, 1 November 1940, 227237-42; ibid., "Press Reaction to the Sirois Report," November 1940, 227297-316.

53 Armstrong, *Politics of Federalism*, 225; Granatstein, *Canada's War*, 165–66.

54 University of Manitoba Archives, Dafoe Papers, box 11, file 5, Skelton to Dafoe, 23 November 1940.

55 LAC, Mackenzie King Diaries, 1 November 1940; ibid., Mackenzie King Papers, Primary series correspondence (J1), W.C. Clark to Joseph Sirois, 15 November 1940, Sirois to Clark, 22 November 1940. See also Granatstein, *Canada's War*, 165–66, Wardhaugh, *Behind the Scenes*, 185; Gibson and Robertson, *Ottawa at War*, Dexter to Dafoe, 8 November 1940, 91.

56 Mackenzie King to the Premiers, 2 November 1940, printed in the conference proceedings: Canada, *Dominion-Provincial Conference, 1941* (Ottawa: King's Printer, 1941), v–vi.

57 The Prime Minister wrote to all the premiers. See, e.g., LAC, Mackenzie King Papers, Memoranda and notes (J4), Mackenzie King to T.D. Pattullo, 2 November 1940, 222750-2; ibid., Primary series correspondence (J1), King to Bracken, 2 November 1940, 239760-2. King's letter to the premiers is reprinted in the introduction of the published version of the 1941 conference. W.L. Mackenzie King to Provincial Premiers, 2 November 1940, Dominion-Provincial Conference, 14–15 January 1941, in *Dominion-Provincial Conferences, 1927–1941* (Ottawa: King's Printer, 1951). The premiers received it. See AM, Bracken Papers, vol. 119, King to Bracken, 2 November 1940; BCA, Premiers Papers, GR 441, vol. 57, file 20, King to Pattullo, 2 November 1940.

58 LAC, Mackenzie King Diaries, 13 December 1940.

59 Gibson and Robertson, *Ottawa at War*, Dexter to Dafoe, 30 December 1940, 111.

60 AM, Bracken Papers, GR 119, King to Bracken, 28 December 1940; BCA, Premiers Papers, vol. 95, file 2, King to Pattullo, 28 December 1940.

61 R.M. Fowler, "Confederation Marches On: A Comment on the Rowell–Sirois Report," *Behind the Headlines* 1, 4 (1940): 1–23; and J.W. Dafoe, "The Canadian Federal System Under Review," *Foreign Affairs* 18 (1940): 646–58.

62 LAC, Mackenzie King Diaries, 6 January 1941.

63 Ibid., 12 January 1941; Granatstein, *Canada's War*, 168.

64 LAC, Mackenzie King Diaries, 12 January 1941.

65 Ibid., 13 January 1941; LAC, Mackenzie King Papers, Primary series correspondence (J1), King to Sir William Mulock, 13 January 1941, 264274-5, cf. Mulock to King 14 January 1941, 264276-7; Granatstein, *Canada's War*, 165.

66 UMA, Dafoe Papers, Dafoe to J.T. Thorson, 19 November 1940, Dafoe to R.M. Fowler, 18 December 1940, Grant Dexter to Dafoe, 30 December 1940, Dafoe to H.F. Angus, 9 January 1941; Ramsay Cook, *The Politics of John W. Dafoe and the Free Press* (Toronto: University of Toronto Press, 1963), 230–31.

67 UMA, Dafoe Papers, box 6, file 1, Fowler to Dafoe, 11 January 1941; ibid., Angus to Dafoe, 13 January 1941.

68 LAC, Mackenzie King Papers, Primary series correspondence (J1), Hepburn to King, 8 November 1940, 244220; Armstrong, *Politics of Federalism*, 225.

69 LAC, Department of Finance, vol. 2701, R.M. Fowler to J.L. Ilsley, 6 January 1941; C.G. Power, *A Party Politician: The Memoirs of Chubby Power* (Toronto: Macmillan, 1966), 193.

70 Armstrong, *Politics of Federalism*, 227.

71 Pattullo to King, 7 November 1940, correspondence in Dominion-Provincial Conference, 14–15 January 1941, in *Dominion-Provincial Conferences, 1927–1941;* Fisher, *Duff Pattullo*, 330.

72 BCA, Premiers Papers, vol. 95, file 2, Pattullo to King, 2 January 1941.

73 LAC, Mackenzie King Diaries, 9 January 1941; Granatstein, *Canada's War*, 168–69.

74 Conrad Black, *Duplessis* (Toronto: McClelland and Stewart, 1977), 234–35.

75 LAC, Ernest Lapointe Papers, vol. 15, file 38, Gouin to Lapointe, 4 January 1941, Lapointe to Gouin, 7 January 1941.

76 UMA, Dafoe Papers, vol. 12, Crerar to Dafoe, 16 January 1941.

77 Mackenzie King, Dominion-Provincial Conference, 14–15 January 1941, in *Dominion-Provincial Conferences, 1927–1941*, 1–10, key quotations in order from 3, 4, 5, 6, and 7 ("crux"), 9. The summary and key quotations are set out and cited in the balanced accounts by Armstrong, *Politics of Federalism*, 226; and Granatstein, *Canada's War*, 169.

78 Saywell, *"Just Call Me Mitch,"* 458–59.

79 Hepburn, Dominion-Provincial Conference, 14–15 January 1941, in *Dominion-Provincial Conferences, 1927–1941*, 10–16, quotation 11–12.

80 Ibid., 11–12, 12–16.

81 Ibid., 16; and Armstrong, *Politics of Federalism*, 226–27.

82 Ibid. The colourful remarks are examined critically in Armstrong, *Politics of Federalism*, passim; and sympathetically in Saywell, *"Just Call Me Mitch,"* 460ff.

83 Godbout, Dominion-Provincial Conference, 14–15 January 1941, in *Dominion-Provincial Conferences, 1927–1941*, 16–17.

84 MacMillan, Dominion-Provincial Conference, 14–15 January 1941, in *Dominion-Provincial Conferences 1927–1941*, 17–18. LAC, Mackenzie King Papers, Primary series correspondence (J1), MacMillan to King, 21 January 1941, 262380, King to MacMillan, 29 January 1941, 262382.

85 Ibid., 18–19. On McNair and the government, see Cory Slumkoski, "A Fair Share," *Journal of New Brunswick Studies* 1 (2010): 128–29.

86 Bracken, Dominion-Provincial Conference, 14–15 January 1941, in *Dominion-Provincial Conferences, 1927–1941*, 20–37.

87 Pattullo, Dominion-Provincial Conference, 14–15 January 1941, in *Dominion-Provincial Conferences, 1927–1941*, 38–39, 40–41.

88 Campbell, "Dominion-Provincial Conference," 14 January 1941, in *Dominion-Provincial Conferences, 1927–1941*, 41–49.

89 Patterson, "Dominion-Provincial Conference," 14 January 1941, in *Dominion-Provincial Conferences, 1927–1941*, 50–51.

90 Solon Low, *Text of an Address* [30 December 1940] *on the Report of the Royal Commission on Dominion-Provincial Relations* (Edmonton: King's Printer), in Alberta Archives, Department of Public Works, box 80, file 00/28.

91 Aberhart, "Dominion-Provincial Conference," 14 January, *Dominion-Provincial Conferences*, 14–15 January 1941, in *Dominion-Provincial Conferences, 1927–1941*, 54–61.

92 See Clark Banack's new account of Aberhart's contradictory stance, rooted in his "premillenialism," in *God's Province: Evangelical Christianity, Political Thought, and Conservatism in Alberta* (Montreal and Kingston: McGill-Queen's University Press, 2016), 111–15, 119–20, and 121–29. Banack agrees with Alvin Finkle, *The Social Credit Phenomenon* (Toronto: University of Toronto Press, 1989), that Aberhart's first administration enacted serious enough "left-leaning" initiatives despite its basic fiscal conservatism.

93 LAC, Mackenzie King Diaries, 14 January 1941.

94 Ibid.

95 *Globe and Mail*, 15 January 1941. This is cited in Armstrong, *Politics of Federalism*.

96 LAC, Mackenzie King Diaries, 14 January 1941.

97 Prime Minister to the Provincial Premiers, 28 December 1940, Dominion-Provincial Conference, 14–15 January 1941, in *Dominion-Provincial Conferences, 1927–1941*, xiii.

98 Mackenzie King, Dominion-Provincial Conference, 14–15 January 1941, in *Dominion-Provincial Conferences, 1927–1941*, 69–71.

99 Dominion-Provincial Conference, 14–15 January 1941, in *Dominion-Provincial Conferences, 1927–1941*, 71. And for the reports of the conference scene, see Armstrong, *Politics of Federalism*, 228.

100 Ilsley, Dominion-Provincial Conference, 14–15 January 1941, in *Dominion-Provincial Conferences, 1927–1941*, 71–73.

101 Ibid., 73–74.

102 Ibid., 71–75, esp. 73–74 and 75.

103 Granatstein, *Canada's War*, 171.

104 McQuesten, Dominion-Provincial Conference, 14–15 January 1941, in *Dominion-Provincial Conferences, 1927–1941*, 75–79. Summary in Armstrong, *Politics of Federalism*, 228–29.

105 Hepburn, Dominion-Provincial Conference, 14–15 January 1941, in *Dominion-Provincial Conferences, 1927–1941*, 79–80. Descriptions of the event are found in Armstrong, *Politics of Federalism*, 229; and Saywell, *"Just Call Me Mitch,"* 461.

106 Aberhart, Dominion-Provincial Conference, 14–15 January 1941, in *Dominion-Provincial Conferences, 1927–1941*, 82–83, quotations 83.

107 Ibid., 80–91.

108 Bracken, Dominion-Provincial Conference, January 1941, in *Dominion-Provincial Conferences, 1927–1941*, 85–87; Mackenzie King, ibid., 103–8; Kendle, *John Bracken*, 179–81.

109 Ibid., 92–99.

110 Stephen T. Henderson, *Angus L. Macdonald: A Provincial Liberal* (Toronto: University of Toronto Press, 2007), 100; T. Stephen Henderson, "A New Federal Vision": Nova Scotia and the Rowell-Sirois Report, 1938–1948," in *Framing Canadian Federalism*, ed. Dimitry Anastakis and P.E. Bryden (Toronto: University of Toronto Press, 2009), 57.

111 Henderson, "New Federal Vision," 52–53; Henderson, *Angus L. Macdonald*, 8.

112 Henderson, *Angus L. Macdonald*, 100; and described in Saywell, *"Just Call Me Mitch,"* 461.

113 Hepburn, Dominion-Provincial Conference, 1941, in *Dominion-Provincial Conferences, 1927–1941*, 80 and 101, the latter statement quoted in Armstrong, *Politics of Federalism*, 229; and Saywell, *"Just Call Me Mitch,"* 461.

114 Saywell, *"Just Call Me Mitch,"* 461.

115 LAC, Mackenzie King Diaries, 15 January 1941; Armstrong, *Politics of Federalism*, 229–30.

116 Lapointe, Dominion-Provincial Conference, 1941, in *Dominion-Provincial Conferences, 1927–1941*, 92–93.

117 Armstrong, *Politics of Federalism*, 3, 198.

118 Mackenzie King, Dominion-Provincial Conference, 1941, in *Dominion-Provincial Conferences, 1927–1941*, 107–8; Paul Martin, *A Very Public Life*, vol. I (Ottawa: Deneau, 1983), 269, 107–8.

119 LAC, Mackenzie King Diaries, 15 January 1941.

120 Lapointe, Dominion-Provincial Conference, 1941, in *Dominion-Provincial Conferences, 1927–1941*, 92; LAC, Mackenzie King Diaries, 17 January 1941.

121 See Norman Hillmer, *O.D. Skelton: A Portrait of Canadian Ambition* (Toronto: University of Toronto Press, 2015), 287, 296, 305, 318, 327; and LAC, Mackenzie King Diaries, 28 and 30 January 1941.

Chapter 11: The Aftermath: 1941–46

1 David E. Smith, "Bagehot, the Crown and the Canadian Constitution," *Canadian Journal of Political Science* 28, 4 (1995): 627.

2 A copy is found in Archives of Manitoba (AM), Bracken Papers, GR 119, F.S. Burchill, "Canada: One Country," *Liberty*, 11 January 1941.

3 Library and Archives Canada (LAC), Department of Finance, RG 19, vol. 22, "Review of Press Comment on Dominion-Provincial Relations Conference," by Miss Costello, May 1941.

4 Ibid.; LAC, MacKay Papers, vol. 8, A. Skelton to R.A. MacKay, 16 May 1941, cover letter attached to the "Review." "Press" meant radio as well as print.

5 AM, Bracken Papers, Gratton O'Leary, "What Does Canada Face Now?" *Liberty*, 15 March 1941.

6 Christopher Armstrong, *The Politics of Federalism: Ontario's Relations with the Federal Government, 1867–1943* (Toronto: University of Toronto Press, 1981), 230.

7 John T. Saywell, *"Just Call Me Mitch": The Life of Mitchell F. Hepburn* (Toronto: University of Toronto Press, 1991), 462.

8 LAC, Department of Finance Papers, RG 19, vol. 22, "Review of Press Comment on Dominion-Provincial Relations Conference."

9 Robin Fisher, *Duff Pattullo of British Columbia* (Toronto: University of Toronto Press 1991), 335–36.

10 Ibid., 334–38; and David J. Mitchell, *W.A.C. Bennett and the Rise of British Columbia* (Vancouver: Douglas and McIntyre, 1983), 62–63.

11 British Columbia Archives (BCA), Premiers Papers, GR 1222, vol. 95, file 4-5, G.M. Weir, 13 February 1941, "The Sirois Report and BC's Social Services," 20 February 1941, "Effect of Sirois Report on Education in BC."

12 Archives of Ontario, Hepburn Papers, RG 3-10, press statement by Premier T.D. Pattullo, 31 January 1941.

13 Fisher, *Duff Pattullo*, 339–43. Despite the prime minister's satisfaction at having the provinces at his mercy, he also agreed with some of the fiscal substance of Pattullo's criticisms. See LAC, Mackenzie King Diaries, 14 January 1941.

14 LAC, Department of Finance Papers, RG 19, vol. 22, "Review of Press Comment on Dominion-Provincial Relations Conference," by Miss Costello, May 1941.

15 Archives of Ontario, RG 1-13, Hepburn Papers, Aberhart to Hepburn, 14 February 1941.

16 John Kendle, *John Bracken: A Political Biography* (Toronto: University of Toronto Press, 1979), 177 and 177–80.

17 AM, Bracken Papers, GR 119, "Conversations Following Collapse of Conference on the Sirois Report," January 1941; Archives of Ontario, RG 1-13, Hepburn Papers, Aberhart to Hepburn, 12 March 1941.

18 Dominion-Provincial Conference, 1941, 85–87, 103–8; University of Manitoba Archives (UMA), Dafoe Papers, Crerar to Dafoe, 16 January 1941; *Winnipeg Tribune*, 22 January 1941, 28 January 1941, 29 January 1941; AM, Bracken Papers, GR 119,

"The Dominion-Provincial Conference and the Sirois Report," radio broadcast by John Bracken, 27 January 1941. See the summary in Kendle, *John Bracken*, 180.

19 AM, John Bracken Papers, GR 119, Stuart Garson, "The Implementation of the Sirois Report," speech to the Manitoba Associated Boards of Trade, 20 February 1941.

20 LAC, Department of Finance Papers, RG 19, vol. 22, "Review of Press Comment on Dominion-Provincial Relations Conference."

21 Ibid.

22 Ibid.

23 UMA, Dafoe Papers, box 14, file 2, Fowler to Dafoe, 11 January 1941; ibid., box 1, file 1, Dafoe to Angus, 9 January 1941.

24 UMA, Dafoe Papers, T.A. Crerar to Dafoe, 16 January 1941.

25 Ibid.; Queen's University Archives (QUA), Crerar Papers, box 104, Dafoe to Crerar, 19 January 1941. The editorial is quoted in Ramsay Cook, *The Politics of John W. Dafoe and the Free Press* (Toronto: University of Toronto Press, 1963), 231–32.

26 UMA, Dafoe Papers, box 14, file 1, Angus to Dafoe, 11 February 1941.

27 LAC, MacKay Papers, vol. 8, Angus to MacKay, 28 January 1941.

28 Ibid., Mackenzie King Diaries, 15 January 1941.

29 Ibid., 18 January 1941.

30 LAC, Department of Finance Papers, RG 19, vol. 2701, Ilsley to I.J. Kinley, 7 January 1941.

31 Walter L. Gordon, *A Political Memoir* (Toronto: McClelland and Stewart, 1977), 38–39.

32 F.W. Gibson and Barbara Robertson, eds., *Ottawa at War: The Grant Dexter Memoranda* (Winnipeg: Manitoba Record Society, 1994), 78; R.B. Bryce, "William Clifford Clark, 1889–1952," *Canadian Journal of Economics and Political Science* 19, 3 (1953): 421.

33 David Slater, *War Finance and Reconstruction: The Role of Canada's Department of Finance, 1939–46* (Ottawa: n.p., 1995), 48–49.

34 J.L. Granatstein, *Canada's War: The War Policies of the Mackenzie King Government, 1939–1945* (Toronto: University of Toronto Press, 1974), passim.

35 LAC, Mackenzie King Diaries, 26 March 1941.

36 Cited in Irwin Gillespie, *Tax, Borrow and Spend: Financing Federal Spending in Canada* (Ottawa: Carleton University Press, 1991), 81. Another view is found in Colin Campbell's thorough work, "J.L. Ilsley and the Transformation of the Canadian Tax System: 1939–1943," *Canadian Tax Journal* 61, 3 (2013): 650–54.

37 Granatstein, *Canada's War*, 174; Robert Wardhaugh, *Behind the Scenes: The Life and Work of W.C. Clark* (Toronto: University of Toronto Press, 2010), 199–210. And the synthesis, Shirley Tillotson, *Give and Take: The Citizen Tax-Payer and the Rise of Canadian Democracy* (Vancouver: UBC Press, 2017), 170–204. The great expansion

of federal spending is illustrated in Livio De Mateo's survey, *A Federal Fiscal History, Canada 1867–2017* (Vancouver: Fraser Institute, 2017) 32–45, www.federal-fiscal -history-canada-1867-2017. Provincial and municipal net revenues equalled federal net revenues in 1939; by 1945 they were less than one-quarter of the federal total. See *Historical Statistics of Canada,* 2nd ed., ed. F.H. Leacy (Ottawa: Canadian Government Publications Centre, 1983), Series H1-18, H92-112 and H113-122.

38 QUA, Crerar Papers, 104, Crerar to Dafoe, 8 March 1941; Dexter to Dafoe in Gibson and Robertson, *Ottawa at War*; UMA, Dafoe Papers, box 11, file 5, Skelton to Dafoe, 13 May 1941.

39 UMA, Dafoe Papers, box 8, file 2, Dafoe to Skelton, 20 May 1941.

40 Ibid., Dexter to Dafoe, 13 May 1941; Gibson and Robertson, *Ottawa at War,* 168.

41 AM, Bracken Papers, GR 119, "Proceedings at the meeting of Representatives of the Provinces with Representatives of the Dominion," 18–19 December 1941.

42 Archives of Ontario, Conant Papers, RG 3, box 417, excerpts of minutes of meeting of Dominion-Provincial Conference, 30 September 1941.

43 Saywell, *"Just Call Me Mitch,"* 479.

44 "The fundamental problem of getting an average standard of public service in the majority of Canadian problems at no more than an average rate of taxation, still remains be solved," Winnipeg *Tribune,* 16 January 1942.

45 AM, Bracken Papers, GR 119, "The Dominion-Provincial Taxation Agreement Compared with the Recommendations of the Rowell-Sirois Report, Address to the Winnipeg Board of Trade," 12 February 1942; AM, Bracken Papers, GR 119, Garson to Sandy Skelton, 11 February 1942, Skelton to Garson, 26 February 1942.

46 Bracken's quixotic move is examined in Kendle, *John Bracken,* chap. 12.

47 LAC, Mackenzie King Diaries, 26 October 1942.

48 P.E. Bryden, *"A Justifiable Obsession": Conservative Ontario's Relations with Ottawa, 1943–1985* (Toronto: University of Toronto Press, 2013), 10.

49 See Raymond Blake, *From Rights to Needs: A History of Family Allowances in Canada, 1929–1992* (Vancouver: UBC Press, 2009); Peter Neary, *On to Civvy Street: Canada's Rehabilitation Program for Veterans of the Second World War* (Montreal and Kingston: McGill-Queen's University Press, 2011); Heather MacDougall, "Into Thin Air: Making National Health Policy 1939–45," in *Making Medicare: New Perspectives on the History of Medicare in Canada,* ed. Gregory P. Marchildon (Toronto: University of Toronto Press, 2012), 41–69.

50 Peter Neary, "Ian Alistair Mackenzie," *Dictionary of Canadian Biography,* vol. XVII, 1940–1950.

51 See Canada, Special Committee on Social Security, *Report of the Advisory Committee on Health Insurance* [Heagerty Report] (Ottawa: House of Commons, March

1943); and L.C. Marsh, *Report on Social Security for Canada* (Ottawa: King's Printer, [March] 1943). The Heagerty Report on Health Insurance is well summarized by MacDougall, "Into Thin Air," 41–69. The Marsh Report has been reprinted and extolled by Allan Moscovitch, *Report on Social Security for Canada* (Montreal and Kingston: McGill-Queen's University Press, 2017), ix–xxx. Opposition to Heagerty is noted in MacDougall, "Into Thin Air," 53, 57, etc.; cf. Slater, *War, Finance and Reconstruction*, 187ff; and Robert Bothwell et al., *Canada 1900–1945*, 390. On Dexter, see his memo of 21 March 1943, in Gibson and Robertson, *Ottawa at War*, 405.

52 Charlotte Whitton, *The Dawn of Ampler Life* (Toronto: Macmillan, 1943), 1–84, and critiques 87–128 and appendix summarizing the two federal government reports.

53 H.M. Cassidy, *Social Security and Reconstruction in Canada* (Toronto: Ryerson, 1943). See also H.M. Cassidy, *Public Health and Welfare Reorganization: The Postwar Problem* (Toronto: Ryerson, 1945), 23–29.

54 Bryce, "William Clifford Clark," 421.

55 J.W. Pickersgill, *The Liberal Party* (Toronto: McClelland and Stewart, 1962), 48.

56 QUA, Dexter Papers, Dexter memorandum, 1 March 1945, also cited in Gibson and Robertson, *Ottawa at War*, 496ff.

57 Skelton's mid-war work on reconstruction planning is examined in Colin Campbell, "J.L. Ilsley and the Transition to the Post-War Tax System," *Canadian Tax Journal* 63, 1 (2015): 10–13. Mackintosh's work is examined in Grant, *W.A. Mackintosh*, 268–98, esp. 285–88, and the "White Paper" is accessible online at http://fraser.stlouisfed. org/. Clark's work in the 1944–46 period is reviewed in Wardhaugh, *Behind the Scenes*, 261–65, 297–99, and 305–11.

58 Canada, Dominion-Provincial Conference, *Proposals of the Government of Canada*, August 1945 (Ottawa: King's Printer, 1945), 7–8, 47. The broader context is found in Robert Bothwell, Ian Drummond, and John English, *Canada since 1945: Power, Politics, and Provincialism* (Toronto: University of Toronto Press, 1982), 91–98.

59 Canada, Dominion-Provincial Conference, *Proposals of the Government of Canada*, August 1945 (Ottawa: King's Printer, 1945), 9–21.

60 Ibid., 21 and 21–27.

61 Ibid., 27 and 27–46.

62 Ibid., 47–49, 50–52.

63 See Bryden's recent study of Ontario's policies, *"Justifiable Obsession,"* 22–33. See also Campbell, "J.L. Ilsley and the Transition to the Post-War Tax System," 29–34. Drew's comment is quoted in Dale Thomson, *Louis St-Laurent: Canadian* (Toronto: Macmillan, 1967), 171. One of many examples of the interprovincial commitment to continue the process was an exchange between Stewart Garson and Chester Walters.

See AM, Garson Papers, Garson to Walters, P2356, 1943–45, 16 August 1945, Walters to Garson, 16 August 1945.

64 QUA, Dexter Papers, Grant Dexter, "Memo to George [Ferguson] and Brucie [Hutchison]," 26 September 1945.

65 Ibid.

66 Marc Gotlieb, "George Drew and the Dominion-Provincial Conference on Reconstruction of 1945–6," *Canadian Historical Review* 66, 1 (1985): 27–47; and Bryden, *"A Justifiable Obsession,"* 22–33.

67 BCA, BC Economic Council Papers, 110/3, 29 and 30 August 1945, Perry to Hart, Hart to Perry, 6 September 1945, Neil Perry to John Hart, 18 September 1945, Hart to Air Priority DoT, Ottawa (arranging a Hansen visit), 25 September 1945, Alvin Hansen to Neil Perry, 10 October 1945, Hansen to Perry, 18 and 19 October 1945, Hansen to Perry, 5 December 1945, Perry to Hart, 110/2, Alvin Hansen to John Hart, 13 June 1946.

68 Campbell, "J.L. Ilsley and the Transition to the Post-War Tax System."

69 See the accounts in Granatstein, *Canada's War,* an Ottawa-centred study; Campbell, "J.L. Ilsley and the Transition to the Post-War Tax System," 43–48; and Bryden's Ontario-centred, *"A Justifiable Obsession,"* 22–33 for complementary accounts of what was on the table. Bryden's account of the efforts of the provinces, the role of Skelton, and the disappointment of the outcome leads to the conclusion that the 1946 sessions ended in "vitriol." See also Marc Gottlieb, "George Drew and the Dominion-Provincial Conference on Reconstruction of 1945–6," *Canadian Historical Review* 66, 1 (1986): 46–77. See also LAC, Mackenzie King Diaries, 6 May 1946.

70 Archives of Ontario, Ministry of Treasury, Economics, and Intergovernmental Affairs, Drew Speeches, George Drew to the Canadian Club, Winnipeg, 17 June 1946. Ontario's remarkable about face on matters of federalism is shown in Bryden, *"A Justifiable Obsession,"* chaps. 1 and 2.

71 Archives of Ontario, L.M. Frost to J.M. Macdonnell, 24 July 1946.

72 See Campbell, "J.L. Ilsley and the Transition to the Post-War Tax System," 48ff. At the federal level Family Allowances and Veterans' Benefits were implemented, though not without great provincial irritation. See Blake, *From Rights to Needs;* and Neary, *On to Civvy Street.*

73 AM, Garson Papers, P-2356, files 2–6, 1941–47, file 3, Garson to Graham Towers, 13 January 1943, Towers to Garson, 23 February 1943, Garson to C. Walters, 14 April 1943; ibid., file 6, Garson to J.W. Pickersgill, 12 November 1945, Garson to S. Thompson, 18 December 1945; Saskatchewan Archives Board, Tommy Douglas Papers, R33-1, file 23, 773A, M.C. Schumiatcher to T.C. Douglas, 29 July 1945, G.E. Britnell to C.M. Fines, 9 May 1945, Britnell to Fines, 20 June 1945, J.W. Corman to

All Ministers, 16 July 1945, Douglas to King, 25 July 1945; ibid., 773B, "Suggested Topics for Dominion-Provincial Conference," 8 March 1950, T.K. Shoyama to Douglas, 3 May 1950; ibid., 773C, "Condensation of Correspondence [1946–50]," "Suggested Topics for Dominion-Provincial Conference," 8 March 1950.

74 QUA, Dexter Papers, additions, vol. 1, Macdonald to Grant Dexter, 1 November 1945, Macdonald to J.R. Stirrett, 11 June 1946, Macdonald to Grant Dexter, 21 December 1946. Macdonald's continuing support for the Rowell-Sirois Report is confirmed in Stephen T. Henderson, *Angus L. Macdonald: A Provincial Liberal* (Toronto: University of Toronto Press, 2007).

75 LAC, Institute for Research on Public Policy, "Ottawa Decides, 1945–1971," interview with J.W. Pickersgill, Gordon Robertson, Robert Bryce, Mitchell Sharp, and Louis Rasminsky, 28 February 1989.

76 Ibid., Mackenzie King Diaries, 31 January 1946.

77 Angus L. Macdonald to Mackenzie King, 5 December 1946, 32, T.C. Douglas to Mackenzie King, 12 July 1946, 53, and "Press Statement" by D.C. Abbott, 25 January 1947, 64–67, in Canada, Dominion-Provincial Conference, *Correspondence since the Budget of 1946* (Ottawa: King's Printer, 1947), passim.

78 P.E. Bryden, "The Obligations of Federalism: Ontario and the Origins of Equalization," in *Framing Canadian Federalism*, ed. Dimitry Anastakis and P.E. Bryden (Toronto: University of Toronto Press, 2009), 75–79. See also Bryden's more recent "St-Laurent's Intergovernmental Relations Strategy," in *The Unexpected Louis St-Laurent: Politics and Policies for a Modern Canada*, ed. Patrice Dutil (Vancouver: UBC Press, 2020), 156–72.

Conclusion: Appraising Rowell-Sirois

1 Ronald M. Burns, "The Royal Commission on Dominion-Provincial Relations: The Report in Retrospect," in *Canadian Issues: Essays in Honour of Henry F. Angus*, ed. Robert M. Clark (Toronto: University of Toronto Press, 1961), 149–53. Returning to academe years later, Burns wrote a book somewhat more sympathetic to the piecemeal tax rental system: *The Acceptable Mean: The Tax Rental Agreements, 1941–1962* (Toronto: Canadian Tax Foundation, 1980).

2 Brief summaries are Robert Wardhaugh, *Behind the Scenes: The Life and Work of W.C. Clark* (Toronto: University of Toronto Press, 2010), 354–45, 360–63; P.E. Bryden, *"A Justifiable Obsession": Conservative Ontario's Relations with Ottawa, 1943–1985* (Toronto: University of Toronto Press, 2013), 64–73; and Mary Janigan, "St. Laurent and Modern Provincial Equality," in *The Unexpected Louis St-Laurent: Politics and Policies for a Modern Canada*, ed. Patrice Dutil (Vancouver: UBC Press, 2020), 243–60. The shift to equalization is summarized in Robert Bothwell, Ian Drummond,

and John English, *Canada since 1945: Power, Politics, and Provincialism* (Toronto: University of Toronto Press, 1982), 151–53.

3　Library and Archives Canada (LAC), Department of Finance Papers, RG 19, memorandum on federal-provincial financial relations, 4 August 1950.

4　Ibid.

5　Ibid., vol. 3440, memorandum on review of dominion-provincial financial arrangements, 20 October 1950.

6　Ibid., memorandum on federal-provincial financial relations, 4 August 1950.

7　Ibid., memorandum on review of dominion-provincial financial arrangements, 20 October 1950.

8　Ibid., RG 19, memorandum on federal-provincial financial relations, 4 August 1950. Bryce continued to hold the views he helped to express in 1950. In his history of the Department of Finance written in 1986, he expresses the same views of the commission: backward-looking, unfair to the wealthy provinces, both vague and overly bureaucratic. It was, as he said in an interview, "dreadful." See R.B. Bryce, *Maturing in Hard Times, Canada's Department of Finance through the Great Depression* (Montreal and Kingston: McGill-Queen's University Press, 1986), 218–19; and LAC, Institute for Research on Public Policy Collection, Robert Bryce Interview, 28 February 1989, 21 February 1990, "Ottawa Decides, 1945–1971."

9　Canada, Canadian Intergovernmental Conference Secretariat, "First Ministers Conferences, 1906–2004" (Ottawa: n.p., n.d.), http://www.scics.ca/en/.

10　H.A. Innis, "The Rowell-Sirois Report," *Canadian Journal of Economics and Political Science* 6, 4 (1940): 571; J.A. Corry, "The Federal Dilemma," *Canadian Journal of Economics and Political Science* 7, 2 (1941): 215, 226.

11　Barry Ferguson and Robert Wardhaugh, "Reconsidering Rowell-Sirois and Rethinking Canadian Federalism," in *Constructing Tomorrow's Federalism*, ed. Ian Peach (Winnipeg: University of Manitoba Press, 2007), 40–43. A lone dissenter in the 1940s was an American political scientist, Luella Gettys, but hers was a rare case of an expert in both American and Canadian federalism. Gettys had written a critique of the Canadian conditional grant system and read the report as a contribution to the analysis of federalism and a proposal to rebuild provincial governmental autonomy. See Luella Gettys, "Canadian Federalism," *American Political Science Review* 35, 1 (1941): esp. 103–5.

12　W.A. Mackintosh, "Federal Finance," *Canadian Tax Journal* 1, 4 (1953): 335–39 and 417; H.F. Angus, "An Echo from the Past: The Rowell Sirois Commission," *Canadian Tax Journal* 1, 4 (1953): 439–49. See also Gettys, "Canadian Federalism."

13　Ronald M. Burns, "The Royal Commission on Dominion-Provincial Relations: The Report in Retrospect," in *Canadian Issues: Essays in Honour of Henry F. Angus*, ed. Robert M. Clark (Toronto: University of Toronto Press, 1961), 149–53.

14 Donald V. Smiley, "The Rowell-Sirois Report, Provincial Autonomy, and Post-war Canadian Federalism," in *Canadian Federalism: Myth or Reality*, ed. J. Peter Meekison (Toronto: Methuen, 1968), 47–65.

15 See a number of important works: most notably J.L. Granatstein, *Canada's War: The War Policies of the Mackenzie King Government* (Toronto: University of Toronto Press, 1974); J.L. Granatstein, *The Ottawa Men: The Civil Service Mandarins 1935–1957* (Toronto: University of Toronto Press, 1982); Bothwell et al., *Canada since 1945;* and Doug Owram, *The Government Generation: Canadian Intellectuals and the State, 1900–1945* (Toronto: University of Toronto Press, 1986).

16 Four exemplars are Christopher Armstrong, *The Politics of Federalism: Ontario's Relations with the Federal Government, 1867–1943* (Toronto: University of Toronto Press, 1981); John Kendle, *John Bracken: A Biography* (Toronto: University of Toronto Press, 1981); Stephen Henderson, *Angus L. Macdonald: Provincial Liberal* (Toronto: University of Toronto Press, 2007), and P.E. Bryden, *"A Justifiable Obsession": Conservative Ontario's Relations with Ottawa, 1943–1985* (Toronto: University of Toronto Press, 2013).

17 T. Stephen Henderson, "'A New Federal Vision': Nova Scotia and the Rowell-Sirois Report, 1938–1948," in *Framing Canadian Federalism*, ed. Dimitry Anastakis and P.E. Bryden (Toronto: University of Toronto Press, 2009), 51–52, 66–67.

18 V.C. Fowke, "The National Policy Old and New," in *Approaches to Canadian Economic History*, ed. W.T. Easterbrook and M.H. Watkins (Toronto: McClelland and Stewart, 1969), 237–58; Maureen Eden and Maureen Molot, "Canada's National Policies: Reflections on 125 Years," *Canadian Public Policy* 19, 3 (1993): 232–51; and Neil Bradford, *Commissioning Ideas* (Toronto: Oxford University Press, 1998), passim. The policy shift was, in part, endorsed by another federal inquiry, the Macdonald Commission, which looked into the Canadian economy. See Greg Inwood's excellent *Continentalizing Canada: The Politics and Legacy of the Macdonald Royal Commission* (Toronto: University of Toronto Press, 2005).

19 The approach to federalism as "watertight compartments" was no longer useful. To use a metaphor employed by an American scholar, rather than a "layer cake," federalism should be viewed as a "marble cake." The much-reprinted essay was originally published as Morton Grodzins, "The Federal System," in *Goals for Americans: Programs for Action in the Sixties*, Henry F. Wriston, chairman of editorial board (Englewood Cliffs, NJ: Prentice-Hall/American Assembly, 1960), 265–84.

20 E.R. Black, *Divided Loyalties: Canadian Concepts of Federalism* (Montreal and Kingston: McGill-Queen's University Press, 1975), 3.

21 The agenda of this era of the "welfare state," or "compensatory liberalism," is noted in many works, for example, Bryan M. Evans and Charles W. Smith, eds., *Transforming*

Provincial Politics: The Political Economy of Canada's Provinces and Territories in the Neoliberal Era (Toronto: University of Toronto Press, 2015), especially its introduction. A classic (Canadian) analysis of modern welfare state liberalism, written on the eve of its eclipse, is C.B. Macpherson, *The Life and Times of Liberal Democracy* (New York: Oxford University Press, 2012 [1977]).

Index

Note: "(f)" after a page number indicates a photograph or illustration; subentries of "Commission" and "Report" refer to the Rowell-Sirois Commission and Report, respectively, and are capitalized in the index for clarity.

Macmillan, Hugh, 30
Macmillan Commission (1933), 70, 101
McNair, J.B.: and implementation con-
ference, 256, 259, 276–77; King on,
259. *See also* New Brunswick
McPherson, Ewan, 41–42
MacQuarrie, Josiah, 124, 126
McQueen, Robert, 24, 87
McQuesten, Thomas, 153, 159, 242, 262–
63, 264
Major, W.J., 104
Mallory, J.R., 136–37
Manitoba: agricultural economy, 103;
Bank of Canada report on, 60–62,
63; borrowing by, 107; brief (*Manitoba's Case*), 95, 103–9, 125; British
Columbia, 235–36; call for return to
Rowell-Sirois, 292; conflicts with
federal government, 16; creation of,
191; debt, 105, 106, 136, 274; and
default/bankruptcy, 42, 55, 56, 57, 58–
59, 274; disallowance and, 16; experts,
team of, 104; federal loans to, 32; at
final hearings, 186; financial situation,
52–53, 56–58, 103; and fiscal responsibility, 29; freight rates and, 103;
Great Depression in, 102–3; and
Green Book intergovernmental
consultations, 290; Hepburn on,
150; high-dollar policy, 105; and
implementation of Report, 241–42,
256–57; and Loan Council, 41–42;
municipalities, 275; and National
Adjustment Grant, 275; and national
commission proposal, 55; at National
Finance Committee meeting, 52–53,
55; National Policy/national policies
and, 104, 107; and need for commission, 67; planning position on

Commission, 84; poverty in, 103;
preferential treatment for, 103; preliminary reponse to Commission,
95, 96, 116; public hearings in, 102–
9; public works in, 105; and relief,
105; on Report, 235–36; Schools
Question, 108; and sidelining of
Rowell-Sirois, 283; social policy, 106;
tariff and, 103, 105, 106, 107, 108–9;
and tax rental agreements, 283; taxation in, 105, 108; temporary grant to,
63–64; unemployment in, 28, 103,
106, 108. *See also* Prairie provinces
Manitoba Act (1870), 16
Mann, Thomas, 159
Manning, Ernest, 291
Maritime Bank, 16
Maritime provinces: briefs/
presentations, 96; and compensation,
82, 164, 229; and compensation for
past underfunding, 229; and Duncan
Commission, 53, 54; federal fiscal
system and, 42; financial situation,
239; Great Depression and, 7, 26;
hearings, 122; on implementation of
Report, 241; and National Policy/
national policies, 8, 11, 42, 141; preliminary meeting with Commission,
97; press reports in, 232; representative as commissioner, 69, 73, 74;
Rowell on, 130–31; Saunders's research study on economic history
of, 184; studies, 122; subsidies for,
22; trade through ports, 164; and
Wartime Tax Agreements, 282;
White Commission (*Inquiry into
the Readjustment of the Financial
Arrangement between the Maritime
Provinces and the Dominion of*

and final hearings, 186; and Green
Book intergovernmental consultations, 290; hearings in, 122–27; and
Loan Council, 42; national policy and,
47–48; per capita income, 126; preliminary meeting with Commission,
97; and proposed national commission, 54; Provincial Economic Inquiry
(Jones Commission), 33, 42, 47–48,
105, 122–23, 124, 126, 164; on Report,
235; and Report implementation,
256; *Submission*, 124–27; support for
Rowell-Sirois, 292; and tariff, 126.
See also Macdonald, Angus L.;
MacMillan, A.S.; Maritime provinces

old age pensions: in Bennett's New
Deal, 36; conditional grants and, 23;
dominion-provincial conference on
finances and social security and, 294;
federal government and, 106, 125,
226, 294; federal vs. provincial governments and, 227; Old Age Pensions
Act (1927), 18
O'Leary, Grattan, 271
Ontario: attitude toward Commission,
79, 82–83, 97, 142, 145, 169–74, 180,
186, 291; attitude toward Report, 234–
35; brief/submission (*Statement by
the Government of Ontario to the
Royal Commission on Dominion-
Provincial Relations*), 149, 152–54;
and compact theory of Confederation, 98; Confederation and, 153;
debt, 43; Drew as premier, 283–84;
equalization and, 147; and federal
government, 16, 144, 154; federal
government and presentations by,

157–58; and federal transfers, 157;
on federal-provincial relations, 152;
Great Depression and, 26, 147; and
Green Book intergovernmental consultations, 290; health services in,
243; hearings, 142–43, 148–59; on
implementation of Report, 241, 242–
44; inequitable fiscal system and, 153;
and Loan Council, 41, 43; manufacturing economy, 8; media on Report,
233; medical/hospital care in, 153;
and National Adjustment Grants,
221–22, 269, 291; and national commission proposal, 54; at National
Finance Committee meeting, 53, 54;
national policies and, 145; and natural resources, 19; and projected
plenary/round-table, 180, 186; and
provincial autonomy, 20, 145, 262–
63; and provincial rights, 144; Quebec
alliance with, 145, 146; and Report
implementation, 254–55, 262–63;
and representation on Commission,
254; revenue, 19; role in building up
Canada, 153–54; role within federal
system, 156; and royal commission
proposal, 50–51; social life at hearings, 154–56; social services in,
283; spending, 153; suspension of
cooperation with Commission, 171–
72; tax transfers and, 221; and taxation, 149, 153–54, 157, 269; and
unemployment aid/insurance, 146,
154; and Wartime Tax Agreements,
282–83. *See also* central provinces;
Hepburn, Mitchell
Ottawa hearings, 117–22, 165–67
Owram, Doug, 55